Criminological Theory

An Analysis of Its Underlying Assumptions

WERNER EINSTADTER

STUART HENRY

Eastern Michigan University

Harcourt Brace College Publishers

Fort Worth   Philadelphia   San Diego   New York   Orlando   Austin   San Antonio
Toronto   Montreal   London   Sydney   Tokyo

Publisher	Ted Buchholz
Senior Acquisitions Editor	Christopher P. Klein
Senior Project Editor	Cliff Crouch
Senior Production Manager	Kathleen Ferguson
Art Director	Scott Baker
Electronic Publishing Coordinator	Cathy Spitzenberger

Library of Congress Catalog Card Number: 94–76733

International Standard Book Number: 0-15-500329-1

Address for editorial correspondence: Harcourt Brace College Publishers
301 Commerce Street, Suite 3700
Fort Worth, Texas 76102

Address for orders: Harcourt Brace, Inc.
6277 Sea Harbor Drive
Orlando, Florida 32887

Phone: 800 / 782-4479, or
(*in Florida only*) 800 / 433-0001

Printed in the United States of America

4 5 6 7 8 9 0 1 2 3 4   066   9 8 7 6 5 4 3 2 1

This book is intended as an analytical overview of criminological theory. It is designed to give upper-level students a clear understanding of the underlying assumptions of criminological thought by examining the ideas of its various theories on human nature, societal structure, criminal law, criminal behavior, crime causation, and criminal justice policy. It shows how criminological theories are constituted and how particular theorists' ideas contribute to an overall theoretical framework.

We believe that it is vitally important for students and anyone concerned with issues of crime to have a clear, comparative understanding of the core concepts and theories of crime before they attempt to:

1. evaluate these against research evidence;
2. apply them to particular crimes; and
3. consider the substance of criminal justice policy.

Without understanding the assumptions on which a particular theory rests it is impossible to comprehend its meaning. Without a clear idea of its internal logic it is impossible to understand the connections between ideas about causes and their implications for policy. This book, then, is a bare-bones approach to ideas about crime, society, and the nature of human beings, and it attempts to lay the foundation for more substantive and applied considerations.

We are not concerned, however, with the minutiae of contributions that each theorist has made to criminological thought, nor with how one interpretation of a particular theorists' work differs from another, or from the original. This is a task better suited for professional criminology journals or the classic monograph. Indeed, such a task may be almost impossible to assess and undoubtedly leads to disagreement and controversy.

Nor are we concerned with guessing the intention of particular authors' works, or with speculating about their commitment to the ideas that they express. We are not examining the extent to which a particular theorist is pure. It will be clear from our examination of the literature that most theorists implicitly subscribe to more than one position, simultaneously. To pretend that they are representatives only of a particular perspective would add to the distortion that already dominates the field. Certainly other criminologists may take particular theorists as representatives or exemplars of a theoretical framework. This is not our task. Instead we suggest that some theorists have gained a reputation for being associated with certain theoretical perspectives. We are not concerned with contributing to the development of a hierarchy of criminological thought, involving, as it must, the privileging of some statements over others. Indeed, our argument is that a textbook interpretation of a theoretical perspective may make its own contribution to the selective refinement of criminological theory. We recognize that we too are involved in this process. However, we are concerned with the extent to which theoretical ideas are constituted as logical frameworks for the analysis of crime and society's response. Any single framework must necessarily be an ideal type. We are interested in presenting the culture of criminological theory (which we discuss in Chapter 1). As a result we draw on three crucial resources: original writings, journal articles and, importantly, and so often omitted, textbook discussions. Our view aims to capture the central themes of each perspective as presented in all three of these sources. We hope to have struck a balance rather than being biased toward any one resource.

Finally, and perhaps most importantly, this is a book about the logic of ideas, rather than their verification or validity. The reader will have to look elsewhere for the test, although our inclusion of a short evaluation of the main criticisms should help launch interested students in the right direction. However, our central aim is to identify the ideal or typical logical frameworks of theoretical perspectives on crime, free from the distracting detail of empirical research. We believe that only when the theory is clear can other tasks, such as testing, verification, assessment, and integration, begin.

We assume that students reading this book will have had some exposure to criminological ideas, typically through an introductory criminology course. If not, reading any standard introductory text is recommended. In addition, students who wish to achieve a greater theoretical depth will also benefit from consulting an edited collection of original works. Finally, because our analytical approach to criminological theory is concerned with common ideas organized around core assumptions, students who want to retain the integrity of a particular theorist's ideas would benefit from consulting Martin, Mutchnick and Austin's (1990) *Criminological Thought: Pioneers Past and Present,* Jacoby's (1994) *Classics of Criminology,* or even Hermann Mannheim's (1960) classic *Pioneers in Criminology.*

Acknowledgments

Textbooks are collaborative efforts. Not only do they draw on the published wisdoms of others, they unwittingly rely on the insights and experiences of a host of colleagues. They would be intellectually poorer without the scrutinizing questions of friends, spouses, reviewers, and, most importantly, students. An exhaustive list of those we should thank would read like an award ceremony producer's nightmare but some do deserve a special mention. Foremost we thank Jock Young of Middlesex University, England, for without his original outstanding analysis "Thinking Seriously About Crime," we might well have written a different book. While we are not wholly in agreement with Jock's current "realist" direction (See Chapter 10), we have enormous respect for his pioneering criminology. We also thank both Stanley Cohen of the Hebrew University, Jerusalem, and Marty Schwartz of Ohio University, whose communications and published insights have tempered our soaring postmodernist zeal. Kathy Daly of the University of Michigan and Dawn Currie of the University of British Columbia strengthened our understanding of the feminist contribution. We thank them for devoting the time to what is not a feminist text. However, in keeping with the feminist perspective we have tried to infuse our chapters with gender awareness. For clarification on his power-control theory we thank John Hagan of the University of Toronto.

Early encouragement in our project was received in conversations and communications with Piers Beirne. In its making this book has gained sustenance from our colleagues at Eastern Michigan University, particularly, Gregg Barak and Joe Rankin, whose collegiality and constructive commentary made our task that much easier. Thanks to Lee Doric–Henry of Wayne State University for help with the original artwork. Thanks also to Laura Einstadter for her help in locating some obscure sources. Finally, we thank our various peer reviewers, whose tough but appreciative criticisms made this a far better work than it might otherwise have been: Theron T. Bowman, Texas Christian University; Theodore C. Chirocos, Florida State University; Dennis R. Longmire, Sam Houston State University; Robert Mutchnik, Indiana University of Pennsylvania; Melvin C. Ray, Mississippi State University; Calvin J. Swank, Youngstown State University; and Carol Thompson, Texas Christian University.

CONTENTS

The promotion of a great idea may be of greater value
than the complete proof of its validity.
—*Robert H. Gault*

Not all memorable personages of science or philosophy are necessarily honored
for their well received contributions; and certainly not all are respected for the
validity of their ideas. It seems that in science we at times need a few good
"bad" examples to help show us which way not to go.
—*Randy Martin, Robert Mutchnick, and Timothy Austin*

[We] have been both victims and perpetrators of deficient conceptions, if not
damaging misconceptions of social conditions. To that extent problems have
been... literally of our own making, our responsibility.
—*Barry Smart*

CHAPTER ONE

The Analytical Framework

This chapter introduces our analytical framework and the various criteria we use to examine the theoretical models elaborated in each of the subsequent chapters. Our framework draws on the analytical approach developed by some sociologists and criminologists for theorizing about law, crime, and criminal justice. In particular we have used Jock Young's classic paper "Thinking seriously about crime: Some models of criminology" as a point of departure (see also Davis, 1975; Empey, 1982; and King, 1981, for similar approaches). Young (1981: 250) argues that theoretical models or perspectives compete, each having "its own intellectual history and each flourishing, with powerful support and a substantial body of research." Similarly, in his now classic distinction between models of the criminal justice process, Packer (1968: 217) captures the essence of our analytical approach when he argues that models represent "an attempt to abstract separate value systems that compete for priority in the criminal process."[1]

However, abstracting and theorizing are not neutral processes: "Theory is a selective rendering of the world, as it categorizes reality in selective ways" (Davis, 1975: xii). As such, criminological theory generates "blind spots" that among other things obscure their "very real consequences for controlling human conduct." It is our intention to illuminate these blind spots by systematically examining different theoretical perspectives with the same set of critical questions about their underlying assumptions. These questions ask of each theory, What are the core ideas about humans and society, and about crime and criminal etiology,

---

[1]Several commentators (e.g., Michalowski, 1977; Young, 1981) employ the concept of *paradigm* rather than those of model, perspective, or school. In its simplest form the term *paradigm* refers to scientific thought that shares commonly accepted concepts and similar elements in common, including definitions of research problems and even researchers working to test empirically these assumptions for the purpose of validating theory. Thus a paradigm is "a school of thought within a discipline that provides the scientist with a model for choosing the problems to be analyzed, the methods for analyzing them, and the theoretical frameworks for explaining them" (Curran and Renzetti, 1994: 34). An elaborated discussion of the notion of paradigm was developed by Kuhn (1962, 1970) in expounding on the history of science, in which he saw paradigms as stable periods of the scientific development of "normal science" that eventually succumb to a buildup of anomalies before they enter a crisis during which several paradigms compete for prominence. Use of the concept, particularly in social science, has been subject to some controversy (Ritzer, 1975; Barnes, 1981). We tend to agree with Turner (1986: 31) that "the concept of paradigm has been so overused that it has lost any meaning." Partly because we do not examine all the elements of a paradigm (e.g., methods) and partly because of the controversy, we prefer the terms *perspective* or *framework,* which we use interchangeably.

and what are the preferred or implied criminal justice policies, correctional philosophies, and crime control practices?

Because of their different ideological stance, not all theoretical approaches make their assumptions explicit. In many cases these have to be teased out. For example, because they focus on individual choice, classical theorists have little to say about crime causation. Similarly, because of their belief in the individual nature of crime causation, biological theorists have little to say about society's role in the genesis of crime. Such silences obscure very real assumptions harbored by theorists. One of the main purposes of our systematic analytical approach is to elucidate these assumptions. We admit at the outset, however, that our interpretations of the theories and perspectives we analyze are subjective.[2]

ANALYTICAL DIMENSIONS AND CORE QUESTIONS

The following five interrelated analytical dimensions are at the heart of any criminological theory, whether or not these assumptions are made explicit by theorists.

Human Nature and Human Behavior   This dimension addresses criminologists' assumptions about human freedom and constraint: whether people choose their actions or whether their actions are determined by internal or external forces; whether humans are *naturally* individuals or social and cultural products; whether people are isolated beings or socially interconnected; and whether they are different from or similar to other species. This dimension also identifies the behavior assumed to follow from such assumptions.

Society and the Social Order   In this category we consider criminological views of society: whether these assume a consensus, or conflict; whether society is seen to be composed of groups, classes, or cleavages; and whether such divisions form a hierarchy of power. We also consider theorists' assumptions about the state and its relation to the wider socioeconomic order.

The Role of Law, the Definition of Crime, and the Image of the Criminal   Ideas about the nature of criminal law and its role in defining the subject of criminology are the focus of this dimension of criminological theory. Do theorists assume that criminology should be restricted to a legalistic arena or do they think it should include any

---

[2]We have attempted to take a representative sample of the literature from each theoretical position. Biases aside, because space does not permit an exhaustive analysis, our selections may differ from other researchers'. Our objective, too, is complicated by the overlap that exists between theorists' contributions. We therefore encourage students to select and analyze their own materials, using the criteria we identify.

activity subject to regulation? Should criminology include the normatively deviant? Does the law or do agents of social control define crime? Is crime limited to that which the state defines as offensive or is it based on a broader definition of social harm? Moreover, is harm assumed to occur to individual or collective victims? Does the definition of crime also include victimless crimes and harms against the state?

Criminological theorists also imply or express images of the kind of person that commits offensive behavior. We might have considered this issue as a subcategory of the theorists' views of human nature; however, in our judgment, thinking about who is criminal *follows* decisions about what is offensive behavior. Typically such behavior is met with questions such as, "What kind of person would do such and such?" Finally, are offenders assumed to be the same as non-offenders or do they constitute several distinct and different types? Are crime and criminals viewed as real or as socially constructed categories?

Causal Logic   Much criminological thought is based on assumptions, propositions, and hypotheses about the cause of crime. Do crime and deviance stem from the choices individuals make in varying socially structured contexts or would some be rule breakers in any context? Are criminal behaviors determined by internal or external forces over which actors have little control? How do these causes produce crime? Do they operate independently or interactively? Is cause an appropriate tool of analysis? Alternatively, is our search for causes part of the solution or part of the problem of crime?

Criminal Justice Implications   This analytical category focuses on the procedures for determining culpability and for administering justice, the correctional ideology that guides the administration of justice, and the intervention techniques used to enforce it. Our concern here is not theories of social control per se but the models of criminal justice that are implied by and that are logically consistent with particular theories of crime causation. These theories may favor systems of justice and control that have already been constituted (by practitioners, politicians, lawmakers, etc.), or they may suggest their own. Typically theorists build on or critique the existing institutional forms, suggesting additions or new emphases that reflect their own ideological assumptions. What roles are played by the differing elements of the criminal justice system as shaped by the policy implications, philosophy of intervention, and criminal justice practitioners operating from within a particular theoretical framework? Does the system *implied by a particular theory* urge that police, for example, protect the public, afford rights of due process, fight crime, or divert offenders from the system through preventive intervention? Do formal procedures guarantee justice, as professed by some theorists, or can procedures alone not guarantee justice in an unjust society, as held by others.

Criminal Justice Policy and Correctional Ideology[3]   This subdimension explores the policy implications of theories of causation. What are the assumptions that logically follow from the different theories of crime causation? Is the policy implication directed at the individual or the wider social context? What policies toward crime do the various theorists recommend? The relevant debate is between advocates for different ideological positions justifying state intervention. These justifications, rationales, or philosophies for the use of state power will be defined in more detail later, but for the present purpose they can be organized according to five broad philosophical categories: (1) punitive philosophies, such as punishment, retribution, incapacitation, and deterrence, whereby offenders are harmed or deprived by the state with the aim of preventing them or others from committing future offenses; (2) therapeutic philosophies, such as treatment and rehabilitation, whereby offenders are forced or helped to refrain from future offending; (3) compensatory philosophies, such as restitution and reparation, whereby the offenders are forced to make amends for their past offenses; (4) conciliatory philosophies, such as mediation, whereby offenders and victims are encouraged to resolve their disputes; and (5) philosophies of social change, such as institutional reform and celebration, whereby crime and deviance are seen as indicators of structural, societal, or community pathology that requires social and organizational change. (see Black, 1976, for a similar analysis.)[4]

Techniques of crime control. Finally, we outline the logical techniques implied by theory and its associated policy and correctional ideology for implementing intervention or sanctioning. We consider to what extent the same methods can be justified under different philosophies. For example, prison can serve more than one ideology or philosophy simultaneously, providing, for example, incapacitation, punishment, deterrence, and/or rehabilitation (see Shover, 1979; Shover and Einstadter, 1988).

It should be remembered, however, that the theories we consider have different emphases in terms of these analytical categories. For some theoretical frameworks we provide greater detail in a particular analytical section because the theory either better lends itself to such analysis, or its assumptions are more clearly spelled out in the original sources. For others we combine categories where this is appropriate. Let us now look in more detail at what is meant by each of our analytical dimensions. In particular, we examine the range of theoretical positions that are taken within each of these dimensions.

---

[3]The term *correctional ideology* is defined by Shover and Einstadter (1988: 6) as "broad, abstract assumptions and beliefs about crime and how best to deal with it."

[4]Black (1976: 2) calls these categories "styles of social control" represented in law. He identifies the penal, compensatory, therapeutic, and conciliatory, suggesting that the first two are accusatory in nature, whereas the last two are remedial, designed to help and ameliorate. He fails to consider the fifth category, which we include here to address the structural level of intervention.

Human Nature and Human Behavior

Much has been claimed about human nature and what is essential to the concept of being human. We believe that assumptions about this are implicit or explicit in every criminological theory and have important implications for criminal justice practice. As Bartol (1991: 2–3) says, "Where crime is at issue, a society which believes that humans are by nature aggressive and violent will have different methods of social control than a society which believes they are by nature peaceful, loving and friendly." Without a clear exposition of these assumptions any understanding of particular theories will be obscured. The range of characteristics that have been attributed to humans is vast. We will not document all of them here but only indicate those that criminologists have taken to be important in their thinking about crime. At the outset it should be clear that conceptions of humans typically occur by way of an analogy that tends to represent what is seen as their essential characteristics. To gain a better grasp of what is at issue when considering assumptions about human beings, let us look at some examples of ideas on human nature.

In his encyclopedic review of the topic, Volkart (1964: 306) suggests that one approach to human nature is to reduce it to a cluster of essential needs required for humans to survive, as in Malinowski's (1944: 75) definition of human nature that "all men have to eat, they have to breathe, to sleep, to procreate and to eliminate waste matter from their organisms." But any approach that focuses solely on a limited range of biological endowments tells us little about what is distinctly human, since the same approach can be used to describe all animal organisms. This leads us to the issue of whether humans are *no different* from animals, as implied in Machiavellian and Hobbesian philosophy, *different by degree* from animals, as in Darwinian and Marxian philosophy and recent sociobiology, or *fundamentally different* from animals as some neurobiological and cognitive theorists have proposed (see Bartol, 1991: 4–6; Adler, 1967).

Another assumption made about human nature is that people are seen in varying degrees of isolation from or connectedness to one another. The theories range from those that envisage us as separate entities, units, individuals, even as "social atoms," to those holding the idea that we are social beings or, in some cases, "ambassadors" for our "species" who represent a wider social formation. For example, Cooley (1909) argued that human nature is not something existing separately in the individual but is a reflection of the images derived from interaction with others in group life. He saw human self-identity as derived from the communication we have with others. Just as a mirror ("looking glass") reflects our physical appearance, so group life reflects our social appearance (hence his concept "the looking glass self"). Goffman (1959) uses the analogy of drama, theater, and the stage to show this interconnectedness between humans as both actors and audience.

Some theorists, such as Marx (1844: 126), envisage us as partly separate individuals with the potential to be universal and free but also as dependent on one another and forming a greater social whole, which Marx calls a "species-being" and in which we are bound to each other and to the social history of our past (Marx, 1852: 115). Within this frame of reference, the extent to which we cooperate or compete, the degree to which we are all in agreement or opposition, is also critical to our identity and our survival as humans.

A related assumption in criminological theory is the extent to which human beings are assumed free to act toward others or whether they are assumed to be driven by forces, either external or internal. As Young points out (1981: 250–51), the issue here is the age-old question of free will versus determinism: "of whether the act was committed willfully as part of a process of reasoning … or whether it was non-rational, invoking determining factors outside rational control." In other words, do we have the capacity for voluntary action and if so is this based on rational goal-directed choice or random, haphazard stumbling that may subsequently be rationalized? Alternatively, is it the case that human action is somehow generated, shaped, or channeled by forces over which we have little control, which, indeed, are part of some grand or not so grand plan? And if humans are determined by forces, do these come from inside a person, such as their biological constitution or personality (internal determinism) or from outside the person in their physical or social environment (external determinism)? (See Bartol, 1991: 6–10.)

Important, too, has been whether our behavior is essential to our nature. Are we no more than a series of instances of what we do, or are we separate from our actions, such that we act roles, play scripts, and interpret our parts from the vantage point of an inner self?

A related issue concerns whether human types are real or is "typing" a socially constructed category that we impose on the behavior of others and from which we impute an underlying difference that may not have any real existence. A belief in the reality of social types postulates that "there is not one human nature but many—as many as there are cultures, societies and social groups" (Kretch and Crutchfield, 1948: 47).

It is clear from this brief excursion into some of the ideas about the essence of human beings that what is "human" is open to many interpretations. It is equally apparent that criminologists rely on a number of these assumptions or models of humans in constructing their theories of crime. In examining criminological theories we need to establish what combinations of elements have been assumed or even boldly stated.

Society and the Social Order

Just as "a society's social, political and economic structures are based on fundamental premises about human beings" (Bartol, 1991: 2), so its political and especially legal institutions are based on particular assumptions about society. Indeed, it has long been recognized that no answer to the question "What is law?" is possible without a theory of society. Therefore, it is appropriate for us to consider criminologists' views of society before turning to their assumptions about law and their definitions of crime.

Society refers to the totality of relationships among people which recurs as a distinct pattern of institutions and culture. In referring to the concept, most theorists follow the nineteenth-century sociologists Comte and Spencer in believing that society is more than the sum total of individuals who constitute it. Thus, for many sociologists, "a society is a cluster, or system, of institutionalized modes of conduct ... modes of belief and behavior that occur and recur ... across long spans of time and space" (Giddens, 1987: 8). However, disagreement exists about precisely what behavior and institutions make up a society, about how or even whether the totality is sustained in an orderly manner, and about whether it exists through interactive relations of cooperation or conflict: all are central issues.

Young (1981: 251) states that "all criminological theory, at least implicitly, involves a theory of social order." However, like sociologists, criminologists differ in their perceptions of how society is constituted. Like their views concerning human nature, theorists' views of the way society is structured and how it functions shape their explanations of crime. There are several models of social order.

For some theorists, what holds society together as an integrated whole and gives it cohesive order is consensus or agreement, based on either consent or assent of the majority, and arrived at either voluntarily, ideologically, or coercively. Consensus refers to the social condition whereby members of society agree on the basic values and norms that constitute the moral order. Consensus may prevail whether power is concentrated or dispersed. Thus we may envisage a pyramid-like hierarchy, with power concentrated among a few. (See Figure 1-1). This hierarchy gains assent from the subordinate majority, providing it with authority to rule. Alternatively, though less common, is a model of society exhibiting relatively equal distribution of power, albeit with a division of labor based on gender distinctions, as in some nonindustrial subsistence economies or hunting-and-gathering societies, where common values prevail. (See Figure 1-2.)

In contrast, in a pluralist model, society is perceived as fluid, composed of a variety of groups, each with its own interests. (See Figure 1-3.) Interests may be economic, but they can also be based on status and prestige, ideology, religion, and politics. Some of these interests are in harmony, others in competition, and still others in conflict. Pluralists see the interactions between interests as the dynamic driving force of society. From this perspective society is viewed as a dynamic entity, interacting, conflicting, growing and ever-changing.

In a further variant, society is envisaged as being composed of classes of people who share similar economic and social circumstances. As a result, members of these classes have different life experiences, placing them in different strata, which in turn hierarchically order the society. (See Figure 1-4.) In some versions of this view there are many strata, whereas in others there are only a

SOME MODELS OF SOCIETY

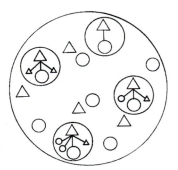

Figure 1-1   Consensus Acephalous Society

Individuals and
patriarchal households.

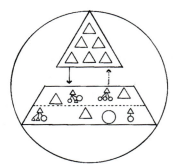

Figure 1-2   Consensus Power-Hierarchy

Two levels: Dominant economic and political elite; masses giving assent.

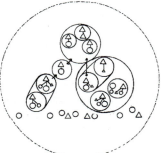

Figure 1-3   Pluralistic Structure

Alliances formed between individuals and
families having similar interests and
beliefs, who conflict with others similarly
formed, in a struggle for dominance.
Consensus of the whole weakened.

Legend

Conflict

Consensus

Weak Consensus

Domination/Control

Influence

Female

Male

Family

Government Agency

Corporation

few. Those at the top of the hierarchy possess the most power while those at the bottom possess the least. Some theorists emphasize economic power as the pervasive force that shapes the social order, whereas others give more credence to political and social power as the overriding determinant. Moreover, order in such a hierarchically structured society may be maintained by coercion of the few over the majority. More subtle ideological means may also be employed whereby assent to existing arrangements is generated by various strategies designed both to gain the assent of the subordinated and to mystify the conflict over substantial inequalities in the distribution of wealth. One version of this model sees an economically powerful elite controlling a political-administrative apparatus. (See Figure 1-5.) Another version depicts real separation between a semi-autonomous state and economic elites, each of which is fragmented into conflicting interest groups. (See Figure 1-6.)

The Role of Law, the Definition of Crime, and the Image of the Criminal

Law, particularly criminal law, is at once the expression of the integration of society, the means to enforce society's cooperative existence, and evidence of its disunity. Law expresses integration insofar as it contains the formal codification of mandates, dictates, and customs declared acceptable within a society by those in positions of power. Though it is questionable whose values or standards are reflected by the rules that comprise the substantive criminal law, it lays down both what is *expected* and what is *excepted* by the members of a society and specifies what conduct is believed to be against the interests of the society as a whole, as represented by the state (as opposed to civil law, which specifies harms to the individual). Procedural criminal law specifies how the state will deal with violators and how the penalties specified for those convicted of violations will be administered.

The behavior prohibited by the substantive criminal law, whether based on the will of a king, the revelations of a divinity, the carefully considered wisdom of justices, or the lobbied labors of legislators, is crime. Crime is an act prohibited by law that is subject to punishment. However, what is defined as crime has varied historically and culturally. For example, Sutherland and Cressey (1961) reveal that at different times it has been a crime to print a book professing the medical doctrine of circulation of the blood; drive with reins; sell coins to foreigners; have gold in the house; and write a check for less than a dollar. Some consensus criminologists view changes in the content of criminal prohibitions "desirable in order to reflect changes in public sentiments or judgments of public needs and values" (Hall Williams, 1982: 2). Conflict criminologists see such change as a means to adjust state social control mechanisms to maintain existing power relations.

The variability of crime alerts us to the relativity and socially constructed nature of the definitional process. Similarly, the existence of crime reminds us that all people do not conform to lawful behavior.

SOME MODELS OF SOCIETY (continued)

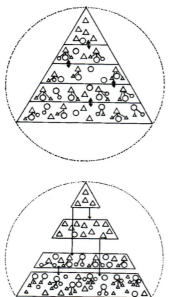

Figure 1-4   Class Hierarchy

Multiple levels: Upper classes of economic and political elite; middle classes; lower classes and politically powerless.

Figure 1-5   Power-Class Hierarchy

Multiple levels: Corporate economic elite; small business, corporate managers; political administration (government); subordinated powerless masses.

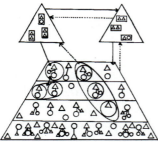

Figure 1-6   Dual Power Class Hierarchy

Multiple levels: Power divided between relatively autonomous economic and political elites. Economic elite composed of conflicting corporations dominating class hierarchy and controlling political elite. Political elite composed of conflicting dominant agencies influencing government and dominating class hierarchy.

Class hierarchy containing a plurality of interest groups more or less organized, influencing economic and political elite.

Legend

←——→	Conflict
⌒	Consensus
⌒ (dashed)	Weak Consensus
——→	Domination/Control
·····→	Influence
○	Female
△	Male
(family symbol)	Family
▭	Government Agency
⊓	Corporation

Not surprisingly, then, criminologists have differing views about the content of their subject. Early debates in criminology were concerned with what should define crime for the purpose of criminological study. There were those who argued that the whole field of criminology should be restricted to the study of what is *legally* defined as crime (Michael and Adler, 1933; Jeffery, 1956). Others wished to narrow this focus further to include only those *convicted* of criminal offenses (Tappan, 1947). Even today some warn about the tendency of criminologists to stray too far from the focus on behavior prohibited by criminal law on the grounds that "simply because one disapproves of certain behavior does not make it criminal if the law still permits it, however reprehensible the behavior may be" (Hall Williams, 1982: 3). However, one of the main limitations of such legalistic approaches is that they prevent the criminologist from examining or questioning existing social arrangements or institutions (Schwendinger and Schwendinger, 1970; Quinney and Wildeman, 1991: 3–4). These approaches concentrate on crimes of the powerless and omit any consideration of the process of law creation, as well as what we now take to be crimes of the powerful, such as corporations engaged in price fixing, consumer fraud, tax evasion, and crimes by government agencies such as police corruption. Importantly, criminologists adopting a strict legal definition also exclude consideration of crimes by the state, and other more broadly based pervasive harmful activities (e.g., institutionalized racism and patriarchal oppression).

As a result some, most notably Sutherland (1949: 511–15), wished to expand what counted as crime to include activities that were both "socially injurious" and those for which there was the provision for penalty, regardless of whether it was implemented through a regulatory code rather than the criminal law. Sutherland believed that the crimes of corporations were a legitimate arena of criminological study.

More recently, the expansion of criminology is seen in the move to replace the narrower concept of crime with that of deviant behavior. However, even this does not necessarily avoid the problem of state power, for,

> [b]y adhering to dominant definitions of deviance as abnormal, theorists fail to critique the social order that generates these stereotypes. As a result deviance research displays excessive concern with the problems formulated by administrators or enforcement groups. This trivializes the research product, reducing it to a rhetoric for elites that justifies their dominance over powerless groups. (Davis, 1975: xxii)

For these reasons, other theorists include in their definition of crime, the realm of social control, as well as harms such as racism, sexism, and the exploitation and violation of human rights, seen as "social injury" (Schwendinger and Schwendinger, 1970). For example, in a discussion on state crime Cohen (1993: 98–101) says we need to refine our concepts of human rights violations in terms of Von Hirsch and Jareborg's (1991) notion of crime as "intrusion" into others' human rights (such as the right to physical integrity, material support, freedom from humiliation, privacy, and autonomy). He argues that the category of violator must be expanded, on *moral* grounds, to include corporations and the state.

In our analysis of criminological theory we shall be especially concerned with the criminologists' definition of crime. Is it strictly legalistic or is it founded on a broad definition of social harm? We shall be concerned with whether criminologists believe that the subject of criminology is based on concrete notions of harm to individual victims, more abstract concepts of harms to the state, or victimless crimes deemed harmful to morality, and whether it includes crimes of the powerful and harms to human rights.

An important implication of the way theorists define crime is the image they present of the criminal who commits such behavior. As part of our analysis of definitions of crime we shall consider the construction of criminal types by theorists. We shall thus be concerned with the kinds of people presented as lawbreakers, especially in what Cohen (1966: 42) called "kinds-of-people" theories, which propose offender typologies and associate them with different kinds of crime.

Causal Logic

The purpose of all theory is to understand and explain. No matter what the underlying basis of a theory, its basic aim is to build a logical framework to explain a particular phenomenon. A primary device used in Western schools of thought is the concept of cause. The nature of cause has been the subject of philosophical debate and scientific discourse for centuries. *Causality* has been defined as the "relation between two events or states of affairs in which one brings about or produces the other" (Quinton, 1977: 92). A simple definition of *cause,* as criminologists use the concept, is "the forces or conditions that shape and influence humans to commit criminal acts." The concept of cause enables humans to explain what has happened, to predict when it will happen again, and to prevent future occurrences through the control of other events.

Just as law and definitions of crime follow from the concept of society, so criminological ideas about the causes of crime closely follow assumptions made about human nature. Theorists who see human nature as an individual phenomenon will likely develop causal explanations at the individual level.

Broadly speaking, there are two polarized positions at the individual level of explanation. The first is that criminal behavior is not caused but freely chosen. Accordingly, choosing crime is like choosing any other behavior, and though there may be situational opportunities, essentially people choose to break laws to satisfy motives. The range of such motives is endless. The following attempt to classify the basic rewards people seek demonstrates the innumerable induce-ments of the behavioral choice to commit crime.

> **Intrinsic rewards:** to enjoy fun and excitement; to obtain thrills; to get high; to satisfy curiosity. **Personal and psychological rewards:** to relieve pain, stress, tension or boredom; to establish identity; to compensate for missing expecta-tions; to cope; to avoid or escape responsibility; for self-preservation or self-defence. **Economic, monetary or material rewards:** to make money; to obtain goods and services; to correct economic injustices; to compensate for lost economic ben-efits. **Interpersonal or social rewards:** to achieve status, to earn honor and pres-tige; to repay favors; to gain acceptance; to fit in or feel normal; to stand out; to express resentment to others; to prove group loyalty; to fulfill traditional role expectations; to compete or to meet a challenge. **Political rewards:** to beat the system; to take control over one's life; to dominate or express power over others; to gain freedom. **Religious or moral rewards:** to satisfy ethical beliefs. (Henry, 1990: 145–46)

Importantly, these motives may also be satisfied by choosing to commit legal activities, so they tell us little about what causes crime nor about why some peo-ple choose legal rather than criminal behavior to satisfy the same motives. Thus theories that offer motives as causal explanations may not be explaining crime so much as describing human behavior per se.

The second position at the individual level of explanation for explaining the origins of crime is held by theorists who believe that criminal behavior is *caused* rather than freely chosen. Any motives could be causal if they were assumed to drive or predispose the individual to commit law-violating behavior rather than conforming behavior. From the perspective of internal determinism, both biological and psychological theories of crime have been proposed. The biological version includes theories that assume crime is the consequence of a variety of conditions such as internal genetic or chromosomal abnormalities, brain chemistry malfunction, metabolic or hormonal changes, dietary prac-tices, drug or substance ingestion, and so on. Moreover, some of these biological approaches assume that physical abnormality is often visible in the appearance of the individuals afflicted or can be revealed through screening or tests. The psychological and psychiatric theories of personality that operate at the indi-vidual internal level assume that crime is the product of a malformed or psy-chotic personality.

Other psychological theories, to the extent they rely on assumptions about human development, move to another level of analysis in their assumptions about cause. Insofar as others are involved, whether these are family or small groups, the explanation for crime shifts to the external level. At this level of explanation the cause of crime might be seen as a consequence of poor social-ization, imitation, social learning, reinforcement, or more general processes of social interaction. These processes either commit a person to conform to a sub-culture of law violation or else provide them with the skills and rationalizations to neutralize any internalized commitment to conformity. Although these pro-cesses involve interaction and cognition that have an outcome in a person's iden-tity, they fall into what is typically referred to as the micro level of analysis.

Criminologists who use a larger canvas and attempt to explain crime as a social phenomenon point to certain generating conditions within the culture and/or social structure itself as the causal nexus. Social structure, culture, and social institutions are concepts favored by theorists who give priority to the importance of models of society rather than models of human nature. This is referred to as macro-level analysis. These macro-level explanations of crime cau-sation assume not only that the forces predisposing or driving persons to crime are outside the control of the individual but also that they are above the level of individual intervention. Such approaches see crime as a product of the conflict between different cultures, the distribution of differential means to goal fulfill-ment; the inequalities of the social structure; and separation, fragmentation, and alienation in social life. Whereas individual, micro-level analysts often assume that causes can be scientifically diagnosed, macro-level analysts believe that the social framework, together with its accompanying ideological beliefs, prevent these causal forces from being easily seen. As a result, their analyses often require a critical method to penetrate the "veil of obscurity" surrounding con-ventional criminological interpretations of the world.

Yet others reject this dichotomy between macro and micro levels of analy-sis. They contend that while social and psychological determinants are of impor-tance in explaining crime, as is the wider social context, the conscious actor is left out of the equation. This, they argue, is a serious omission, because people do not simply commit crime in stimulus-response fashion but, rather, take conditions that affect them into account and actively shape their behavior accordingly. Some, such as social interactionists, argue that criminal behavior is created within a limited social context and is ongoingly constructed as people are con-fronted by crime-enabling situations.

Whatever level of analysis is adopted in criminological theories, some con-sideration must be given to the model of causation that is adopted by the theo-rist. Even those assuming individual free choice have to give some consideration to the situational and circumstantial opportunities that operate as factors to constrain or enable choices. This issue is of particular importance to those theo-rists who operate with either internal or external levels of analysis of cause.

Four basic models of causality are possible. Simplest is the model that assumes a single sequential linear causal chain such as A causes B, B causes C, C causes D, D causes E, and E causes Y. For example, unemployment (A), causes poverty (B), which creates stress (C), leading to family conflict (D), which can result in crimes (such as domestic violence) (Yi) or can lead to inadequate socialization of children (E), which can lead them to go astray with peers who engage in gang activity (Yii). (See Figure 1-7.)

A second type of causal explanation is multiple causality, in which a range of factors are either necessary or sufficient when occurring together to cause crime. Thus A + B + C + D may cause E, which causes Y. An example (see Figure 1–8) is that a combination of failure to develop an attachment to conventional parents (A), underachieving in school (B), conflict (unrelated) within the family (C), and alienation from the family (D) may cause an identification with a peer subculture (E) that in turn leads to gang-related activity.

A third type of causal explanation is the interactive model. Here causal factors are seen to influence each other such that crime is the outcome of a process. As Cohen (1966: 44) points out, unlike theories that emphasize mixes of multiple causes, interactive process theories do not treat the interaction as a single episode but as a process that "develops over time through a series of stages." For example, as a result of several different issues building up from childhood to adolescence a teen may come to resent her family and have weak attachments to them (A). A disregard for their admonitions about the value of school work may lead to underachievement at school (B), which results in disciplinary measures and further disrespect and disregard by the teen for her family, to the point where arguments and conflict ensue (C). As a reaction to this situation an adolescent may feel alienated from her family and its values (D) and be open to the support of similarly situated peers (E). This identification and association take time away from conventional activities such as school work and result in declining grades and further family conflict, reinforcing the strength of perceived alienation and more deeply entrenching the adolescent in her peer culture. Some of the peer culture's activities are gang related and the teen's deepening commitment to them involves her participation and resultant trouble with the law, which further reinforces the original factors contributing to family disaffection and alienation as the cycle repeats again and again more intensely. (See Figure 1-9.)

Finally, a fourth model of causality is that of dialectics. Here it is less appropriate to talk of interaction than *codetermination.* Each of the causal "entities," rather than being discrete, incorporates a part of the others so that when one changes the others change because some of the one is the other. Thus A is comprised of some of B and C, but B + C do not equal A. Likewise B is comprised of A and C but some of B is unique to itself. So in our delinquency example (see Figure 1-10), the defining characteristics of a dysfunctional family include the quality of parental attachment, the extent of internal conflict, and the experience of alienation (A). Together these are also *a part of* institutional achievement such as school achievement (B). This is because school work and attitudes toward authority are constructed not just in school but also in the family and the home. These are not only separate but also overlapping. Similarly, the peer subculture and gang delinquency (Y) are not only a street culture, they are also part of the

TYPES OF CAUSALITY

Figure 1-7   Linear Causality

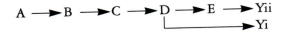

EXAMPLE

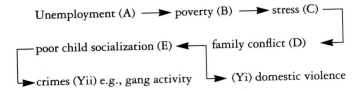

Figure 1-8   Multiple Causality

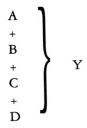

EXAMPLE

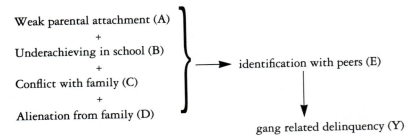

TYPES OF CAUSALITY (continued)

Figure 1-9   Interactive Causality

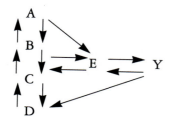

EXAMPLE

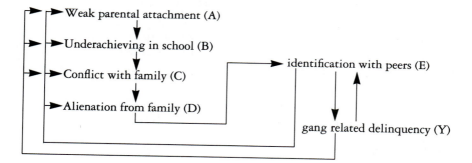

Figure 1-10   Dialectical Causality

EXAMPLE

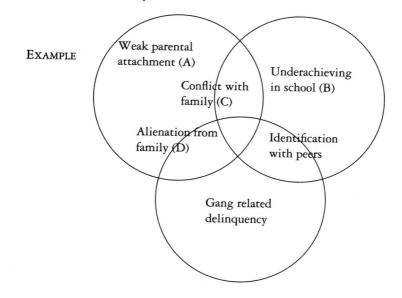

informal relations of school work and home life. As Matza and Sykes (1961) pointed out, the values of the members of delinquent subcultures overlap with and are drawn in part from the wider institutions of the dominant culture such as school and the family. Thus the more these values are asserted, the more their contrasting opposites are defined and made available. Nowhere is this relationship better expressed than in Matza's (1964) notion that the law contains the seeds of its own neutralization, whereby the more precisely the law specifies the conditions of its applicability, the more precisely it identifies the exceptions, the more complex it becomes, and the more available become the ways to evade conforming to the law, especially to those subject to its controls. So in this case the delinquent outcome is codetermined by all of those areas of life with which the teen relates and is not confined to his or her peer subculture.

In addition to adopting various models of causality, criminological theorists also have notions of the varying strengths of causal factors that comprise their models. Thus causes may be described as "necessary" in that without them the crime would not occur. They may be said to be "sufficient" in that with them alone the crime may occur. Other adjectives used to describe the relative strength of causal factors include *predisposing, conditional, contingent, precipitating, primary, secondary,* and *tertiary.* Interestingly, it is rare for criminological theories to specify the strength of the causal components of their theory. This is usually left to empirical researchers to establish.

Criminal Justice Implications

Assumptions made about crime causation have direct implications for criminal justice policy and about how actions toward offenders are justified, which in turn colors the way the institutions and procedures of justice will be used. Whereas a society may punish offenders based on specifications in criminal law, criminological theorists are concerned with overall policy, based on the logic of their theoretical analysis. Policy deals with crime as a phenomenon rather than with particular instances of lawbreaking. Thus, whereas a judge is formally constrained by the specifications of criminal law, and whereas policymakers deliberately choose strategies for policy after reviewing the evidence of alternatives, *criminologists are primarily concerned with policy that is consistent with or implied by their analysis of its cause.* For criminological theorists, then, the main constraints on policy and the accompanying correctional ideology come not from law, political expediency, or empirical efficacy, but from the logic of their own theoretical analysis.

Although policy, philosophy, and criminal justice are interrelated—some may say confused—it is important to specify what we take each to mean before proceeding. For our purposes the following definitions will apply:

Criminal justice policy refers to the overall prescription for addressing law violation that follows logically from a theory's causal analysis of the crime problem. Such policy includes (1) a correctional ideology (Shover, 1979; Shover and Einstadter, 1988) that incorporates (a) philosophies that justify the use of state power against offenders (based on the desire to achieve one or more desired outcomes or goals), and (b) strategies for action to be taken in relation to the offender, which may or may not include the victims, the community, social institutions, and the state itself; (2) an administrative apparatus, the criminal justice system, for processing offenders; and (3) actions in the form of crime control techniques (e.g., punishment, treatment, reorganization of institutions) to be applied, in conformity with the rules of the administrative system, to satisfy the goals of the philosophies and strategies previously specified (which we shall discuss below, under Criminal Justice Policy and Correctional Ideology).

Crucial to any understanding of the response of society (through its state agencies) to crime is the recognition that, while the *form* of the criminal justice system and techniques of crime control may continue to exist over long periods of time, their *content* and use in any particular historical period will depend on the policy, correctional ideology, and its associated philosophies prevailing at the time. This, in turn, depends to some extent on the popularity and favorableness of particular theories of crime causation. In other words, criminal justice and crime control techniques can be seen as "empty colorless frameworks" (to adapt from Renner's [1904] view of the law), whereas the policy, correctional ideology, and philosophy form the varying hues that make these frameworks meaningful. The interrelatedness of the form and content comprises what is typically referred to as a *model of criminal justice.* Thus commentators refer to the "medical model," the "crime control model," the "classical due process model," the "rehabilitative model," and so forth, as shorthand ways of describing the confluence of these various elements as they are implied by a particular theory or adopted in practice by different governments. Let us briefly look at criminal justice and correctional ideologies before examining the techniques of crime control.

The Criminal Justice System   As mentioned above, the criminal justice system is an institutional and procedural framework representing one means whereby the state responds to the event of crime. The system comprises procedures for processing those accused of breaking criminal laws, a means of determining whether an offense has occurred, and whether those accused committed the alleged offense, and rules specifying what should happen at each stage of the process (procedural rules).

A variety of models for how the criminal justice system should and does operate have been identified by criminologists. These include the due process, justice, crime control, bureaucratic, medical or rehabilitation, status passage, nonintervention, and radical or power models. King (1981) has described how a court is configured differently under six of these, which he terms "theoretical process models" (see Table 1-1).

Table 1-1   King's Six Process Models of Criminal Justice: The Court

PROCESS MODEL	SOCIAL FUNCTION	FEATURES OF COURT
Due Process Model	Justice	-Equality between parties -Rules protecting defendant against error -Restraint of arbitrary power -Presumption of innocence
Crime Control Model	Punishment	-Disregard of legal controls -Implicit presumption of guilt -High conviction rate -Unpleasant experience -Support for police
Medical Model	Rehabilitation	-Information-collecting procedures -Individualization -Treatment presumption -Discretion of decision makers -Expertise of decision makers or advisors -Relaxation of formal rules
Bureaucratic (Administrative) Model	Management of Crime and Criminals	-Independence from political considerations -Speed and efficiency -Acceptance of records -Minimization of conflict -Minimization of expense -Economical division of labor
Status Passage Model	Denunciation and Degradation (Shaming)	-Public shaming of defendant -Priority for community values -Agents' control over the process
Power (Radical) Model	Maintenance of Class Domination	-Reinforcement of class values -Alienation and suppression of defendant -Deflection from issues of class conflict -Differences between judges and judged -Contradictions between rhetoric and performance

Adapted from Michael King, *The Framework of Criminal Justice* (London: Croom Helm, 1981), p. 13.

Each of these have different priorities and depend on the criminal justice policy goals, which in turn are shaped by the analysis of cause (see Criminal Justice Policy and Correctional Ideology below). King (1981: 13) points out that, depending on which model has priority, there can be different effects upon components of the system such as law enforcement or the court. For example, the overall policy goal of the classical due process model is to administer justice. Therefore, the court will emphasize equality between the parties, protect the individual's sovereignty by assuming innocence, and provide rules protecting defendants against error and the arbitrary use of power. In contrast, a court influenced by the medical model will aim to rehabilitate the offender. As a result its procedures will be extensively developed with regard to diagnosis, prediction, and treatment. It will incorporate various information-gathering procedures and use experts' advice to determine the individual therapeutic needs of the case. Each of these models of criminal justice is shaped by what King refers to as a social function and what we refer to as correctional ideology.

Criminal Justice Policy and Correctional Ideology
In the history of criminological writing perhaps no other issue has more pages devoted to it than what goals should be served by sanctioning the convicted offender and what justifications exist for intervening in individuals' lives. Recently termed "correctional ideologies" (Shover, 1979; Shover and Einstadter, 1988), these philosophical assumptions are powerful determinants of penal strategies and appropriate crime control techniques.

Depending on the historical era, the political context, and the emergence of fashionable theory in criminology, different philosophies of punishment arise and become dominant, although never exclusively so. For example, during the 1950s and the early 1960s rehabilitative philosophies predominated. The more conservative era of the 1980s revived a punitive model of "just deserts." However, during the 1960s retribution was not abandoned, neither was rehabilitation absent in the 1980s. The major thrust of the philosophy of punishment reflected the dominant correctional ideology. Though ideologies and their constitutive philosophies change over time, few are ever totally abandoned and newer versions of thinly disguised old ideas may gain renewed currency and popular acceptance.

The range of philosophies that justify state or societal action in response to the problem of crime is vast. Most are concerned with justifying specific action taken against individual offenders, in light of assumptions about causality, although some also justify intervention to change the society. Young (1981) has argued that the major dichotomy in the issue of philosophies is whether to punish individuals or to treat them. However, the list of philosophies in Table 1-2, though not exhaustive, is indicative that their possible objectives are much greater than this simple division.

Table 1-2   Correctional Ideologies: Philosophies of Intervention and Their Policy Objectives

PHILOSOPHY OF SANCTIONING OR INTERVENTION	OVERALL POLICY OBJECTIVES
Prevention	Removing the conditions, motives, or incentive for crimes before they occur.
Incapacitation	Protection of the public by removing the offender's capability of committing further crimes.
Deterrence	Preventing crime either generally or specifically. General deterrence involves symbolic use of public punishment aimed at affecting the future actions of all potential offenders. Specific or individual deterrence is aimed at affecting the future behavior of particular individuals who have already offended or specific offenses that they might otherwise choose.
Retribution, or Just Deserts	The idea that offenders deserve to be punished for their offenses based solely on the harm caused by the act, thus equating the balance of harm.
Conciliation	Resolving the conflict or dispute between offender and offended.
Restitution	Returning the situation to its pre-offense standing with regard to individual victims.
Reparation	Compensation for the offense to be paid to the state or community for the harm caused to collective victims.
Rehabilitation	Interventions designed to change or correct the offenders' future behavior.
Treatment	Interventions designed to cure individuals of the cause of their offending.
Diversion	Providing alternatives to criminal justice system effects to avoid stigmatizing the offender.
Decriminalization	Removing offenses from the criminal code.
Celebration	Using the occasion of crime as an indication of the need for social, institutional, or structural change.

Techniques of Crime Control   The criminal justice system culminates in a range of actions or dispositions in the form of practices and techniques that can be used to accomplish policy and philosophical objectives. Criminal law is nothing without a specification of sanctions to enforce conformity. These typically take the form of penalties, infliction of pain or deprivation, or inducements and therapeutic treatments designed to produce behavioral change. But, like the behaviors prohibited, the severity of the sanctions or extent of the treatment varies. For example, although in seventh-century England most offenses, including murder, were subject to a variety of fines and monetary compensations, by 1819 there were 223 offenses subject to capital punishment. These included robbery, burglary, and housebreaking, as well as some forms of vandalism, deception, and impersonation, and "many other acts, more or less reprehensible, some of which had not even been crimes, let alone capital ones, before" (Hibbert, 1963: 71). By 1896 there were only 4 capital offenses on the English statutes (Earle, 1896: 149). Moreover, changes in social organization and technology render some punishments less obvious than others at different historical periods. For example, at first sight it seems that in the sixteenth and seventeenth century bilboes, stocks, and the pillory were no more in use than today is the ducking stool, the whipping post, or branding and maiming. The close-knit social relations that allowed these techniques to be used to invoke shame are no longer as apparent, although calls by MADD (Mothers Against Drunk Driving) for the names of drunken drivers to be published and decried in the news media may indicate that technology has merely changed the form of certain punishments. And the experience of wearers of the modern-day electronic tether may be comparable to those whose ankles were clamped in the bilboes (Earle, 1896). Indeed, recent developments in information technology bringing about the "virtual community" may see the emergence of branding through the electronic bulletin board!

By *techniques of crime control* we refer to the actual sanctions or enforcement techniques or intervention and change strategies administered to the individuals, institutions, or the wider social structure with the aim of limiting the amount and extent of crime. Though the philosophies outlined above are linked to the type of causal analysis that is at the heart of criminological theory, it is important to recognize that the technique used to control crime and to meet the philosophy is not the same as the philosophy itself. The two are often confused. Moreover, techniques of control may be suggested singly or in combination. Nor do techniques of control necessarily reflect a single perspective. Similar methods of attempting to control crime may be implicit in different theoretical perspectives but serve different philosophical objectives. For example, the technique of levying fines can be used as a punishment, as a deterrent, as retribution, and, if paid to the victim, even as restitution. But fines do not satisfy the goals of treatment nor those of incapacitation (except in the case of property forfeiture, since here the property, such as drug-making equipment or transportation, is necessary to continue the crime). Similarly, family therapy or counseling might serve to correct offenders, satisfying the philosophy of rehabilitation and prevention, but these are questionable for exacting retribution and do not generally attempt to deter.

It is clear, therefore, that some techniques may serve one or more philosophies while others, such as community service, may serve a single philosophy, such as reparation. It is worth noting that of all the available techniques of crime control, prison is the one that is claimed to satisfy the most wide-ranging set of philosophies. This might account for its universal popularity as a sanction, regardless of its effectiveness or ineffectiveness.

Policy, correctional ideology, procedures, and sanctions are closely inter-related. They are contingent upon the overall logic of the theoretical analysis. This can be clearly illustrated with an example. Suppose the criminologist's perspective on crime is that of biological positivism. Within this perspective crime, such as the rape of a female, may be seen as the product of genetic defects that produce high testosterone levels among certain members of the male population. From this perspective laws recommending punishment for sexual crimes might be questioned on the grounds that punishing the sick for their illness is not going to cure them. Nor for that matter is it going to prevent other similarly sick people from committing sexual crimes. The policy recommended by those subscribing to biological theory, therefore, would need to reflect the individual nature of the cause. The primary policy, therefore, might stress a correctional ideology emphasizing the philosophies of prevention and treatment—in other words, a medical model. Theorists would likely suggest that the criminal justice system provide for preventative procedures that require people to be screened at an early age for suspect genes. Those found to have them might be required either to submit to a variety of clinical crime prevention (control) techniques, such as genetic engineering, hormone-reducing drugs, or chemical or surgical castration. Alternatively, they might be segregated from others to prevent reproduction of their genes. A similar range of crime control techniques could be used to implement a treatment philosophy aimed at curing the convicted sex offender: chemical castration would be an option instead of prison.

In contrast, a socialist-feminist theory of crime might begin with a view of society as patriarchal, as subordinating women as objects of control. From this perspective male offenders might be considered as acting out their gender-structured masculinity. Clearly, there would be little place for correctional ideologies emphasizing individual biological treatment. Prevention of the problem would also be an appropriate policy aim. However, strategies would be designed to intervene at various levels in the social structure. The criminal justice policy of such a perspective would likely involve interventions designed to eliminate the domination of male attitudes in centers of power. Actions might include a ban on media portrayals denigrating women and glorifying machismo and might also require interspersing women's studies throughout the school curriculum.

It is also important to recognize that because of the bureaucratic inertia in institutional systems, there is a recurring discovery and resurrection of techniques of crime control. Importantly, because no theoretical perspective or correctional ideology predominates, the criminal justice systems found in practice typically contain elements of several competing models of criminal justice (reflecting the several competing theories from which they are derived). This can create considerable confusion, conflict, and poor morale among criminal justice practitioners, who may resolve and simplify their dilemma by making a commitment to, or even championing, one approach or even one favored technique.

Evaluation of the Theories

As we explained from the outset, it is not our main purpose to evaluate the various theoretical perspectives on the basis of how well they are supported by research evidence. That task has been undertaken by numerous introductory criminology texts and research monographs, and it constitutes the bulk of the content of professional criminology and criminal justice journals. Indeed, such evaluation would require that we accept a particular commitment to positivist research methodology that is inconsistent with the methodological implications of some of the theoretical approaches we examine. Nonetheless, we are concerned that students get a sense of the overall empirical validity of the different approaches. Therefore, we provide a summary of the major empirical findings without assessing the relative merits of the studies. However, we are concerned with the logic of the various theoretical frameworks. Thus at the end of each chapter we explore a number of critical assessments that have been made of the theories. Our purpose is not to provide an exhaustive critical review but rather to highlight some of the problems that theorists have left unresolved. In reading these sections, the student should remember that "Criticism is rarely disinterested. What passes for detached assessment is often a partisan advocacy of the reviewer's own work" (Downes and Rock, 1982: 70).

A COMPARATIVE ANALYSIS

Overall, then, our analysis of theories according to the foregoing categories is designed to show both how these theories are similar and how they are different. Such an approach enables the reader to compare the theories' assumptions about key issues. For purposes of clarity we will not be very concerned with how particular theories have been differently interpreted, and only superficially with the extent to which they have been empirically supported. Instead we will be primarily interested in identifying the key assumptions contained in the writings of certain theorists insofar as they indicate their position on the major dimensions we have identified above. As indicated in Table 1-3, it may be helpful to recognize that criminology takes a multidisciplinary approach to its subject and that each of the theoretical frameworks we consider has roots in wider disciplinary inquiry.

Table 1-3   Multidisciplinary Roots of Criminological Theory

THEORETICAL FRAMEWORK	DISCIPLINARY ROOTS
Demonological Theories	Theology Paganism
Classical and Rational Choice Theories	Economics Rational Philosophy
Individual Positivism I: Biological Theories	Biology Genetics Neurology Anthropology
Individual Positivism II: Personality Theories	Psychiatry Psychology
Sociological Positivism I: Social Ecology Theories	Geography Sociology Anthropology
Sociological Positivism II: Strain Theories	Sociology Economics Anthropology
Social Process Theory I: Learning, Bonding, and Social Control Theories	Psychology Social Psychology Sociology
Social Process II: Interactionism, Labeling, and Social Constructionist Theories	Philosophy Social Psychology Sociology
Critical Criminology I: Conflict, Anarchist, and Marxist Theories	Philosophy Political Science Sociology Economic History
Critical Criminology II: Feminist Theories	Philosophy Sociology History
Critical Criminology II: Postmodernist Theories	History Philosophy Sociology Feminism Linguistics Literature

Let us now turn to the first of these frameworks, demonology, which has its roots in both theology and paganism. Interestingly, demonology contains the seeds of subsequent ideas about crime. Here in this primary and historically most far-reaching framework, lies the fundamental contradiction between "free will," in the idea of contracts with the devil, and determinism, in the notion of soul possession.

CHAPTER TWO

Demonological Theories

It might seem somewhat curious to begin our analysis of criminological theory with a look at pre-criminological thought. However, much can be learned from a cursory, yet analytical, examination of the ideas about crime that preceded the rise of classicist rational logic in the seventeenth century and that still have serious professional advocates today.[1] Paradoxically, the logic relied on by demonology has considerable parallels in subsequent criminological thought. Indeed, within demonology is contained both a precursor of the classicist idea of freedom of choice and a forerunner of the deterministic idea of causality (Pfohl, 1985). The concept of freedom to choose is reflected in the notion of "temptation to evil." However, this freedom is somewhat limited, not least by the assumption of human susceptibility to evil forces and the recognition that any compact made with the Devil cannot voluntarily be rescinded.

Thus several commentators (Szasz, 1961, 1973; Sarbin and Miller, 1970; Suchar, 1978; Henderson, 1982; and Asch, 1985) have recognized that demonology, as a complete explanatory framework, has more in common with the determinism of scientific criminology. This determinism can be seen primarily in the idea of "demonic possession" but is also implied in the assumption of the relative powerlessness of humans to resist a driving force and in the reverence for uniquely qualified persons to harness, defuse, or control the force (i.e., professional psychiatrists, medical practitioners, "diviners," "witch finders," or Catholic priests). These experts are perceived to have special powers to diagnose the cause of the force and to conduct formal testing procedures both to confirm its presence and to effect its removal, often at the expense of the carrier. Moreover, positivistic and demonological theories also share the view that multiple causes can produce a wide range of deviant behavior. Until relatively recently, the insane were popularly believed to be possessed; now they are generally

---

[1]We are not implying that there is a linear relationship between demonology and modern criminological thought. We are essentially concerned with theoretical frameworks that, as we have seen, coexist at several points in time. However, it is worth pointing out that the content of particular frameworks differs in certain respects, depending on the historical period and the cultural context in which it is manifest. For example, the pagan European view of demonology and witchcraft that existed prior to the ninth century was different from the religious and fantasy views that arose in the fifteenth century and that prevailed into the seventeenth century. Indeed, while folklore upheld the pagan view that did not relate witches to the Devil, later they were seen as very much the Devil's project. It is essentially this viewpoint we shall discuss here, as it is imbued with Western civilization's logic. For a general discussion of the earlier conceptions of witchcraft and witchcraft in other cultures see Mair (1969).

portrayed as diseased. However, as we shall see, there are still serious advocates, largely Christian psychologists and pastors, who take the view that mental illness is the work of the Devil.[2]

BASIC IDEA, CENTRAL MOTIF, AND MAJOR THEORISTS

Demonology, the subject of books by numerous authorities, even kings (e.g., by King James I in his early-sixteenth-century *Daemonologie*), has been described as "the spiritual explanation" (Vold and Bernard, 1986; Holman and Quinn, 1992), "the prescientific view" (Barnes and Teeters, 1943), the "natural depravity view" (Yablonsky, 1990: 425), and even as a "pseudo-science" (Mair, 1969: 223). However, demonology is essentially a theological theory of crime.

The essential idea of demonology is that any malevolent interference in the ongoing nature of life, including human relationships, is seen as the result of demonic forces. Demons themselves emanate from various supernatural or "otherworldly" powers. At various times the source has been said to be the tormented souls of women who died in childbirth, or of those who expired from suicide, or the dead but not yet buried. Ultimately, in the West, since the rise of Christian theology, demons were the agents or servants of the deeper force, the Devil, the chief demon, the proverbial "root of all evil" and the antithesis of God. Whatever their source, all these forces of evil are generated from powers outside those whom they subsequently invade.

Nonconforming behavior was brought about either through "temptation" or "possession" (Pfohl, 1985: 20–21). Temptation resulted from a weakness of faith in God and from the implied weakness of humans for worldly, especially carnal, pleasures. These pleasures were aroused by devilish temptation and were exchanged in a "compact" made with the Devil. This pact sealed the sale of their soul. Those who signed such a pact were designated as witches. "Possession" in contrast, left humans with little choice in their allegiance with the world of darkness, since humans were here seen to be "taken over," "seized," and "directed to evil" against their will. Whether temptation ultimately led to possession was an issue in some dispute.

A rudimentary societal policy to combat demonic forces underlies the correctional ideology of the philosophies of "protection," and "exorcism." As in the subsequent medical model of prevention and cure these are effective only when the authoritative persons administer precise, sacred, and ritualistic "spells," "charms," and "talismans," either to ward off, or to chase out, the demons.

---

[2]For example, Crabtree's (1985) theory of multiple personality distinguishes multiple personality disorder from demonic possession but recognizes both and sees each requiring a different type of intervention. See also the arguments in defense of demonology by Wilson (1989), and for a general review of exorcism in the modern world see Goodman (1988).

Historically, such "control practices" could only be performed by specially gifted persons, typically holy men, witch finders, or other "cunning folk." With the formation of nation states and of centralized religious authority, the job of demonic control became increasingly centralized: "Divinely ordained officials administer ritual punishments that purge offenders of demonic influence and restore God's blessing upon the entire community of the faithful" (Pfohl, 1985: 28). Even today it is claimed that specialists in exorcism or spiritual counseling are necessary to deal with those possessed, and often these are priests of the Catholic Church.

Where the source of behavior is seen to be in the displeasure of various gods, rather than the proactive work of the Devil, the societal response embodies a philosophy of "appeasement" through sacrifice and symbolic displays of deference, rather than exorcism. Similar is the idea that unless one undergoes a religious conversion to Christianity, one will continue to be vulnerable to evil (Colson, 1980, cited in Vold, 1986: 8). Contemporary theologians see Christian counselors as those best equipped to combat the necessary "spiritual warfare" and that exorcism is one of their essential tools. (For recent reviews of exorcism see Baker, 1974, and Goodman, 1988).

HUMANS, HUMAN NATURE, AND HUMAN BEHAVIOR

Demonology has a limited view of human agency. Humans are seen as (1) open to ideas and suggestions, (2) vulnerable to the force of evil, and (3) liable to be possessed by demons or the Devil. Historically, as Suchar (1978: 39) points out, "the belief in demons existed alongside the rationalistic understanding of human choice and volition." Humans were all capable of sinning. However, although evil spirits or demonic possession were responsible for some sins, they were not responsible for all. A distinction was made that some were possessed while others, such as witches, were considered to be willing or desirous to do evil. As we have seen, the notion of possession presents the extreme deterministic possibility that a "person is believed to be literally taken over by the devil or some evil spirit. Once possessed, a person may be viewed as no longer responsible—as no longer able to choose between good and evil, sin or conformity" (Pfohl, 1985: 21). For other persons, demonology is less deterministic, assuming that "humans are afforded some measure of choice" (Pfohl, 1985: 20). An element of individual choice is implied for deals made by ordinary people on such weighty matters as contracting to sell their soul to the devil. Humans are seen by some, in accord with St. Thomas Aquinas, one of the founders of natural law theory, as being implanted before birth with a "soul" that provides us with reasoning power, rationality, and morality. These ideas have parallels with much later classicist thought, which claims that humans are equally endowed with the ability to reason and can each rationally calculate.

Under demonology humans are also seen as having a vulnerability and susceptibility toward evil. Because of Adam and Eve's fall from grace over the issue of "forbidden fruit," "we are said to be weakened and seducible by the multiple forms taken by the devil—sloth, anger, lust, pride, envy, gluttony, greed" (Pfohl, 1985: 21) but are generally prepared to resist such temptation. Again, resistance to demonic temptation implies a degree of will, as does "deciding to seek spiritual help" (Holman and Quinn, 1992: 44). Resistance is also assisted by the dictates of law and the state, by family and adherence to conventional values and institutions, and crucially by a belief in God as the superior supreme being. Reflected here, from an *analytical* standpoint, is control theory's basic idea that all humans are susceptible to rule breaking unless cajoled or persuaded to do otherwise. Religiously, insofar as present-day Christian fundamentalist theologians are concerned, faith in God represents the light; turning out the light allows in the darkness, in the form of drugs, pornography, and other forms of sin. So people have the power to resist crime by having faith in God.

VIEW OF SOCIETY AND THE SOCIAL ORDER

To those sharing a demonological view, society represents God's kingdom on earth. The state of a society is seen as the outcome of the battle between powers; not class, status, or party powers, as in conflict theory (which demonology's approach to society nonetheless anticipates), but the powers of "good and evil" (Pfohl, 1985: 20). Thus Barnes and Teeters (1943: 2–3) point out that: "the condition of any community [is] regarded as in large part, determined by the struggle between good and evil spirits." Mair (1969: 198) points out that the stronger the belief in a single God personifying all goodness, the stronger the belief in a single Devil personifying all evil, although not all theology conforms to this pattern.

The social order during the politically dominant era of Christian theology was feudalism, the concentration of power and wealth divided between the secular elite that comprised the monarchy and their manorial lords, and the spiritual elite embodied in the Church. The Church decided moral matters and had both the persuasion and power to expunge dissenters either directly or through its influence over civilian powers (Suchar, 1978: 37).

In the past, the idea of community consensus was strong and the resistance to change brought a fear of instability. For Erikson (1966) the appearance of the devil in, for example the witchcraft accusations in 1692 in Salem, served a symbolic function of reaffirming social boundaries at a time when the society was experiencing fragmentation and a shift in religious belief to a more liberal Puritanism.

THE ROLE OF LAW, THE DEFINITION OF CRIME, AND THE IMAGE OF THE CRIMINAL

The Christian theology informing the version of demonology that we examine here sees the law operating on a hierarchy of levels. The thirteenth-century ideas of St. Thomas Aquinas are indicative. For Aquinas the highest law is *eternal law,* that of God himself. Beneath this is positive *divine law,* the codification of that law into written religious texts. These lay the foundation for the commands and prohibitions of *natural law,* which is held to be universally valid and unchangeable. Finally, beneath natural law is *human law* and its codification in the law books.

Perhaps not surprisingly, the offenses committed as a result of demonic possession or witchcraft, even where this is not an offense per se, are considered not simply to be against humans or human law, but against God. As Pfohl (1985: 21) says, the deviant act is "believed to harm more than a particular or immediate victim." It is, "a transgression against God ... it is also an act against the whole order of nature itself, against the entire cosmos." In this sense the common interests of all are defended by the Church against "cosmic disruption" (ibid.).

In European witch trials the actual offense was often heresy, based on the prohibition against making a pact with the devil.[3] What was defined as heretical was what the Church saw as any deviation from its doctrine and practice, and from faith in God. Suchar (1978: 37) says that "definitions of heresy were usually broad enough to include anyone who incurred the displeasure of Church officials for whatever violation of conventional behavior." He cites Sumner quoting a twelfth-century definition: a heretic is a person who "in any way differed, in mode of life, from the faithful in general," whether this be in conversation, language, dress, or manners (ibid.; Sumner, 1906: 242–43). In matters of sexuality, deviance was equated with sin, and homosexuality in particular "was defined as a person in a supernatural state and being possessed by devils" (Bell, 1971: 248, cited by Suchar 1978: 40). As Szasz (1973) says, there was no distinction made between homosexuality as a state of being and practices such as sodomy and heresy.

It has been argued by some that definitions of heresy were shaped by bureaucratic church interests. For example, Currie (1968) argues that the emphasis on the discovery, conviction, and execution of witches in Europe was

---

[3]However, as Mair (1969: 184) argues, witchcraft in African cultures is also part of an ordinary person's "explanation of misfortune in terms of the ill will of neighbors," especially ill will from those with whom one had quarreled (see Macfarlane, 1970). Indeed, in some non-Western cultures, the belief in witchcraft is not a deviation from the accepted religious or moral beliefs but an intrinsic part of the "magico-religious complex" (Mair, 1969: 181, 185).

based on the fact that upon conviction witches' property was confiscated by the Church and its officials. Thus "the bureaucratic officials had a vested interest in the deviance of witches as well as in a continuing supply of them" (Higgins and Butler, 1982: 57).

From the demonological perspective criminals are seen as evil, sinners, supernatural pawns, buggers, and heretics. In spite of condemnation for original sin, which is weakness in the face of temptation, the person committing an offense is sometimes the subject of sympathy, especially if he or she were possessed or "afflicted" with an evil force allowed in by virtue of weakness of spiritual faith. Criminals, therefore, are seen as, "puppets of the supernatural" (Vold and Bernard, 1986: 32), the medium of devils, "forced to perform their evil will" (Yablonsky, 1990: 425). Under certain circumstances, however, the human agent, as witch, is more active and thereby more responsible (Suchar, 1978: 39). As active agents, witches have the ability to turn themselves *voluntarily* into cats or werewolves and are said to be accompanied by various helpers, in the form of "imps," "goblins," or "familiars," typically cats, dogs, or other creatures known to have suckled at the witches' variously placed nipples.

CAUSAL LOGIC

Within the framework of demonology, the cause of crime and deviance is held ultimately to be a supernatural force that directs its carrier to commit harm toward others, against God and against the cosmos. Where the supernatural force is seen as the Devil, he is held to be antagonistic toward humans insofar as they represent and serve God. Around the year 400 St. Augustine argued that, "Evil (crime) resulted from influences of the devil ... Criminals were possessed by the devil" (Masters and Roberson, 1990: 54, 55). Beginning in 1692, America's Massachusetts Bay Puritan Colony experienced three crime waves that were blamed on the Devil (Erikson, 1966).

Though it was both the force and the person that together committed the act, for many it was the demonic force that was primarily responsible for the crime. Interestingly, a gender distinction was also made. Thus, as Barnes and Teeters (1943: 2) point out,

> Criminals were regarded as persons whose acts were instigated by evil spirits ... The criminal was a person who did the bidding of the evil spirits and thus translated their malicious intent into specific and menacing human activity ... the criminal was a man who succumbed to diabolical temptation. The worst of all criminals was the witch who had made a contract with the devil.

For St. Thomas Aquinas (around the year 1250) evil, in the form of crime, occurred because human appetites toward worldly pleasures were enticed by the Devil to overcome our conscience embodied in our God-given soul.[4] In this endeavor the Devil had helpers, an "army of demons" (Suchar, 1978: 38) in the form of evil angels

> who had the ability to unite themselves to bodies and to communicate their knowledge and commands to men. They were a hierarchically organized army in the service of Satan working for the perdition of the faithful. Satan and his hosts could tempt human beings into their service. (Kors and Peters, 1972: 8, cited by Suchar 1978: 38)

All people were held to be subject to "satanic promptings," which if given a positive response, would result in some degree of possession by the powers of darkness (Omand, 1977). However, not all people were equally susceptible to possession, since the fervently faithful could resist. Nor were all equally subject to the harms of those possessed. Traditionally, the poor believed they were victimized by witches and devils: "Preoccupied with the fantastic activities of these demons, the distraught, alienated, and pauperized masses blamed the rampant Devil instead of the corrupt and the rapacious nobility (Harris, 1974: 238, cited in Higgins and Butler, 1982: 18).

More recent political theologians and fundamentalist commentators concentrate their attributions of Devil-inspired crime to particularly horrific crimes—such as in the claim by the reverend Pat Robertson that the Jonestown murder—suicide of nine hundred persons in Guyana was a result of the demonic possession of their leader Jim Jones (Higgins and Butler, 1982: 18)—or to disturbed deviant behavior. At least one academic researcher has reportedly studied the relationship between narcotics and Satan and theorizes that "drug addicts become 'outright apprentices' of the devil" (Yablonsky, 1990: 425).

Most of the recent demonological analysis, however, relates to the role of demons in the etiology of mental illness. Bufford (1989), for example, argues that mental illness and demonic possession are separate phenomena that may occur together or separately and influence each other. Page (1989b) argues that psychological and demonic explanations of certain types of aberrant human behavior may be complementary and compatible. Others have identified criteria in the Scriptures that can be used to differentiate demonic possession from mental illness (Virkler and Virkler, 1977). For some, demonizing is defined as a spiritual-psy-

---

[4]It has been pointed out that this view has parallels with Freudian psychoanalysis, whereby "demonic powers" are the unconscious fears, fantasy, guilt, and hostility that are a "natural part" of humans, and the psychotherapist is the successor to the exorcist in relieving the patient of these "bad" forces (Henderson, 1976; Gettis, 1976). Earlier, Freudian analysis was invoked in a re-interpretation of the Salem witchcraft accusations, where these were explained as hysteria (Starkey, 1949).

chological illness of a person who is willing either consciously or unconsciously, to have Satan enter, organize, and take control of the person's psyche and soul because a part of the self seeks dominion over the total self (Southard and Southard, 1985; Southard, 1986). However, not all who believe in possession take the view that this has to emanate from the single Satanic source. One recent commentator (Crabtree, 1985) suggests that most possessions are not demonic but are caused by blood relatives who may be dead or alive.

CRIMINAL JUSTICE SYSTEM IMPLICATIONS

To determine the presence of evil forces a set of procedures was established that can be construed as parallel to the secular criminal justice system.[5] Elements of the "demonological" criminal justice system include, divination, torture, the use of oracles, trial by ordeal, and, of course, the Inquisition. The hallmark of demonological "justice" is some system, usually formal and ritualized, for determining whether the untoward behavior exhibited by an accused is indicative of the presence of demons or evil spirits, or whether the person possessed is a witch. In the first stage of the process in suspected witchcraft accusations, persons with alleged special powers, known as "diviners," "witch-finders," or "cunning folk," are available for consultation. Diviners "are believed to posses a God-given 'second sight' such that they can trace the origins of evil spirits and spells. The expert testimony of a diviner is, however, open to challenge. In this sense the role of diviner is much like that of a psychiatrist in a contemporary criminal trial within our own society" (Pfohl, 1985: 22).

Use of these special persons is followed with a trial by ordeal. As Mair (1969: 181) points out, the crime of witchcraft is "impossible to detect by everyday means, is treated differently from other crimes, and the ordeals which traditionally provided one means of detection could inflict great physical suffering." In the case of witchcraft, whether the accused was guilty might be decided by the "swimming," "floating," or "ducking" ordeal:

> A witch, bound and cross-bound with her right thumb tied to her left toe and her right toe to her left thumb, would float if flung into a pond. If she did float she was pulled out to be punished as a witch; if she did not her relatives had the com-

---

[5]In this regard it is important to realize that even within periods of fervent demonology, many offenses were not interpreted within this framework. They were not seen to be caused by supernatural forces and were not subject to the special processes we discuss here. A parallel may be drawn with the modern system of criminal justice with respect to those offenses said to result from mental illness, subject to mental health diagnostic procedures and to treatment, as opposed to the majority of other nonmedicalized offenses. On the relationship between diagnosing deviance and mental illness as witchcraft see Szasz, 1973.

fort perhaps of knowing that, even though dead, she had been proved innocent to their own satisfaction if not always that of her accusers (Hibbert, 1966: 45).[6]

Other ordeals included trial by fire, in which the accused was asked to hold white-hot irons or coals for a specified time, and trial by immersion in boiling oil, among others (Suchar, 1978: 41).

Ordeals such as these, then, were a form of divination or discovery of the evidence for possession and, though extremely hazardous, did not have to, nor did they always end in death. The cruelty of these procedures was considered necessary to elicit the truth. This was also true for torture.

The usual purpose of torture as part of a witch trial was to elicit a confession of guilt.[7] Mair (1969: 183) says that

> witch trials are described as determined attempts to secure, by confession under torture if there is no other way, evidence that the accused person has not only been guilty of murder but has also consorted with the Devil in obscene and blasphemous rites and sexual embraces.

A commonly employed device for achieving such information or confessions was "the rack," on which people would be stretched. By the late sixteenth century in England torture was becoming popular in criminal trials. Hibbert (1966: 39) informs us that it could also include other techniques such as a body-pressing appliance known as the "Scavenger's Daughter," "a device that crushed the body until the blood spurted out of the nostrils and the tips of the fingers instead of stretching it 'until the bones and joints were almost plucked asunder.'"

The idea of torture was not only to obtain information, or a confession, but to force people to plead guilty or not guilty:

> Admissions of deviance were literally produced by the disembodiment of deviants from their present sinful state. The reactions of suspected deviants to the searing pain of inquisitional torture were studied as a sign from above as to

---

[6]It is important to point out that "ducking" was not only used as an ordeal but also as a punishment for "scolding women" and for kindred offenders, such as slanderers, as well as for scolding men and even quarrelsome married couples, who were tied to the ducking stool back to back (Earle, 1896: 11–12). Similarly, other procedures, such as torture, were not used exclusively in witchcraft trials but were also employed in secular trials when dealing with ordinary offenses, just as it is today by some state governments (see Cohen, 1991).

[7]Cohen (1991: 90), in a critical review of the modern-day use of torture says it has typically been justified on utilitarian grounds that it is necessary as a method "of obtaining information, intelligence, testimony, confessions or evidence." In contrast, he argues that, as in the case of slavery, "the only morally defensible position about torture is abolitionist."

whether the accused was guilty of a particular act. While the guilty eventually cried out admissions, it was believed that God fortified the innocent to persevere during the ordeal of their diagnosis. Thus it was entirely possible that the innocent might ultimately be vindicated only by the steadfast endurance of pain until death. (Pfohl, 1985: 23)

However, it was recognized that "witchcraft may be stronger than counter-magic, and so impair the judgment of divination or ordeal ... (and) that the Devil may confer on his subjects a gift of taciturnity which enables them to refuse confession even under torture" (Mair, 1969: 224).

In sixteenth-century England, though torture was used to get confessions, the ordeal was a private procedure, not part of a court trial. Courts were to take no account of the results of ordeals, but the judges and justices did rely on rumor, opinion, witnesses, and, importantly, manuals containing what today we would call "profiles" of stereotypical witches. The main criterion for confirming witchcraft seems to have been the discovery of marks or spots, such as warts or moles, on the accused's body, supposedly made by the Devil and through which he was supposed to have entered (Mair, 1969: 193). In the United States of the seventeenth century and especially in the Salem witchcraft trials, suspected and accused witches, in addition to being identified by physical marks, ordeals, and confessions, also were assessed by "spectral evidence." According to Pfohl (1985: 24), "This involved reports of persons who had supposedly seen 'floating specters,' or ghostly forms which had taken the shape or appearance of one of the accused. The basis for this particular identification strategy was the belief that the devil cannot assume the shape of an innocent person."

Criminal Justice Policy and Correctional Ideology

In the demonological model, the basic philosophy justifying intervention involved prevention and exorcism, but punishment was also seen as warranted. An important distinction was made between humans and spirits. Punishment of those who survived a witchcraft ordeal was directed at the person, not the spirit, both for their original sin in making a pact with the Devil and for the harm they committed against another. As Mair (1969: 181) says, "the person found guilty, unlike the fantasy witch, is an ordinary human being, and if he is punished, it is for what he is held to have done, and not for being intrinsically unworthy to exist."

Prevention was aimed at self-protection. Protection was taken either against the possibility of being seduced by the Devil and thereby becoming a witch, or against the witchcraft practices of another. The latter form of protection was typically against the undetected witch.

Perhaps the more interesting justification for intervention in demonology was for the purpose of removing the source of evil. Even when acts on the body of a person, from a secular vantage point, may have looked like punishment, their purpose "was to purge the body of a sinner of traces of the devil and thereby restore the body of the community as a whole to its proper relation to God, [to] remind participants of the supreme reality of God's will and, by purging evil, restore humans to their proper relationship as servants of the divine" (Pfohl, 1985: 25).

The evil could never be completely eliminated because it was the Devil. However, it could be chased out. The aim of intervention under exorcism was to remove the evil source from its present "site" in the person possessed. If this was not possible, the site was to be expunged or incapacitated, which typically meant death or at least exile or banishment.

Techniques of Crime Control

If the accused survived the torment of torture and the trial, they were then subject to various techniques designed to satisfy the correctional ideology for the control of crime (evil). From a secular perspective, these too were often barbarous. However, like some twentieth-century psychiatric treatments such as electric shock or lobotomy, it was often difficult to distinguish them from punishment. Perhaps most symbolic were the various techniques used to conduct exorcism.

As Crabtree (1985) describes the ritual, exorcism was not a pretty process. It could involve violence, vomit, stench, and levitation as well as the expression of unrepentant hatred. Moreover, if it failed to be effective, either the carrier had to be removed from the community, or else their life had to be forfeited. Death was not so much to punish them but to frustrate the Devil and close down one of his vehicles for evil on earth. As Masters and Roberson (1990: 54) point out, "If exorcism failed to drive the devil out of the "sinners," they were turned over to civil authorities, and "capital punishments and other brutal punishments were used to eradicate the devil." Indeed, among the capital offenses of Massachusetts in the years 1641–43 they cite that "if any man or woman be a Witch, that is, hath or consulteth with a familiar spirit, they shall be put to death" (Masters and Roberson 1990: 56). But even death as a technique had the larger and somewhat therapeutic purpose of freeing the human spirit from the Devil's clutches. Whether the devil was also freed in the death of his subject is questionable since, in some cultures, signs of the Devil's invasion were met with death by strangulation as a prelude to burning, which was done "to prevent the escape of the evil spirit" (Higgins and Butler, 1982: 17).

In sixteenth-century Europe witches were nearly always burned, not least because this or drowning had been advocated since 1485 by the Dominican monks Heinrich Kramer and Jakob Sprenger (1485–86) in the classic *Malleus Maleficarum (Witch's Hammer)*. The burning of witches is said to be justified because of its effect of destroying the witch completely. Hibbert (1966: 45) quotes one authority on the European witch hunts of the Inquisition, saying that by the sixteenth century

> witches were burned no longer in ones or twos but in scores and hundreds. A bishop of Geneva is said to have burned five hundred within three months; a bishop of Bamburg six hundred, a bishop of Wurzburg nine hundred. Eight hundred were condemned, apparently in one body by the senate of Savoy. (Hibbert, 1966, quoting H. C. Lea, 1906)

As Pfohl (1985: 25) explains, burning also "evoked an image of hell as the final resting place for unpurged sinners," and so burning functioned to symbolize the dominant perception of the social order.

Less severe techniques of control are more apparent in the present-day manifestations of demonological perspectives than in its historical record. However, historically, gentler techniques included the pursuit of spiritual guidance; sacrifice; appeasement or atonement; and enforced pilgrimages to religious shrines; as well as placement in monasteries, convents, and hospitals (Rosen, 1968: 142; Suchar, 1978: 39). Indeed, the early use of the prison under the concept of "penitentiary" is derived from the idea of penitence, meaning regret of wrongdoing and willingness to atone for it. It was for this reason that persons were often placed in solitary confinement, since this "would force them to reflect on their crimes and spiritually develop to a point where they could resist demonic temptation or seek the protection of a benevolent spiritual force (God)" (Holman and Quinn, 1992: 44).

Recent approaches to demonic possession recommend exorcism (Page, 1989a; Omand, 1977) and usually involve some form of pastoral counseling. One commentator, for example, claims it is necessary to keep up the spiritual war with Satan and his minions and argues that Christian counselors are the only mental health workers appropriately equipped for this warfare (Wilson, 1989). Indeed, some see little distinction between demonic possession and psychopathology, arguing that psychotherapy is part of the larger ministry of the Church (Bach, 1979).

EVALUATION

As a theoretical framework demonology is essentially a belief system and, as such, is not readily testable. Pfohl (1985: 19) has noted that although the perspective, "functions as a powerful explanation of the causes, consequences and control of deviant behavior" in earlier historical and in some contemporary tribal societies, "in our own Western society such a perspective is apt to be viewed as little more than superstition." Indeed he says that "judged by naturalistic standards of the secularized modern world, the demonic perspective is very inadequate" but points out that a more accurate assessment is that it relies on beliefs, "no longer believed in as much as other beliefs" (p. 36). In spite of this it should not be thought that demonology was accepted by everyone, even in its heyday. Mair

(1969) points out that even in the fifteenth century, critics challenged aspects of its own logic. Thus one such critic, a Puritan Elizabethan clergyman, George Gifford, was particularly critical of the powers of "cunning folk" or witch finders who he believed were themselves inspired by Satan and were no less culpable than witches. The Devil knew when disasters would befall and stirred up trouble between persons so that they would think they had been bewitched, resulting in false accusations. Believing that the Devil was responsible, said Gifford, served as a convenient excuse to avoid responsibility for one's own ungodliness:

> Gifford maintains that people evade the searching of conscience by ascribing to witches what is in fact deserved punishment, and that the "cunning men" to whom they go for remedies are themselves sent by the Devil to distract them from attention to their sins and reliance on the scriptures for guidance. (Mair, 1969: 185)

Perhaps the most insightful criticism comes from analysts like Szasz (1973) who, in their comparison of witchcraft and positivism, echo sixteenth-century Gifford in seeing demonology as a political process of "scapegoating" misfortune onto innocent but different others or onto uncontrollable forces. Scapegoating makes us feel normal and good about ourselves. Its modern-day versions include racism, homophobia, and the idea of "Evil Empires." "By providing a hated symbol of the abnormal and antisocial, the witch strengthens cultural conceptions of normatively approved social behavior" (Peoples and Bailey, 1988: 321).

Some recent commentators such as Holman and Quinn (1992: 44) claim that the spiritual school is "no longer accepted by most people today" even though "it dominated society up until the late 15th century." However, recent assessment is less dismissive of demonology than one might think. We have seen that as a practitioner-supported view, it was pervasive until well into the seventeenth century and that it continues today, among Christian psychologists and pastors, especially in relation to what is manifest as mental illness. Thus Yablonsky says that while "the concept of demonology is generally believed to be of no value by most criminologists," the continued belief by a large part of society makes "demonology a consideration in treating criminals in many communities even today" (Yablonsky, 1990: 425). Some support for this view is reflected in a 1990 Gallup poll in which "55 percent of the respondents said they believed in Satan, and 49 percent said they thought people are sometimes possessed by the Devil" (Turque and Chideya, 1991: 62). It is remarkable that as we enter the twenty-first century, demonological scapegoating is still for some a framework explaining crime. For feminist critics, however, this is no surprise. Some have challenged the whole assumption about witchcraft, denying that it is not evil. Rather, some have argued that at least "white" witchcraft promotes healing, encourages positive ways to change body images, and provides ways for women to confront dying (Forefreedom, 1992). They argue that the bad press witchcraft has received is part of the stereotypical attack attempting to control powerful women (ibid.), and especially their sexuality (Bullough and Bullough, 1977).

In the next chapter we consider classical theory, whose early strands were articulated and developed in the era of the Enlightenment. Classical theory became and continues to be the foundation of all Western jurisprudence and, as we shall see, maintains a profound influence on criminological thought.

CHAPTER THREE

Classical and Postclassical Rational Choice Theories

Introductory criminology texts often begin their discussion of criminological theory with a discussion of the "classical school" of criminology. However, they sometimes merge and confuse two sets of dissimilar ideas and assumptions and refer to these both as *conservative*. In contrast, the classical school we discuss here, as we shall see below, is attributed to the eighteenth-century work of legal scholars such as Cesare Beccaria and Jeremy Bentham. It was a *radical* reaction to the predominant pre-Enlightenment practice of criminal justice. Whereas classical theory developed what became known as the "due process model" of justice, the existing system of state justice against which it was arraigned and which more aptly deserves the term *conservative*, was essentially a "crime control" approach. Packer (1968) makes the distinction between the due process and crime control models. Valuing social order over procedure at the expense of individual rights, the conservative crime control approach (which we do not develop in this book[1]) favors many laws against morality, victimless crime, social order, and the state. It assumes the accused guilty rather than innocent and uses any means, often torture, to obtain convictions, believing rules of procedure impede swift convictions. It is concerned with general rather than individual deterrence and uses publicly administered, severe sentences to symbolically punish arbitrarily selected offenders and to instill fear in others. Its arbitrary, discretionary, and punitive approach embraces the death penalty for a wide range of offenses. This conservative approach to crime control, which classicism criticized and displaced, finds present-day advocates in the more fanatical politicians and media pundits, as well as some academics, notably, Van den Haag (1975) and Wilson (1975). Because of its emphasis on an element of individual free choice as a "cause" of crime and because of its focus on punishment, the crime control model is often confused with classicism. However, as we shall see, classicism and neoclassicist developments are based on a very different set of assumptions and offer a fundamentally more measured analysis of crime and justice, relying, as they do, on humans' capacity for rational thought, rather than assuming an animal instinct of fear.

---

[1]For a good overview see Young, 1981: 274–80.

Table 3-1   Related Theories *

Neoclassicism
Humanitarian rationalism
Administrative criminology
Justice model
Just deserts model
Due process model
Economic theory of crime
Wealth maximization theory
Time allocation theory
Rational choice model
Situational choice theory
Routine activities theory

*Theories that take a perspective similar to or overlapping with the model that we develop in this chapter.

BASIC IDEA, CENTRAL MOTIF, AND MAJOR THEORISTS

Classical criminology is essentially an economic theory of crime that focuses on the criminal act as defined by law. The key idea is that people are more or less free to choose crime as one of a range of behavioral options. The relative attractiveness of any choice is affected by the costs associated with criminal action. These costs may be structured into the criminal justice system. Thus importance is placed on legal justice and justified punishments in arranging the rational, cost-benefit calculation that is seen to govern both individual behavior and society's response. Additionally, costs may be an outcome of situational and contextual constraints that can be manipulated in order to reduce the opportunities to commit crime.

During the twentieth century the original conceptions of classical theory have been developed, adapted, clarified, or even re-created, such that there are now many criminological theories sharing a similar perspective (see Table 3-1). As we examine these developments throughout this chapter, the differences between these versions of classicism will be clarified. Indeed, as is true for each of the theoretical frameworks developed here, few if any theorists have adhered to any single set of theoretical assumptions.[2] Writers whose work can be considered as constituting a classical perspective, whether this be framed in the context of jurisprudence or economics, span a period of 240 years. Table 3-2 lists those who founded a classical perspective during its emergent period of 1748–1813.

---

[2]See especially, Beirne (1991) on the issue of Beccaria's dual positions derived, on one hand, from the free-willed rationality reflecting the ideas of Montesquieu and Rousseau and of the Enlightenment and stemming, on the other, from Locke and Hutcheson, from whom Beccaria drew his determinism and science of humankind.

Table 3-2   Founders of Classical Theory

THEORIST	MAJOR WORK	DATE
Montesquieu	*De l'Espirit des lois (The Spirit of the Laws)*	1748
Voltaire	*Lettre a M. d'Alembert (Letters)*	1762
Beccaria	*Tratto dei Delitti e delle Pene (Essay on Crimes and Punishment)*	1764
Bentham	*An Introduction to the Principles of Morals* and *Legislation*	1765 1789
Howard	*The State of Prisons*	1777
Marat	*Plan de legislation criminelle*	1780
Kant	*Foundations of the Metaphysics of Morals*	1785
Romilly	*Observation on the Criminal Law*	1810

In addition, there are a number of recent writers who are considered revivalist classicists, neoclassicists or postclassicists. The key works of these writers are included in Table 3-3.

Whether founders or current advocates, classical theorists share a similar critical challenge to existing systems of law and justice, being opposed to social arrangements that give a large role to the state, to inconsistencies and arbitrariness in the administration of justice, and to unlimited severity of penalties. Beccaria (1764a: 16), for example, was particularly critical of interpreting the spirit rather than the letter of the law since "the erring instability of interpretation" introduces too many variations in outcome. He said that it was better to fix the ambiguities of language in the law than to interpret it. Beccaria was also opposed to torture and was generally, although not in every case, opposed to the death penalty.

Advocates of the traditional classical position proposed reforms of criminal law and the administration of justice, particularly the reform of certain types and degrees in severity of punishments. These reforms were directed at influencing the conditions and alternatives available when humans made behavioral choices.

More recent contributors to classicist theory also criticize the arbitrariness of perspectives that rely on rehabilitation and treatment and any of the numerous ways that discretion and inconsistency infiltrate the administration of justice. Thus Andrew Von Hirsch (1976) and the American Friends Service Committee (1971) criticized a prevailing humanist-inspired tendency to substitute treatment

Table 3-3   Theorists Using Rational Choice Explanations of Crime

THEORIST	MAJOR WORK(S)	DATE
Contemporary Neoclassicists		
American Friends Service Committee	*Struggle for Justice*	1971
Fogel	*We are the Living Proof: The Justice Model for Corrections*	1975
Von Hirsch	*Doing Justice*	1976
Economists of Crime		
Becker	"Crime and Punishment: An Economic Approach"	1968
Tullock	"An Economic Approach to Crime"	1969
Reynolds	*The Economics of Criminal Activity*	1973
Ehrlich	"Participation in Illegitimate Activities: An Economic Analysis"	1973
	"The Market for Offenses and the Public Enforcement of Laws"	1982
Sullivan	"The Economics of Crime"	1973
Heineke	*The Economics of Crime*	1978
Simon and Witte	*Beating the System: The Underground Economy*	1982
Schmidt and Witte	*An Economic Analysis of Crime and Justice*	1984
Postclassical Rational Choice and Routine Activities Theorists		
Clarke	"Situational Crime Prevention"	1983
Cornish and Clarke	*The Reasoning Criminal*	1986
	"Rational Choice Theory"	1987
Cohen and Felson	"Social Change and Crime Rate Trends"	1979
Felson	"Routine Activities, Social Controls, Rational Decisions and Criminal Outcomes"	1986
	"Routine Activities and Crime Prevention in the Developing Metropolis"	1987
Cooke	"The Demand and Supply of Criminal Opportunities"	1986
Roshier	*Controlling Crime*	1989

interventions for punitive responses, arguing that in spite of rehabilitation advocates' emphasis on understanding and concern, their model was often more cruel than that of the punitive approach. Moreover, these commentators despise the "discriminatory use of penal sanctions" and the "wide margins of discretionary power in the hands of police, district attorneys, judges, correctional administrators, parole boards, and parole agents" (American Friends Service Committee, 1971: 124).

The modern neoclassical position, then, attempted to arrest what they saw as a growing drift toward discretionary sentencing, and sentencing disparities resulting from the growth in rehabilitation and treatment. They were concerned about limiting sentencing discretion.

In the postclassicist position the major concern is to move away from the criminal justice system as the only provider of incentives and disincentives (Roshier, 1989) and to consider the wider environment as a smorgasbord of choice opportunities available to the potential offender (Heineke, 1978; Schmidt and Witte, 1984).

Two related developments have occurred more recently that have extended this approach. Known variously as *situational choice theory* (Clarke and Cornish, 1983: 48; Cornish and Clarke, 1987) and *routine activities theory* (Cohen and Felson, 1979; Felson and Cohen, 1980; Felson, 1987), these theories have some of their "roots in the ecological tradition" and some in "control theory" (Krohn, 1991: 300) but their view of humans is no less than the "rational man" of classical theory.[3] Another variant of the routine activities explanation is Cohen and Machalek's (1988) "evolutionary ecological theory," in which biological and personality differences shape the choice of behavioral strategies for needs fulfillment.

Versions of the economic opportunities models take a wider view on the obstacles to opportunities for crime, including such measures as increasing environmental and situational impediments to choosing crime as well as augmenting the opportunity costs of crime by providing legitimate skills training, reductions in poverty, and increased job opportunities.

HUMANS, HUMAN NATURE, AND HUMAN BEHAVIOR

In the early classical theories of crime, humans are seen as independent, free-thinking, and rational decision makers who can control their own destiny by defining their self-interests. They are hedonistic (pleasure seeking) and self-seeking, motivated to maximize their gain from each other. Their behavior is

> the result of individual choices motivated by two conditions: pleasure and pain. According to the doctrine these two polar motives are present in virtually every choice a human makes, and people will choose the behavioral alternative that maximizes the amount of pleasure and reduces the amount of pain. (Meier, 1989: 92)

---

[3]We analyze ecology theory in Chapter 6 and control theories in Chapter 8.

The categories of pleasure and pain are seen as discreet and mutually exclusive, and as Beirne (1991: 807) points out, depend much on Locke's (1689) "sensationalism" in which "all things painful are, by definition bad and all things pleasurable, good." For Bentham, however, pleasure and pain meant more than simple sensual experiences. For him there were four sources of pain and pleasure: physical, political, moral, and religious. Pleasure or pain "from the ordinary course of nature" is physical, and at this level, it is indeed sensation. However, at the hands of a judge or representative of state power it is political; at the hands of "chance persons in the community" it is moral or popular; at the hands of a "superior invisible being" it is religious. Moreover, pleasure exists in at least fourteen categories (Bentham, 1765b: 23). For example, among his fourteen types of pleasure is "justice," which is defined as the state in which pleasure is allocated to the virtuous. Further, pleasure and pain have each a variety of "circumstances" by which Bentham meant qualities, which include "intensity," "duration," "certainty or uncertainty," and "propinquity or remoteness."[4]

The prevailing ideas about humans during the eighteenth century, according to Vold and Bernard (1986: 19), included the notion that "Human will was … a faculty or trait of the individual that regulates and controls behavior … In general the will was free—that is, there were no limitations to the choices that an individual could make." Few, however, subscribe to the idea of an absolute freedom of will, although some make this the assumed starting point of law (Fogel, 1975). Beirne (1991) questions the nature of the voluntarism in Beccaria's notion of will, suggesting that this "is a determined will, rather than a free will." There is no question that a determined will is an accurate description of Bentham's (1765a: 11) view in which human behavior is "determined" by the categorical imperatives of pleasure and pain:

> Nature has placed mankind under the governance of two sovereign masters, pain and pleasure. It is for them alone to point out what we ought to do, as well as to determine what we shall do. On the one hand the standard of right and wrong, on the other the chain of causes and effects, are fastened to their throne. They govern us in all we do, in all we say, in all we think: every effort we can make to throw off our subjection, will serve but to demonstrate and confirm it.

However, it may be said, as in Meier's interpretation above, that free choice was believed to relate to the actions taken to satisfy what was a driven desire or need, rather than determining the desire or need per se. Moreover, the idea of specifying goals also suggests some degree of freedom over needs as well as the means

---

[4]These are important qualifications specifying conditions that shape experience and ultimately the choice of behavior, as we shall see below.

to achieve them. Beccaria's observation that "every act of our will is always proportionate to the strength of the sense data from which it springs" (cited by Beirne, 1991: 808), does not so much deny the presence of free will but suggest that free will is not the only aspect of human beings that must be considered. Indeed, Beirne (1991: 812) recognizes this in his conclusion that Beccaria "subscribed to a notion of human agency simultaneously involving 'free' rational calculation *and* 'determined' action." Consistent with the ideas of the early classicist period, as Vold and Bernard (1986: 19) state, "God and the Devil could influence will—and so apparently could nature, that is impulses or instincts—yet in the specific action of the individual the will was free." They claim that nowhere in his thesis did Beccaria question this prevailing view of human nature and human behavior (ibid.: 20).

Likewise, the related idea of pure rationality in the exercise of will is problematic. Young (1981: 257) argues that the conception of a nonrational human has always been implicit in classicist thought, albeit justified "on the grounds that they are either *pre*-rational (e.g., children or juveniles) or *sub*-rational (the aged and infirm)" and that what is considered nonrational varies historically. Moreover, the neoclassicism that emerged from failed attempts to implement a pure version of Beccaria's principles in the post–French Revolutionary Code of 1791 and that culminated in the Code of 1819 included exceptions and discretion on the basis of age, mental condition, and circumstances (Vold and Bernard, 1986: 26). This is testimony to the recognition of a variability of rationality among humans. For Bentham, rationality is exercised as people engage in a "felicity calculus" in which they assess "the relative pains and pleasures of an act and its consequences" (Bonn, 1984: 73, referring to Bentham, 1789). In other words, they weigh pleasures against their pain and *choose* the former; their choice is goal directed and aimed at maximizing their sense of well-being or utility.

The very idea of utility in Bentham is more than simply the well-being of any individual, since any individual's well-being must not be at the expense of others. Utility produces benefit, advantage, pleasure, good, or happiness, or conversely it prevents pain, mischief, evil, or unhappiness. Utility can aid the community. This may be the community as a whole or an individual. In the latter case, since the community is the sum total of individuals, each individual's happiness adds to the happiness of the community and each individual's unhappiness detracts from it. Thus Bentham's notion of rational calculus is more than purely hedonistic since it can operate in a socially aware way such that "people are seen to act in a responsible manner, to be aware of their actions and to understand the consequences of their actions" (Bonn, 1984: 73).

More recent economic theories of crime (Becker, 1968; Sullivan, 1973) reveal a similar division of ideas about human nature, expressed in the differences between the market or resource allocation model, which is part of wealth maximization theory (Becker, 1968; and Ehrlich 1973; Ehrlich, 1982; Brower and

Ehrlich, 1987) and time allocation theory (Heineke, 1978; Schmidt and Witte, 1984). In wealth maximization, humans rationally seek to maximize utility, which is defined solely in terms of individual wealth; leisure is even reduced to monetary equivalents. In time allocation, utility also depends on the value of time, which may vary from person to person and may have a social or psychological, as well as monetary, value. Indeed, like Bentham, the more sociologically aware economists argue that rational calculation is made, based on a variety of satisfactions, including status and prestige, style and image, taste, comfort, and convenience. The cost-benefit calculation involves assessing the *composite* total reward of an action in relation to the *composite* total cost, including the various probability calculations of likely success. This model of rational choice stresses that it is *perceived* rewards and *perceived* sanctions rather than actual rewards and sanctions that are important in any calculation and "that so-called 'rational behavior' means that actors behave *as if* they were maximizing their own expected utility" (Heineke, 1988: 303–305; our emphasis). People do their best to calculate the outcome "given their reading of present and future possibilities and given resources" (Sullivan, 1973: 142). If there is an acceptable probability of success, they likely will take the risk.

Under situational choice and routine activity theory, humans are defined as pleasure seeking, self-interested rational actors who make choices about their behavior in circumstances of constraint. According to rational choice theory, the offender is seen as "choosing to commit an offence under particular conditions and circumstances" (Clarke and Cornish, 1983: 49). The choice model "does not see decision-making as always being fully rational or even properly considered; instead the model employs notions of 'limited rationality' in which economic explanations of crime are modified by taking cognizance of other motivational and cognitive factors" (Clarke and Cornish, 1983: 50). Thus, like noncriminals, offenders are variable in their motives, which may range from desires for money and sex, to excitement and thrill seeking. Their ability to analyze situations and to structure their choice, to switch between substitutable offenses may also vary, as may their specific skills to carry out a crime (Cornish and Clarke, 1987).

In a variation of routine activities theory Cohen and Machalek (1988) accept that humans have the ability to reason. However, unlike situational choice and routine activities theorists, they argue that humans differ in their physical and behavioral traits and are *limited* in their use of rational thought. Indeed, they claim that it is "unnecessary to assume that criminal acts are perpetrated by rational calculating individuals who understand fully the strategic implications of their chosen actions" (Cohen and Machalek, 1988: 479).[5]

---

[5]These assumptions make it questionable whether Cohen and Machalek's theory is classifiable under the rational choice framework or more appropriately considered a version of integrated theory (see Chapter 13).

While free will may not, therefore, have been seen as fully free, nor rationality fully rational, it is important that the notion of "free will" secures the "driving seat" in traversing the conditions of behavioral choice, since without such a view the clarity and logic of the classical and postclassical arguments rapidly dissipates.

VIEW OF SOCIETY AND THE SOCIAL ORDER

Society is viewed by classicists as a consensus about the desirability of "protecting private property and personal welfare" (Taylor, Walton, and Young, 1973: 2). The society becomes a highly stratified hierarchy based on a "social contract" (Hobbes, 1651; Rousseau, 1762; and Locke, 1690). This contract is assumed between free rational individuals who calculate (though not without varying degrees of persuasion) that it is in their interests to sacrifice a part of their freedom (liberty) to the state so that they may enjoy the rest in peace, security, and freedom from "original chaos" (Beccaria, 1764a: 12). Original chaos here is taken to refer to an assumed state of anarchy or disorder that it is believed would prevail if no social contract existed. Such disorder is more typically referred to as the "war of all against all (Hobbes)" (Taylor, Walton, and Young, 1973: 2). As Von Hirsch (1976: 47) explains, "To realize their own freedom ... members of society have the reciprocal obligation to limit their behavior so as not to interfere with the freedom of others." However, there is some ambiguity of interpretation about how freely the social contract is entered into. Beccaria did not believe that individuals choose to enter a social contract for, as he says,

> No man ever freely sacrificed a portion of his personal liberty merely in behalf of the common good. That chimera exists only in romances. If it were possible, everyone of us would prefer that the compacts binding others did not bind us. (Beccaria, 1764a: 11)

"It was, thus, necessity that forced men to give up part of their personal liberty" (ibid.: 12). Likewise, Beirne (1991: 798) describes the portion of liberty given up as "a 'deposit' that no citizen can ever 'withdraw' from the 'common' store or from the 'public treasury'" and that has to be "defended against the private usurpations of each particular individual."

Although it was deemed in everyone's general interest to be forced to give up part of their liberty in "exchange" for the freedom to accumulate wealth, it was also deemed in everyone's interest that the sovereign state not be so strong that it would usurp the very individual freedoms it was supposed to protect: "They believed ... the state, should play a limited role—accorded only that power necessary to protect individuals' rights and liberties ... based on a consensus between rational citizens" (Young, 1981: 257).

Only after such a forced giving was it possible to have "a kind and civilized society" (Maestro, 1973: 158), a "peaceful society in which justice would prevail" (Bonn, 1984: 73). Beccaria, following the ancient Romans such as Cicero and the Scottish philosophers Locke and Hutcheson (Beirne, 1991: 796) held the idea, subsequently made famous by Bentham, that this society would optimize utility for all, bringing "the greatest happiness for the greatest numbers" (1764a: 8). Moreover, with the "social state" comes an increase in "sensibility" and gentleness of spirit. So it was thought.

THE ROLE OF LAW, THE DEFINITION OF CRIME, AND THE IMAGE OF THE CRIMINAL

Law for Beccaria is not derived from Divine Will. It is not to be confused with God's law for the control of sin but is man's law for controlling "the harm done to society," "the nation," or "the public good" (Beccaria, 1764a: 14, 64). Laws for Beccaria (1764a: 11, 53) are "the conditions under which independent and isolated men united to form a society" under which they "agree to support and defend one another." These conditions should be such that all are bound by the contract of mutual obligation under which contracts useful to "the greatest number" should be observed (Beccaria, 1764a: 8). The contract should reflect the "natural rights of man," which are independent of the state and the church and should preserve the individual's freedom to choose. For Bentham, the concern is with the "collective human rights of society" that are to be protected, rather than the rights of individuals or social interest groups (Galliher, 1989: 345). The purpose of law then, according to Bentham (1765a: 158) is to increase the general well-being:

> The general object which all laws have, or ought to have, in common, is to augment the total happiness of the community; and therefore, in the first place, to exclude, as far as may be, everything that tends to subtract from that happiness: in other words, to exclude mischief.

Making the law proscribing behavior and penalizing the offender should be separated from the power of the state and the arbitrariness of the judiciary. Thus "for Beccaria, the authority of making penal laws could only reside with legislators who represented the whole society and were united with the people they represented by a social compact" (Bonn, 1984: 73). Beccaria argued that the "power to enact penal laws can only be invested in the 'Legislator' who represents all members of society" (Monachesi, 1955: 41). Bentham's view was that the sole purpose of legislation was the happiness, in terms of "pleasure" and "security," of a community of individuals. His utilitarianism meant that, not only was it necessary to proscribe behavior in law but the law should also "prescribe the specific punishments for the specific crimes" (Bonn, 1984: 73); otherwise it would not be possible for potential lawbreakers to make the rational calculation.

The preference was for a minimal amount of clearly written statutory law to avoid both "evils" of obscurity and interpretation. Bentham also recognized that law, insofar as it involved punishment, was pain. It was "the artificial production of pain and pleasure by the legislator; since pain is an evil, it is important that he should never produce it except to provide an overplus of pleasure" (Everett, 1970: 23).

Crime is defined by the legal code such that there is no crime without law, and law is based on the "injury" or "harm done to society." Harm is limited by Beccaria to the economic marketplace (Beirne, 1991: 798), where it refers to restrictions on the freedom of the atomized individual's ability to accumulate wealth. For Beccaria it was necessary "to restrain men from encroaching on the freedom of one another defined and established by the terms (laws) of a social contract (Monachesi, 1955: 40). But for Bentham harms were behaviors that caused pain. He discusses twelve categories of pain whose measurement was necessary, though difficult, in order to give legislators a basis on which to decide whether to prohibit an act. He believed that no act ought to be an offense *unless* it was detrimental to the community. An act is detrimental if it harms one or more members of the community.

A corollary of the belief that law is concerned with acts that are defined as criminal, rather than with criminal actors, is that the law "should not be involved in the control of any activities which do not harm others, do not contradict their self interest or threaten the Social Contract" (Young, 1981: 259). Thus as Young points out, there can be no crimes against the morality of society, nor can there be crimes where there are no victims. For example, personal drug consumption, prostitution, and homosexuality, insofar as they involve mutual consent, should not be criminal offenses in the pure scheme of classicist thinking.

Theorists differ on what crimes in particular were given consent and thus the extent to which they were crimes. As Beirne (1991: 781, 799) points out, whereas Voltaire denied that suicide was a crime, Beccaria was less certain. He was more concerned with clear crimes against property, such as theft, counterfeiting, smuggling, and indolence. Monachesi (1955: 44) suggests that Beccaria proposed basically three categories of crime, based on the seriousness of their harm to society. In order of seriousness these were (1) crimes against the state; (2) crimes that injure the security and property of individuals; and (3) crimes disruptive to the public peace. Bentham elaborated a list of categories of offenses he considered to be of five classes, each with special characteristics: public offenses, semipublic offenses, self-regarding offenses (offenses detrimental only to the offender), offenses against the state, and multiform or anomalous offenses. Each should carry a punishment determined by the circumstances. Bentham declared that only harms to others should be criminal offenses; cases of public morality and transactional crimes where "consent has been given" should not be subject to the criminal law (Bonn, 1984: 74). In considering what is defined in law, therefore, there is no concern with those who commit crime, only with those acts that harm others.

It should be clear from the discussion above that classical thinking does not consider the criminal as a special kind of person. Those who commit crimes are rational, hedonistic, free actors, no different from noncriminals, except that they break the law. Beccaria believed that all people are "by nature self-seeking" and, therefore, "all people are liable to commit crimes" (Martin et al., 1990: 17). Lawbreakers are those who choose to limit others' freedom as defined by law. In Clarke and Cornish's (1983) rational choice theory, the offender's choices are limited and other motivational factors are considered (see Chapter 6 for development of this idea).

CAUSAL LOGIC

Free choice, lack of the fear of punishment, ineffective criminal justice systems, available unguarded targets, and opportunistic situations provide the components of causality under a rational choice explanation. Crime is the outcome of the reasoning process of rational calculation. There is a perception that the benefits or pleasure of crime outweighs the costs or pain resulting from the consequences of it. According to Meier (1989: 92), "Beccaria believed that crime was a reflection of materialism and represented the offender's attempt to improve the material conditions in his or her life," whereas he says Bentham believed criminals chose to violate the law because they desired "money, sex, excitement, revenge, or any other such gain." Indeed

> the decision to commit crime ... is similar to deciding to undertake conventional actions, such as starting a new career or choosing a college. Motivation may stem from a number of different sources or needs, including greed, revenge, envy, anger, lust, thrill-seeking, or bravado. (Siegel, 1989: 96)

Interestingly, and entirely consistent with the logic of this model, is the observation that inappropriate and excessive punishments can be the cause of crime. Thus if punishments or obstacles are made too severe or restrictive, additional crimes may be chosen in order to avoid the consequences of the outcome. What this means is that adjustments of the criminal justice system or situational environments might be themselves, indirectly, the cause of crime. Even Beccaria recognized this in his observation that excessive punishments will result in extra crimes, in an escalating spiral whereby the "severity of punishment itself emboldens men to commit the very wrongs it is supposed to prevent; they are driven to commit additional crimes to avoid the punishment for a single one" (1764a: 43), with the result that "punishments will punish the crimes that they themselves have caused" (Beccaria, 1764b: 16). Moreover, Beccaria argued that, "to prohibit a multitude of indifferent acts is not to prevent crimes that might arise from them but to create new ones ... For one motive that drives men to commit real crime there are a thousand that drive them to commit those indifferent acts which are called crimes by bad laws" (Beccaria, 1764a: 94). Clearly, perception of the meaning of motives and even of punishment as motive was a vital, if less often considered, assumption in the causal analysis of classical theory.

Routine activities and situational choice theorists also recognize the importance of perception in rational calculation and see this structured by situational constraints and opportunities. The routine activities perspective (Cohen and Felson, 1979; Felson and Cohen, 1981; Felson, 1986, 1987) assumes that there are potential offenders who are motivated to commit crime and it concentrates on "the manner in which the spatio-temporal organization of social activities helps people translate their criminal inclinations into action (Cohen and Felson, 1979: 589)." Three factors are important: (1) an offender, (2) a suitable target, and (3) no guardian to guard against crime (Felson, 1987: 911). The approach "considers how everyday life assembles these three elements in space and time (ibid.)." When these three elements converge, crime occurs. Thus, rather than a discretionary and inconsistent criminal justice system reducing effective controls and lowering costs, these theorists see environmental situations providing or denying crime opportunities or facilitating or suppressing the criminal event. They also recognize the role of perception in rational calculation. They argue that a number of factors will lead to criminal activity, including: a low perception of the probability of apprehension and punishment; the belief that punishment is uncertain, negotiable, or of low severity; and relatively low expectations of gains from legitimate work and high expected gains from illegitimate activities, in a context where moral reservations are absent.

A similar approach is taken in Clarke and Cornish's (1983: 8) situational or rational choice theory, whereby criminal behavior is seen "as a function of choices and decisions made within a context of situational constraints and opportunities." As Siegel (1989: 113) says in his review of the rational choice position:

> Offense and offender characteristics are interactive. Each offense has its own properties, including risk and payoff; each offender has a unique set of skills and needs. The interaction between the offender and offense provide[s] a basis for selecting among alternative courses of action and therefore structure[s] the offender's choice of behavior.

In their related theoretical development Cohen and Machalek (1988) combine assumptions about rational calculation with several other ideas from ecological, biological, psychological, and structural theory to present an analysis that sees crime as the outcome of limited behavioral choice based on the set of behavioral strategies that people develop over time. Crime is the use of accumulated and available alternative behavior strategies to satisfy needs by expropriating others of valuables, whether these be property, power, sex, or prestige.

CRIMINAL JUSTICE SYSTEM IMPLICATIONS

To deal with the concept of the rationally calculating offender, the prevailing system of arbitrary laws and procedures needed to be reformed. Beccaria criticized existing laws as only representing the "interests of a few powerful members of society" and complained about the unequal punishment, by the same courts, of people guilty of the same crimes (Galliher, 1989: 23). Because of its arbitrariness, uncertainty, severity, abuses, errors, not least those resulting from the barbaric use of judicial torture, he saw the existing system as a "massive obstacle to human liberation" (Quinney and Wildeman, 1991: 46). And both Beccaria (1764a: 24) and Romilly saw justice as a lottery shot through with "chance and subterfuge."

Young (1981: 254) says the classicists were motivated by the belief that "just as men were governed by Reason, so too ought the systems of government, legislation and law by which their common conduct was governed." Thus the classical thinkers wanted

> a "rational system," derived not from the jumble of precedent and custom and tradition but from clearly defined rational first principles, and set out in a systematic form. Its operations should be certain and predictable, so that men could calculate the "benefits" and "costs" of wrong-doing as they did the profit and loss of a financial transaction. (Ibid.)

Such a "due process model" (Packer, 1968) has certain underlying assumptions or core features:

Sovereignty or primacy of the individual rather than primacy of the state or society is assumed as is the presumption of innocence. This means that "the security and privacy of the individual may not be invaded at will" and that "the alleged criminal is not merely an object to be acted upon but an independent entity in the process who may ... force the operators of the process to demonstrate to an independent authority (judge and jury) that he is guilty of the charges against him" (Packer 1968: 219). A related implication of this assumption is that any pain, such as torture, or other deprivations inflicted before a trial to establish guilt or innocence are unwarranted. As a result of rules designed to protect the individual, the criminal justice process has been seen as "an obstacle course. Each of its successive stages is designed to present formidable impediments to carrying the accused any further along in the process" (Packer 1968: 223). Moreover, those acquitted after a trial, even if they have been detained in custody "ought not to be branded with infamy" (Beccaria, 1764a: 19).

Separation of powers is maintained between the legislature and judiciary. There is established an independent judiciary such that "a third party be given the duty of determining whether in fact a violation had occurred ... a magistrate is needed to resolve the issue" (Monachesi, 1955: 40). In other words "there is the assumption, implicit in the ex post facto clause that the function defining conduct that may be treated as criminal is separate from and prior to the process of identifying and dealing with persons as criminals" (Packer, 1968: 218).

Public accusations rather than secret allegations are required.

Public prosecution is required such that the criminal justice process is invoked by officials of the criminal justice system (Packer, 1968: 219).

Rules limiting investigation are imposed such that "there are limits to the powers of government to investigate and apprehend persons suspected of committing crimes" (Packer 1968: 219). These take various forms, including rules of police procedure, limits on police power, limitations on the length of time an individual can be held in custody during investigations, and what is acceptable evidence. In addition there are rules preventing probable guilt and others restricting guilt to factual determinations by officially designated authorities having the jurisdiction to hear the case within a specified period, and only then if the accused is of criminally responsible status and has not been previously tried for the same offense. Moreover, there must be a "statute of limitations that relieves citizens of 'uncertainty' regarding their fate" (Beirne, 1991: 801, citing Beccaria, 1764b: 56).

Equality before the law. Beccaria believed that there should be equality before the law and between parties in dispute: "The individual is responsible for his actions and is equal, no matter what his rank, in the eyes of the law" (Taylor, Walton, and Young, 1973: 2). Further, he argued that "the laws of a society apply equally to all members of society regardless of their station" (Monachesi, 1955: 41). To Packer the process is "a contest between, if not equals, at least independent actors." He also assumes that there should not only be equality of treatment before the law, but equality of access to legal defense and the means to scrutinize the process (Packer, 1968: 219; 226–27).

Restraint in the use of arbitrary power by the state, judiciary, or its institutions is required.

A rule-based system is designed to eliminate discretion. Under this system all laws are enforced irrespective of the status of the accused or the victim (Galliher, 1989: 23) and "mitigating circumstances or excuses are, therefore, not to be allowed or entertained in court" (Taylor, Walton, and Young, 1973: 2). This

means that there are strict and logical rules limiting judicial discretion and constraining judicial action to no more than "negation or affirmation of fact,"
"determining whether a person has or has not acted contrary to law," and with
"no right or authority to interpret penal laws" (Monachesi, 1955: 42). Indeed
Beccaria held that

> No magistrate, who is himself a member of society, can with any justification
> inflict upon another any penalty not ordained by law. Nor can any magistrate,
> regardless of circumstances, either increase or decrease, or change in any fash-
> ion, the punishment prescribed by law ... It is the duty of the magistrate to
> inflict such penalties exactly as they have been described (in law). (Monachesi,
> 1955: 41)

This principle also implies the need for a precise and clear wording of statutes,
"written in a language so as to render them completely understandable to the
people" (Monachesi, 1955: 42).

An adversarial trial is desirable to ensure equality of inquiry, an impartial investigation of the evidence, and a "formal, adjudicative, adversary fact-finding
process in which the factual case against the accused is publicly heard by an
impartial tribunal and is evaluated only after the accused has had a full opportunity to discredit the case against him" (Packer, 1968: 223). Such a trial relies
on many rather than few independent witnesses, for "the credibility of a witness ... must diminish in proportion with the hatred or friendship or close relationship between himself and the accused" (Beccaria, 1764a: 23).

The right to be represented by a supporter, a friend, or legal counsel is guaranteed.

Efficiency and fairness in protecting individual rights are assured.

Certainty of detection and efficient police rather than mere police presence is preferred.

Certainty of punishment over severity of punishment is a goal since, "The certainty
of a punishment, even if it be moderate, will always make a stronger impression than the fear of another which is more terrible but combined with the
hope of impunity" (Beccaria, 1764a: 58). Also, "It is not cruelty nor severity,
Beccaria believes, that renders punishment an effective deterrent, but rather its
certainty ... that leaves a lasting impression on the minds of men" (Monachesi,
1955: 44–45). This is because "men are more frightened by an evil which is
inevitable even though minor in nature," than they are by one more severe, if it
is accompanied by the hope that one might escape that punishment" (Beccaria,
1776: 114). It is believed that only with certainty of apprehension and fixed

laws can citizens "calculate precisely the ill consequences of a misdeed" (Beccaria, 1764b: 12). As Young (1981: 262–63) says in his characterization of the classicist perspective:

> The law is an instrument, not only of control, but also of education. And "educating the public" into the calculus of law-abidingness requires that irregularities, due to either lack of detection or evasion of penalties or irrational prison regimes, should be eliminated. Any deviation from strict disciplinary uniformity simply encourages crime, either through ineffective control or by propagating injustices which cause citizens to question the justice and impartiality of the Social Contract.

Celerity, meaning the swiftness of prosecution in the administration of justice, is desirable since the closer the offense is associated with the consequences (albeit consequences artificially constructed in the form of penalties or sanctions) the greater is believed to be the educational impact.

Trial by a jury of peers is believed to be fundamental. However, for Beccaria the equality of peers was modified such that where a crime had been committed against another individual, "half the jurors should be the equals of the accused and half the peers of the victim" (Beccaria, 1764b: 27).

Rights of appeal against a sentence should be guaranteed and be based on a review of the case by an independent body. Though seemingly appropriate from the perspective of promoting a sense of justice, appeal is not conducive to certainty of outcome. Indeed, once a judge has determined whether a law violation has occurred "no appeal should be permitted" (Monachesi, 1955: 42), save those appeals that are for the protection of a defendant against abuses and error resulting from overlooking facts or from a violation of rules of investigative conduct.

Criminal Justice Policy and Correctional Ideology

Underlying the classicist reform of the criminal justice system is a correctional ideology that emphasizes the prevention of crime through a form of deterrence: to fairly administer a universal system of justice based on equal treatment before the law, in order that individuals accept responsibility for their offending and *choose* not to offend. The proposal is to optimize rather than maximize the efficiency of criminal justice, especially enforcement and court hearings, making it visible, certain, and swift, but not at the expense of individual rights, which need to be protected at all times throughout the process. As Packer (1968: 224) says of his "due process" version of the model, "the aim of the process is at least as much to protect the factually innocent as it is to convict the factually guilty." In the rational choice model or situational opportunity versions of the perspective, emphasis is placed on manipulating the situational environment to make the choice of crime more difficult and costly (Clarke and Cornish, 1983: 48; Cornish and Clarke, 1987). In the routine activities version of the theory (Cohen and Felson, 1979; Felson, 1987) the implication is that victims themselves should manipulate their lifestyles so that they and their property are less likely targets and are better protected from motivated offenders. The focus, then, is on denying the offender the opportunity to engage in crime by manipulating the local physical environment, through target hardening, environmental design, and other measures.

Three philosophies justifying a punishment intervention pervade original classicist thinking: (a) retribution or just deserts; (b) individual deterrence; (c) prevention. The core ideas are contained in the conclusion to Beccaria's treatise, which states that any punishment should be: "public, prompt, necessary, the least possible in the given circumstances, proportionate to the crimes, dictated by the laws" (Beccaria, 1764a: 99).

According to Beccaria, the basis of the state's right to punish its offenders lies in the forfeiture of a part of their freedom for everyone's protection and security. They agreed to it, insofar as they condone the formation of the state as their protector. The administration of punishment is the prerogative of the state based on a mandate from the social contract (Locke, 1690). While the burden of proof with regard to the degree of intervention rests with the state, it should intervene in convicted offenders' lives as little as possible and only as needed (Von Hirsch, 1976).

Most of the versions of this model believe in limiting and fixing the severity or amount of punishment. Bentham's argument is compelling, claiming that since the aim of law is to eliminate mischief, law itself must limit its sanctions to the most parsimonious necessary to achieve the desired goal: "all punishment is mischief: all punishment itself is evil. Upon the principle of utility, if it ought at all to be admitted, it ought only to be admitted in as far as it promises to exclude some greater evil" (Bentham, 1765a: 158). Indeed, Bentham suggests that punishment should not be used:

1. Where it is groundless; where there is no mischief for it to prevent ...

2. Where it must be inefficacious; where it cannot act so as to prevent the mischief ...

3. Where it is unprofitable, or too expensive; where the mischief it would produce would be greater than what it prevented.

4. Where it is needless; where the mischief may be prevented, or cease of itself ... (Ibid.: 159)

Most contributors to the classicist model believe that it is the harm of crime that warrants the punishment rather than the characteristics of the offender. Recent contributors to the perspective categorically state that the punishment of a guilty offender is in retaliation for his or her crime, and thus they seek to resurrect the idea of retribution. Von Hirsch (1976) believes that the retributive element should be acknowledged as a purpose of punishment and as a precursor to limiting punishments in the interests of justice:

> When we honestly face the fact that our purpose is retributive, we may, with a refound compassion and renewed humanity, limit the degree of retribution we exact. And still we are not happy. Our solution is one of despair, not hope ... The concept of deserts is intellectual and moralistic; in its devotion to principle, it turns back on such compromising considerations as generosity and charity, compassion, and love. It emphasizes justice, not mercy ... (Ibid.: xxxix)

The idea of retribution as "justice" is that when someone infringes upon someone else's rights, he or she gains an unfair advantage over all others in society and as such upsets the assumed balance. Punishment acts as a counterbalance by giving the offender a disadvantage and brings things back into balance. This has nothing to do with deterrence but with an idea of justice; the punishment restores an equilibrium to society of "benefits and burdens" (Von Hirsch, 1976).

Beccaria had a somewhat different orientation in limiting punishment, partly because of the effectiveness of its specific deterrence and partly because of his idea of its being unnecessary and barbaric. Thus he pointed out the folly of unlimited punishment and argued that infinitely severe punishment had an exacerbating effect on crime. He "agreed with Montesquieu that every punishment which was not soundly based upon absolute necessity was tyrannical and that the more cruel and severe the punishment, the more the minds of men grew 'hardened and calloused'" (Hibbert, 1966: 70). This callousness would prove a problem for any hope of deterrence based on awakening "crude and uneducated minds" to rational calculus.

According to Meier (1989: 93), Beccaria believed that punishment should be "sufficient to deter crime but not so severe as to brutalize the offender." The purpose of legal punishment "is to deter, not to punish" (Meier, 1989: 93). Bentham (1765a: 166) too believed that "the value of the punishment must not be less in any case than what is sufficient to outweigh that of the profit of the offence" but it "ought in no case to be more than what is necessary to bring it into conformity with the rules" (ibid.: 169).

As well as describing a process whereby people choose not to commit crime, Bonn (1984: 73) points out that deterrence means prevention and for Bentham prevention was the primary objective. Likewise, Beirne (1991: 804) observes that "Beccaria's penal calculus rested on the view that it was better to prevent crimes than to punish them." Indeed, he refers to punishments as "obstacles that restrain men from committing crimes" (Beccaria, 1764b: 14, cited by Beirne, p. 805). A similar view is held by Bentham, who claims that sanctions are motives, capable of giving a binding force to law but also of influencing the way people act:

> A sanction then is a source of obligatory powers or motives: that is, of pains and pleasures; which, according as they are connected with such modes of conduct, operate, and are indeed the only things which can operate, as motives. (Bentham, 1765a: 34–35)

Some suggest that prevention, secured through deterrence, is based on both individual and general deterrence. Thus Monachesi (1955: 4) says, "The essential end of punishment is ... to prevent offenders from doing other harm to society and to prevent others from committing crimes." Bottomley talks of the classicist "diminution of penalties," fixing punishments based on "their *general* deterrence value" (Bottomley, 1979, p. 124). However, the notion of "just deserts" offered by more recent commentators such as Morris (1974) and Von Hirsch (1976) means that specific penalties must be *just,* based only on what was *deserved* by the last crime or series of crimes, not that they should deter others. Nor should they be based on characteristics of an offender. Indeed, as the Quaker body, The American Friends Service Committee (1971: 146–47) proclaimed:

> The whole person is not the concern of law. Whenever the law considers the whole person it is more likely that it considers factors irrelevant to the purpose of giving punishment.

We should ensure punishment is based only on the crime committed, "on the consequences of the act rather than ... the intentions of the offender" (Conklin, 1989: 58).

To be consistent with the notion that offenders are not punished for the benefit or the effect that punishment has on others' behavior, or used only to promote public safety, it is necessary to abandon all notions of general deterrence from actual instances of punishment. As Young (1981: 261) insightfully observes, because it holds the individual rather than the social order as the priority: "The notion of using punishment to make a *general* example is anathema to classicism." Instead one must rely on the educative effect of knowing *what* the punishment will be:

> Punishment is thus looked upon as an educative process and the types of punishment selected and how they are imposed should always be done so as to make the greatest impact and the most enduring impression upon all members of society, while inflicting the least pain on the body of the offender. (Monachesi, 1955: 44)

An implication of "just deserts," basing punishment only on the crime committed rather than on who is accused, or for the benefit of others' protection against projected crimes, or apparent danger, is that both first and repeat offenders would receive the same sentence (Galliher, 1989: 24; Vold, 1958: 24). As Young (1981: 261) points out:

> Previous convictions of the actor are to be judged irrelevant to the particular act being judged by judicial process, since he or she must be punished only in relation to the specific action for which an accusation has been laid.

Further, punishment must not "be used for reformation, for this would encroach on the rights of the individual and transgress the social contract" (Taylor, Walton, and Young, 1973: 2).

But this was not Bentham's view since he also went beyond deterrence and prevention to include the prevention of "what today is called 'recidivism'" (Bonn, 1984: 74). He indicates that if the offense is one that is repetitive or may have been committed previously without discovery, the punishment must be increased "to outweigh the profit not only of the individual offence, but of such other like offenses as are likely to have been committed with impunity by the same offender" (Bentham, 1765a: 170).

Beccaria (1764a: 64) believed that penalties should be based on the measure of the "harm done to society," rather than on the harm incurred by the victim or the "dignity of the injured person" (ibid.: 65). Thus Meier (1989: 93) says that for Beccaria, the amount of punishment should be based on the severity of the offense such that "serious crimes should receive severe penalties and less serious crimes should receive less severe penalties." Reflecting the preventative over the punitive, the severity of punishments should be based on the principle of proportionality, such that potential offenders choose a lesser crime, because "punishments must be proportional to the interests violated by the crime" (Taylor, Walton, and Young, 1973: 2). Here proportionality has more than one criterion. It can mean that the punishment increases in relation to the degree that misdeeds are contrary to the public good. This is, indeed, a common interpretation of Beccaria:

> the amount and nature of punishment inflicted against transgressors should vary in proportion to the degree to which an act of an individual endangers the existence of society ... punishment ... should be inflicted in measures commensurate with the effects of the crime on society. It follows that the more threatening the crime is to societal welfare and existence, the more severe the punishment should be. The only measure of the seriousness of crimes is the amount of harm done to society. (Monachesi, 1955: 43–44)

This interpretation should not be taken out of context, however. Unless it is remembered that threat to society and the public good refers to violations of individual freedom, then this view of proportionality would be equally consistent with a crime control model in which society is a collectivity and that in turn is reflected by the state. Such a view is not part of the classicist model as we develop it here.[6]

Proportionality can also mean that punishment increases according to the pleasures to be gained from the crimes, which Beccaria describes as "the motives that lead people to crimes" (Beccaria, 1764b: 14). Contrary to the general tendency for classicists to adopt punishments whose severity is based on harm, Bentham takes this argument further, recognizing differences of individual circumstance and thereby the impact of any punishment:

> Owing to the different manners and degrees in which persons under different circumstances are affected by the same exciting cause, a punishment which is the same in name will not always either really produce, or even so much as appear to others to produce, in two different persons the same degree of pain: therefore, that the quantity actually inflicted on each individual offender may correspond to the quantity intended for similar offenders in general, the several circumstances influencing sensibility ought always to be taken into account. (Bentham, 1765a: 169)

This remarkable insight clearly led the way to the variation in penalties that would, if significant, undermine the ability for rational calculation. Indeed, most recent versions of the classicist model reject the variation of punishment based on individual situations and circumstances and propose equal punishments for equal crimes based on a tariff system. Fogel (1975: 254), for example, suggested replacing the broad range of sentences available for particular classes of felony with "determinate sentences," each being "a fixed sentence" with only a narrow range of adjustments allowed for seriousness or mitigating circumstances.

For Beccaria penalties were to be only so severe as simply to deter, only enough as necessary for society's protection: "punishments must not be in excess" (Taylor, Walton, and Young, 1973: 2). Similarly, Bentham believed in limiting punishments but based on potential future gains, arguing that "society should administer a degree of punishment (pain) just sufficient to offset the potential gains (pleasure) of the criminal behavior" (Bartol, 1991: 11). Bentham also believed punishment should be avoided where it has no power to affect the will, where "the evil of punishment exceeds the evil of the offense" and where the same effect can be obtained at a cheaper price (Bonn, 1984: 74).

Punishment should also be prompt in relation to the crime since, as Beccaria (1764a: 56) points out:

---

[6] It is, however, part of the crime control model under conservative criminal justice as we explained at the outset.

the promptness of punishments is more useful because when the length of time that passes between the punishment and the misdeed is less, so much the stronger and more lasting in the human mind is the association of these two ideas, crime and punishment; they then come insensibly to be considered, one as the cause, the other as the necessary inevitable effect.

For Bentham, promptness posed a problem and was a ground for varying the severity of punishment. Recognizing that enforcement is not perfect and that some crimes stand less chance of being prosecuted, Bentham believed that this should be compensated for, in order not to lose the deterrent effect. Thus, he believed there was a need to increase punishment if its application is more remote than the profit of the offense; that is, if the pleasure of the offense is immediate and the probability of punishment is remote, then the magnitude of the punishment (pain) should be commensurably increased.

For economic theorists the model has the implications that it is necessary to change perceptions of the value of relative gains from the legitimate system and devalue those from the illegitimate system. Though this can clearly be achieved by increasing security and effectiveness of the criminal justice system, it can also be achieved, as time allocation theorists argue, by moral education. Moreover, both time allocation and wealth maximization theorists recognize that an increase in legitimate opportunities will also bring about the same effect. For example, Ehrlich (1982) argues that crime control requires only the imposition of deterring punishments or the promotion of legitimate earning opportunities that affect the relative profitability of participation in illegitimate activities for all potential offenders, with no attempt at individual control.

Techniques of Crime Control

Bentham (1765a) believed that the type of punishment used should be that which is most efficacious in terms of how well suited it was to the offense. Some punishments have different effects because they are qualitatively distinct. The effect of the punishment will depend on the motive for the offense: "the punishment most subservient to reformation will be the sort of punishment that is best calculated to invalidate the force of that motive" (ibid.: 181). Hence, those offenses that are the result of "ill will" and those motivated by an "obstinate refusal to do something lawfully required" are best prevented and reformed by a punishment that provides confinement on a "spare diet." Offenses resulting from "indolence and pecuniary interest" (theft, embezzlement, fraud) are best punished by "penal labor." Bentham considered capital punishment "unsatisfactory because the pain it imposes is greater than the purposes that it accomplishes" (Geis, 1960: 59). Likewise for Beccaria the death penalty is neither useful nor necessary. He found it brutal, contrary to the preventative aims of deterrence, not least because it was less effective than the prospect of a lifetime sentence. Only in the extraordinary case in which "a nation is recovering or losing its liberty" (Beccaria, 1764a: 46) is the ultimate sanction conceivable, for example, "when it is evident that even if deprived of liberty he [the political criminal] still has connections and power such as endanger the security of the nation" (ibid.). Indeed, Beirne (1991: 789) points out that though opposed to the death penalty in general, Beccaria believed that "capital punishment is justified if (1) an incarcerated citizen is still a threat to society, (2) a citizen's mere existence could produce a revolution dangerous to the state, or (3) a citizen's execution deterred others from committing crimes. Although Beccaria argues that the last of these options does not hold true, he does not attempt to defeat the justification in the other two cases. He points out, instead, that such cases are rare exceptions.

Moreover, under circumstances of stable government, neither Romilly nor Beccaria believed death to be the most potent form of punishment (Hibbert, 1966: 75). It was little more than a "passing spectacle" (Monachesi, 1955: 46). As Beccaria (1764a: 46–47) says, "It is not the intensity of punishment that has the greatest effect on the human spirit, but its duration, for our sensibility is more easily and more permanently affected by slight but repeated impressions, than by a powerful but momentary action." For both Bentham and Romilly as far as murder was concerned, the death penalty was a "sad necessity," and for Montesquieu "it was the repugnant 'remedy of a sick society'" (Hibbert, 1966: 70, 75).

Moreover, Beccaria (1764a: 53) believed that lawbreakers and "anyone who disturbs the peace … must be excluded from society—must be banished from it." Instead of death or banishment, classicists prefer prison because time served can be adjusted and staged at different levels for different offenses. But this does not also preclude the expenditure of equivalence time in the service of others: "the temporary subjugation to society of the labor and the person of the criminal" (Beccaria, 1764b: 40). Nor was Beccaria averse to the use of corporal punishment for crimes of violence against persons (Beirne, 1991: 801). However, it was prison that offered the most discretely adjustable form of punishment, that unlike death did not exercise "all its power in an instant" but spread out unhappy moments of perpetual slavery over a lifetime." For Bentham prison time should be spent in a way that was constructive toward personal reform, while also being watched continuously and supervised impersonally. Thus his "panopticon" included "provision for prisoners to work and to be taught profitable trades" (Bonn, 1984: 74, referring to Ignatieff, 1978).

More recent commentators argue that prison, when used, should itself also embody the motif and principles of the classical due process model. Instead of ending at the point of imprisonment, due process should ensure that prisoners are handled in a lawful manner and not be subjected to the abuses of treatment in the belief that this may help or cure them in the future.

So prisons should be recognized for the coercive punishment and deprivation of liberty that they embody (Morris, 1974; Fogel, 1975). Indeed, Fogel (1977: 127) laments that "it is a sad irony in our system of criminal justice that we insist on the full majesty of due process for the accused until he is sentenced to prison, then justice is said to have been served." If we do not continue to serve due process during prison time to release, what constructive lesson can the convicted offender have derived from the punishment?

Classical theory also prefers fines, because they can be equalized and staged in progressive severity. One commentator points out that rather than punish, Beccaria prefers to prevent crime and, in this regard, even proposes "perfecting the system of education" (Beccaria, 1776: 156).

In contrast, the routine activities approach centers on satisfying the philosophy of prevention by taking into consideration the continued development and change of the modern metropolis in planning crime control through "situational crime prevention" strategies (Clarke, 1983). Situational crime prevention is based on "target hardening," that is, making property less vulnerable to criminal exploitation. Surveillance, environmental management, and using measures that make crime like robbery less likely, such as paying by check rather than cash, are suggested strategies (Clarke, 1983: 227).

A combination and extension of all these ideas may be found in the "rational choice perspective" (Clarke and Cornish, 1985; Cornish and Clarke, 1986; 1987). If proper situational measures are taken that would hinder or reduce the success of crime, the probability of crime is reduced. For example, where prevention is the paramount aim, the techniques of crime control include a variety of environmental manipulations such as

> steering column locks on cars, flat fare and "no change" systems on public transport, cheque guarantee cards, the control of alcohol sales at football matches, supervision of children's play on public housing estates, vandal resistant materials and design, "defensible space" architecture, improved lighting, closed-circuit television surveillance, and the employment of doormen, caretakers and additional shop assistants. (Clarke and Cornish, 1983: 48)

For routine activities theorists it is necessary to "harden" and thereby reduce the availability of suitable targets, to increase the presence of capable, caring, intimate guardians of potential victims, such as friends, relatives, and neighbors and to adjust victim behavior and lifestyle to make people less vulnerable during their routine activity. Also, changes to the legitimate opportunity structure are implied. This suggests that increases in formal wages, the creation of new jobs, increases in the desirability of jobs, better job training and work placement programs as well as financial subsidies, would prove effective inducements to increase the perceived gain from law-abiding activity and thereby raise the opportunity costs of crime. However, these measures would also need to be accompanied by increased security systems and an expansion of the criminal justice system in ways that would raise the perceived cost of criminal alternatives.

EVALUATION

Beccaria's ideas are said to have provided "the intellectual foundation for modern democratic societies" and the starting point for legal reform (Galliher, 1989: 24), which included bringing an end to cruel punishments such as public executions and torture (Maestro, 1973). His approach is credited with replacing public torture and execution with imprisonment. Beccaria's famous essay *Dei delitti e delle pene* has been evaluated as "a tightly reasoned attack upon the prevailing systems of administration of criminal justice," whose "rapier-like thrusts at the barbarism and inhumanity of the penology of his day," is seen as "tremendously significant" in bringing about the present-day system (Monachesi, 1955: 38, 49). The modified neoclassicist conception of the earlier classicist vision is "the major model of human behavior held by agencies of social control in all advanced industrial societies" (Taylor, Walton, and Young, 1973: 9–10). Young (1981: 258) further points out that it "continues to be influential in contemporary thought" and that "the doctrine of the limited state ... forms the cornerstones of modern legal and constitutional traditions." Indeed, as an explanatory framework the perspective explains white-collar and corporate crime better than it explains street crime (Box, 1983), although any crime with a pecuniary motive is also readily explainable, such as some theft and burglary.

However, in spite of such positive evaluations, the perspective was and remains controversial and provocative. Moreover, in spite of his almost universal adoration, Beccaria's contribution has been challenged by some as being less profound than that of his contemporaries (Newman and Marongiu, 1990), and as politically conservative rather than radical and pioneering (Jenkins, 1984: 112). Nonetheless, Beccaria's original position "aroused the hostility and resistance of those who stood to gain by the perpetuation of the barbaric and archaic penological institutions of the day" (Monachesi, 1955: 38). Indeed, by 1765 for his trouble Beccaria had invoked accusations of "sedition," "impiety," and "heresy," and his essay was condemned to the Pope's list of banned reading for its "extreme rationalism" (Beirne, 1991: 782). It was criticized by Ferri for being more interested in the diminution of punishments than in the diminution of crime. Bottomley (1979: 3) says of the classical school that, "more attention was paid to equating the penalties imposed upon specific criminal acts, as such, rather than to investigating individual motivation."

Some of the most devastating criticisms of the perspective stem from the observation that it assumes formal equality between people but ignores inequality of persons and structure:

the emphasis on private property, on the just rewards for entrepreneurial skill and the "right" to accumulate wealth, produced an actual social structure in which the basis of rights and benefits was very unequally distributed throughout society ... Classicism ... failed both in theory and practice to square the significant divergences between formal and substantive equality. (Young, 1981: 258)

As a result, says Young (1981: 264), classicism has "constantly to confront all the contradictions that flow from a legal philosophy based on formal equality which is required to operate 'justly' in conditions of substantive inequality." He concluded that in reality, the classicist model is "more just" for some than it is for others: "For whereas the rich offender may be cushioned by his or her wealth, the poor offender, with the *same* sentence but little to fall back on, is punished *in fact* disproportionately" (ibid: 266). As a result, classicism allows those who can afford punishment to buy license to crime.

A corollary of assumed formal equality is that law, and in particular punishment, is presumed to be perceived the same way, irrespective of a person's social class position. Clearly this is not so, and it is argued that classicism fails to consider the differential satisfaction people obtain from the same criminal act and, further, it fails to consider the differential pain experienced by the same sanctions (Galliher, 1989: 25). However, as we saw earlier, some classicists, notably Bentham, recognized this problem, so he revised the idea of equal punishments to take account of "circumstances."

Classicism also fails to account for the differences in people's ability to use reason, to calculate their interests, and to set goals and objectives. It fails to consider irrational behavior or spontaneous crimes or to consider the role of peer groups and their different effects on the rational calculus. Bartol (1991: 12) points out that the assumption among commentators that classicists believed in free will is contradicted in their own writings by the assumption, especially evident in Bentham, that "people are *driven* toward the acquisition of pleasure and the avoidance of pain, independent of any freedom of will, and he cites Bentham, who discusses pain and pleasure as the "two sovereign masters" of mankind. Beirne (1991) similarly points out the science of human nature inherent in some of Beccaria's passages. Beirne (1991: 807) argues that his adoption of Locke's "doctrine sensationalism" and Condilliac's development of this doctrine show that humans are born as blank slates and become what they are through "their sensory reactions to external stimuli." Thus Beirne interprets Beccaria's position as being "resolutely opposed to any notion of free will," implying that "human agents are no more than the products of their sensory reactions to external stimuli" (ibid.).

It is clear that these two ideas, though apparently contradictory, are capable of being held simultaneously. It is possible for people to be driven by desires and a search for pleasure while simultaneously choosing between a range of perceived satisfactions and avoiding perceived dissatisfactions, whether these be seen as costs or whatever. However, we might agree with Beirne's (1991: 813) assessment that "classical criminology" is an invention, that "was not the creation of Beccaria, Bentham, and others, but the retrospective product of scholarly self-aggrandizement," which, "as an identifiable set of assumptions about crime and punishment ... was not actually denominated until the 1870s" by thinkers "keen to distance their invention of scientific criminology from that of Beccaria's 'outmoded discourse of free will.'" However, we believe Beirne's is a description of a process of theory construction that is no less true of later theories than it will likely be of future ones.

A final criticism against the traditional classicist position comes, perhaps surprisingly, from economic rational and situational choice theorists who believe that the problems with classical theory have more to do with their limited vision of what counts as costs and benefits, than to do with the rational model of human nature. In his postclassical perspective, Roshier (1989: 16), for example, argues that

> In general, the classical perspective contained a peculiarly narrow view of what it actually is that controls human behavior. It was concerned solely with the formal legal apparatus and relied on very specific mechanism of control ... there is no particular reason inherent in the classical view of human motivation to assume that this is the only possible means of control. Beccaria just happened to think it was. There was no consideration at all given to the possibility of disincentives operating in the informal social context, and a total neglect of social and economic *incentives* of all kinds.

These recent theorists, however, embrace an expanded rational choice model. By concentrating chiefly on the decision-making process of offenders confronted with specific contexts, the focus of the effort to prevent crime shifts from broad social programs to target hardening, environmental design or any impediment that would persuade a motivated offender from offending. One criticism of this focus is that if crime is somehow prevented by situational measures in one area, the offender will go elsewhere to commit his offenses, a notion that has been termed "displacement." According to Cornish and Clarke (1987: 934), rational choice theory "assumes that the offenders respond selectively to characteristics of particular offenses—in particular, to their opportunities, costs, and benefits—in deciding whether or not to displace their attention elsewhere." Hence, displacement is an unlikely outcome. Most potential offenders are seen as being crime specific; a shoplifter is not likely to become a robber if he or she reasons that the probability of successfully shoplifting has been reduced to a minimal level. Cornish and Clarke (1987: 935) assert that "the readiness with which the offender will be prepared to substitute one offense for another will depend upon the extent to which alternative offenses share characteristics which the offender considers salient to his or her goals and abilities."

Criminal justice policy that is oriented to the rational choice theory becomes simpler and possibly more economical than the broader social interventionist changes required in the more social ecological analyses. It is an approach that has a good fit with high-tech advancements and also has an inherent, intuitive, and nonthreatening "security" appeal to legislators since it is simple and does not challenge existing social arrangements. However, rational choice and its variants come close to blaming the victim in shifting the focus to those who must change their ways to accommodate predators. Because the routine activities of people are involved in crime, as well as certain "attractive" targets, the responsibility for avoiding criminal victimization rests with the potential victim. Feminist critics have been particularly vocal in challenging this assumption in the case of rape and sexual assault.

As products become more and more portable, increased responsibility rests with persons to make them resistible to theft, presumably to deter motivated offenders. Lacking certain guardianship presence, the routine activities of people may converge with those motivated to commit crime and result in victimization. While a certain amount of prudence is necessary, the perspective carried to its logical extreme can lead to a siege mentality and a society that is geared to ever-increasing oversight and surveillance, fortification of homes, restrictions on freedom of movement, and the proliferation of guns for alleged self-defense. Given the propagation of surveillance cameras and other devices, the current tendency seems to be the full development of a watched and monitored society.[7] Though this may be considered necessary by some to reduce crime, the evidence that it does is not clear, but the social and emotional cost is high.

In the next chapter we turn to the positivist reaction to the original classical arguments on free will and the embrace with determinism and the scientific method to investigate a world assumed to be governed by natural laws. In doing so, we reveal that "positivist criminology creates almost a mirror image of classicism: free-will disappears under determinacy, equality bows before natural differences and expert knowledge, and human laws that are created become scientific laws that are discovered" (Young, 1981: 267).

---

[7]For further discussion of the implication of this trend, and the issues of privacy raised by it see Einstadter and Henry (1991), Einstadter (1992), and Pfuhl (1992).

CHAPTER FOUR

Individual Positivism I: Biological Theories

Individual positivism is seen as a break from classicism, each being fundamentally different in their assumptions about human nature. They are also different in their use of data, with positivism being "characterized by methods, techniques and rules of procedure rather than by substantive theory" (Gottfredson and Hirschi, 1987: 10). However, they are similar in their belief about the importance of rational thought and causal logic for understanding criminal behavior.

The essence of positivism in criminology is well expressed by Barnes and Teeters (1943: 174): "Not until we recognize the fundamental truth that the individual is made a delinquent by forces beyond his control operating on his structure, can we make much progress in understanding such behavior and correcting it." Clearly positivism allows for such forces to emanate both from within and outside the individual. We shall discuss the ideas of sociological positivists who see these forces emerging primarily from outside the body/mind, in later chapters. Here we are concerned with those theories that see predisposing criminal forces primarily located within the individual (although not to the exclusion of the physical environment); hence the category of "individual positivism." Such theories are basically of two types, depending on whether they see the force located in the (1) biological or (2) psychological makeup of the individual. Biological and psychological approaches to individual positivism differ in significant ways in their explanation of these forces, a difference popularly characterized as being between "nature and nurture." Cohen (1966: 42–43) calls both these versions of individual positivism "kinds-of-people" theories:

> Insofar as the situation plays a role, it is treated as a triggering or "precipitating" circumstance, releasing a tendency that is already fully formed, and which would probably find expression sooner or later anyway ... The central task of such theories is to devise a classification or typology of personalities, of which each type has a propensity to certain kinds of behavior. One or more of these types may be prone to deviance in general, or to some specific type of deviance. These types may be conceived in terms of biological characteristics, either hereditary or acquired, or in terms of purely psychological characteristics, such as personality structure, temperament, or dominant underlying needs.

Cohen (1966: 43) says that if the answer to the question of how some people become the kinds of people who commit crime or deviance is not some biological antecedent, "the answer takes the form of a theory of personality or development."

Biological theories consider the direct effect of physical and physiological process on behavior and the indirect effect of environment on *the brain* whose processes then control behavior. In contrast, psychological theories consider the combined effect of these forces and developmental processes on the functioning of *the mind* and examine how the processes of mind affect behavior. (We will return to this issue in discussing human nature. For the present, it is important to realize that in these theories the brain and mind are seen as different but related entities and that the brain's physiological processes are the province of biology and neurology, the mind and its mental processes the province of psychology.) For this reason we shall consider these theories in separate chapters, while recognizing their similarities relative to other theoretical approaches to crime. Here we shall consider biological theories. In Chapter 5 we shall analyze psychological and psychiatric theories of personality, and in Chapter 8 we focus on theories of learning and bonding.

Table 4-1   Related Theories*

Positive school
Italian school
Craniology
Faculty-phrenology
Constitutional theory
Body-type theory
Criminal somatology
Biocriminology
Sociobiology
Biosocial theory
Neobiology
Biopsychology
Genetic theory
XYY Chromosome theory
Endocrinological theory
Hormone theory
Evolutionary r/K theory

*Theories that take a perspective similar to or overlapping with the model that we develop in this chapter.

BASIC IDEA, CENTRAL MOTIF, AND MAJOR THEORISTS

The professed "scientific approach" to the biological study of crime is captured in the idea that some people are "born criminal" or at least inherit a predisposition to crime which may become manifest when the individual is exposed to certain "triggering" environments. Biological theorists believe that humans are significantly determined by biological forces beyond individual control and that our behavior reflects a prewritten code. For many of the early theorists, such as Ferri (1886), there was no free will. Indeed, criminal anthropologists of the Lombrosian School, "equated positivism with materialism (or naturalism)," examining crime as a phenomenon of the natural world of matter, and "espoused an absolute determinism, denying any role whatsoever to free will" (Rafter, 1992: 527). For this reason, from the outset it became fundamentally important for these theorists to "discover" the biological difference between conventional, conforming, or "normal people" and "deviants" who, under identical conditions or environments, are unable to follow the same rules. They did this through systematic empirical-observational, scientific research, more often of offenders than of controls. As a result, there was a shift of emphasis from studying the offense or crime to studying the offender or criminal, an idea begun in the early eighteenth century with Gall's phrenology: "The measure of culpability, and the measure of punishment cannot be determined by a study of the illegal act, but only by a study of the individual committing it" (Gall, quoted by Ellis, 1901: 31). The image of the criminal as defective is placed in an evolutionary environmental context. As humans develop over time they become less criminal, most learning how to adapt to the environment. In some early theories the criminal is seen as an underdeveloped atavistic "throw-back" to an earlier stage of human evolution, a reminder of where we have been.[1]

At various times and among different theorists, there have been different ideas of what precisely causes crime (Table 4-1 lists examples of the range of different theories and Table 4-2 lists the key works of biological theorists). These theorists share a common concern to identify the defective biological attributes that make some people prone to deviate *under certain environmental conditions.* The defects are considered to have different sources and sites such as chromosome pattern, hormone imbalance, or genetic makeup. Within this framework the appropriate model of criminal justice is medical, that is, relying on epidemiological research oriented to prevention, combined with diagnosis of the one or many causes, and prescription to "treat" the defect. It is significant that the diagnosis of cause requires qualified experts and can mean that different people who break the same rules or laws (e.g., theft) might do so as a result of different defects. The logical policy toward convicted offenders is to remove them from society and/or to correct or cure the defect. Each type of defect has its own group of treatments, which might need to be administered for differing lengths of time to effect a cure. The result, according to biological explanations, is that the same crime can result in differing "sentences" of treatment.

---

[1]"Atavism" was first used by Darwin and comes from the Latin, *atavus,* meaning "ancestor."

Table 4-2   Theorists Using Biological Explanations of Crime

THEORIST	MAJOR WORKS	DATE
della Porte	*The Human Physiognomy*	1586
Lavater	*Physiognomical Fragments*	1775
Pinel	*A Treatise on Insanity*	1806
Gall	*Les Fonctions du Cerveau*	1810
Caldwell	*Elements of Phrenology*	1824
Pritchard	*A Treatise on Insanity*	1835
Esquirol	*Des malades mentales*	1838
Maudsley	*The Physiology and Pathology of the Mind* *Responsibility in Mental Disease*	1867 1874
Lombroso	*L'Uomo Delinquente (The Delinquent Man)* *Crime: Its Causes and Remedies*	1876 1911
Dugdale	*The Jukes: A Study in Crime,* *Pauperism, Disease, and Heredity*	1877
Ferri	*The Theory of Imputability and the Denial of Free Will* *Criminal Sociology*	1878 1886
Benedikt	*Anatomical Studies upon the Brains of Criminals*	1881
Garafalo	*Criminology*	1885
Henderson	*An Introduction to the Study of the Dependent, Defective* *and Delinquent Class*	1893
MacDonald	*Criminology*	1893
Ellis	*The Criminal*	1897
Drahms	*The Criminal*	1900
Goring	*The English Convict*	1913
Goddard	*The Kallikak Family: A Study in the Heredity* *of Feeblemindedness* *Feeblemindedness, Its Cause and Consequences*	1913 1914
Lange	*Crime and Destiny*	1919
Kretschmer	*Physique and Character*	1921
Hooton	*Crime and the Man* *The American Criminal*	1939 1939

Sheldon et al.	*The Varieties of Human Physique*	1940
	The Varieties of Temperament	1942
	Varieties of Delinquent Youth	1949
Glueck and	*Unraveling Juvenile Delinquency*	1950
Glueck	*Physique and Delinquency*	1956
Hutchings	"Genetic factors in criminality"	1974
Mednick	*Genetics, Environment and Psychopathology*	1974
Mednick and Christiansen	*Biosocial Bases of Criminal Behavior*	1977
Mednick and Shoham	*New Paths in Criminology*	1979
Gabrielli and Mednick	"Genetic Correlates of Criminal Behavior"	1983
Mednick, Moffit, and Stack	*The Causes of Crime: New Biological Approaches*	1987
Hurwitz and Christiansen	*Criminology*	1983
Jeffery	*Biology and Crime*	1979
Jeffery	*Criminology*	1990
Jeffery	"Biological and Neuropsychiatric Approaches to Criminal Behavior"	1994
Ellis	*Genetics and Criminal Behavior*	1982
Ellis	"Criminal Behavior and r/K Selection: An Extension of Gene-Based Evolutionary Theory"	1988
Wilson and Herrnstein	*Crime and Human Nature*	1985

HUMANS, HUMAN NATURE, AND HUMAN BEHAVIOR

From the biological perspective, humans are seen as inheriting a biological and genetically determined constitution that makes them both broadly similar and yet also uniquely different. Human behavior is seen as an outcome of the interaction between biology and environment, mediated by brain function and intelligence. According to the now discredited "craniology" or "faculty phrenology" theory of Franz J. Gall, each human faculty and function is governed organically by a specialized section of the brain indicated by bumps on the cranium (Fink, 1938: 2-3). Interestingly, contemporary theory still holds that various regions of the brain control parts of the body. According to Jeffery (1993: 7), a leading contemporary advocate of biological criminology, "the brain is divided into sensory, motor, and associational areas which allow sensory information to be taken into the body, organized and stored neurochemically, and then used to control the motor which in turn is connected with the muscles and glands ... The brain also controls the emotional aspects of behavior as found in violence, anger, fear, sex, hunger, thirst and so forth." Jeffery (1994: 20–21) clearly distinguishes between three models of the relationship between human behavior and environment. Two of these, introspective psychology, or mentalism, and behavioral psychology are not our concern here since they deal with the effects of environment on mental process or its effect directly on human behavior. (See Chapter 5). In the third model, there is an integration between biology and psychology whereby "the environment interacts with the individual by means of the brain, and the brain in turn controls behavior. This is an *Environment*→ *Brain*→ *Behavior* model of behavior, sometimes referred to as an *Environment*→ *Organism*→ *Behavior* approach" (Jeffery, 1994: 21).

Most people possess a similar range of attributes and capabilities. However, according to Jeffery (1993: 6), within the human population there is considerable individual variation because "no two individuals possess the same genetic structure", each being the combination of 50 percent of the chromosomes from each parent. Moreover, individual differences transcend group differences such that intragroup differences (between members of an ethnic group) will be greater than intergroup differences (between ethnic groups). However, several biological criminologists do not hold this view. For Wilson and Herrnstein (1985), the reason why Japan has a low crime rate is because of constitutional traits inherent in the Japanese. And for Rushton (1987; 1990) a genetically oriented racist theory of crime prevails, according to which a hierarchy of criminal races exists, based on correlations between crime and racial type. Rushton insists that the pattern of correlated variables, particularly for crime, places Mongoloids above Caucasoids, who are above Negroids.

A central issue in understanding the biological version of individual positivism is the view of humans as having inherited genetic characteristics that are manifest in a given environment. Many texts, particularly those critical of biological criminology, often misstate the theory as biologically deterministic. This, according to Nelkin (1993: B1), is partly because, in trying to convey the importance they attach to their work, many geneticists use "overblown rhetoric and misleading metaphors" that distort the view of biology in the popular culture. Nelkin (ibid.: B1) shows that geneticists repeatedly define the gene as the essence of identity, as the basis of human differences, with the body a carrier for a set of genetic instructions or program hereditarily transmitted across generations. She says that these ideas are then magnified in media images of crime which emerge with headlines about "criminal genes" and predispositional explanations implied in such titles as: "Is Crime in the Family Tree?" (ibid.: B2). These same images present "DNA as the essence of the person," as "the most powerful force in shaping behavior," and as "a natural" basis of social stereotypes. Such images carry over into textbook accounts of biological theories of crime, with the result that the subtleties of environmental interaction with genes is lost. It is easy to see how these same simplistic ideas can be employed to justify racist and sexist claims about the nature of crime.

Those who hold biological views of criminal predisposition are rarely this unsophisticated. Shah and Roth (1974: 108), for example, claim that human behavior is the result of a *combination* of heredity and environment. They point out that there is a wide range of biological factors that are in continuous inter-action with their organism's environment and that it is the interaction of these causes that must be understood. Di Tullio (1969a: 13), similarly, claims that, "the human person is a synthesis of an evolutionary process chiefly connected with hereditary forces and of a formative process chiefly connected with envi-ronmental and cultural forces," and Fishbein and Thatcher (1986: 240) see a "dynamic interaction between physiology, biochemistry, the environment and behavior." Thus the genetic process is succinctly explained:

> Located in the cell's chromosomes are genes, which are the blueprints for inher-itance ... genes are transmitted from parent to child in an unaltered fashion. The genetic constitution is determined by a number of pairs of genes, half of each pair coming from the father and the other half from the mother. The total set of genes of one individual is called the genotype and the individual, as it develops from the interaction of genotype and environment, is called the phenotype ... There is a continual interaction between genetic and environmental factors. A person's environment depends to a certain extent on his own choice ... Environmental fac-tors may also be shaped and modified by the person ... by his individuality. Conversely, the influence which the environment exercises on the person will depend on his susceptibility and on other personal characteristics ... Thus both genetic constitution and environment are functionally interdependent. (Hurwitz and Christiansen, 1983: 47–48)[2]

This basic position at the root of biological approaches to crime implies that humans themselves, and their behavior, are not predetermined by genetics nor for that matter by the environment in isolation, but emerge as an interactive out-come of both. It implies, also, that humans are open to change through manip-ulations or interventions in their environment and are not, as is traditionally posited, predetermined to a particular destiny. That this point is lost in simpli-fied critical commentaries frustrates biological criminology's supporters. As Jeffery (1993: 6) expresses it: "It is not Genes OR Environment, but Genes in INTERACTION with Environment. It is not heredity or environment, but heredity and environment." Moreover, he asserts that "genes do not cause behav-ior ... Genes in interaction with the environment create a brain and nervous system. The relationship is ENVIRONMENT–BRAIN–BEHAVIOR, and not GENES–BEHAVIOR." The result is that "environment determines the manner

---

[2]The total set of all human genes is known as the human genome, and attempts to map these and their relationship to disease and dysfunction are known as the genome project.

in which the genetic systems develop into phenotypes or organism, but environmental factors can also alter genetic structures," as in the case of substances or toxins that interfere with normal human development (ibid.: 1993:7).

However, in Jeffery's version of biological theory (unlike Hurwitz and Christiansen's) the process for this interactive engagement is highly mechanistic and even extends to broad complex social-environmental encounters such as poverty: "Experience enters the body via the sensory system, is processed by the brain, and the brain then sends information to the motor system as behavioral adaptions of the individual to the environment" (ibid.). For others (Fadiman and Kewman, 1973), the process is more interactive, showing how the electro-chemical processes of the brain are affected by the environment. The latest assumptions about human mental process, for example, suggest that an important part of the brain is at the electro-chemical conjunction of hundreds of millions of nerve endings, called "synapses." Through these unions of nerve endings pass chemical substances known as "neurotransmitters," such as serotonin and dopamine. Neurotransmitters are generated and stored in neurons in the brain but released by electrical signals given off by nerve fibers. Stimulating these nerve fibers, then, which can happen as a result of numerous environmental encounters (such as jogging, laughter, etc.), releases neurotransmitters, which travel toward receptors, which, in turn, react to the neurotransmitters, triggering a series of electrochemical events. Through such a process the brain eventually sends information to increase, decrease, or otherwise change various behaviors, changing the impact of the environment on the organism.

VIEW OF SOCIETY AND THE SOCIAL ORDER

For the biological positivists, society is seen as part of the environment, although its organization is a reflection of the normally distributed attributes of the population. Since people are differently endowed, for a given environment, those with superior abilities will dominate those with less capability. According to Martin et al. (1990: 123), Sheldon, for example, accepted "the inevitability of 'survival of the fittest' ... for various psychological patterns." Thus society is a hierarchy, based on natural ability in a given environment. As Katz and Chambliss (1991: 246) say in their critical analysis of the biological view, "individuals, classes, races and countries in power obviously were superior to those who, on the bottom of the status hierarchy only had their defective genes to blame." They further argue that for biological theorists:

> The characteristics of society are seen simply as the sum total of the characteristics of its individual members, and the individuals, in turn, the product of their genetic codes. Societies are aggressive because the individuals in these societies are aggressive.

Jeffery (1993: 7) describes this as a "systems approach" or "a cell to society" approach. Society is the ongoing outcome of people's various adaptions to the behaviors produced by others' adaptions.

The differences between individuals are distributed as a normal curve and that which corresponds to the normal part of that curve constitutes a social consensus. Nowhere is this better reflected than in the way law is treated by biological theorists and in their shared view about what is deviance.

THE ROLE OF LAW, THE DEFINITION OF CRIME, AND THE IMAGE OF THE CRIMINAL

In biological theory, law is conceived as a reflection of the consensus of society. Garafalo (1914) for example, rejected legalistic definitions and stated that law should be based on the concept of "natural crime" that "offends the community" because it is "antisocial in nature." Crime is a deviation from normal behavior that is prohibited by law, but, said Garafalo, it must be harmful and an offense against the basic moral sentiments of a society.[3] Behavior lags behind law, so some deviation will not be criminalized at any one time. From the biological view science can measure what is normal and therefore can aid in forming law and in detecting and curing crime.

According to this view, the criminal is someone who breaks laws naturally and will break norms and laws in any society. The criminal is different from the noncriminal by being defective and, by implication, inferior. Criminals are born with a nature favorable to crime. Many are "latent criminals" who are predisposed to lawbreaking, drug taking, and so forth, and whose natural deviance or criminality will become manifest under certain conditions. Indeed, many of Lombroso's "born" criminals were epileptic, "with the disease latent and merely awaiting to become active under certain conditions" (Barnes and Teeters, 1943: 163). According to Maudsley (1874) people "go criminal, as the insane go mad, because they cannot help it" (Maudsley, quoted by Scott, 1973: 211). For Lombroso (1876), criminals could be identified because they were distinct physical types who exhibited certain physical marks or features, which he called "stigmata." These included a slanting forehead, long ear lobes or no ear lobes, a large jaw with no chin, heavy supra-orbital ridges, excessive hairiness of the body or an absence of hair, and extreme sensitivity or nonsensitivity to pain (Barnes and Teeters, 1943: 162). Possession of multiple physical abnormalities made them atavistic or "born criminals." Possessing five out of eighteen of these characteristics was enough to qualify a person as a born criminal with the somatological characteristics of primitive man. Moreover, Lombroso and Ferri identified several

---

[3]The Italian Penal Code is still based upon Lombroso's model of the born criminal, as some have critically observed (Cesaro, 1988).

other types of offenders, including the insane criminal; the epileptic criminal; habitual criminals; criminals of passion, which included political cranks; and the occasional criminal.

Classifying criminal types is the hallmark of the early biological approaches. Later this is exemplified in the somatotype theories of Kretschmer (1921), who saw distinct physically different types,[4] and the body-type theorists Sheldon et al. (1940). Sheldon related psychological temperament to physical constitution on a continuum of types from imperfect to well balanced, depending on the strength of each component as measured on a seven-point scale.[5] Deviations from the norm were associated with personality deviations (Martin et al., 1990: 123). These theorists identified three basic types of persons, based upon their physical appearance (see Table 4-3). For Hooton (1939a; 1939b), civilians were biologically superior to criminals, who made up an incorrigible, inferior class. Others, however, recognized them as physically superior. For Sheldon et al. (1940) these hereditary criminal types could be identified by the age of 6.

In addition to typing criminals, specific family research identified degenerative or "socially bankrupt" families to which generations of criminals could belong and through whom the hereditary trait of crime and degeneracy was thought to be passed, such as the Jukes and the Kallikaks (Dugdale, 1877; Estabrook, 1916; Henderson, 1893; Goddard, 1912). For these theorists and, indeed, Garafalo (1914), criminals were defective psychically rather than physiologically. Their mind was seen as a product of their biology, influenced by a congenital or inherited element which was different from that of normal, noncriminal people.

In her review of criminological anthropologists Rafter suggests that criminals were classified into a hierarchy of types "putatively derived from biology and then used to establish gradations within the criminal class," which were "in fact, derived from social class and then attributed back to biology" (Rafter, 1992: 538–39).

Others acknowledge the universality of delinquency as a typical phase of development among adolescents. They seek to explain why some do not mature out of crime in terms of genetic predisposition. These theorists construct a typology based on developmental types among adolescents, as in DiLalla and Gottesman's (1989) distinction between *continuous antisocials,* who are delinquents who continue their criminality as adults; *transitory delinquents,* who are delinquents but not criminals; and *late bloomers,* who are criminals but not delinquents.

---

[4]Schafer (1976: 52) points out that both Kretschmer and Sheldon heavily relied on the earlier typology of body type and mental illness formulated by Kraepelin (1883).

[5]This was later used by Glueck and Glueck (1950) in their monumental longitudinal study of delinquency.

Table 4-3   Major Body-Type Theories

DESCRIPTION	NAME OF SOMATOTYPE	CRIME/DEVIANCE
Type 1 Soft, rounded face; medium height; rotund; thick neck; soft hands; overweight. Relaxed, sociable, tolerant. Motivation dominated by the gut.	Pyknic (Kretschmer) Endomorphic (Sheldon) Personality type: "Viscerotonia"	delinquent, manic-depressive, occasional fraud
Type 2 Strong muscle and bone; firm; sturdy; wide shoulders; deep chest; tapering trunk. Lack of sensitivity; assertive, dominant, aggressive.	Athletic (Kretschmer) Mesomorphic (Sheldon) (Glueck and Glueck) Personality type: "Somatotonia"	delinquent, schizophrenic, habitual, violence, and robbery, homicide
Type 3 Thin, fragile, light, delicate; developed nervous system; large brain. Thoughtful, tense, reserved, inhibited.	Leptosome or Asthenic (Kretschmer) Ectomorphic (Sheldon) Personality type: "Cerebrotonia"	schizophrenic, habitual petty theft

For those who see the problem of crime as a problem of brain processes, the familiar classification of abnormality through mental illness serves as the starting point of the image of criminals as being abnormal. Those who are abnormal because of mental disorder are classified as suffering from psychosis, personality disorder, or neurosis. Psychotic disorders are seen to stem either from "some organic condition or some functional disorder which has no [known] organic origin," and neurotic disorders "occur when a person's personality is seriously disturbed by some non-organic, non-functional condition which seriously affects the patient's performance and behaviour" (Hall Williams, 1982: 44).[6] Psychiatrists view psychoses as affecting the personality at several levels, which include consciousness (e.g., illusion and distortion), memory (e.g., loss), thinking (e.g., inability to deduce logically), intelligence (e.g., impaired), emotions (e.g., exaggerated), and the whole personality. Indeed, it is typical to include a third separate category called "personality disorder."[7]

---

[6]Neuroses are seen by many as diseases that, unlike psychoses, do not produce radical changes in personality or anatomy and that can be objectively perceived by those suffering them (Hurwitz and Christiansen, 1983: 95).

[7]Since personality disorder and functional psychosis have no known biological basis, we consider these categories as part of the psychological theory of crime in the next chapter.

CAUSAL LOGIC

The cause of crime, according to the biological theory, is an interactive *combination* of biological defectiveness, predisposing a person to criminal behavior, and an environment in which the predisposition becomes manifest. The range of causal agents varies. Crime may be caused because the defectives are (a) impelled to anger, (b) susceptible to addiction, (c) subject to impaired brain functions, such as learning ability limiting their capacity for socialization, or have difficulty controlling their behavior, or (d) are excited by environmental stimuli. Moreover, once present the trait can be passed on through heredity. For example, Mednick and Finello (1983) argue that studies of the autonomic nervous system suggest diminished response to frightening stimuli in those classifiable as antisocial and that genetic, physiological, and biochemical factors are causal agents in criminal behavior.

Specific hypothesized causes or defects that have been suggested include mental deficiency (Goring, 1913); feeblemindedness, which was an earlier term for mental defective (Goddard, 1912); physical inferiority (Goring, 1913; Hooton, 1939a; 1939b); XYY chromosome pattern (Jacobs, 1965; Telfer, 1968); brain disorder/dysfunction, perhaps revealed by electroencephalograph (Hare, 1970; Hare and Connolly, 1987; Hippchen, 1978; Moyer, 1976); race (Ferri, 1886; Garafalo, 1914; Hooton, 1939a; 1939b; Rushton, 1990); low IQ (Goddard, 1912; Hirschi and Hindelang, 1977; Wilson and Herrnstein, 1985) or learning disabilities (Hippchen, 1978); biochemical and hormonal imbalances (Schlapp and Smith, 1928; Dalton, 1961); defective genes (Jeffery, 1978; 1993; Mednick and Christianson, 1977; Mednick et al., 1987); blood chemistry disorders, such as low blood sugar (Hippchen, 1978); ecological stimuli or deficiencies or excessive sugar consumption; allergens; or vitamin and mineral deficiencies (Hippchen, 1978; Hoffer, 1978; Wunderlich, 1978; Dorfman, 1984). Environmental contexts are not often discussed in great detail beyond particular negative physical environments such as drugs but, when a more expansive view is taken, have included: geographical location, temperature, and climate (Ferri, 1886).

The causal logic of the now discredited phrenology and early constitutional theory is often misunderstood. Physical stigmata were not thought to cause the crime but were considered indications of its presence and gave a means whereby it could be detected within the individual. Thus phrenologists (Gall, Spurzheim) believed the tendency to crime was one of the characteristics of behavior detectable through bumps on the head. Early Italian School anthropological theorists (Lombroso, Ferri, Garafalo) and others believed the defect was reflected in physical appearance or "bodily makeup" (indicated by physical stigmata, or body types), somatypes such as mesomorphs having more crime-prone personalities (Kretschmer, 1921; Sheldon et al., 1949; Glueck and Glueck, 1950; Cortes and Gatti, 1972) as well as incurring more mental disease. In Lombrosian theory, then, it was not the stigmata that caused crime; this merely indicated that a person was criminal. The crime was caused by atavism, which rendered a person less developed and as a result he or she could not adjust to the rules of modern society. Atavistic criminals were "throwbacks":

> a reversion to a primitive or subhuman type of man, characterized physically by a variety of inferior morphological features reminiscent of apes and lower primates, occurring in the more simian fossil men and to some extent preserved in modern "savages." (Wolfgang, 1960: 247)

As Schafer (1976: 43) says, "The lack of adjustment to modern (that is, nineteenth-century) social norms leads these atavistic men to clashes with their society, and these clashes are the crimes."[8]

Others, such as Goring and Goddard, rejected the born criminal per se, believing that it was not crime that was inherited but the feeblemindedness inherent in degenerate stock: "The criminal is not born; he is made. The so-called criminal is merely a type of feeblemindedness, a type misunderstood and mistreated, driven into criminality for which he is well fitted by nature" (Goddard, 1912: 8). Goring (1913) believed that the essential difference between criminals and the general population was their intelligence, which for the criminal was defective. For later anthropologists, too, such as Hooton (1939b), crime was the combined outcome of low-grade organically inferior organisms with the environment. Hooton (1939b), moreover, argued that constitutional and environmental factors operate on physical and mental inferiors and that "differences in constitutional type ... undoubtably are agents in determining the choice of offence" (Hooton, 1939a: 308).

Following the attempts to link constitution and crime, several theories of crime causation consider a hormonal or endocrinal perspective. Endocrinal (ductless) glands, such as the pituitary, thyroid, pancreas, adrenals, and gonads (ovaries/testes), produce hormones partly in response to neurochemical processes in the brain that are, in turn, affected by feedback from these same hormones, as the whole system moves toward a state of equilibrium. The production of hormones can affect both physical and mental processes and temperament, with the suggestion that "disturbed production" of hormones or "abnormal secretions," are significant crime factors (Hurwitz and Christiansen, 1983: 79). Some theorists suggested that the endocrinal disturbances may have affected the offender as an unborn child during the mother's pregnancy (Schlapp and Smith, 1928: 28-29). Moreover, the irregularity of specific glands has been tied to specific crimes, such

---

[8]There is some similarity between this interpretation of Lombroso and the later ideas of culture conflict.

as the pituitary, gonads, and adrenal in the crime of murder, and pituitary and thyroid in the crimes of robbery, deceit, and theft (Kinberg, 1935; Berman, 1928, cited by Hurwitz and Christiansen, 1983: 81).

The idea that crime is caused by hormonal imbalances has been more recently applied to explain some women's crime. In the theory of premenstrual tension, for example, a deficiency of the hormone progesterone just prior to menstruation "has been suggested as significantly influencing the behavior of certain women, who become disoriented and commit acts which are 'out of character'" (Hall Williams, 1982: 37).

The XYY Chromosome theory argues that a chromosomal imbalance exists in which some persons are endowed with an additional Y chromosome (sex determining). These "super-male" chromosomal persons were claimed to be more aggressive when found among populations of prisoners and mental patients (Jacobs et al., 1965; Telfer et al., 1968; Nielsen, 1968; 1971; Griffiths, 1971). This aggressiveness was not necessarily seen as producing more violent crimes but more crime generally (Montague, 1968; Schafer, 1976: 55).

Some theorists came to recognize the limitations of general constitutional theory, arguing that it is not a single genotype (the total set of genes) that provides the thrust toward crime but a variety of phenotypical characteristics that are more or less inherited. In other words, the cause is individual genotype in developmental interaction with the environment (Rosenthal, 1975). Indeed, Kessley and Moos (1970) argue that to claim a single chromosome is capable of specific behavioral effects fails to consider the broad range of environmental factors and ignores the fact that the phenotype is the result of the interaction and integration of the genome with the environment. Thus Jeffery (1993: 6) argues that there are no specific genes for murder, rape, or robbery nor for any other specific behavior.

One of the more recent genetic theories of crime causation is Ellis's (1987, 1989) evolutionary theory of r/K selection. This argues that crime is a product of a particular pattern of selective reproduction known as r/K selection. R-selected organisms produce large numbers of organisms after a short gestation period with minimal risk and give each offspring little or no care. Ellis (1989) argues that males are more R-selected than females, that males throughout the mammalian order exhibit R-selected characteristics and that as a result are more prone to crime than females.

The analysis of cause has shifted between monolithic or single-cause theories and multicausal or multifactor theories. However, in the latter case, the theory of cause remains linear and, for most recent theorists, consistent with Ferri, interactive with the environment. As Di Tullio (1969b: 53) expresses it, "the currently prevailing theory is that all criminal phenomena are the expression of a complex of closely fused individual and environmental causal factors ... The task is not to insist on the purely sociological or biological nature of crime, but rather to analyze the way the sociological factors combine with biological factors in the development of a single criminal phenomenon." For example, Jeffery (1993) believes that criminal behavior can result when the electromagnetic processes of the brain are sufficiently disturbed by genetics, chemicals, or environmental factors to cause abnormal perceptions, judgments, and behaviors that may lead to crime. This combined causal or coproduction approach has been described as the "diathesis-stress" model when explaining mental illness: "The model suggests that severe stress acts to trigger an illness to which the individual was vulnerable: neither the biological disposition nor stress alone can cause mental disorder but, mental disorder can or will result from their combined action" (Holman and Quinn, 1992: 87). Ellis (1988) has applied a similar integrated approach to crime, arguing that it is important to consider the interrelationship between the neurochemical processes of the brain that control behavior and to recognize that this process is itself controlled both by genetic *and environmental* factors, which can include both physical environments such as drugs or injury as well as experiential learning environments.

Again one must be reminded of the harmful potential this causal logic can create. The denigration of some categories of people as "inferior" (which historically has been typically persons of color) can easily lead to draconian policies and techniques of crime control, based on the "public good" of ridding society of defective dangerous elements, a rationale legitimated in the name of science. How a criminal justice system intended to protect individual human rights can be adapted to the repression of those diagnosed as defective will become apparent in the succeeding dimensions of our analysis.

CRIMINAL JUSTICE SYSTEM IMPLICATIONS

The kind of criminal justice appropriate from the biological perspective is based on the "medical model" for the diagnosis and treatment of disease. In this model crimes are simply "an occasion for social intervention," in which the court's role should be to put scientific "knowledge to practical use in the way in which it deals with offenders" (King, 1981: 19–20). The court process

> should resemble that of a clinic, where the successive objectives are diagnosis, prognosis, treatment and cure; hence the medical model. Ideally a court which operated according to the principles of this model would begin with the assumption that every person who appeared in the dock was in need of treatment and that the court was able through its expertise to provide such treatment itself or refer the defendant to some other agency where the appropriate treatment would be available. It would then set about collecting information about the defendant's family background, ... education, ... medical history, ... work record, ... previous encounters with the criminal law ... [and] present situation. All this information

would be analysed by officials who, through their expertise, qualifications and experience were skilled in diagnosing the causes of the defendant's anti-social behavior, predicting the likelihood of further anti-social acts and proposing the appropriate course of treatment. (King, 1981: 20)

Thus we can summarize the criminal justice system under the medical model as comprising certain key elements:

1. information collection
2. individualized diagnosis
3. considerable discretion, based on diagnosis of cause
4. experts as judges and jurors and expert witnesses as advisors
5. due process displaced by scientific method and expert judgment
6. prediction
7. treatment presumption
8. treatment selection
9. sentences to be indeterminate
10. right to appeal limited to further authoritative opinion

Illustrations abound of advocates for such an approach to criminal justice in the early statements of criminal anthropologists. Garafalo (1914), for example, was opposed to juries that represented popular bias and ignorance, and he felt that "the only way to reform the jury is to abolish it" (Jones, 1986: 97). Similarly Ferri (1897) wanted to replace the jury system with a panel of experts composed of doctors and psychiatrists. Interestingly, Lombroso, Ferri's father-in-law, "was often called to testify as an expert witness in criminal trials" (Curran and Renzetti, 1994: 44).

More recently, some biological theorists have lamented that diagnostic procedures are not available for criminal offenders. For example, Fishbein and Thatcher (1986: 259) observe that "the unfortunate reality for those who come into contact with law enforcement authorities by virtue of their dysfunction is that the appropriate treatments are unavailable or inaccessible as, indeed, are the most rudimentary facilities for diagnosis."

Criminal Justice Policy and Correctional Ideology

From our general discussion of the approach to criminal justice it is clear that several philosophies of intervention combine to provide the mainstay of biological criminology's correctional ideology. These are protection, prevention, rehabilitation, and treatment. In this context the philosophy of prevention means "preventing the crime *before* it occurs, rather than waiting for it to occur" (Jeffery, 1994: 27). This involves screening the general population for potential indicators of future trouble in the manner that public health checks for signs of illness and disease. Fishbein and

Thatcher (1986: 259) believe that "screening" for underlying problems causing anti-social behavior, "should be initiated during the early stages of development," preferably "in the formative years." Clearly, such a philosophy claims to justify intervention without specific reason, on the grounds that it benefits both the public and the individual good. Such an approach, in its pure form, provides few legal safeguards since, as with medicine generally, invasive testing practices, which in any other context would themselves be criminal acts, are here legitimate on the grounds of scientific necessity. Indeed, rather than protecting the individual or using scientific procedures to understand the problem of crime, Jeffery (1994: 28) believes we should use them to discover the offender. He says "the question is not 'What disease does the person have?' but 'What person has the disease?' We should not ask 'How many men are criminal?' but rather 'What men are criminals?'" (ibid). Jeffery concludes that "we must move from a punitive to a preventative framework. There must be major changes in the legal system, which would relate criminal law much more to science and technology and much less to prisons and executions; otherwise our high crime rate will continue in the future" (Jeffery, 1994: 28).

Once criminals have been identified, the biological perspective's policy is to rehabilitate the convicted offender through diagnoses and prescription of a cure for the defect. The justification for intervention is to treat the cause of the crime in order to rehabilitate the offender and reintroduce him or her back into society: "Restoration of the defendant to a state of mental and social health whereby he will be able to cope with the demands society makes of him and refrain from conduct which might cause further intervention to be necessary" (King, 1981: 20).

From this perspective sentencing is a treatment, with the length of sentencing indeterminate, based on expert assessment of when the person is cured. This policy reform was lobbied for by both Lombroso and his student Ferri. Indeed, for Ferri "crime is like sickness," "the remedy should be fitted to the disease. It is the task of the criminal anthropologist to determine in what measure it should be applied" (Ferri, 1886: 386).

Ferri justified punishment in terms of self-defensive preservation against criminals who would destroy it through their defiance of law and the social danger that this creates. Although treatment/cure is the hallmark philosophy of the approach, it should not be forgotten that the logic of the perspective included the possibility of incurability with the idea that philosophies of elimination, expulsion, or exile are justified on the grounds of "social hygiene." Ferri proposed to satisfy hygienic or preventative goals; therapeutic, reparative, and repressive goals; as well as elimination. His argument was that offenders were not morally responsible and that all notions of punishment or retribution for moral culpability should be eliminated. Garafalo believed in elimination as well as enforced reparation (Parmelee, 1918: 193). Indeed, he believed that the "safety of the community" was the criterion for determining whether elimination should be permanent or temporary.

Techniques of Crime Control

Several procedures and techniques are suggested to detect potential criminals. One such is screening potential offenders before they commit offenses (Mednick, 1979: 45). The potential value of "screening clinics" occurs in several biological theories. Jeffery (1978), for example, believes that we must develop a private criminal justice system based on early diagnosis and preventative treatment for medical and biological disorders known *or* suspected to be associated with crime such as genetic defects, learning disabilities, and malnutrition. He argues (Jeffery, 1993: 7) that "neuropsychiatry offers a unique opportunity to develop diagnostic and prevention techniques within an interdisciplinary criminology which would make use of CAT scans, PET scans, MRI scans, and EEG tests." He (ibid: 8) claims that this would help minority populations understand why they are being disproportionately victimized:

> Crime prevention programs including pre and postnatal care, early help for underweight infants, well baby clinics, nutritional programs, neurological examinations for brain injuries, examinations of lead contamination in children, examinations for learning disabilities and hyperactivity and other public health projects, would be of great help to the black community ... It might be better to invest our dollars in these programs rather than in building dozens of new prisons.

Such an approach would pay particular attention to alcohol and drug use by pregnant women and "other medical problems that could lead later to behavioral problems" (Jeffery, 1994: 28).

Once potential offenders have been identified, and actual law breakers convicted and diagnosed, the control objective of treating the offender is achieved through using surgery or drugs. For example, lobotomies and castration were popular in the 1930s through the 1950s. Drug treatments have been designed to correct biological or hormonal imbalances. They have included vitamin stimulants in diet, Ritalin for hyperactivity, chemical castration for rapists, and hormone treatment for premenstrual syndrome, or PMS. Castration was related to hormonal theory in that it was seen as removing the glands that produced sex hormones. It has been typically used on chronic sex offenders and homosexuals, although in Germany it has also been used to treat crimes against property. However, as Hurwitz and Christiansen (1983: 81) point out, since "castration removes a decisive physical requirement not only for abnormal but also for normal sex life," it cannot be seen to "regulate a glandular abnormality, nor even suppose one."

The logic of the analysis early on led several theorists to the view that some offenders were beyond treatment. Ferri (1886) proposed surgical operations and the death penalty to eliminate permanently those unfit for social life or who could not adapt to it, as did Garafalo (1914) and others much later. Thus eugenics (improvement of the race through better breeding) was proposed, including sterilization for the untreatables or feebleminded (Dugdale, 1877). Indeed, Hooton (1939a, 1939b) believed that the physical inferiority of the criminal stock made it necessary that they be eliminated: "Only by sterilizing these defective types and breeding a better race does he think it possible to check the growth of criminality" (Barnes and Teeters, 1943: 166), and "the elimination of crime can be effected only by the extirpation of the physically, mentally, and morally unfit, or by their complete segregation in a socially aseptic environment" (Hooton, 1939b: 309). Reviewing the policy on the feebleminded as late as 1943 Barnes and Teeters (1943: 179), though themselves opposed to it, observe that "many of the more progressive students of the problem recommend that the idiot group should be painlessly exterminated. They are a definite burden to both their relatives and to society." The eugenics movement not only promoted selective breeding, restricted marriages, and sterilization but also pressed for restrictive legislation to prevent the immigration of inferior stock. By the early 1940s Barnes and Teeters (1943: 180) reported that "Of some 33,000 defectives who have been sterilized, over 13,000 operations have been performed in California." By its end the eugenics movement was responsible for the involuntary sterilization of 64,000 people (Katz and Chambliss, 1991: 247).

Other techniques, though, could lead to the same end as elimination or eugenics. Expulsion to penal colonies via transportation (Garafalo, 1914) or segregated isolation in reservations so that criminals could not contaminate the rest of the population (Hooton, 1939a) was recommended, as was selective breeding to strengthen the mental and spiritual fibre of the race and eliminate its degenerative physical scourges (Sheldon, et al., 1940).

Most recently the prospect that genetic mapping will identify the genetic source of criminal behavior, along with developments in genetic engineering, has given a new impetus to this approach. However, some of the believers in gene-environment interaction advocate that once the genetic causes have been identified via screening at an early age, elements in the environment, such as "toxic element concentrations, socioeconomic status, prenatal care, neurological impairments, and learning disabilities" can be "manipulated on a wide-scale basis to prevent the onset of behavioral or forensic disorders in the general population" (Fishbein and Thatcher, 1986: 258). Others, also recognizing the intervention value of the environment in gene-environment causality, invite voluntary participation in a clinical program that would counsel prescreened offenders through career choices and channel them into "relatively challenging, varied and demanding occupations that have the element of excitement that most chronic offenders seem to crave" (Mednick, 1985: 61). One can only guess that it would be acceptable to allow the less criminally inclined to drift into boring, repetitive, low-status positions!

EVALUATION

The early biological theorists have been criticized as representing the ideas of "conceptual dinosaurs" (Martin et al. 1990: 130), who lived in a stone-age era of criminology (Walker, 1974). But even within their own time and conceptual framework, they were highly controversial, and several "lacked confidence in the scientific centerpiece of their doctrine" (Rafter, 1992: 536). Hooton (1939a: 3) dismissed phrenology as a "pseudo-science," while Sheldon et al. (1940: 12) said it "had neither the calipers nor coefficients of correlation." Yet Sheldon's own approach was described as a "new Phrenology in which bumps on the buttocks take the place of bumps on the skull" (Washburn, 1951, cited by Sutherland and Cressey, 1966: 131).

Admittedly, Lombroso has been heralded as the "father of modern criminology," "one of the pillars of criminological thought" (Martin et al., 1990: 21), the first of "the holy three of criminology" (Schafer, 1976: 42). Indeed, he has been celebrated for providing the unprecedented impetus to hundreds of students of crime (Sellin, 1937: 898–99) and for providing provocative ideas that merit him "a place of honor in his own field" (Wolfgang, 1972: 288). However, he was also condemned and criticized methodologically for failing to use adequate control groups and for using dubious correlational techniques. Whereas Tarde's (1886) devastating statistical attack on Lombroso "undermined the popularity of Lombroso" in Europe (Wilson Vine, 1960: 298), it was Charles Goring's scholarship that destroyed the credibility of the "born criminal" in England and the United States. Goring's (1913) studies of over three thousand English recidivists using a control population of university students and military personnel "dealt a lethal blow" to Lombroso's theory since it found his criminal stigmata just as frequently in noncriminal populations (Sheldon, 1940, et al.: 304). Lombroso's work was said by Goring to be "an organized system of self-evident confusion whose parallel is only to be found in the astrology, alchemy, and other credulities of the Middle Ages" (Jones, 1986: 107). Even Hooton (1939a: 13) agreed with the adverse criticism of Lombroso, rejecting his atavistic and degenerate theory and denouncing his seriously flawed research methods. As is so often the case in biological theory, the major unexplained problem was "that there were many who presented the same anomalies as the 'born criminal' who lived honest lives, and that many men who did not present these anomalies behaved like 'born criminals'" (Hibbert, 1966: 217).

Goring and Goddard's feeblemindedness theory was revealed to suffer a similar logical flaw in claiming that, because they are susceptible to suggestion, the feebleminded are even more able to be socialized into conventionality than normal types (Barnes and Teeters, 1943: 179), so they are less likely rather than more likely to be offenders! Of course the theory was also completely undermined by the evidence that most offenders are not mentally defective.

Hooton disposed of Goring's work as unscientific and for containing distorted results in "conformity with his bias" (Hooton, 1939a: 17). Hooton's own neo-Lombrosian theory wilts, in the majority opinion, from "a highly critical rejection" as a result of circular reasoning that makes the theory dubious and unconvincing, not least because it completely ignores social explanations. Indeed, upon its publication, Sutherland criticized Hooton's work on numerous methodological counts, such as poor sampling, unrepresentativeness, bias in the control group, and for inadequately drawing from prison populations the sample of criminals which preselects only those inept enough to be convicted and sent to prison and omits all those who escape arrest as well as white-collar criminals who are seldom sent to prison (Sutherland, 1939: 911–14). Most insightful was Merton and Montague's (1940: 385) observation that

> Hooton has been forced into the un-American position of espousing the cause of the angels ... What we wish to do here is to suggest that the differences between the angels and the criminals are only skin deep; that the criminals may not have sprouted wings as the angels have done, not because it was not in them to do so, but because their wings were clipped before they were ready to try them.

More generally it has been observed that, "if the results of criminological anthropological research are reviewed, it must be recognized that they are very meager. The original contention that serious criminals show physical degenerative stigmata is dead" (Hurwitz and Christiansen, 1983: 74). Indeed, as Katz and Abel (1984) point out, a major problem with biological theories of heredity is that precisely what is inherited is never made very clear.

Ferri received a better press than most of his contemporaries and was seen as "overshadowing his master" (Schafer, 1976: 44), although he also suffers from the contamination of being Lombroso's student.[9] His was an approach seeking to reconcile and compensate for Lombrosian ideas with those recognizing multiple social factors. But even his contemporary Garafalo (1914: 132) criticized his classification scheme as "without scientific basis and lack[ing] homogeneity and exactness." Subsequently, "efforts to study crime from a multi-factor approach have been severely criticized but still command powerful support" (Hall Williams, 1982: 13).

Some theories, such as XYY chromosome theory, have been almost completely discredited by the evidence, not least since the majority of carriers were found to be *less* rather than more aggressive than fellow XY prisoners; *more*

---

[9]His reputation was not helped by becoming an Italian fascist and supporter of dictator Mussolini. Sellin (1960: 377) says of Ferri: "As for Fascism, he saw something of value in it, so far as criminal justice was concerned, because it represented to him a systematic reaffirmation of the authority of the state against the excesses of individualism, which he had always criticized."

prevalent among prison officers than prisoners; and *more* prevalent in the general population who have never committed crime (Sarbin and Miller, 1970; Clark et al., 1970; Fox, 1971). Hurwitz and Christiansen (1983: 47), though generally favorable to biocriminology, state that, "the connection between chromosome abnormalities and crime, however, seems dubious." Some have suggested that many of the XYY studies are based on faulty methods and inadequate controls and that "positive generalizations about genetic impulsion toward criminal behavior is more an enthusiasm of journalists than genetic scientists" (Moor, 1972: 520; see also *"New York Times"* in Schur, 1969: 14; Nelkin, 1993).

In contrast, evidence from twin studies and adoption studies shows consistent, if limited, support for a genetic component shaping at least convictions for crime. Moreover, these also suffer from serious methodological difficulties. Twin studies are based on the hypothesis that identical twins, resulting from the fertilization of a single ovum by a single sperm (monozygotic), have identical genotypes and therefore are more likely to exhibit criminal behavior when one twin is criminal than are fraternal twins, who result from the simultaneous fertilization of two separate ova by different sperm cells (dizygotic) and therefore have different genotypes. Some support for this hypothesis based on "concordance rates" (rate of agreement) and "twin coefficients" is found in the work of Christiansen (1974; 1977a; 1977b). Methodological problems with these studies include problems of twin classification that is not reliable; the reliance on official conviction statistics as a measure of criminality; the paucity of criminal twins; the compounding of sampling errors through pooling of small sample studies; difficulty in explaining why the majority of twin partners of criminal twins are *not* themselves criminal; and confusion of environment, particularly the differential child development patterns between identical and fraternal twins, with genetic effects. Both Walters (1992) and Hurwitz and Christiansen (1983: 61) conclude that the later studies show a less clear picture than the earlier ones. Describing his own Danish twin study Christiansen said, "The high discordance among monozygotic twins[10] demonstrates that criminality is only to a limited extent, contingent upon heredity or similarity of environment" (ibid: 64). Walters (1992: 606) in an overview of research found that "higher quality studies and those published in 1975 and later provided less support for the gene-crime hypothesis than lower quality studies and those published prior to 1975." As Katz and Chambliss (1991: 249) point out, identical twins growing up in the same household are "often dressed alike, treated alike and able to confuse friends and teachers." Thus it may be the environmental conditions that explain why identical twins are more likely than

---

[10]This showed 64.2 percent *discordance* for men and 78.6 percent *discordance* for women among monozygotes and 87.2 percent *discordance* for men and 95.7 percent *discordance* for women among dizygotes.

same-sex fraternal twins to act alike. Further, studies of twins' imitation of anti-social behavior, and twins' influence on each other's behavior, have indicated that the genetic influence on registered criminality may be more modest than previously thought (Carey, 1992). Indeed, some studies have found that when environmental effects are controlled for, the difference in criminality between different twin types is not significant (Dalgard and Kringlen, 1976). Even the study of identical twins separated early in life and reared apart in different environments, which seems to offer a way out of the environment problem,

> do[es] not, on the whole, change any of the general conclusions about comparison of monozygotic and dizygotic twins. Criminality as such is not hereditary, nor are the predominantly biological factors of criminality with which these studies have been concerned ... No study carried out up to now can be said to have provided conclusive evidence of the dominance of genetic over environmental factors" (Hurwitz and Christiansen, 1983: 70–71)

Though showing some support for biological theory, adoption studies are "less favorable to the gene crime hypothesis than those produced by family and twin studies" (Walters, 1992: 606). Adoption studies compare the criminality (again based on conviction data) of adoptive sons with that of their fathers relative to a control, with the weakly supported hypothesis that, if genetic influence is present, there will be a greater probability of the son being criminal when the biological father is also criminal than among cases in which the biological father is not criminal or in which the adoptive father is criminal (Hutchings and Mednick, 1975; Mednick and Volavka, 1980; Gabrielli and Mednick, 1983; Mednick et al., 1984)[11] Again, methodological problems abound, not least of which are the adoption process's classification and selection procedure, which matches biological and adoptive homes on the basis of family income or socioeconomic status (Walters, 1992; Walters and White, 1989; Kamin, 1985; Lewontin, Rose, and Kamin, 1984); adoption failing to take place shortly after birth (Walters, 1992: 597); and the reliance on official crime statistics as a measure of criminality.

The idea that secretions of the endocrinal glands in some persons leads to increased crime as a result of fear and aggression (Molitch, 1937) has been rejected as being without foundation and untenable when applied to criminality (Wolfgang and Ferracuti, 1967: 199; Hurwitz and Christiansen, 1983: 80).

---

[11]Studies done on the adoptive children of criminal women show that the risk of criminal conviction is greater for the biological children of criminal women than those of criminal men, a finding that researchers suggest shows a genetic predisposition (Baker et al., 1989).

Finally, the more recent racially based criminology of Rushton (1990) and Wilbanks (1987) has been subject to intense methodological criticism. Gabor and Roberts (1990a; 1990b), for example, criticize Rushton for failure to discuss the nature and substance of crime, for inferring causality from zero-order correlations, and for doing so for a small range of offenses in which blacks are overrepresented. Upon reanalysis, they argue, little support is found for a genetic explanation of crime.

Overall biological theory generally tends to do better in explaining convictions for a small number of sexual crimes, and it seems that it may play a part in explaining some forms of violent crime, such as aggressive offenses that result from brain damage (Mednick et al., 1988). However, as Schur (1969: 15) has said,

> Certainly it is possible that systematic long-term research may reveal that some highly aggressive acts are in part genetically determined. Yet ... our knowledge of violent crime suggests that this is quite inadequate as a general explanation. Given the social and situational components of most violence in America, such "internal" factors are likely to have significance in only a very small proportion of violent offenses. And clearly the extension of such explanation for crime in general is totally unwarranted.

Indeed, even supporters of biocriminology find no evidence that biological factors play a causal role in violent crimes in general (Mednick et al., 1988). Biological theory has been claimed to be able to explain some forms of crime resulting from insanity or some delinquency resulting from attention disorder such as hyperactivity. For example, given that use of psychotropic drugs to block dopamine receptors in the brain controls certain psychotic problems such as schizophrenia, it would be easy to conclude that "overactive dopamine synapses" were the cause. However, as Holman and Quinn (1992: 87) point out: "Overactive dopamine synapses may be the *result* of schizophrenia, rather than the cause. A dopamine-blocking agent may merely be controlling a symptom of the underlying disorder rather than alleviating the cause." Similarly, Empey and Stafford (1991: 163–64) argue that although most modern biological theorists accept that genes alone do not cause crime, and, as we have seen, argue for an interactive explanation between genes and environment, the way these factors interact can be crucial. They point out that, rather than indicating, for example, that poor and minority children's biological and intellectual impairment is biological in origin, the evidence suggests that the biological impairment may be the result of socio-economic context:

> Poverty and ignorance reduce the likelihood that poor mothers will receive adequate nourishment and prenatal care while they are carrying their babies; the lack

of prenatal care, in turn, leads to an excessive number of premature births; and premature births then further enhance the likelihood of greater impairment.

Moreover, summarizing the aggregate research literature on crime and mental illness, they argue that linking violence to mental illness is "unfounded." A similar conclusion was reached by Hurwitz and Christiansen (1983: 92), who, after reviewing the evidence, state "that the statistical correlation between insanity and crime is weak," and by Monahan and Steadman (1983), who found little evidence to support the view that the mentally ill were more criminal than the rest of the population. Indeed, Holman and Quinn (1992: 83, 84) argue that "although the media focusses much attention on psychotic killers and rapists, they are actually quite few in number. In fact seriously mentally ill commit extremely few crimes when compared to the 'normal' public, and one is about as likely to be killed by lightning as by a psychotic murderer."[12] They argue that it is the bizarre nature of these crimes that draws disproportionate media attention and results in "the popular misconception that psychotics play a significant role in society's overall crime problem" (ibid.). In other words, in spite of the popular reaction and media interest suggesting that heinous crime is the result of "serious mental problems," criminologists generally still agree with Reckless's (1940: 205) view that mental disorders are relatively insignificant as a cause of crime.

Interestingly, some studies have found evidence of independent contribution of biological parent criminality and urban environment, but no evidence for gene-environment interaction for convicted offenders (Gabrielli and Mednick, 1984). In contrast, other studies have found evidence that genetic factors contribute to individual differences that interact with sociological and environmental conditions, particularly peer associations, to produce delinquent and criminal outcomes (Rowe and Osgood, 1984). Arguably the theory better explains substance abuse, with crime being a correlation of the addiction, rather than crime being itself caused by the biology. For example, a study by Bohman (1978) of Swedish adoptees found that there was a significant correlation between the alcoholism of biological parents and adopted sons. The results show that the genetic explanation for crime is not supported. This is generally the case. There is little empirical support, even in the twin-study and adoption data, when they are critically analyzed. At best what can be said is that genetic differences minimally affect individuals to the extent that, in certain environmental contexts,

---

[12]This might, however, understate the relationship between psychosis and violence, especially since, once diagnosed, psychotics may be committed to institutions and hospitals where their interpersonal violence and violence toward the staff is "absorbed" by the treatment program and seen as evidence of their illness. As a result, the police are rarely notified and these offenders remain hidden from the criminal justice record.

their differences *may* form the basis of lawbreaking activity, with the critical issue being the nature of the gene-environment interaction (Cadoret et al., 1983; Cadoret et al., 1985). Certainly this view is consistent with the more sophisticated of the theoretical advocates.

Overall biological theory has a tendency to medicalize political issues, resulting in a denial of due process rights that is inimical to a democratic society (Box, 1977). This is mobilized by the media and appeals to those who see a quick-fix solution to problems of crime and violence. As Nelkin (1993: B2) says,

> Stories about "bad genes" offer hope that those predisposed to crime or addiction can be identified and controlled. As one writer puts it, crime could be reduced if we determined which persons were biologically predisposed and took "preemptive action" before they committed crime. And another remarks: "It seems pointless to wait until high-risk prospects actually commit crimes before trying to do something to control them" ... genetic explanations that can be mapped and catalogued or deciphered from nature's text seem more objective, and less ambiguous, than environmental or social explanations. They seem to provide hard ways to codify what is normal or deviant, to justify inequities on the basis of "natural" characteristics, and to differentiate "them" from "us." They appeal as a solid, apparently neutral guide to social policy ... if certain people are defined as inherently and irretrievably problematic, society is absolved from responsibility. Why worry about rehabilitation, remedial education or social support ... Defining people as "predisposed" to immutable traits could justify discriminatory social practices. If we believe that there are "criminal genes," for example, this could sanction the use of tests to predict dangerousness, overriding issues of justice or fairness. And if the concept of genetic determinism is extended to groups, this could compromise the rights or obligations of classes of people.

Most disturbing is that, historically, this is precisely how the theory has been used by totalitarian regimes, whether in Nazi Germany or the former USSR, and extending more recently to forced therapy in the United States (Sagarin and Sanchez, 1988).

In the chapter to follow we discuss psychiatric and psychological theories of personality, which are probably the most frequently referenced theories in popular and media-exposed accounts of extreme and apparently senseless violence, such as random murder, or serial murder. The focus here again is the individual offender, and as in the biological approach, little credence is given to the structural contexts that shape the meaning of crime for those concerned. However, in these theories the first glimpse of movement beyond the individual occurs with a recognition that people are shaped by a developmental process. Unfortunately, as we shall see, the effects of that process are seen by these theorists as a relatively short-lived affair, which results in personality traits as relatively fixed components within an individual.

CHAPTER FIVE

Individual Positivism II: Personality Theories

In the previous chapter we considered theories that gave priority to the interactive effects of biology and environment as a basis of behavior and as an explanation for crime. In this chapter we are concerned with some of the psychological theories that attempt to explain crime as an outcome of personality development. Mindful of Bartol's (1991: xi) caution that "many texts on criminology continue to misunderstand or fail to integrate the psychological perspective adequately or accurately," we shall not lump psychologists together in an "all-encompassing psychological explanation for crime" (ibid.: 2). Instead we will consider the different contributions as they bear on our various theoretical frameworks. We recognize that Freudian and neo-Freudian psychology has been heavily influential in forensic psychiatry and psychiatric criminology but that its concepts "have never found a secure place in mainstream psychology" (Bartol, 1991: 18). However, we believe that any consideration of psychological theories of criminal personality must include Freudian psychoanalytical theory along with other theories offering a positivistic view of personality development, such as those of Eysenck (1977, 1983; Eysenck and Gudjonsson, 1989), and Yochelson and Samenow (1976, 1977; Samenow, 1984). We shall leave the analysis of the major learning and cognitive approaches until our consideration of social process theories in Chapters 8 and 9, where they generally have much more in common with the soft determinism[1] contained in the sociological and social psychological theories of differential association, symbolic interactionism, labeling, and social constructionism.

BASIC IDEA, CENTRAL MOTIF, AND MAJOR THEORISTS

The central idea of psychological and psychiatric theories of criminal personality is that people are shaped by the developmental processes occurring during their formative years, particularly their early childhood (ages 1–5), in ways that predisposed them to crime. These theories claim that most children are subjected

---

[1] As Matza (1964) first described it, and Bartol (1991: 7) reminded us, "*Hard* determinism is the belief that *all* behavior ... is caused (or determined) by forces or events that follow the laws of the universe," whereas "*soft* determinism takes a more moderate position." The latter recognizes that while forces do exist, "there is a considerable amount of *self*-determination, free will, or personal responsibility."

Table 5-1   Related Theories*

Psychological positivism
Psychoanalytic theory
Freudian theory
Organismic theory
Psychogenic theory
Criminal personality theory
Problem behavior theory

*Theories that take a perspective similar to or overlapping with the model that we develop in
this chapter.

to effective socialization patterns, with the result that they are "well adjusted"
to the society of their parents and behave conventionally. Some children, however,
are considered to be inadequately socialized or undersocialized, and some are
thought to have experienced significant events resulting in disturbed personalities that predispose them to develop criminal behavior tendencies. Some of these
children are ineffectively socialized because of inherent learning difficulties stemming either from biological defects that affect the capabilities of their mind, or
from mental illness. Others are considered to suffer from defective patterns of
socialization as a result of their parents' own defective past socialization, or from
the stresses currently on the family from external social environmental problems,
such as poverty, unemployment, and so forth.

Several theories that promote these ideas are accepted by psychiatrists,
psychologists, and psychologically oriented criminologists, all of which see the
etiology of crime in the hypothesized pathological or problem personality (see
Tables 5-1 and 5-2). Not surprisingly, their ideas follow the major established
theories in psychiatry and psychology and are adapted to the special case of
abnormal development. Some theorists, especially those influenced by psychiatry,
see processes of the mind, especially the effects of *mental illnesses* such as the
schizophrenias as significant.[2] Related are the theorists of *criminal personality,* such
as Eysenck and Trasler, who take the view that biological differences render people differently sensitive to sensations and arousal and interfere with adequate
socialization. Others, like Yochelson and Samenow, see criminal personalities as
those with defective thought patterns, such as the inability to think abstractly.
There are also psychodynamic theorists who see criminal personalities resulting

---

[2]In this chapter we only discuss theories dealing with psychological processes. Thus in the familiar tripartite classification of mental illness into (1) psychoses, which includes both (a) organic
psychoses and (b) functional psychoses; (2) personality disorder; and (3) neurotic disorders, we
will not consider neurotic disorders, which few claim to be related to criminal activities. Nor will
we consider organically caused psychoses. We concentrate here on theories of "functional" psychoses, which are those not known to have a physical cause, and on personality disorders.

Table 5-2 Theorists Using Psychological/Psychiatric Explanations of Crime

THEORIST	MAJOR WORK(S)	DATE
Freud	*Civilization and Its Discontents*	1927
	"Criminals from a Sense of Guilt"	1950
Healy	*The Individual Delinquent*	1915
Healy and Bronner	*Delinquents and Criminals*	1926
	New Light on Delinquency and Its Treatment	1936
Bowlby	*Forty-four Juvenile Thieves*	1944
Abrahamsen	*Crime and the Human Mind*	1944
	The Psychology of Crime	1960
Friedlander	*The Psychoanalytical Approach to Juvenile Delinquency*	1947
Aichhorn	*Wayward Youth*	1935
Redl and Wineman	*Children Who Hate*	1951
	Controls from Within	1952
Cleckley	*The Mask of Sanity*	1955
Eysenck	*Crime and Personality*	1964
	Personality Conditioning and Anti-social Behavior	1983
Eysenck and Gudjonsson	*The Causes and Cures of Criminality*	1989
Halleck	*Psychiatry and the Dilemmas of Crime*	1971
Jessor and Jessor	*Problem Behavior and Psychosocial Development*	1977
Yochelson and Samenow	*The Criminal Personality*	1976
Samenow	*Inside the Criminal Mind*	1984

from the child development process itself. Thus several theories in the Freudian *psychoanalytical* tradition argue that poor development or damage of ego and superego result in weak internalized controls over the desires and urges of the id or that overdevelopment of the ego results in excessive repression and a potential for symbolic relief of tension through crime and the resultant punishment it brings. Also important are recent theories of personality that see crime as a result of some traumatic event of varying duration, such as sexual abuse, family conflict, and so forth. These theorists sometimes describe such persons as suffering from psychogenic psychosis. Others refer to this as a "problem behavior syndrome," which falls under the broader category of "emotional problem theories."

In one such theory the underlying cause is alleged to be a combination of unconventional personality and unconventional social environments (Jessor and Jessor, 1977). In this theory an unconventional personality is someone tolerant of a wide range of deviant activity and therefore open to engaging in risk-taking behavior such as drug use and delinquency. In emotional problem theory (or problem behavior theory), an inability to cope develops from one or more life crises (see Masters and Roberson, 1990: 298–302).

Whatever the causal process, for most theorists of abnormal personality the response to criminal behavior consists of intervention to treat the offender, usually through some form of therapy, with a view to correcting the defect and changing his or her personality. Thus psychotherapy, therapy, counseling, and treatment, "refer to a set of procedures or techniques used to help individuals or groups alter their maladaptive behavior, develop adaptive behavior or both" (Bartol, 1991: 363). The form these therapies take vary, depending on the particular theory informing the diagnosis. This can include drug therapy, psychoanalysis, group therapy, family therapy, resocialization, reprogramming thought processes, and counseling.

HUMANS, HUMAN NATURE, AND HUMAN BEHAVIOR

Within the psychological/psychiatric framework humans are seen as biological entities, different only in degree from animals, but have personalities that are shaped by childhood developmental experiences in their family. Human behavior reflects the combination of biological attributes and early socialization experiences mediated through the neurochemical processes of their brain. Indeed, Bartol (1991: 4) admits that "a large segment of the psychological and psychiatric research on criminal behavior is dominated by the belief that human beings are basically animals, controlled by a myriad of biological urges, drives and needs."[3]

There are two central assumptions about humans made in psychological theories of personality. The first is that human behavior is governed by the mind (cognitive function),[4] and the second is that the mind is shaped by biological and/or developmental processes, including the relational environment. The biological process referred to in these theories is based on similar ideas held in biocriminology that we discussed in the previous chapter. It will be recalled

---

[3]Some psychologists disagree with this approach and instead take a view of humans as differing radically in terms of their cognitive functioning abilities. We shall consider these ideas in Chapters 8 and 9, under social process theory.

[4]Here cognitive processes are considered in a very narrow sense, which, while including intelligence and logical, rational thought, does not include the construction of meaning, as in the more cognitively oriented theories discussed in Chapter 9.

that the brain is seen as a highly complex electrochemical organ that is controlled *both* by its own chemical and genetic constitution and by the experiences of human development.

Implied by these assumptions is a vision of mental health or normality as a normal biochemical capability, and as normal cognitive processes with their basis in an alleged consensus among qualified experts about what constitutes serious abnormality. For example, to formuulate their theories Eysenck (1977) and Trasler (1962) draw on Jung's concepts of introversion and extroversion (see also Zuckerman, 1979), and Pavlov's ideas of excitation and inhibition. According to Eysenck and Trasler, human behavior is a result of social learning being affected by conditioning, which is itself affected by inherited personality traits. These psychologists claim to have identified several "personality traits," which they group together to form a "personality type." Dimensions of personality are those of introversion or extroversion, neuroticism and psychoticism, and these can affect a person's "conditioning."

Eysenck (1977), for example, argues that humans inherit various personality traits that remain a fixed entity throughout the life course. Personality traits are permanent patterns that guide how people think and conceive of themselves in their world. Normal human beings are emotionally stable and neither overly introverted nor overly extroverted, although Eysenck believes that the majority of conforming individuals tend to be introverted personalities, since such persons are more amenable to conditioning. The normal personality and that of the introvert tend to conform to society's rules and expectations because of their relatively high level of sensitivity to external stimuli.

Trasler (1962) assumes that people try to maximize pleasure and minimize pain, a process they learn mainly during childhood but at differing rates. People have the capacity for reason but these theorists limit this to a reflex action of conditioned responses to stimuli.

For others, especially those taking a psychoanalytic approach, the type of personality that forms is more a product of early developmental processes than it is of biology, although biochemical processes of the brain are necessary. The relationship is one of biological need, producing a psychological drive, manifested as behavior.

Psychoanalytically oriented theorists assume that humans are formed by being adequately socialized through a series of normal developmental stages to develop moral and social selves. Many theorists with this emphasis adopt Freud's assumptions about humans which suggest that perception, personality, and behavior are the product of an interactive process between components of the mind, developed over time through interaction with the environment.

Freud believed that natural laws governed all human life (psychic determinism) and that free will and rational choice are an illusion or an appearance concealing the essence of reality (Jones, 1953: 366). His view of humans thus was one of a passive reflex apparatus, with no energies of its own, operating only to rid itself of inputs from the body (instinctual drive) and from the environment (reality), these inputs being conceptualized as quantities of energy (subjectively experienced as tension), and the regulative rule formulated as the principle of consistency. Consequently, the fundamental principle of motivation and affect is tension reduction. (Holt, 1968: 4)

Freud assumed that humans possessed minds (psyche) that enabled them to adapt to their environment. However, he believed that psychic processes of the mind cannot exist without the brain's biological processes and that physiological processes precede psychical ones so that "information reaching the mind, whether from the outer world through the sense organs or from the body through the chemical stimuli it provides, must begin as a physical excitation" (Jones, 1953: 368).

In Freudian psychology the mind operates at three levels: the preconscious (a repository of energy and drives), the conscious, and the unconscious. Complicated thought can occur as either conscious or unconscious mental processes. Moreover, thoughts and ideas may remain in the unconscious or may be suppressed by it through opposing and conflicting conscious thoughts of the person.

The structure of the mind is comprised of three components: the id (from *idioplasm*), ego, and superego (Freud, 1923). The id and superego remain largely part of the unconscious, whereas the ego is largely part of the conscious. The id consists of "primary" instinctive urges and desires for immediate satisfaction and gratification such as the desire for food, sex, aggression. The id also gives rise to the "pleasure principle," according to which humans directly seek pleasure, discharge tensions, and avoid the state of "unpleasure" or pain. Freud viewed the id as amoral raw need, reflecting the immature instinctive passions of the (primitive) animal within. The id is also considered the source of drive, energy, creativity, and even positive and negative aggression.

In contrast, the ego and superego are each products of learning by the id that build up and "break off" (Martin et al., 1990: 73) as the id is shaped through interaction with the environment of others and the external world. The ego (or sense of self) forms first as an "outgrowth of the id" (Gibbons, 1992: 151), an adaptive compromise between the id and the external world of reality. The ego is a facilitator of the id, the "executive of personality" (ibid., 151), and represents what is possible in reality (hence Freud's "reality principle"), given the logic of a person's capability and the opportunities and constraints presented by situations. The superego, which emerges from the ego as a "specialized" focus on moral and ethical concerns (Martin et al. 1990: 73), is the unconscious conscience. It comprises internalized cultural norms and prohibitions developed from human interaction and identification with significant others. It is the moral conscience, a "psychic police officer" (Bischof, 1964: 44–47) that "polices the person" (Gibbons, 1992: 151), the conveyor of ideal images, and ultimately an ego-ideal or role model of how to behave in ways that are right and correct (socially acceptable). The superego is seen as controlling the id, largely through unconscious processes, popularly known as conscience.

Between the id and the established superego rests the ego, the conscious, rational, reasoning element of the mind. In Freud's (1946) writing the ego's role is a passive, defensive, mediating, and integrating influence between the unconscious impulses of the id and the demands of the superego.[5] It is assumed that in the hypothesized normal human being, the id and superego are in balance, their excesses controlled by the ego, which retains them suppressed in the human subconscious along with conflicts that arise between them and between them and the wider society.[6] As Hurwitz and Christiansen (1983: 96) explain, "the function of the ego is to direct behaviour so as to supply the satisfactions demanded by the unconscious, but in a socially acceptable form." This typically may occur through delayed gratification, whereby the expression of impulses and thereby the discharge of tension, is delayed until the setting or context is appropriate. In addition, "sublimation" can occur, whereby instinctive id impulses are gratified through substituting socially acceptable behavior, such as athletic sports, art, and so forth, for prohibited behavior.

Normal, nondelinquent children, then, are likely to have their desires met by having them channeled into substitutive forms of satisfaction (Healy and Bronner, 1936). Indeed, Barnes, and Teeters (1943: 243) have said, "the greater part of human progress and most cultural achievements ... have been the product of our ... success in diverting the animal drives of man from direct and selfish forms of expression into constructive and socialized avenues of manifestation. This process psychologists call *sublimation.*"

Another way this conflict resolution and tension reduction occur is through "repression," whereby impulse is banished from the conscious part of the ego but continues to exist in the unconscious mind. As we shall see later, rule-breaking behavior can occur as a result of repression, as it can when either the id, ego, or superego is underdeveloped or overdeveloped in relation to the normal.

Several psychological theories of human mind and personality development consider a process whereby humans progress through a series of stages in their early life. For Freud these stages are associated with the basic sexual drives of the id. The stages begin with an obsession with oral drives (giving initial gratification until age 1), progress through obsession with anal drives (giving erotic

---

[5]Some psychoanalytical theories assume a more active role for the ego, conceiving of it as a goal-oriented planner and fighter, rather than merely a passive resolver of disputes (see Hartmann, 1958).

[6]Freud's concern with conflict was important. He saw it operative not just between the id and superego but also between the ego and id and ego and superego (Holt, 1968: 4).

satisfaction from ages 1 through 3), then phallic drives (occuring between ages 3 to 5) through latency (a period of balance and dormant urges from the previous stages between ages 6 and 12), and end with an obsession with genital drives at puberty, when several hormonal changes occur. By the age of 5 or 6 human personality is considered to be formed. At each stage, behaviors that are obsessive require satisfying and yet produce guilt from socialized norms about appropriate behavior. These must be handled by the ego to minimize or reduce that guilt. Without successful resolution and outlet their energy is repressed into the unconscious and the person is said to be "fixated" at that stage of development. As Martin, Mutchnick, and Austin (1990: 74) state: "On occasions in later life, when the finite store of conscious psychic energy grows low, these repressed reserves may be drawn upon. The price that is paid for the use of this libido is the expression of behaviors representative of the unsatisfied wishes from an earlier stage."

Erickson (1950) extended this analysis to include stages of *ego* development that extended into old age and saw normal development as the successful handling of various "identity crises" by the ego at each of these stages in the life course. Erickson was less concerned with psychosexual transformations and concentrated more on ego development than id development. In his eight stages, a critical one for delinquency was the crisis of identity versus identity diffusion. Erickson argued that adolescents must successfully resolve this crisis with a clear sense of who they are in order to develop.

Others psychologists, not taking either a biological nor psychoanalytical approach to the human personality, include the ideas of Yochelson and Samenow (1976). In their study of *The Criminal Personality,* Yochelson and Samenow assume that humans have free will, but differ in the nature of their thought processes or thought patterns concerning the exercise of this will. Normal human thought processes result in personalities that make responsible, planned decisions. They are relatively content, secure, and confident about themselves, and are concerned about others, wanting to please and protect them. Normal people are able to think both concretely and abstractly and to relate concrete instances to general categories or cases, and build up this knowledge from a series of learning experiences.[7]

Importantly, one group of theories within this overall perspective referred to as "emotional problem theories" does not distinguish between the personalities of the offender and nonoffender, seeing them as having "the same psychological makeup" (Masters and Roberson, 1990: 299). Offenders are "normal human beings whose coping skills have deteriorated" as a result of any number of traumatic events or life crises (ibid.: 300).

---

[7]We saw in the previous chapter, however, that certain theorists, such as Wilson and Herrnstein (1985), see humans as differing in their perception and their abilities to use their rational capabilities, so their rational choices are guided variously by both a view to perceived consequences and by predisposing factors.

VIEW OF SOCIETY AND THE SOCIAL ORDER

As in biological theory, most psychological theories of personality give little attention to society and culture and their "concern for the environment is only as a source of stimuli" (Fox, 1976: 155). Where society is considered, most theorists "tend conservatively to take for granted the existing social order" (Hagan, 1986: 417). Freud, for example, saw society as part of the reality of the world, as an aggregate of minds and dangerous energies, mirroring the individual (Reiff, 1961), as "masses in motion and nothing else" (Freud, 1895: 369). Indeed, the very assumption that humans are hedonistic presumes a society as little more than an aggregate of discrete and oppositional particles. As a consequence of this implied conflict view of humans, Freud (1930) saw society as perpetually threatened with disintegration. However, he saw cultural patterns as universally transmitted by genetic hereditary processes and saw culture as the coercive consensus maker: "Culture has to call up every possible reinforcement in order to erect barriers against the aggressive instincts of man and hold their manifestations in check by reaction-formations in men's minds" (Freud, 1930: 61–62).

Even those more sociologically aware psychologists assume that society is made up of individual personalities. They fail to consider that human nature may be an outcome of the kind of society that exists in any particular historical era. For example, Bartol (1991: 2–3), echoing Nelson (1975) and Eisenberg (1972), asserts that "a society's social, political and economic structures are based on fundamental premises about human beings, their inherent tendencies, abilities, weaknesses and preferences." He also claims that a society's system of social control will vary according to its view of human nature, without considering the reverse a possibility.

Where society is considered by individual positivists, it is viewed as a necessary consensus of values about what is normal and acceptable and what is deviant (Taylor, Walton, and Young, 1973: 47ff., on Eysenck). Young (1981: 268) says that, in general, individual positivists take a functionalist view of the relationship between individuals and the orderly maintenance of society. Their view recognizes individuals as different in terms of abilities, personality, and socialization, such that "an individual's final place in the social order reflects more or less the compound of his or her potentiality and the social skills which have been inculcated into them" (ibid., 269).

Society then, at best, is seen as a control mechanism limiting human self-interests to acceptable forms, as a system for organizing cooperation among conflicting individual needs, and as a reflection of human differences. It is, in short, the outcome, not the maker, of minds.

THE ROLE OF LAW, THE DEFINITION OF CRIME, AND THE IMAGE OF THE CRIMINAL

Within the psychological framework, law comprises the rules designed to protect the ongoing development of society. Crime is the manifestation of those with personality problems, or defective personalities. Criminals are those who are not able to learn the correct ways to behave in any society.

This perspective is responsible for the idea that criminal law should be structured so as to allow those whose criminal behavior is a product of biological and psychogenic causes to be exempted from responsibility for their offenses. The insanity defense is the obvious classical illustration. Ever since the seventeenth century the issue of crime as involuntary action has been raised. By 1760 in England total and permanent absence of reason or total absence of it at the moment of committing a crime was allowed as a defense, but it rarely made a difference to the outcome of a case until the trial of Hadfield in 1800, who was judged insane for attempted regicide (Hibbert, 1966: 227). By 1843 the controversial standard of whether a defendant could tell between right and wrong in relation to the act charged was settled with the M'Naghten Rules. Under these rules sanity was assumed to prevail unless the defense could establish that "at the time of committing the act, the party accused was labouring under such a defect of reason, from disease of the mind, as not to know the nature and the quality of the act he was doing, or if he ever did know it, that he did not know he was doing wrong" (ibid.: 228). A number of legal tests were formulated, all attempting to modify the M'Naghten Rules. In the 1950s a more restrictive modified version of M'Naghten, known as the Durham Rule, was introduced in U.S. federal courts. It provided that the accused was not criminally responsible if his or her unlawful act was "the *product* of mental disease or defect." The legal concept of insanity can include organically caused psychotic conditions, functional psychosis, and personality disorders.

Moreover, the recognition that mental health and mental illness are extreme ends of a dynamic continuum has lead to the introduction to law of the concept of "diminished capacity" and the related notion of "diminished or partial responsibility," whereby the accused can be shown not to have the prerequisite mental capacity to form intent. Used primarily in murder cases, the test gives the jury an opportunity to find an accused guilty of a lesser, but associated, offense (Goldstein, 1967). In effect the test tries to show that the defendant may be responsible, but not totally so, because of his or her mental condition at the time of the crime, allowing for more flexibility than the either "guilty" or "not guilty by reason of insanity" verdicts.

Given that the concept of mental normality is relative and ever-changing, definitions of mental illness center on "the inability of some individuals to adapt to their social environment at the standard or normal tolerance level expected by others in the same social environment" (Holman and Quinn, 1992: 85). Rule breaking is defined on the assumption that the world is divided into normal and abnormal minds. Because the abnormal personality is seen as lacking the ability to conform to conventional rules, these psychological theorists make no distinction between deviance from norms and lawbreaking.

Given the view of human nature from the psychoanalytic perspective, it is not surprising that crime is seen as an epiphenomenon or symptom of an underlying personality disorder. Although significant to the victim, psychoanalytical theorists see the form of crime as less significant than its underlying personality disturbance. Indeed, as Eysenck (1977: 77, 79) claims, behavior that is defined as criminal depends upon the social, cultural, and environmental context of a society, but the *predisposition to deviate* is determined by hereditary and personality traits. Thus as Young (1981: 270) cynically comments: "The criminal or deviant would be a rule breaker in any culture—he would be a pacifist during wartime, an aggressor during peace. It is not necessary for the psychological positivist to explain the content of the norms that are violated, merely the propensity for the individual to violate them." Not surprisingly, rather than the types and content of laws, theorists of criminal personality are concerned with types of offenders.

Psychological and psychiatric theories of personality identify several criminal offender categories, which traditionally include the psychopath, the neurotic, and the psychotic. The psychotic (briefly considered in the previous chapter) is considered mentally ill whose criminal behavior is the outcome of delusions or hallucinations and a distorted sense of reality, as in paranoia, and/or schizophrenia. Typically an offender may claim to be "told by God" to kill.

The psychopath—the sociopath or antisocial personality (see especially Cleckley, 1955)—is seen as emotionally immature, self-centered, fearless, lacking insight, and exploiting situations for the immediate gratification of basic instincts without regard for the harm caused to others. Sociopaths are considered to lack self-worth and social feeling and at the same time feel proud and superior to others. They trust no one and abhor dependency on others. They are defiant and aggressive toward authority and suffer from extreme mood swings. A number of theorists believe that criminals are sociopathic *by definition,* and sociopaths commit crimes. It is this circular reasoning, as well as the lack of clarity in diagnosis that have led some to consider sociopathy and psychopathy a "waste basket" category.

Neurotics are described as torn by inner conflict and turmoil, yet aware of their criminal activity but, against their own interests, do it anyway as an attempt to seek punishment for their guilt and to relieve inner pressure.

In emotional disorder theories the offender could be anyone who has temporarily lost the ability to cope. Such persons are not seen as permanently afflicted but "responding to very subtle psychological factors" that affect normal functioning and "after the offender's coping mechanism is functioning again, the person is not likely to commit crimes" (Masters and Roberson, 1990: 300).

CAUSAL LOGIC

Several of the psychological theories of personality posit a mechanistic and deterministic relationship between the unconscious mind and behavior. Others locate the causal agency in social relationships. Some theories, as we have seen, even give priority to distorted but limited cognitive processes that exercise "free" will in carrying out goal-directed behavior. However, as Masters and Roberson (1990: 284) point out, all of these theories

> assume that there is something wrong with the mind or mental faculties of the criminal that causes him or her to commit crimes. According to these theories, the cause of crime lies within the person. The criminal is not considered normal and is thought of as different from the rest of us. The cause of criminal behavior is, therefore, internal, not external.

Although Freud "does not appear to ever have expressed any opinion on the general theory of causality, he presumably held the simple nineteenth-century view of inevitable antecedents" (Jones, 1953: 366). Criminological versions of Freudian theory certainly present such a causal analysis. As one interpreter says, "Freud's true discovery was that the unconscious has dynamic power, that it possesses a force to make a man act unwittingly and unwillingly ... It is easily seen that crime is not a rational process ... Crime is deeply rooted in the instincts of man, and it is usually an act of the instinctual, impulsive life of the criminal individual" (Zilboorg, 1949: 398, 402). Thus from the psychoanalytical perspective it is argued that, as the outcome of early childhood frustrations and unsatisfied desires, antisocial behavior and deviant behavior reflect a conflict between desires and controls that has not been resolved through expression or sublimation. As Zilboorg (1949: 402) states: "Whenever aggression, which must be repressed and socialized (sublimated), steps beyond the boundaries of sublimation, it becomes crime." Indeed, some, such as Healy and Bronner (1936) and Abrahamsen (1960), see crime and delinquency as a form of misdirected sublimation that provides an alternative response to tension relief and satisfying inner thwarted desires that were not satisfied by parents or family.

Humans can also become fixated at one of the stages of development if they fail to receive adequate gratification and their unsatisfied frustrations manifest in an abnormal interest in satisfying their desires. For example, those fixated at the phallic stage may have an excessive interest in sex to the extent of sexual assault, rape, or prostitution. One version of this sees crime as the outcome of unresolved Oedipal or Electra conflicts whereby boys fantasize themselves as their mother's lover or wanting to grow up and marry their mothers, whereas girls want to marry their fathers. In each stage the same-sex parent becomes the rival the child wishes to destroy and unless this conflict is resolved through subsequent submission to the greater power of their same gender and then through gender identification, the unconscious repressed aspects will emerge in the form of various sexual deviances and offenses.

Alternatively, and this was originally Freud's (1915) notion, crime can be caused by an "unconscious guilt complex" resulting from a fear of authority and a strong or overdeveloped superego. This may cause a person to be possessed by feelings of guilt and to commit rule-breaking activity in order to receive punishment that serves, at least temporarily, to relieve the guilt. This complex is indicated by offenders who unconsciously leave clues to their identity in order to get caught. Violent crime, however, is seen to arise from an internal conflict between the life instinct (called Eros) and the death instinct (called Thanatos), a conflict that the life instinct wins by redirecting the latter outward to others (Monte, 1980).

The Adlerian "individual psychology" variant of psychoanalysis rejected Freud's mechanistic causality and ideas about libido, infantile sexuality, and repressed frustrations as a cause of mental disturbance (Adler, 1931). Adler developed a functional or teleological analysis that saw mental disturbance and criminality arising from goal-directed behavior whereby individuals sought to satisfy unfulfilled longings of infantile inferiority. The normal way of coping with this inferiority complex is through the development of an ever-adjusting individual "style of life" or "pattern of life" that provides a sense of superiority and status. When this fails to relieve frustrations, these are compensated for by exaggerated neurotic behavior replacing the alleged deficiencies. Adler (1931) argued that anyone who lacks an identification with society or who feels the world is against them is prone to develop criminal behavior. Thus, for Adler, the criminal is a destructive rebel.

An idea related to that of displaced sublimation in Freud and compensation in Adler appears in the work of Halleck (1971), who argues that crime provides people with the opportunities for creativity and autonomy denied them by conventional society as well as the excuses necessary to rationalize their guilt.

Several variations of these basic psychoanalytic themes exist, depending on whose version of psychoanalysis is examined. For example, Aichhorn (1935) saw criminal behavior as the result of the combination of the primitive impulsive drives of the id seeking immediate gratification, with weak or underdeveloped ego and superego development (because of failed parental socialization or uncaring or missing parents). This causes a failure to form affective ties, with resulting frustration, repression, and an unconscious search for compensatory gratification that are the source of aggression and delinquency at some later stage in life; hence his concept of "latent delinquency." Aichhorn also believed that delinquency could result when there was a *lack* of superego development because of too much freedom and indulgence by parents.

For Abrahamsen (1944; 1960), other crimes occur when the ego is not merely weak but damaged, resulting in an inability to control the id's impulsive, pleasure-seeking activity. The cause of weak, damaged, or absent superegos, or ineffective or distorted egos was considered to be a failure to connect, identify, and form affectional ties with parents.[8] Bowlby (1946) claimed the root cause was "maternal deprivation," which resulted in the "affectionless character," and Friedlander (1947) similarly saw the primary causes of delinquency in the "antisocial character" as a direct product of the mother's handling of the child. Whatever the cause, Redl and Wineman (1951, 1952) believed the failure to form affective ties with parents created an inadequate superego and a distorted delinquent ego that together produced crime.

One of the more deterministic and mechanistic of the psychological approaches to crime is the personality theory of Eysenck (1977; Eysenck and Gudjonsson, 1989) and Trasler (1962), which sees the development of a criminal, or psychotic personality, as the result of extroversion or low IQ affecting the ability to learn rules or perceive punishments. Eysenck and Gudjonsson (1989: 7), for example, argue that:

> It is not crime itself or criminality that is innate; it is certain peculiarities of the central nervous system that react with the environment, with upbringing, and many other environment factors to increase the probability that a given person would react in a certain anti-social manner.

So, like the biological theory we analyzed in the previous chapter, Eysenck's theory is based on the interaction of biological and environmental factors that determine crime proneness, but this time via personality. Eysenck (1977: 146–47) argues that some criminal behavior is caused by inherited (biological) neurotic or psychopathic personality traits, particularly in those who are both highly neurotic (emotionally unstable) and "showing a tendency toward extroversion" and "impulsiveness." Eysenck argues that being less sensitive to excitation by stimuli, extroverts experience "stimulus hunger" and seek out experiences that provide extra stimulation, such as law-breaking, drug taking, violence, and so forth. In addition, such extroverts are less readily conditioned than introverts and are less likely to develop a conscience. They are also less inhibited by pain since they are less sensitive to it and are also less concerned to avoid it.

Trasler (1962) also incorporates behaviorist principles in formulating his theory of "passive avoidance conditioning." He argues that crime is a result of social learning being affected by conditioning. Like Eysenck, he argues that inherited traits of extroversion or introversion affect this learning, with extroverts learning at a slower rate.

Yochelson and Samenow's (1976, 1977; Samenow, 1984) personality theory states that defective thinking patterns ingrained after birth (see Samenow, 1978,

---

[8]This was the precursor to control theory, which we consider in Chapter 8 as part of social process theory.

1979) produce criminal behavior, with the criminal personality being relatively immune from traditionally conceived environmental influences such as parents, home, peers, and community. These thought processes, which become manifest early in a child's life, form a recurring pattern that leads to a search for immediate excitement and a striving for superiority and power over others. One source of these thought patterns is the conflict between a feeling of worthlessness and the fear of having their perceived inferiority exposed. This conflict produces rapid mood swings and intense anger against society or certain categories of people in it, such as certain races or minorities, for example, "whites," "blacks," "women," and "gays." These groups are seen as challenging the criminal personality's assumed superiority. They are held responsible for the lack of respect the affected personality believes he or she rightfully deserves.[9] This pattern eventually results in lawbreaking, which is justified through these and other self-serving rationalizations.

CRIMINAL JUSTICE SYSTEM IMPLICATIONS

As in the biological theory, psychological positivism's approach to criminal justice also favors the medical model in its processing of offenders. This approach assumes that criminality is related to some aberrant psychological condition that may be treatable. Hence the justice system should be modified to accommodate the expertise of knowledgeable and skilled professionals. As we elaborated in the previous chapter, at its most extreme the medical model calls for "experts" instead of routine judges, common juries, and punitive sentences. The disposition of cases should proceed according to the needs of the offender rather than what the law stipulates. As we saw in the section The Role of Law above, various legal tests may be used to determine whether, indeed, an accused fits the "rational man" assumption of the law. These tests are designed to determine whether the accused's mental state at the time of the crime was such that he or she was able to conform to the required intent necessary for legal guilt. This would apply to all mental states, whether their cause was thought to be organic or functional. Thus under this system due process gives way to "scientific method" and expert judgment; experts are decision makers; and judges are assisted by expert witnesses or are experts themselves. Juries are panels of experts rather than laypersons, and the belief prevails "that judges should not sentence delinquents according to the crimes they [have] committed but according to

---

[9]As we shall see in a later chapter, although cognitive psychologists also see the cause of crime in thought processes, this stems not so much from a defective personality as from a misreading of social cues or distorted perceptions amplified by fear. This can result in crime being perceived as self-defense against some perceived but unreal threat.

the diagnosis of their ills by psychological experts" (Empey and Stafford, 1991: 169). The presumption of treatment and its selection in sentences last throughout the correctional process, based on the use of "professional counseling, psychotherapy and medical care" administered by professional "psychiatrists, clinical psychologists, and social workers" (ibid., 169). In this model penal institutions are to be replaced by hospitals and treatment centers. Finally, any right to appeal is limited to a second authoritative opinion.

Criminal Justice Policy and Correctional Ideology

Within the psychological positivist framework, policy and intervention depend on the particular version of personality theory employed. Most theorists allude to some kind of therapeutic intervention designed to restore the assumed defective personality to that of the assumed normal person. Intervention occurs at the level of the individual and is designed to correct individual behaviors. Thus psychoanalytic approaches involve evaluation and treatment to help the offender uncover the childhood root causes, bring these into consciousness, and train the person to control effectively or correct problems of parental or "maternal" deprivation. Eysenck's personality theory sees the role of intervention through psychiatry as practical, aimed at "the elimination of antisocial conduct, and not cluttered with irrelevant, philosophical, retributory and ethico-religious beliefs" (Eysenck, 1977: 213).

Another intervention philosophy using a psychoanalytic approach is prevention based on the assumption that early prediction is possible. Since "predelinquent traits" are thought to be evident "at a very early age, professional treatment should begin at that time" (Empey and Stafford, 1991: 170). Moreover, preventative intervention for "predelinquents" is to begin by the age of 3 or 4 (Bowlby, 1944) and at least by age 6 in the case of the New York City Youth Board (Craig and Glick, 1963). In some cases this preventative philosophy justifies continuous monitoring throughout school life and treatment in special clinics for those with emotional difficulties (Banay, 1948).

Overall, the impact of psychological positivists on correctional ideology can be seen in the establishment of the very notion of "corrections" and in the rehabilitative approach to crime control. Early psychoanalytical analysis of the emerging role of penology reflected the growing influence of psychological positivism:

> Psychoanalytically oriented penologists have for some time been thinking of the future penal institution as a special type of hospital where the delinquent, the minor and the major criminal, might be cared for and studied and re-educated in accordance with modern principles. (Zilboorg, 1949: 405)

However, the anticipation that prisons were to become correctional communities based on the concept of the "therapeutic community" developed by Jones (1953) for mental hospitals, was never achieved. As we shall see in Techniques of Crime Control, several other treatments designed to fulfill the correctional ideology developed that became part of the societal response to crime.

Techniques of Crime Control

Whereas psychiatrists frequently use drug therapy (and occasionally brain surgery) to treat offenders classified as mentally ill, personality theorists prefer some form of interventionist therapy, which varies depending on their particular theory. In either case these same approaches are carried over as ways to deal with the offender.

In psychoanalytic theory the aim of therapeutic analysis is to reveal the unconscious sources of guilt and free the person from the need to be punished. To do this the psychoanalyst follows several procedures. The procedure of *free association* allows the analyst to access the subconscious repressed problems and allows these to be "ventilated." In *transference* the therapist forms a significant relationship with the offender, with the expectation that he or she will replay similar problematic relationships with the therapist. In positive transference the patient's strong feelings toward the analyst creates an artificial neurosis that can be worked on directly by the therapist. Once this occurs, the therapist is able to work with the offender to resolve the conflicts that develop between the therapist and the offender, in the belief that this will, in turn, enable the problems that occurred in the offender's past likewise to be resolved. In *negative transference* the offender transfers hostile thoughts and actions to the therapist.

In contrast, when the source of crime is a damaged or undeveloped superego as in Aichhorn and Redl and Wineman's theory, a superego or ego-ideal must be reestablished. Thus Aichhorn bases "his treatment techniques ... on providing happy and pleasurable environment, so as to promote the type of identification with adults that the child failed to experience earlier" (Vold and Bernard, 1986: 114), and Redl and Wineman recommend treatment with "unconditional love to promote the identification with adults" that was lacking in the offender's earlier development (ibid.: 116). This treatment is carried out in therapeutic communities or schools where aggression is allowed to be "acted out," even to the extent of allowing destruction of rooms and property; ultimately offenders find that they were still loved although disciplined by the staff. These various approaches to personality restoration have been summarized by one early commentator in relation to the classification of criminals:

> [S]ince no universal treatment will produce good results the problem is to classify criminals and work on them in different manners ... The neurotic should yield best to psychotherapy, the kind and extent varying with the degree of neurosis. The psychopath probably should react best to kindness and love, the lack of which probably causes his lack of maturity ... The psychoids probably need chemical treatment and psychotherapy. (Corsini, 1949: 115)

One variation on therapeutic intervention which is rooted in the psycho-analytic tradition is *family therapy* (Ackerman, 1958). This involves the therapist working through the various conflicts between family members in order to prevent the "emotional feeding" that can result in crime and deviance.

The criminal personality theory of Yochelson and Samenow (1977) rejects the usefulness of any form of rehabilitation based on attempts to reform, since they assume that the crime is freely chosen by dysfunctional thought processes and is rationalized for instrumental protection. These researchers' technique, therefore, involves intervention designed to identify and destroy current destructive criminal patterns of decision making by confronting offenders directly and to alter their thought processes through manipulation of rewards. Consistent with their view of free choice, Yochelson and Samenow believe criminal personalities are only deterable if offenders are taught to deter their own criminal thinking. They believe that this can be achieved by confronting offenders with their behavior as victimizers of society in an attempt to increase feelings of guilt and self-disgust. The researchers also claim to teach how to suppress criminal thoughts and to substitute noncriminal ones in their place (Yochelson and Samenow, 1977).

EVALUATION

The psychiatric end of the psychological framework has been criticized from within the profession of psychiatry by those who argue that there is no reliable method of distinguishing between normal and abnormal minds and that the claim to be able to do so is premised on political and social control interests (Szasz, 1961; 1973; Laing, 1959; 1967). Moreover, much of the psychiatric argument is a tautology (circular reasoning). Behavior is observed and judged to be deviant and it is then used to infer a mental illness which is then designated as the explanatory cause of the original behavior (Wooton, 1959). As some commentators have observed, insofar as personality "traits are of a genetic origin, there may not be much hope of achieving significant alterations" (Hall Williams 1982: 74).

Eysenck's original theory of crime and personality has been shown to be flawed empirically, with no difference being found with regard to extroversion and introversion between delinquents and controls. Some considered the theory to be of "little use for explaining adolescent delinquency and recidivism" (Little, 1963: 160) and others found it "untenable" (Hoghughi and Forrest, 1970: 252). A review by Cochrane (1974) found that empirical evidence fails to demonstrate a relationship between criminality and extroversion, but gives some support to the modified version in which Eysenck includes a third "psychoticism" dimension. However, for others the psychoticism dimension has shown mixed results and has led to the suggestion that it is missing a critical "hedonism" variable (Burgess, 1972). Passingham (1972), who investigated evidence on conditioning, found that Eysenck's theories were unsupported by the data and were methodologically flawed. An overview by Feldman (1977) found that the studies supported a combination of high neuroticism and psychoticism traits, but not high extroversion, and argued that the theory is a better explanation of how some personalities acquire criminal attitudes than it is an explanation of how they maintain them or act them out. Even those sympathetic to the theory, such as Bartol (1991: 54-55), admit that the research evidence is weak. Bartol (1991: 57–58) concludes that although Eysenck's theory is unique in being one of the few attempts by psychologists to formulate a general theory of criminal behavior, "as it now stands, the theory has flaws that could be fatal." Not the least of these is its exclusion of cognitive and social learning factors.

Psychoanalytic theory has also received wide-ranging evaluation. "Freud and his ideas have been ignored, revered, ostracized, rebelled against, ridiculed, defied, modified, remodified, discarded, and resurrected" (Martin et al., 1990: 83). On the positive side, Masters and Roberson (1990: 295) point out that Freud's theory "was a demonstration of the fact that we need to study the mental life of the criminal as a whole and consider the impact of the early experiences on later mental development." In addition, its uncovering of unconscious motivation was a corrective to the idea that all crime was the outcome of conscious rational calculation. However, the negative evaluations of the theory have overshadowed any positive contributions it might have.

Freudian theory has long been criticized for being based on circular reasoning, being untestable, and dependent on post-hoc interpretations of hypothetical and unconscious motives, and in some cases for being fraudulent (Masson, 1984). Freud's theory is certainly essentialist and reductionist, in that qualitative constructions of meaning, including love and affection, are reduced to the pursuit of pleasure and/or tension reduction. Hurwitz and Christiansen (1983: 97) observe that "the whole theory which considers the unconscious need for punishment to be a general criminological phenomenon still lacks sufficient foundation." Sanders (1983: 80) says there is very little evidence of its validity and "no known link between a particular type of subconscious problem and a specific type of crime, nor does the theory explain why people with similar problems vent their anxieties in different ways, only some of which are criminal." In its defense, others have claimed to have tested the general theory and found that it is supported (Fisher and Greenberg, 1981; Kline, 1981). With regard to the efficacy of its proposed treatment techniques, Vold and Bernard (1986: 117) point out that those "who receive psychiatric and psychoanalytical treatment generally have no greater chances of being cured than those who receive no treatment at all," and with regard to the evidence of psychological cause they conclude that "research so far has failed to establish a very large role for the personality as a cause of criminal behavior" (ibid.: 128).

Psychologists offer a similar interpretation of the personality-problem evidence, based on a distinction they make between "undersocialized" and "socialized" delinquency (Glueck and Glueck, 1950). Undersocialized delinquency refers to those who are psychologically troubled before they begin committing offenses as preadolescents, whereas socialized delinquents are those who begin delinquency with their peers at adolescence: "Typically, the offenses committed by these youngsters do not develop into serious criminality, and typically these individuals do not violate the law after adolescence" (Steinberg, 1993: 443). McGee and Newcomb (1992) confirmed the existence of a problem behavior syndrome but found that criminal behavior was more determined by general deviance in adulthood than by its presence in adolescence.

The criminal personality theory of Yochelson and Samenow has been criticized for failing to identify why some offenders think criminally while others do not, for lacking controls, for relying more on assertion with example than on systematically gathered data, for failing to define its terms, and for overgeneralizing from a highly selected group of hospitalized hard-core adult criminals and serious psychopathic juvenile offenders to the general population of offenders (Vold, 1979: 155). Moreover, their 52 identified thinking patterns exclude those who commit corporate and government crimes.

A further criticism of personality theory comes from feminist criminologists who argue that personality-trait theorists have either ignored females in their assumptions about personality or else have based any explanation of the differences between men's and women's criminal behavior on flawed stereotypical myths of women as hapless victims of their gender-role socialization (Naffine, 1985).

In spite of the evidence from studies that have not demonstrated the link between personality traits and crime or delinquency (Waldo and Dinitz, 1967; Tannenbaum, 1977), the search for the criminal personality continues not least because, as Barlow (1990: 38) says, "most people are reluctant to believe that rapists, serial murderers, child molesters, and those who commit hundreds of crimes during adolescence and early adulthood have 'normal' personalities." Part of the reason for this, as Bartol (1991: 2) explains, is that "most people have a limited tolerance for complexity and ambiguity. People apparently want simple, straightforward answers, no matter how complex the issue." However, most sociologists and even some psychologists would agree with Schur (1969: 62) that, however simple or complex its explanation may appear, "there has been a tendency to greatly exaggerate the significance of psychopathology in the analysis of crime problems."

In spite of the consistent lack of evidence both for the theory and for its derived treatments, Empey and Stafford (1991: 170) point out that "as a professional ideology ... few bodies of theory have enjoyed widespread popularity like that of psychodynamic theories." Thus, although psychological/psychiatric theories of crime enjoy popularity, their effectiveness in explaining and dealing with crime so far is at best limited. This should not be taken as an indictment of all psychological theory, however, for as we shall see in subsequent chapters, social learning theory and cognitive theories may have much more to offer.

CHAPTER SIX

Sociological Positivism I: Social Ecology Theories

In the last two chapters we concentrated on what Cohen (1966: 42) called kinds-of-people explanations of crime. In these theories crime results, at least in part, from "inside-the-person" defects or abnormalities. With this chapter we begin to analyze theoretical perspectives that give priority to sociological rather than individual forces in criminal etiology. Insofar as these theories see the social environment as a force shaping human behavior, they are referred to as sociological positivism.

In the first of our four sociological chapters we turn to theories about the socio-spatial environment in which people exist, or what Stark (1987: 893) has called "kinds of places" explanations. From the perspective of these theories (see Table 6-1), crime is seen to be generated by factors "outside-the-person," which are "pathological" conditions of particular communities, areas, or neighborhoods. Put simply, social ecology theories imply that crime is not an individual phenomenon but an environmental one, environment referring to the physical, social, and cultural context of human activity.

BASIC IDEA, CENTRAL MOTIF, AND MAJOR THEORISTS

One of the first sociologically oriented perspectives on crime, the social ecology framework has an intellectual heritage of many years, in which time it has

Table 6-1   Related Theories*

Cartographic school
Environmentalist school
Criminal ecology
Criminal-area studies
Human ecology theory
Social disorganization theory
Concentric-zone theory
Chicago School criminology
Cultural-deviance theory
Kinds-of-places theory
Situational choice theory
Routine activities theory
Evolutionary ecology theory

*Theories that take a perspective similar to or overlapping with the model that we develop in this chapter.

experienced several waves of interest (see Table 6-2). The social ecology framework, which is heavily influenced by human geography and biology, is based on an ecological analogy. Geographers view environment as the structuring of space mediated by culture or subculture. Part of the outcome of such structuring is the patterned distribution of crime.

Crime has always shown an uneven geographical distribution. Rural areas traditionally have less crime than urban areas. Some parts of an urban area, such as a city, have greater involvement in crime than others. Within the city there are "criminal areas." This is as true today as it was of the nineteenth-century "rookeries of London" (Mayhew, 1861; 1981; Booth, 1891; Tobias, 1972; Brantingham and Brantingham, 1981). Spatial variation in crime rates is a universal feature of industrialized societies and is trans-global, some nations, such as Japan, Switzerland, Costa Rica, and Nepal, having less crime than others (Adler, 1983).

The uneven distribution of crime was first noted by a French lawyer and statistician (Guerry, 1833) and a Belgian mathematician and astronomer (Quetelet, 1835). Called "moral statisticians," or "social physicists" (Rennie, 1978), they investigated the effects of a range of demographic, situational, and environmental factors, such as season, climate, population, poverty, and geographical distribution, on the crime rate and concluded that it was *societal conditions* that caused crime. Quetelet's "thermic law of delinquency" showed that violence was more prevalent in the southern nations and in warmer seasons, whereas property crimes were more prevalent in northern countries and in the winter.[1] In England, Fletcher (1848) demonstrated statistically that crime spread through neighborhoods "contaminated" by existing criminals,[2] and Glyde (1856) associated crime with population density. However, it was Guerry (1833) who provided the first social ecology of crime by using maps to relate crime to locality and social factors.

To explain the patterned effect of social behavior, and particularly criminal behavior, the geographical perspective was supplemented with insights from biology. Early European biologists had indicated that the ecology of plant life could also explain human organization. The term *ecology* (from the Greek *oikos,* meaning "household" or "living place") refers to the interrelationship between organisms or species of organisms and their natural physical environment. When applied to the relationship between humans and their community environment, this conceptualization is termed *social ecology* or *human ecology* (Faris, 1944;

---

[1]Quetelet (1831) ultimately came to believe, however, that the reason why societies had crime was because an unhealthy morality was manifest in biological defects that predisposed them to a crime (Beirne and Messerschmidt, 1991: 302–303).

[2]A similar idea was contained in Burt's ideas about the reproduction of crime and it was to be resurrected again in Shaw and McKay's (1942) "cultural transmission" explanation for crime, which we discuss later in this chapter.

Table 6-2   Theorists Using Social Ecology Explanations of Crime

THEORIST	MAJOR WORK[S]	DATE
	Cartographic School	
Guerry	*Essai sur la Statistique Morale de la France*	1833
Quetelet	*Physique Sociale*	1835
	Social and Human Ecology	
Mayhew	*London Labour and the London Poor*	1861
Booth	*Life and Labour of the People in London*	1891
Park and Burgess	*The City*	1925
Thrasher	*The Gang*	1927
Alihan	*Social Ecology*	1938
Shaw and McKay	*Juvenile Delinquency and Urban Areas*	1942
Hawley	*Human Ecology*	1950
Morris	*The Criminal Area*	1957
Suttles	*The Social Order and the Slum*	1968
Baldwin and Bottoms	*The Urban Criminal*	1976
Gill	*Luke Street*	1977
Brantingham and Brantingham	*Environmental Criminology* *Patterns of Crime*	1981 1984
Stark	"Deviant Places: A Theory of the Ecology of Crime"	1987
Sampson	"Communities and Crime" 1987	
Bursik	"Urban Dynamics and Ecological Studies of Delinquency"	1984
Bursik and Grasmick	*Neighborhoods and Crime*	1993

Hawley, 1950): "Just as plants, insects, and animals translate a physical terrain into a mosaic of distinct communities, so men [and women] become separated into a network of unlike communities which form an intelligible whole" (Downes and Rock, 1982: 59). Social ecology, then, is "the attempt to link the structure and organization of human community to interactions with its localized environment" (Haggett, 1977: 187).

Moreover, the analogy seemed not only to explain the maintenance of equilibrium by communities but also the dynamics of social change. From a Darwinian-inspired viewpoint European biologists argued that "human communities, like plants, grew by experiencing the coming together of many different individuals. These communities changed over time and ultimately declined as they were gradually superseded by other incoming individuals, who adopted different forms of social organisation" (Heathcote, 1981: 353). The importance of the ecological analogy was that it sensitized researchers to the idea that competition and cooperation coexist in the same geographical space. Thus Warming's (1909) study of the symbiotic interdependence of plant communities argued that those of predominantly the same species living in the same "community" were "in competition with nature, but not each other. Those with several different species, however, would often compete for limited resources more among themselves than with the environment" (Walker, 1994: 49).

In its extreme this position was "environmental determinism," a label given to the work of University of Chicago sociologists in the 1920s and 1930s who used an ecological analogy to explain crime. Recognizing the criminological significance of the ecological analogy allowed these sociologists to challenge substantially the prevalent biological and personality theories. They asked, If crime is a result of individual defects, why do some geographical areas have rates of crime consistently higher than other areas? Further, "how is it that neighborhoods can remain the site of high crime and deviance rates *despite a complete turnover in their populations?*" (Stark, 1987: 893). Is there something criminogenic about the environment or broad spatial context? The answer is: *"There must be something about places as such* that sustains crime" (ibid.).

Chicago sociologists set out to study that "something," firsthand, experiencing the lives of the city residents, as they lived it, from their perspective, by living with them but also by relating their life histories and biographies to the wider patterns documented through statistical data gathering.[3] Studies by Park and Burgess (1925) and Shaw and McKay (1931; 1942) turned the city of Chicago into a laboratory for an ethnography of urban life and culture, "a detailed anthropological mapping of the social territories that made the city," examining the structure and culture of groups, gangs, and subcultures that emerged in particular areas (Downes and Rock, 1982: 54). Park applied the ecological

---

[3]This combined qualitative and quantitative methodology derived from their philosophical awareness of the relevance of both subjective and objective knowledge. In particular Park's sociology was derived from a combination of the American pragmatic philosophies of William James, Charles Pierce, and John Dewey, which elevated experientially gathered knowledge over philosophical thought as the best road to truth. But equally important was the formal sociology of Georg Simmel, whose influence on Park was to sensitize him to explore the objective "structure" of social activity, or the "architecture of experience," that comprised those elements independent of its setting (see Downes and Rock, 1982: 55–58; Martin et al., 1990: 93–113).

analogy to explain how people in human communities "work together for common goals and at the same time compete for scarce resources," and how "a stronger group would disrupt the community through change and eventually reestablish order by replacing (succeeding) a previous dominant group" (Walker, 1994: 49). The Chicago School explained crime as a group phenomenon arising naturally in certain urban sectors. They recognized that a social group "also involves a geographical area whose physical characteristics have a marked influence upon the conduct of both individuals and subgroups" and that "the crime problem is not exempt from the influences of physical surroundings and geography" (Schafer, 1976: 86).

As an explanation of crime the perspective came into disrepute, in part for its denial of human agency and because of its (a) reliance on official definitions of crime, (b) use of official statistics as a measure of levels of crime (Baldwin, 1979; Davidson, 1981: Nettler, 1984), (c) inability to account for relatively high rates of crime and delinquency in stable, working-class communities (Bursik and Grasmick, 1993b: 277), and (d) its almost complete ignorance of the political economy (Davis, 1975). However, the social ecology approach experienced a revival in England in the 1970s and in the United States in the 1980s and 1990s. The revised approaches compensated for the weaknesses of the original analysis, adding victimization data, spatial analysis, and, in some cases, the metaphor of geometry (Brantingham and Brantingham, 1978; 1981; 1984; Stark, 1987) and a consideration of community, neighborhood, and inequality as the basic conceptual units (Blau and Blau, 1982). This has involved a conceptual coalescence with varieties of conflict theory that have "politicized" its analysis (Morris, 1957; Rex and Moore, 1967; Gill, 1977; Bursik, 1986; 1988; 1989; Bursik and Grasmick, 1993a; 1993b; Sampson, 1987; Sampson and Wilson, 1993).[4] The revision recognizes the crucial role that political and economic power plays in structuring crime-prone neighborhoods. It is toward an analysis of the social ecological theory as an explanation for crime that we now turn.

HUMANS, HUMAN NATURE, AND HUMAN BEHAVIOR

The ecological perspective sees human behavior as determined by social conditions that affect the social and physical environment of which humans are a part. They are viewed as conformist, acting in accordance with group values and norms. However, humans are also believed to be capable of operating in a wide variety of social roles that shape their view of the world. Behavior was seen by Chicago School sociologists as relative, a view which implied that there are

---

[4]We discuss conflict theory in Chapter 10. For the purposes of the current discussion, conflict theory is the view that a critical factor in shaping community development is the capability of the powerful to define what is crime and deviance and to impose those definitions through law and criminal justice on the powerless.

limitations on free will and on humans' "freedom of action" (Davis, 1975: 46). However, unlike the ideas about human nature held by classicists and economists, social ecologists recognize that people are not just free rationally calculating atomic beings; they have imaginations and meaningful social worlds, but these are shaped by the social environment: "The imagination is not free to create anything which it may choose to devise. It is constrained by the capacity of the world to answer back and impose itself on thought" (Downes and Rock, 1982: 56).

Part of the constraint on individual freedom, according to ecology theory, comes from the interdependence of humans and the reflection of this in their natural tendency to form organized communities. Hawley (1968: 331) argues that because of the "naked state" in which they come into the world and their "long period of postnatal maturation" humans are interdependent in their search for sustenance from the environment, having the capacity to expand life to the maximum determined by the circumstances. From this perspective, humans, either as individuals or groups, take their identity from the functions and relationships that they perform for the whole unit of which they are a part (Hawley, 1950).

This apparent environmental shaping of human nature does not mean, however, that social ecologists renounce the idea that humans *also* make rational choices. Rather they believe that human behavior is the outcome of an environmentally structured choice.

VIEW OF SOCIETY AND THE SOCIAL ORDER

For social ecologists society is a conglomerate of human communities, each formed through functional systems of relationships that emerge in localized territories (Hawley, 1950). Thus social ecology has a view of society as

> a social system determining the actions and attitudes of its individual members ... through their effective socialization into a consensus of its "shared value system" of attitudinal and behavioral norms ... an external organic reality characterised by a constraining morality which determine[s] social order." (Heathcote, 1981: 341–42)

The central hypothesis is that human "organization arises from the interaction of population and environment" and that the environment provides both the ultimate challenge to human existence as well as the resources to meet that challenge over time through cooperative, self-sustaining forms of a social organizational whole (Hawley, 1968: 330). But this functional consensus masks an underlying diversity, which early social ecology theorists saw and described. What on the surface appears to be all one mass, a veritable urban jungle, on closer examination is revealed to be rooted in different economic and cultural soils. Again, the ecological analogy is the instructive metaphor:

Instead of being a homogeneous expanse of dense growth extending thousands of miles, as it appears from the air, the jungle is actually a composite of as many as 200 different kinds of forests packed tightly together. Each forest is composed of its own species of trees and plants ... Once you get away from that perception of all green, then you can see a diversity of habitats right there in the jungle (*Washington Post,* March 22, 1985).

Chicago School social ecologists of the 1920s and 1930s suspended the perception of the "all green" consensus to delve beneath the appearance into the mosaic of life worlds of society's inhabitants. But they also recognized that the multiplicity of social forms made up a whole and in time the whole would absorb the differences of its parts. The differences between the varieties of groups were magnified in the groups' struggle for space and in their attempt to adapt and survive. As in the ecological analogy, whereby the struggle for survival in plant and animal communities maintains the ecological balance, so too, from the Chicago School's perspective, says Davis (1975: 43), "the human community developed ... through symbiosis, or mutual dependence, differentially positioned groups were interrelated by biotic balance, an unending process of adjustment and readjustment."

Given the mix of nationalities, with its differing sets of norms and values, a diverse plurality of values prevailed, with the expectation that cultural conflict would arise. Conflicts were found to occur between ethnic groups which served to strengthen them (Davis, 1975: 53).

The pluralistic vision of culture conflict in relation to crime was implied in the notion of the "struggle for space" and emerged in the writing of Sellin (1938), who drew from the work of students of the Chicago School to inform his analysis. Sellin saw society as a mix of cultures whose conduct norms, or rules of behavior expressing values, were in conflict with those of other cultures. Within this conflict and transformation, some groups would emerge as dominant. Thus was formed a natural hierarchy and an early recognition of conflict as power. For Hawley (1968: 333) power emerges in the form of functional dominance:

Functional units having direct relations with environment, and thus performing the key function, determine or regulate the conditions essential to the functions of units having indirect relations with environment. Dominance in other words is an attribute of function ... Power is held in varying degrees by all other units, in measures that vary inversely with the number of steps removal from direct relation with the unit performing the key function.

Although he recognizes the possibility of powerful interests forming through unions between units, these are not seen as reflective of autonomous power but of units in a similar functional position in relation to the environment.

The early ecological approach, like the society from which it emerged, did not accommodate to the diversity of cultures and subcultures nor recognize that power could be created through dysfunctional interests. Rather it represented at best an acceptance of the established mainstream values and a pressure toward relinquishing "old ways," and at worst a rationalization and justification for those who dominated others, culturally and organizationally. Hence there is a theme of conservatism in these social ecologists' perception of society. As Williams and McShane (1988: 42) say, "Chicago School theorists were, at heart, *consensus* theorists ... the assumption was that consensus, or a natural conformity to cultural lifeways, was the initial pattern of human behavior":

> This is demonstrated in their appreciation of diversity in human behavior, yet it was a patterned diversity, one shared by the members of the culture to which one belonged. It was only where one group came into contact with another that conflict developed. And of course, they recognized that society is made up of a variety of cultural groups; therefore conflict is simply a fact of life.

THE ROLE OF LAW, THE DEFINITION OF CRIME, AND THE IMAGE OF THE CRIMINAL

Within the ecological perspective law is taken as the standards and rules of the dominant mainstream culture of society as formulated by its political institutions. Law defines what crime should be, and, implicitly or explicitly, the perspective seems to offer no challenge to the types of definitions of crimes that are made. Since the roots of the perspective lie in functionalism, one would expect a consensus of values in interpretation of the law. Moreover, the perspective does not concern itself with law as such but does place some emphasis on the control features of law and how these operate. Indeed, Shaw and McKay (1931: 114–15) claim that respect for the law is an "acquired attitude" emerging in the context of stable and consistent social standards, and this fails to develop where chaos and confusion prevail.

The social ecological perspective acknowledged the force of diverse cultures and their traditional and conflicting customs. Some cultures or groups developed sufficient power to be able to have their own culture's rules and values dominate as the law in their neighborhood. The result is that simply by following their own culturally acquired norms subcultural members may break the law of their host country. Indeed, as Downes and Rock (1982: 66–68) point out, a constant theme in the social ecologists' perspective is that "crime is an unremarkable consequence of normal conditions," deviance being no more than diversity, a "surrogate social order," that serves as an alternative to conventional institutions.

In the traditional social ecological perspective criminals are those who are in a state of transition through fragmented social organization. They are envisaged "as a small minority occupying the margins of society ... and [are] depicted as existing in a state of social disorganization within these marginal areas" (Heathcote, 1981: 342). In this perspective criminality need not be a permanent state. Delinquents can mature and thereby escape it, but they can just as easily be locked in.

In recent versions of ecology theory (Cohen and Machalek, 1988), criminal behavior is not abnormal but a natural expression of diverse behavioral strategies stemming from normal social organization and interaction. Delinquents "are portrayed as inherently sociable people whose response to parental indifference and neighborhood demoralization is the development of alternative forms of organization" which "happen to be delinquent according to the standards of the larger society" (Empey and Stafford, 1991: 184, citing Kobrin, 1971: 124).

CAUSAL LOGIC

Quetelet, influenced by the positivism of his era, believed that causal relationships, similar to the laws of physics and astronomy, would be found to explain general events in social life, and particularly the phenomenon of crime (Beirne and Messerschmidt, 1991: 299–300). He believed that societies "give birth" to crime when they undergo rapid changes in the economy and relative deprivation (Quetelet, 1831: 38). Thus for him it was society that was the ultimate cause of crime, not individuals.

Social ecology's causal theory has a base in human geography with its notion of the relevance of culturally defined space to social organizational forms, but it is also influenced by the individual positivists' claim that "environmental factors" are an important trigger for those predisposed to crime. As we have seen, individual positivists argue that crime is an interactive outcome of individual and environmental factors. However, from the social ecology perspective, crime does not have to be premised on inherent predispositional traits. Indeed, social ecology advocates claim that it can be the product of human interaction with the physical and social environment. Thus the traditional perspective does not focus on the individual offender, but attempts to explain variations in the *rates* of crime and delinquency by relating these to types of *spatial area* and to the cultural adaptions people make when living in these areas.

The early sociologists Park and Burgess (1924) used the ecological model to describe the structure of the new urban communities. Burgess (1925), for example, argued that the growth of cities followed a specific pattern. Growth came in concentric waves or circles from the center of the city outward as pressure from the center threatened to encroach surrounding spaces of lower intensity activity. The city center was the area of highest density occupancy, and highest intensity land use, those surrounding it were successively of lower intensity land use. Each area in a circle was considered to be distinct, with its own individual social characteristics. Of importance here is the notion that these were "natural" (distinct neighborhoods) or "biotic" areas, terms borrowed from plant ecology. These areas were distinguished from one another by the physical and economic characteristics that tended to be stable over time. Burgess (1925) also argued that this equilibrium was maintained by mobility. Although he recognized that both cultural and economic factors contributed to this process, the best indicator was the distribution of land use and values (Bursik, 1986: 37).

Using the basic model developed by Park and Burgess, Shaw and McKay (1942) explained crime and delinquency in the context of the rapidly changing face of the city of Chicago and the urban environment in general. They divided Chicago into five concentric zones representing diverse areas of the city growing from the center outward. Zone 1 was the central financial and business district, known in Chicago as "The Loop." Zone 2 was the area immediately surrounding the central business district. This area was termed the "interstitial" area, the "zone of transition," or even "the twilight area" because it was "in between" periods of social organization (Walker, 1994: 51). It was a previously desirable residential area that changed as business expanded and industries settled in the area. There was a steady physical deterioration of residences as the central business district and industries expanded and absent landowners held on to their property for speculative reasons. Here the greatest turnover of the population occurred, with new groups replacing the earlier immigrant group, who were able to move to residences in more favorable neighborhoods. The zone of transition, with its dilapidated buildings served as the only neighborhood affordable to the newly arrived immigrants, and conveniently close to their factories. It was considered a temporary abode until economic mobility and assimilation into the mainstream of society became possible. For a variety of reasons, however, some became trapped in these neighborhoods; age, language problems, infirmity, and insufficient skills were conditions that made mobility for many difficult, if not impossible.

Zone 3, titled "workingmen's homes," or the area of "respectable artisans," consisted of rooming and boarding houses where salespersons and other workers lived. It also was the zone where those who could escape the deteriorating conditions of Zone 2 were likely to move. Zone 4, "suburbia," was the residential zone of the middle classes with single-family homes and apartment residences. Finally, Zone 5, "exurbia," was the commuter zone, where upper-class, upper-income residents lived in relative opulence in large single-family homes.[5]

Shaw and McKay, employing official records, used special maps to record the distribution of juvenile arrests, residences of truants, physical deterioration, incidence of tuberculosis, and infant mortality, in an attempt to discover if there

---

[5]More recently, as a result of urban renewal and gentrification, some cities have developed multiple centers and others have businesses dispersed along transportation routes.

were patterns to these social maladies and reasons for their existence. The zonal model predicted that Zone 2, because of its physical and economic conditions, would be the natural area of criminality and residences of criminals. Shaw and McKay found, indeed, that, at least as far as "official" rates were concerned, crime and delinquency were greatest near the center of the city in Zone 2 and declined with distance from the center, with Zone 5 experiencing the least incidence. The pattern persisted over forty years, no matter which ethnic group or nationality moved into an area during each new wave of European immigration. Moreover, it was subsequently confirmed in studies of 18 other cities (Shaw and McKay, 1942) and in studies by other researchers (Schmid, 1960; White, 1932; Longmoor and Young, 1936; Lottier, 1938–39).[6] The general conclusion of these studies was that

> the highest rates are usually found in the congested and disorganized urban sections lying next to the central business and warehouse areas, and the lowest rates in the outlying suburban and residential districts." (Barnes and Teeters, 1943: 141)[7]

As a result of these findings of stability in the incidence of crime and a distinct clustering in particular geographical areas, Shaw and McKay sought to explain crime and delinquency as a product of disintegrating neighborhoods. Though several factors such as poverty, economics, and ethnicity seemed to correlate with these areas as some commentators have noted (Bursik, 1986; Kornhauser, 1978; Tittle, 1983; Bursik and Grasmick, 1993b), Shaw and McKay posited only an indirect causal relationship between these factors and rates of crime. Thus, for them, it was not so much an area's economic impoverishment that produced crime, since this existed in other areas such as the rural South, unaccompanied by significant levels of crime. Nor was crime caused by particular ethnic groups who occupied these areas. Rather it was the outcome of *social disorganization.*

For most residents of these areas, population changes and dilapidated living arrangements undermined (a) traditional stable structures, (b) established coping behaviors, and especially (c) traditional control institutions. It was the general conclusion that in these areas there was little or no community feeling, a predominance of transitory impersonal relations, and an absence of intimate ties. The usual institutions of informal social control, such as the family, family net-

---

[6]Lottier showed how robbery rates decreased as one moved away from the city center but increased again as one came to nearby cities, regardless of their size.

[7]Some contradictory evidence such as that of Davie (1937) showed that both Cleveland and New Haven did not conform to the same pattern of crime distribution, and Lander (1954) found no evidence of it in Baltimore. Moreover, the more general implied connection between crime and delinquency was related to the density of populations, an idea questioned by the examples of low-crime, high-population societies like Japan.

works, extended kinship ties, school and community organizations, were no longer ineffective.

In addition, ethnic culture based on these institutions had its authority undermined. In the conflict and confusion over values and the relative isolation of ethnic identities, parents lost the respect of their children, who were in conflict with them over mixed value systems. As Whyte (1943) found, "Children of immigrants, adapting more rapidly to the change in culture than did their parents and grandparents, were often embarrassed by their families and drew away from them" (Williams and McShane, 1988: 35). This resulted in parents' loss of control over their children.

Given the clash between various ethnic groups, there was little cooperation in attempting to solve common problems (Kornhauser, 1978). Shaw (1951: 15, cited by Siegel, 1992) summarized the position:

> The successive changes in the composition of population, the disintegration of the alien cultures, the diffusion of divergent cultural standards, and the gradual industrialization of the area have resulted in a dissolution of the neighborhood culture and organization. The continuity of conventional neighborhood traditions and institutions is broken. Thus, the effectiveness of the neighborhood as a unit of control and as a medium for the transmission of the moral standards of society is greatly diminished.

It was this breakdown in the self-regulatory structure of the community that became known as *social disorganization*, a condition in which people compete and distrust each other. At the same time it was assumed that the poorer neighborhoods were insulated from other areas, with the consequence that the more conventional value system of the dominant culture did not permeate the walls of their social isolation. Such insulated neighborhoods were considered relatively unintegrated into the wider culture and structure and therefore were unable to deal with their problems.

Social disorganization was also considered to lead to the experience of *personal* disorganization (Durkheim's sense of anomie or absence of moral authority and guidelines). This could also lead individuals to crime, delinquency, and mental illness, especially depression and suicide.

High rates of delinquency, then, were seen in part as a reflection of the inability of the community to regulate itself (Bursik, 1986: 38). But that is not all they were. It is important to recognize that the early social ecologists were *not* proposing a deterministic argument that environment causes crime. Rather, as with their views on human behavior, crime was behavior chosen in a particular environmental context. As Walker (1994: 54) says, Shaw and McKay's findings do not indicate, therefore, that certain ecological characteristics result in residents' abandonment of conventional values, increasing the level of delinquency. They suggest, rather, that people who live in high delinquency areas are subject to a variety of contradictory standards, values and behaviors rather than one (usually law-abiding) environment. As a result, residents may choose a delinquent life-style rather than a conventional one.

In other words, crime is an environmentally structured choice for those seeking to survive in socially disorganized neighborhoods.

Instead of suffering this personal disorganization individually, some were attracted to a collective, unregulated, unofficial "community" solution. Insulated from the dominant culture and alienated from their parents' traditional cultures, some immigrant youth formed their own new primary support groups, some of which took the form of gangs. Thus Thrasher (1927: 33) saw the gang as offering "a substitute for what society fails to give, and it provides relief from suppression and distasteful behavior. It fills a gap and affords an escape."

Gangs developed their own delinquent traditions that were passed on to new members. As a consequence the youth peer group became the major influence in the life of the child and delinquency often became an accepted and valued form of behavior. Once established, delinquency and gang subcultures continued in the neighborhood and a tradition was initiated that stayed, no matter which ethnic group was dominant at any particular moment. In residential neighborhoods that had a higher economic status and where there was a low rate of crime and delinquency, Shaw and McKay believed that the norms and values of the child's social milieu were conventional. In contrast, in the lower economic areas "a powerful competing system of delinquency values exists" (Shaw and McKay, 1942: 437). It was when the conventional values were weakened that the competing system took hold.

This breakdown of institutional controls within the area or neighborhood, leading some to choose delinquency, and the development of norms and values that encourage delinquent and criminal behavior, over time generate a subculture of delinquency. Delinquency was thereby transmitted to future occupants of the neighborhood, from generation to generation, in what became known as the process of *cultural transmission.*

> Successful criminals in the area … demonstrated both the success and the normality of their way of life. They thereby became a model for ambitious youths, themselves lacking legitimate opportunities to attain such wealth. Subsequently a criminal tradition becomes normative to the area, and one which approximates to a state of "social disorganization" in the Durkheimian sense of a lack of a uniform set of cultural standards conforming to that of wider society, and of a community thereby ceasing to act as an effective agent of social control on its members. Under

such circumstances, criminal activity becomes tolerated and accepted. (Heathcote, 1981: 357)

In an early use of differential association theory (which we discuss in Chapter 8), Shaw and McKay (1942: 436) assert with regard to this process:

> This tradition is manifested in many different ways. It becomes meaningful to the child through the conduct, speech, gestures, and attitudes of persons with whom he has contact. Of particular importance is the child's intimate association with predatory gangs or other forms of delinquent and criminal organization. Through his contacts with these groups and by virtue of his participation in their activities he learns the techniques of stealing, becomes involved in binding relationships with his companions in delinquency, and acquires the attitudes appropriate to his position as a member of such groups.

Not all ethnic groups, however, were found to be equally vulnerable to social disorganization and its related substitutions of community with gangs. By importing strong cultural traditions some ethnic groups, such as the Chinese, showed an ability to resist disorganization and adapt to their environmental conditions. Moreover, some cities showed different patterns of development. It became apparent that certain ethnic groups were less involved in delinquency and crime than other groups. As Shaw and McKay (1942: 440) admit in their conclusion, foreshadowing control theory (which we discuss in Chapter 8):

> In communities occupied by Orientals, even those communities located in the most deteriorated sections of our large cities, the solidarity of Old World cultures and institutions has been preserved to such marked extent that control of the child is still sufficiently effective to keep at a minimum delinquency and other forms of deviant behavior.

But these and other groups, such as the European Jews, were considered special cases in the overall pattern of crime and deviance that the deteriorated community fostered (Hayner, 1933; MacGill, 1938).[8]

Contemporary social ecologists have generally retained the position that prioritizes place over person in their explanation of crime. Stark (1987: 905), for example, argues that high crime among blacks is not universal. He points out that a large proportion of blacks in the South live in the suburbs and rural communities where there are physical features conducive to low crime rates. The

---

[8] The failure of the Chicago School to fully acknowledge the significance of stable communities with low delinquency rates in areas of high social disorganization was subsequently seen as a major flaw in the approach (Lander, 1954; Heathcote, 1981: 360).

majority of blacks in northern cities live in those "areas where the probabilities of *anyone* committing a crime are high" (Stark, 1987: 906). Others have argued that crime needs to be discussed in terms of social/ecological characteristics that include the site of both the crime, the offender's residence, and where the offender was arrested, among several other factors (Georges-Abeyie, 1981: 100–101).

Recent years have seen an elaboration and extension of social ecology theory, reflected in the idea that changes in certain elements of urban design would reduce crime (Jeffery, 1971; Gardiner, 1978; Clarke and Mayhew, 1980). A more focused idea was that building design and place impact rates of crime since they can affect territorial and personal space (Newman, 1972; 1973). More recently, geographers have explored crime patterns and associated environmental factors (Harries, 1980; Georges-Abeyie and Harries, 1980; Davidson, 1981; Lowman, 1986).

As Brantingham and Brantingham (1981: 18) point out, recent environmental criminology must be distinguished from the work of the early part of the twentieth century. There has been a shift to considering crime as discrete criminal events and more generally a "shift from the sociological to the geographical imagination" (ibid.: 18). The geographical imagination "asks the individual to recognize the role of space in his own biography, to relate the spaces he sees around him, and to recognize how transactions between individuals and between organizations are affected by the space that separates them" (Brantingham and Brantingham, 1981: 20, citing Harvey, 1974). The key here is the emphasis on different forms of space, whether within situations, neighborhoods, or within cities, between cities, between regions, and between countries. But different types of space create different opportunities for crime. This, too, is recognized as part of the decision-making process of potential offenders as they take into account certain crime targets, as we saw in the discussion on rational choice theories of crime (Chapter 3).

The causal logic of this theory has been modified by combining the insights of conflict theory with the community approach. Morris (1957) and Bursik (1988), for example, combine conflict theory and social disorganization theory to show how political decisions, such as the decision to construct new housing projects in already deteriorated neighborhoods, can further destabilize a community, increase its residential turnover, and further undermine its ability to self-regulate, thereby facilitating delinquency. Morris (1957), for example, demonstrated the importance of government housing policies to the generation and concentration of delinquency in certain areas. In his study in the South London city of Croydon, it was found that the political decision by local government housing authorities to concentrate their problem tenants together in older and less desirable housing resulted in the formation of delinquent areas around the concentration.

Similarly, Bursik and Grasmick (1993a, 1993b) suggest that the early approaches (and by implication situational choice and routine activities theories) fail to explain the neighborhood and community-level differences and omit the crucial role of power, economic deprivation, and neighborhood composition in the causal chain shaping the ecology of an area. Bursik and Grasmick (1993a) and Sampson and Wilson (1993; Wilson, 1987) show how changes in economic patterns produce inequality by concentrating poverty in an immobile underclass in inner-city neighborhoods as the more successful move out to the suburbs.

Economic forces such as de-industrialization, the shift from manufacture to low-paid service sector employment, and the "flight of the affluent" (white and black) from inner cities, leave these neighborhoods devoid of their most skilled members. What remains is a residual "concentration and isolation of the most disadvantaged segments of minority populations in central city neighborhoods of older industrial cities" (Bursik and Grasmick, 1993b: 264). In such communities there is increased isolation and lack of neighborhood identification. Not only is there the traditional disorganization but also there exists a direct affect on crime as "an alternative means of gaining economic and social sustenance from the environment" (Bursik and Grasmick, 1993b: 266; 1993a: 65–70). For a community to be viable it is necessary to obtain external resources and political support.

The inability to secure these resources and the relative absence of "political brokers" can be affected by a range of factors, not least of which is the perception that an area is "bad." This, in turn, can lead to a limited ability for economically marginal neighborhoods to exercise effective public control (Moore, 1978). The overall impact is a perceptual discrediting of these neighborhoods, resulting in increased police controls and further fragmentation. Miller (1981), for example, argues that it is the perception of crime for a neighborhood, whether true or not, that leads to fear and a resultant decline in neighborhood property values and an increase in neighborhood instability. This in turn can then lead to a failure of funding or, as Bursik (1989) shows, an exacerbation of social disorganization by political decisions that add unstable developments to an already deteriorated community. The political decision to concentrate low-income families into these stereotyped problem areas creates "hierarchies of desirability" (Gill, 1977: 5). A "bad" public reputation emerges of both the area and its residents via reported incidents in the media that then expose these residents to further policing, cast further suspicion on them, and thereby amplify the problems of disorganization and control (Morris, 1957; Gill, 1977; Armstrong and Wilson, 1973; Scraton, 1981).

For Suttles (1968; 1972) the stereotyped public image of an area is internalized by the residents in such a way that it begins to construct their self-identity, resulting in what he defined as a "defeated neighborhood." This is a community whose residents withdraw from public participation, "out of shame, mutual fear and an absence of faith in each other's concern" (Suttles, 1972: 239). Some have suggested that crime is related to these residents' negative perception of the quality of life in their neighborhood and that what begins as property crime escalates to violent crime as the fear–disillusionment–isolation–crime–fear cycle deepens (Reiss, 1983). For others, this collective disillusionment is the product of a political exclusion from power and the resources that provide honor. Heathcote (1981: 367) summarizes this new direction as "the essential recon-struction of Chicago theories ... to include ways in which relatively powerful interest-groups ... can use political and economic power to manipulate and main-tain the disadvantage of other less powerful and less well organized groups."

From these theoretical developments and extensions we can see that the relevance of ecology to crime has not lost its impact and adherents. The causal logic remains the same: the environment, now more specifically defined, is part of the causal chain. What has been added is political power and its ability to exploit public stereotypes in ways that sustain rather than dismantle the social dis-organization, fear, and self-respect of neighborhoods with crime problems.

CRIMINAL JUSTICE SYSTEM IMPLICATIONS

Based on the assumption that human motivation to commit crime cannot be changed and that humans act rationally given their environmental context, the social ecology perspective is relatively silent on the criminal justice system and its procedures for processing offenders. Social ecologists do, however, have signif-icant policy implications for intervention that form part of their correctional ide-ology. Primarily their policy is one of prevention by manipulation of the environment and the person's place within his or her social space.

Criminal Justice Policy and Correctional Ideology

Initially, some social ecologists felt that intervention was unnecessary as the cause, transitional areas, would eventually improve with the cessation of immigration and ethnic groups becoming integrated into American society. Crime, at least the excessive area crime resulting from social disorganization, would eventually whither away. Davis (1975: 48–49) describes the Chicago School's position: "The melting pot, in time, would eradicate urban pockets of deviance. Even the slum, the lowest point of urban disorganization, would rise from its submerged status and be absorbed into the urban order."[9] These early theorists, therefore, felt little needed to be done, other than to facilitate the assimilation process of immigrants into the mainstream.

Others took a more active stance. They felt that the decision-making pro-cess leading to criminal behavior might be shaped by purposeful modifications

[9]In so far as urban renewal and "gentrification" of the slum has occurred, it might be thought that in some areas the slum has in fact risen up. But even here the effect on area crime is mixed. In a study of five U.S. cities McDonald (1986) showed that gentrification did not uniformly reduce the crime rate. While crimes against the person were reduced, property crime was not.

in environmental structures. Theirs was essentially a "correctionalist" stance, says Heathcote (1981: 343), which embodied the positivist notion that:

> since all forms of social disorganisation are abnormal and "pathological" to a healthy society they can, by definition, be largely eradicated by making planned adjustments to the structure and processes of that society, and thereby to the individuals within it.

Put simply, it was necessary to intervene to change the conditions of an area so as to reduce the causes of disorganization and thereby crime. As Empey and Stafford (1991: 185) point out, these conditions were interpreted by government commissions[10] primarily as "poverty." But there were those, including Shaw himself, who argued that community organization was the key. Some even went so far as to suggest that those residents most affected by disorganization be moved to new geographical areas.

Techniques of Crime Control

The implementation of policy in the social ecology perspective focuses on techniques for prevention. Early efforts attempted large-scale programs essentially to change the cultural and social milieu. Consistent with the preventative emphasis, the Chicago School gave rise to what was the forerunner of all community approaches to crime prevention, the Chicago Area Project, a model duplicated but never quite equaled (See Kobrin, 1959; Schlossman and Sedlak, 1983). Based on Shaw and McKay's findings, the purpose of the project was to organize communities and to use their indigenous leadership in crime prevention programs. It was argued that community members were in the best position to know what the community needed. It was felt that community leadership and social control, lost because of social disorganization, could be restored if residents got into prevention. If residents organized local programs for their children, were more involved with established institutions such as the school, labor unions, clubs, and law enforcement agencies, then crime would be reduced. Efforts were made to improve the appearance of neighborhoods, implement recreational activities, organize summer camps, and provide more effective law enforcement. The program gave rise to community organizers and street-gang workers who became models for subsequent efforts. Thus the early thrust was to avoid the criminal justice system.

Recent research has supported the notion that a form of community organizing does make a difference to disorganized areas, especially with regard to

---

[10] The two main commissions were the National Commission on Law Observance and Enforcement, reporting in 1931, and the President's Commission on Law Enforcement and the Administration of Justice, reporting in 1967.

the cooptation of gang activity. For example, Bursik and Grasmick (1993b: 280) have described research by Erlanger (1979) on Los Angeles gangs and by Dawley (1992) on Chicago gangs that demonstrates that where gangs themselves are able to solicit funds from outside their community to develop community-based improvement programs, these areas experience both a reduction in crime and a reduction in the fear of crime. These social movements for neighborhood change are likely to be successful to the extent that they can establish ties with other community groups with similar interests and who have already established ties (though not necessarily monetary) to political and business leaders (McCarthy and Zald, 1987; Bursik and Grasmick, 1993a: 156–57; 1993b: 279).

EVALUATION

In general, social ecological approaches have enjoyed considerable influence, a long history, and praise over the years. Guerry's (1833) foundational work was heralded as the first scientific criminology (Morris, 1957). Given the unique geography of the city, the Chicago School's idea of zonal development had considerable legitimacy. Its adherents were very influential as the forerunners of important naturalistic ethnographic research methods using an urban base. Their focus on different neighborhoods and ethnic enclaves, heralded the start of subcultural theory and resulted in some of the early and now classic monographs on the life process of deviance, delinquency, and crime, such as Shaw's (1930) *The Jackroller,* Anderson's (1923) *The Hobo,* Thrasher's (1927) *The Gang,* and Zorbaugh's (1929) *The Goldcoast and the Slum.* These narratives lent a qualitative, human dimension to criminology and gave it a realism that was absent in the larger-scale positivistic studies. Arguably, their combination of both qualitative and quantitative measures in these early works has never been excelled (Short, 1969). Finally, the policy off-shoot of Shaw and McKay's work, the Chicago Area Project, has had considerable influence on the importance of community involvement in crime prevention.

There has, however, been serious criticism of the social ecology theory, attacks on its qualitative and allegedly unsystematic methodology, and much debate about the value of its research, particularly in its agenda for policy development.

From the outset there was an objection to using a plant metaphor to explain the formation and change of human communities. Such an analogy to human ecology not only distorts the reality of human organization but is weakened when forces such as technology, class, and power are acknowledged (Alihan, 1938). Hence from the beginning the dominant assumption underlying ecological work was in question.

Ecological studies generally are seen to have several inherent problems and limitations that affect their usefulness. Davidson (1981: 87–89), for example, says there is a fundamental methodological problem of false or spurious results. What may be observed on the aggregate level may not be the case for individuals. Drawing conclusions for individuals from aggregate data is known as the *ecological fallacy,* a common problem even in sophisticated research (Alihan, 1938). Ecological studies are empirical and, no matter how methodologically sophisticated, tend to be theoretically weak (Baldwin, 1979), not least because of their tendency to infer causality from correlation, which is known as the *problem of causal order* (Hirschi and Selvin, 1967). Ecological studies are not dynamic. Their data tend to specify a point in time without taking into account the process that led to the criminal acts in the first place. Lastly, Davidson (1981: 88) contends that ecological studies place "too much emphasis on relatively simple demographic, social and economic indicators which themselves may have quite complex relationships to the underlying causes of crime."

One of the most crucial theoretical criticisms is that the central explanatory concept, social disorganization, is presented as both a description of a condition and the cause of that condition. In other words, the explanation is a tautology.

Moreover, just as early individual positivists did not use controls when examining criminal populations, neither did the Chicago School examine the assumed "organization" of noncriminal areas. As Kobrin (1971) argues, they failed to show that residents in more desirable neighborhoods of the city were any more organized in problem solving or more integrated as a community. However, recent research in England by Sampson and Groves (1989) has confirmed that communities characterized by low supervision, low participation in organizations, and few friendship networks have higher rates of delinquency than those with the opposite characteristics.

In addition, it has been pointed out that the ecological determinism of some early work stood in stark contradiction to the researchers' own ethnographic findings (Davis, 1975). Some argue that the Chicago School's "appreciation of overlap was minimal" in that their ethnographies "exaggerated the separation between deviant and conventional worlds, drawing barriers too densely" (Matza, 1969: 70). At the same time, they failed to consider the differences between groups of the same income level living in similar areas (Robison, 1936; Morris, 1957: 88).

Others have claimed that (1) the theory's ethnographic methods were more journalistic than scientific, (2) the macro-level data gathering was based on too insensitive and artificial a unit of measurement (one square mile), and (3) this research relied exclusively on official records of the police and courts and on legal definitions of delinquency. The failure to appreciate undetected crime and unprocessed offenders made the logic of the theory suspect (Robison, 1936). Davis (1975: 60) comments that "the greater visibility of lower class offenders combined with the lack of institutional safeguards to protect their privacy, exposed this population to agency detection and control." Because of this, the ecological distribution of crime patterns may have reflected little more than the ratio of private to public space available to residents. If this be the case, the greater crime rate is merely a measure of the concentrations of those with the lowest access to private space, whose lives are played out in the fish bowl of public and police visibility.

Recent research by Smith (1986; Smith and Jarjoura, 1988) suggests another mechanism. In a 60-neighborhood study of three major cities Smith found that police were more responsive to complaints by victims in low-crime areas, where they were *less* likely to file police reports, than in high-crime areas. This would suggest that police amplify the process of disorganization in the high-crime areas, while strengthening the integration of community in low-crime areas. Indeed, a major criticism of the social ecology theories is that in accepting the official definition of street crime as the crime, early researchers ignored how officials constructed these rates. By allowing a greater influence of the residents of organized communities in defining what counts as crime, the crimes of the middle class and the powerful, perpetrated behind the closed doors of suburban privacy, were overlooked, distorting both the conception and the measurement of crime.

Shaw and McKay's assumption of a stable ecological pattern has also been challenged (Schuerman and Kobrin, 1986). Bursik (1986) demonstrates that although the process of ethnic succession described by Shaw and McKay may have been correct for the period of their study, Chicago has changed considerably because of the development of suburbs, especially since the 1940s. Moreover, Bursik and Webb (1982) were able to show that, contrary to Shaw and McKay's contention of stable delinquency patterns, neighborhoods experiencing racial change had high delinquency rates, even though the rates may have been lower prior to the change in racial composition. According to Bursik (1986) the same difficulty that beset Shaw and McKay's work has been true of later ecological studies: their reliance on the assumption of stability without taking into account the changing ecological nature of the city. Indeed, in a recent replication of Shaw and McKay's study in Little Rock, Walker (1994) found that though the main tenets of the disorganization hypotheses were confirmed, changes in the nature of the city and surrounding urban areas have undermined the geographic elegance of the original concentric-zone hypothesis: "Modern urban cities have a much more decentralized, service-oriented form of industry" which has "changed the pattern of residential areas" and consequently dispersed the distribution of delinquency. But Walker found that official delinquency was still correlated with physical and population dimensions of disorganization.

How certain neighborhoods develop into high-crime areas is still not clear. Schuerman and Kobrin (1986) studied high-crime areas in Los Angeles over a twenty-year period and distinguished three stages in a cycle of deterioration: *emerging, transitional,* and *enduring.* Neighborhood deterioration seems to antedate a rise in crime, but at a later stage crime tends to forerun further physical decline. Rising crime rates and neighborhood deterioration were foreshadowed in Los Angeles by a number of indicators, such as "a shift from single to multiple-family dwellings, a rise in residential mobility, unrelated individuals and broken families, the ratio of children to adults, minority group populations, females in the labor force, and non-white and Spanish surname population with advanced education" (Schuerman and Kobrin, 1986: 67). This, then, also challenges the notion of stability in earlier studies and adds a developmental process to area studies. According to these researchers, only in emerging crime areas is there any possibility of successful intervention. Once an area has had a high crime rate over several decades, it is an area considered "lost" for purpose of crime reduction (Schuerman and Kobrin, 1986: 98).

Perhaps the most damning criticism of the Chicago School is its naive ignorance of power and uncritical acceptance of the political economy. Park, for example, saw segregated and isolated communities and the emergence of social hierarchy as the outcome of a "spontaneous" evolutionary process (Martin et al., 1990: 102, 104). Similarly, Shaw and McKay glossed over the political process involved in the creation of the area conditions. For example, much of the property in the high-crime areas in Chicago was owned and controlled by absentee landlords who had no interest in keeping up their tenants' lodgings because they held the property for speculative profit. Though this was known, it was not acted upon (Snodgrass, 1976). Similarly, the so-called natural areas of the city were actually planned and highly regulated by statutes and ordinances (Suttles, 1972). Furthermore the political, economic, and social forces that created both the business district and the social disorganization of the zones of transition were ignored, thus treating the symptoms rather than the cause (Snodgrass, 1976). Moreover, as we have mentioned, there was a conservative/liberal slant to Park and Shaw and McKay's work that only allowed them to see policy development within the established parameters of the system and so prevented a critique of the politics of business (Davis, 1975: 45, 61; Vold and Bernard, 1986).

Finally, Portes and Stepick's (1993) Miami research challenges the whole notion that social disorganization is the inevitable "rite of passage" for new waves of immigrants. Their study of Cuban, Nicaraguan, and Haitian immigration into South Florida between 1965 and 1990 shows that instead of immigrants adapting to the ecology of the city, the reverse can also be true: Miami has been transformed and, because of the absence of an entrenched elite, the immigrant entrepreneurs have created their own enclave of Cuban business. Instead of being fragmented and disorganized, the new waves of immigrants have displayed a "bounded solidarity," not least in response to their hostility to the Castro regime. Moreover, instead of entering the lowest rung of the city, the Cuban immigrants have taken over significant sections of its economic and political structure, displacing white Americans, who have "fled" because of Latino success rather than fear of crime. At the same time indigenous blacks have moved to the lowest rungs of what the Cubans have transformed into a bicultural Anglo-Cuban city. Based on their Miami study, Portes and Stepick argue that economic behavior and the choice about where to live "is 'embedded' ... in a context of values, loyalties, and relationships that makes such choices more than a simple process of rational decision making." They claim that a neglected dimension of traditional social ecological theories of adaption "is the 'social capital' that immigrants bring—the extent to which the ties that are created enable a particular group to overcome discrimination, to find niches in the economy and so on" (Coughlin, 1993: A11).

However, in spite of all its deficiencies, some consider the early abandonment of the social ecological framework as a whole to have been "premature" (Bursik and Grasmick, 1993b: 277) and unwarranted (Downes and Rock, 1982: 73) and, as testimony, point to its endurance and recent revival. Many of its supporters believe that the ecological approach has often been misunderstood. Its movement toward an integration with conflict theory and issues over powerful decision makers marks a refreshing liberation from contemporary individual-level analyses. However, this new direction fails to consider the connections between political officeholders and corporate speculators as crimes in themselves and therefore fails to address the creation of social disorganization as a byproduct of corporate and government crime.

In the next chapter we stay with the concept of crime as the product of normal people being put in abnormal situations, but instead of abnormality of place, culture conflict, social disorganization and deviant reorganization, our examination of strain theory looks at the inequalities in the economic opportunity structure and particularly at those whereby normal people are denied a legitimate economic position in the social structure.

CHAPTER SEVEN

Sociological Positivism II: Strain and Subcultural Theories

In the previous chapter we analyzed theories that gave causal significance to the spatial environment in organizing and disorganizing communities. Crime was seen as a problem of adaption to environmental change and was particularly acute in places of greatest change, such as the city. Here we turn to a group of theories that also see crime and deviance as an adaption—a normal response to abnormal circumstances. However, rather than focusing on various areas or community environments, they locate the causal force to adapt in the organization of the whole society, that is, in its social structure. Crime and deviance are thus seen as normal adaptive responses to the kind of structural organization that a society adopts. Particularly important in this organization is (1) the division of labor, (2) the nature and distribution of occupational roles, and (3) the opportunities available to obtain them. What we have termed structural-strain theory is also referred to as anomie theory and is part of the functionalist tradition in sociology. (See Table 7-1.)

Functionalism has been a dominant, overarching perspective that has had a long history with roots in both sociology and anthropology. We will be concerned only with its use in attempts to explain crime or deviance. We will concentrate on the ideas of two major sociological theorists, Emile Durkheim and Robert K. Merton, and their explanation of crime in relation to social structure. We will also examine the work of theorists who have followed in this tradition. Although there is some disagreement about the extent to which they can all be classified as strain theories (Cullen, 1988), we will give special attention to the

Table 7-1 Related Theories*

I. Structural Strain Theories

Sociological positivism
Structural functionalism
Anomie theory

II. Subcultural Strain Theories

Differential opportunity theory
Blocked opportunity theory
Delinquent subculture theory

*Theories that contain themes similar to or overlapping with the model that we develop in this chapter.

145

ideas of the subcultural theorists Albert Cohen, Richard Cloward, Lloyd Ohlin, and to revisions made by the leading contemporary strain theorist, Robert Agnew. (See Table 7-2.)

BASIC IDEA, CENTRAL MOTIF, AND MAJOR THEORISTS

The central idea of strain theory is that the universal goals a society may establish for its members may not be achievable by some, and not satisfying to others. Even those who are able to achieve societally prescribed goals may be unsatisfied in any long-term sense. The cause of this inability to reach satiable goals is either the unequal opportunities some are afforded by a society's social organization or a failure of its culture to clearly define and limit what individuals can achieve. In such circumstances of cultural and structural misalignment (called strain), crime and deviance may be a normal adaptive response.

Strain theory is rooted in both functionalism and its close relation, systems theory. Traditionally functionalism asserts that all "recurrent social activities have the function of maintaining a social system" (Whitaker, 1965: 127).[1] The analogy is to an organism where all parts function to maintain the whole. From this perspective, even some level of crime is normal and functional in that it serves to allow governments to clarify central societal values and norms. Crime, or at least the societal reaction to it, reminds people what is acceptable behavior, thereby serving to integrate the whole (Durkheim, 1893).[2]

According to Durkheim's version of anomie (which, as we shall see later, has differences from the way Merton applied the concept), a state of uncertainty or "anomie" is produced when changes in society upset its balance by failing to provide clear guidelines for how individuals successfully integrate into the whole. This, in turn, can create "excessive" crime.

Anomie can result from several sources. For Durkheim, a particularly important precondition of anomie was cultivating individual freedoms while removing or diversifying moral and normative restraints—a characteristic of the emerging capitalist society of the nineteenth century. This condition freed individuals to pursue the satisfaction of personal appetites, only to find that

---

[1]A word about the notion of function is in order here. The concept of "function" has a special meaning in sociology but is often used with imprecision. According to Martindale (1960) it is best thought of as "appropriate activity" or "system determined or system maintaining activity." The critical point of this position is the view that social life is fundamentally incorporated in systems. In these systems, any item is to be judged in terms of its determination by the system and its place in maintaining the system (Martindale, 1960: 445).

[2]We will elaborate this idea below when analyzing strain theorists' views of society.

Table 7-2 Theorists Using a Structural-Strain Explanation of Crime

THEORIST	MAJOR WORK(S)	DATE
Durkheim	*Division of Labor in Society*	1893
	Suicide	1897
Merton	"Social Structure and Anomie"	1938
	Social Theory and Social Structure	1957
Cohen	*Delinquent Boys*	1955
Cloward	"Illegitimate Means, Anomie and Deviant Behavior"	1959
Cloward and Ohlin	*Delinquency and Opportunity*	1960
Dubin	"Deviant Behavior and Social Structure"	1959
Elliot, Huizinger, and Ageton	*Explaining Delinquency and Drug Use*	1985
Agnew	"A Revised Strain Theory of Delinquency"	1985
	"Foundation for a General Strain Theory of Crime and Delinquency"	1992

these are insatiable, ever-receding desires. As one commentator says of the societal goal of money as a measure of success in contemporary society:

> There is no "stop sign" in society that says "Okay, you've reached your monetary goal, you can stop." Thus while we can look backwards and see progress relative to where we were, if we look *ahead,* we cannot see ourselves any closer to an ultimate goal than when we began. This state of affairs in society is an anomic one. (Sanders, 1983: 94)

The discovery of infinite insatiability produces individual dissatisfaction, social fragmentation, and social conflict (Durkheim, 1893). According to Durkheim, crime also results from malintegration of people's skills and abilities to the available positions in society (as in his notion of "forced" division of labor).[3] It is this version of Durkheim's anomie that has similarities with Merton's view.

In Merton's (1938) strain perspective, crime and deviance occur when structures of opportunity are mismatched to culturally prescribed aspirations. As

---

[3]This is in contrast to his ideal of a meritocratic "spontaneous" division of labor wherein people are allowed to rise to positions that exactly match their abilities and talents and are subject to the moral regulation from communities comprised of members of their occupational profession.

a result many people are not able to achieve culturally defined goals through the socially legitimate means available to them.[4] According to Merton, in a well-integrated society there are adequate means available for all who desire to pursue successfully the culturally prescribed goals:

> A well regulated, or stable, society has a balanced equilibrium between means and goals. In a stable society, both means and goals are accepted by everyone and are available to all. Social integration effectively occurs when individuals are socialized into accepting that they will be rewarded for the occasional sacrifice of conforming to the institutionalized means and when they actually compete for rewards through legitimate means. Malintegrated, or unstable, societies stress the goals without stressing the means, or vice versa. (Beirne and Messerschmidt, 1991: 377)

Beirne and Messerschmidt point out that for strain theorists, the lack of fit occurs because the ideology and the reality are in conflict. The ideology promotes insatiability (unlimited aspirations, "the sky's the limit") through a cultural emphasis on a universal capability to succeed. The ideology rewards this nebulous and illusive pursuit of success while punishing as failure anything less than continuing the attempt. In contrast, the reality of class, racial, and gender divisions does not (1) provide universally available legitimate means to achieve, so that many are without sufficient power or resources to compete; (2) provide sufficient openings in the social structure; and (3) provide any idea of what the end point, "success," looks like nor any affirmation when it has been achieved. Under these circumstances of structural strain (anomie), many people experience what seem to be blocked legitimate opportunities. In response to the continuing demand to achieve, they turn to illegitimate means. Put simply, they cheat. Whether they cheat alone or with others is what distinguishes Merton's theory from the ideas of subcultural strain theorists, who see the adaptive response as a collective enterprise.

HUMANS, HUMAN NATURE, AND HUMAN BEHAVIOR

In strain theory humans are seen as rational actors, not in the utilitarian sense of having "free" will, but as actors whose *choice* of behavior is influenced by societal

---

[4]In Merton's analysis *means* refers to the methods and resources used to achieve goals. There are legitimate means, such as education, competing for employment, and saving toward financial security, and there are illegitimate means, such as working off-the-books, dealing drugs, evading taxes, and so forth. We shall see later that others have interpreted the concept of means more liberally than we present it here. Merton originally wrote his essay, "Social Structure and Anomie" in 1938. Later he expanded on the original essay and compiled a number of his publications in a volume entitled *Social Theory and Social Structure,* which was published in 1957. This volume was revised and enlarged in 1968. Here we draw from all three sources.

structures, cultural definitions, and interactive processes. According to Young (1981: 281) strain theorists look at humans as "rational problem solving individuals placed in determined frameworks." Thus, the extent of "choice" is an open question since strain theory's recognition of agencies capable of socializing individuals, such as the media, family, school, or peers, can imply that humans are the subject of manipulation and that choice is a token one.[5]

Humans, then, are deemed capable of learning society's objectives and values (cultural goals) and of internalizing these through a socialization process that goes on within the different strata of society. They thus begin life as rational but social blanks, open to cultural prescription and influence, moldable with regard to the objects of their attention. As Empey and Stafford (1991: 227) say, "Strain theory assumes that people are either inherently social at birth or that human nature is the product of interaction in intimate groups." For Durkheim human appetites are present from birth and are naturally insatiable,[6] but can be heightened or diminished by the *social structure.* Even though Durkheim believed that some are born defective and are incapable of socialization, these persons are in a minority. The majority are subject more to structural conditions than to forces from within. In Merton's reformulation of Durkheim, the appetites of individuals are *culturally* rather than structurally induced (Bartollas and Dinitz, 1989: 170; see also Martin et al., 1990: 218).

Thus, as in individual positivism (Chapters 4 and 5), people are subject to forces, but in this perspective the forces lie primarily in the organization of society and its allocation of resources and opportunities, rather than within the person. This idea is seen in strain theorists' assumptions that societal processes directly impinge on humans to drive or pressure them in specific directions. Thus a sociological positivism replaces the rejected biological and psychological positivism.

A revised strain theory, however, developed by Agnew (1985; 1991a; 1991b; 1992; and Agnew and White, 1992) implies somewhat different assumptions about human nature that are more akin to a behaviorist pain-pleasure principle. Agnew introduces the notion that humans can gain pleasure in their pursuit of a variety of goals, but they can also experience frustration and anger in their attempts to avoid pain, especially if their opportunities to avoid pain are blocked. Agnew adds a psychological reactive element to the model of humans with his incorporation of ideas on personal stress, frustration-aggression, and behavioral learning (Agnew, 1992). Agnew also diverges from the goal-directed behavior of traditional strain theory by introducing the social-psychological

---

[5]See Beirne and Messerschmidt (1991: 378), especially on the "choice" of conformists in Merton's theory. See p. 159 ff of this chapter.

[6]This assumption, consistent with Hobbesian theory, leads to the development of control theory that we discuss in the next chapter.

notion of equity and justice in human interaction: "Individuals do not necessarily enter into interactions with specific outcomes in mind, but rather with the expectation that a particular distributive justice rule will be followed" (Agnew, 1992: 55). He points out that the traditional strain literature focuses on the individual's outcomes and goal pursuit, whereas the notion of "equity" suggests that the individual's inputs also have to be considered. Individuals who assess their own ability to accomplish outcomes as limited are likely to accept limited outcomes as fair. Conversely, those who assess their own abilities as expansive are likely to see limited outcomes as unjust. Moreover, this is a comparative process with reference to those with whom one interacts in significant relationships. This is an important modification of traditional strain theory, since it acknowledges that societal-level forces that may cause strain may not universally apply because they can be modified by individual and interpersonal assessments.

VIEW OF SOCIETY AND THE SOCIAL ORDER

From the strain perspective society has three major elements: a structure, a culture, and a system of maintaining order. The structure is comprised of both classes and institutions. It is seen as a system of interrelated parts that function to maintain the whole in a state of balance. Certain needs and requisites must be fulfilled for society to function in an orderly manner and to maintain equilibrium. Society is perceived to function like a machine whose interrelated parts make coherent operation possible. Adler et al. (1991: 110) give a good illustration: "Imagine a clock with all its parts finely synchronized. It functions with precision. It keeps perfect time. But if one tiny weight or small spring breaks down, the whole mechanism fails to function properly." However, unlike a machine, such as a clock, society as a system is capable of making adjustments to correct states of structural imbalance. The metaphor is that of an organism whose various components function to sustain the whole. Thus component social institutions, such as the family, education, religion, law, and so forth, are seen as functional equivalents in maintaining the life of the whole society (Parsons, 1937). Should any institution fail to perform its function or no longer be capable of carrying it out, another institution will fill the void. In this way society maintains itself in equilibrium.

Moreover, from this perspective all societal phenomena serve some function, otherwise they would not exist. Without implying that each societal process is necessarily intrinsically socially acceptable, any lasting societal process is deemed to serve some functional purpose (serves "manifest functions"), and, as we shall see later, this is also true for crime, which, although undesirable in itself, serves certain "latent functions" (Merton, 1961). The terms *manifest functions* and *latent functions* have a special meaning in this context. *Manifest* refers to a function that has an outcome that is its clearly intended purpose. For example, one of the manifest functions of the police is to arrest lawbreakers. However, the very existence of a police force may have the unintended consequences of creating situations in which bribery and corruption become possible. This, in turn, may allow the police to "license" informally key informers, who provide a stable flow of convictions (Klockars, 1974; Henry, 1977). Thus an unintended latent function of the existence of a formal police force is the stabilization of a "professional" class of offenders.

In general, the social order is perpetuated through the process of socialization that inculcates members into the basic culture and into its associated norms and standards of behavior. The culture comprises established goals and central values aimed at producing an overall desirable outcome. Traditional strain theorists assume that a moral consensus exists concerning these values and goals. For example, culture for Cohen (1955) refers to commonly shared knowledge, beliefs, values, codes, and tastes that are patterned and perpetuated over time. Examples of what he depicts as core values include ambition, individual achievement, working hard, thinking and planning ahead, being polite, controlling aggression, deferring gratification, and respecting others' property. Through interaction within the family and other social institutions, societal members become aware of the norms and values stressed within that society and thus become the bearers and perpetuators of the system.

However, there is disagreement among strain theorists about both the degree of consensus and the nature of legitimate norms and values, especially when they become translated into shared culturally defined goals. Referring to the United States, Merton's classical strain theory is held to have a narrow set of common goals embodied in the pursuit of the "American Dream." The most prominent of the goals making up the American Dream is "monetary success." Cohen (1955) and Cloward and Ohlin (1960) recognize a greater diversity of goals, including middle-class lifestyles, status symbols, and even the possibility of the inverse or alternatives to these, as peer-defined prestige goals replace societally defined cultural goals. These "subcultural" versions of strain thus recognize the potential for conflict, rather than consensus of goals, as different strata, classes, or groups formulate their own subcultural variations on the so-called general consensus.

In contrast to what Agnew describes as these "classic strain" perspectives, "modern strain theorists" such as Elliott et al. (1979, 1985) assert that "adolescents pursue a variety of different goals that vary from adolescent to adolescent and from group to group" (Agnew, 1991b: 279). These goals also differ, depending on whether they are achievable immediately or in the long range and whether more than one goal is held simultaneously. For adolescents, goals may include such things as educational attainment, peer group popularity, and being liked by the opposite sex. Indeed, the "revised" strain theory of Agnew recognizes that, rather than an emphasis on a single goal of materialism or status and prestige,

there exist a diversity of goals that might include those providing more immediate satisfaction. That for adolescents important goals are "popularity with
peers, good grades, doing well in athletics, and getting along with parents,"
says Agnew (1985: 153) "allows strain theory to explain middle class delinquency." It is worth pointing out, as do Williams and McShane (1988: 63), that
although Merton is characterized as focusing on the most prominent goal, material success, he used this only to have "a consistent example throughout his
work." He recognized the possibility of diverse goals, and was more concerned
with "extreme emphasis on achievement ... whatever the character of the goals"
(Merton, 1968: 220).

A major consideration in the view of society held by strain theorists is the
nature of social order. Theorists taking the strain perspective recognize the existence of both classes and groups in the constitution of society but disagree about
the importance of their role. Strain theorists envisage a crude and overlapping
hierarchical class system, with classes differentiated by wealth, by access to the
means to obtain wealth, and by social status. Theorists, such as Merton refer to
lower classes and working-class strata, but for others like Cohen, class is little
more than a status hierarchy of families. The classical strain theorists tend to give
a greater role to "class" position and class inequality in differentially structuring
the opportunities available, than do the modern and revised versions. The latter
tend to emphasize group, gender, race and ethnicity, and other subcultural, structural, and even situational components in their analyses.[7] For example, Agnew
(1991b: 282) talks of an "aversive situation" for adolescents, which may include
the following indicators of "environmental adversity":

> (1) the extent to which parents scream, slap, threaten, nag, ignore and withdraw
> love privileges; (2) the extent to which teachers lose their tempers, make negative
> comments and talk down to students; (3) the extent to which students find school
> boring and a "waste of time." (Agnew, 1991b: 282)

Agnew's revised strain theory also implies that there is a diversity in the distribution of power within the social structure that is based on grounds other than
class, such as gender or age. Thus adolescents, for example, are considered more
constrained by institutional structures than, say, adults, and that, as a result, have
goals that are directed to the avoidance of pain rather than achieving pleasure:

> One of the distinguishing features of adolescents is that they lack power and are
> often compelled to remain in situations which they find aversive. They are com-
> pelled to live with their family in a certain neighborhood; to go to a certain school;

---

[7]To be fair, Cohen (1955: 137–47) earlier acknowledged these different structural dimensions,
in particular, gender, which, when combined with class, results in different cultural goals for boys
and girls.

and, within limits, to interact with the same group of peers and neighbors. (Agnew, 1985: 156)

From this two consequences follow. First, cultural goals are likely to be diverse and include activities such as escape from pressure and having fun in walking out of situations ("exiting"). Second, social institutions, such as the family, may not be as functional as traditional strain theory assumes.

However, in all these versions of strain theory there is little attempt to relate the analysis to the wider structural context, as in Durkheim's linking of anomie as a general moral deregulation to the transformation of society after the Industrial Revolution or even Merton's connection of strain to the Depression of the 1930s.

THE ROLE OF LAW, THE DEFINITION OF CRIME, AND THE IMAGE OF THE CRIMINAL

For Durkheim, law represents the expression of society's collective consciousness, whereas for Merton it is the formalization of institutionalized norms, the means of integrating the members of society, and the mechanism for maintaining social order and resolving conflicts. Structural functionalists are less concerned with the creation of law or the reason for its existence than with its institutional role in society, which for Parsons (1937) was, like religion, "integrative." New laws are seen as a reflection of societal values, which often lag behind cultural-structural change. Though some functionalists see law as open to change, others, particularly some systems theorists, see law as a self-referential, self-sustaining, autonomous system that resists external influence. The latter view reflects the functionalist's idea that law serves a stabilizing function, resisting the effects of attempts at sudden or dramatic change, although it also suggests that what is stabilized is the institution of law itself, rather than the wider social structure.[8] This does not imply that strain theorists subscribe to an overly determinist vision of law. Rather, law provides the basic framework within which the friction of day-to-day interaction is minimized.

Generally strain theorists take the substantive law as a given, "the will of the people" (rather than adopting the classical ideas that law is the command of a sovereign power formulated as independent and logically consistent rules). For example, Holman and Quinn (1992: 219) observe, when interpreting Merton's anomie, that the "acceptable means of attaining goals are determined by *regulatory norms* ... The most important of these regulatory norms are enacted as laws in modern societies." The main focus, however, is not with law but with why certain populations choose not to follow the law. One of the major theoretical and

---

[8] See especially Teubner (1988). For a discussion of the different approaches taken by systems theorists to law and for a critique of autonomous self-referentiality, see Evan (1990).

conceptual weaknesses of strain theory is its neglect of what constitutes law and crime.

A number of assumptions have been made about the nature of crime by strain theorists. It is important to remember in reviewing these assumptions that reference is to crime as a phenomenon, not to individual criminality, a concept that Merton, like Durkheim, had rejected as a basis for theoretical analysis (Merton and Ashley-Montagu, 1940). Moreover, in the revised versions of the theory, crime typically means conventional "street crime" as measured by official statistics. Further, even when the definition of crime is expanded to include "white-collar crime" as in Agnew's (1991b) analysis, no attention is paid to *how* definitions of crime in law are constructed and why some groups' illegitimate opportunities are defined as "less serious" than others. As we shall see later (in our evaluation), this omission considerably affects the usefulness of much of the researchers' attempts to test the theory.

One of the most interesting discussions on the nature of crime from the structural strain perspective lies in Durkheim's assertion that crime is a normal feature of society. In his *Rules of Sociological Method,* first published in 1895, Durkheim writes:

> [Crime] is an inevitable though regrettable phenomenon arising from the incorrigible wickedness of men; it is to assert that it is a factor in public health, an integrative element in any healthy society. (Durkheim, 1982: 98)

He argues, further, that crime is normal because it is impossible for a society to exist without it.

> Crime ... consists of an action which offends certain collective feelings which are especially strong and clear-cut. In any society, for actions regarded as criminal to cease, the feelings that they offend would need to be found in each individual consciousness without exception and in the degree of strength requisite to counteract the opposing feeling. (Durkheim, 1982: 99)

Were this possible, he argues, there would still be crime; it would merely be of a different form. Even in the most moralistic of societies crime would still be present.

> Imagine a community of saints in an exemplary and perfect monastery. In it crime as such will be unknown, but faults that appear venial to the ordinary person will arouse the same scandal as does normal crime in ordinary consciousness. (Durkheim 1982: 100)

In Durkheim's view, no society is such that everyone is alike or thinks alike because we all have different biological makeups and we occupy different areas in space. Hence some divergence is inevitable. This, however, must be seen as a positive feature since it allows for creativity and social change. All societies must allow for some deviance to prevent stagnation. Some crime, therefore, becomes inevitable. Crime is *necessary* for societal change. Durkheim uses the example of Socrates, who, according to Athenian law, was rightfully condemned. "However, his crime—his independence of thought—was useful not only for humanity but for his country." Thus crime may serve the purpose of going beyond the status quo and "prepare a way for a new morality. ..." (Durkheim, 1938: 71)

Obviously not all crime is of this nature; it is the principle that deviation from accepted norms can bring about change that is important. Indeed, Durkheim argued that if the rate of crime in a society were to drop precipitously this would be cause for concern, because it would mean that the society had become too authoritarian and did not allow for sufficient deviance for its own ability to adapt to change. On the other hand, a rate of crime that exceeded normal expectations might also indicate that something was amiss in the structure of social relations. Durkheim's functional rebel indicated a type of deviance that signaled problems within the social structure, such as the continued presence of hereditary positions in a society that allowed social mobility based on ability.

Crime, then, is also a barometer or indicator of broader social conditions. Though certainly disturbing in the individual case, as a phenomenon it is like pain, an unpleasant experience but normal and necessary to indicate a condition needing attention. Death in the individual case is a tragic event, but it is normal for society. Durkheim perceives crime in a similar way.

Merton's view continues this sense of the normalcy of crime. However, his strain theory sees it as a normal response to an abnormal situation: an adaption or adjustment to societal contradictions. As Empey and Stafford (1991: 227) observe: "It also sees delinquency as an expression of conformity to shared values and standards" and explainable "by values that all Americans share be they young or old, black or white, lower or middle class." For Merton, then, most criminals are not different from noncriminals. They are simply those who have followed society's goals but have been frustrated in their attempt and so have deviantly adapted to their structural situation of strain.

CAUSAL LOGIC

For Durkheim the cause of crime is both in the individual and in society. Durkheim developed the concept of "anomie" that would prove to be highly influential in later formulations concerning structural-functional explanations of crime and deviance. In his work on suicide, *anomie* (deriving its meaning from a Greek term meaning "lawlessness") describes a state of "normlessness" or "rudderlessness"[9] that arises when there is a disruption in the ongoing social order, such as sudden shifts in the economy like depression or recession or, conversely, when there is high inflation. At these junctures of rapid social change, Durkheim reasoned, the control mechanisms of social norms are no longer effective. They have lost their meaning. The result is that normative checks on personal ambitions are no longer operative. The unanticipated personal upheavals that are caused by these societal conditions may lead to suicide or other deviations. Society, under such circumstances, is in a state of disruption that affects individual behavior because the controlling mechanisms of society cease to curb aspirations. For Durkheim, then, anomic conditions *create* a loss of control over preexisting aspirations, which become unlimited and result in a disjunction between these now rampant ambitions and the possibility of achieving them.[10]

Durkheim observes this tendency within individuals who pursue aspirations for self-satisfying ends with little regard for others, but he says this is magnified by industrial societal cultures that ignore or deemphasize the moral and the collective whole, and do not replace it with a substitute. Thus the cause of crime for Durkheim is a combination of (a) the breakdown of the traditional moral structures of the family, kinship networks, the community, and traditional values of deference to authority; (b) a "forced" (rather than "spontaneous") division of labor; (c) the celebration of the individual or the "cult of individualism"; and (d) the failure to adapt the social structure fast enough to accommodate rapid social change. The result is that

> From top to bottom of the ladder, greed is aroused without knowing where to find ultimate foothold. Nothing can calm it, since its goal is far beyond all it can attain. Reality seems valueless by comparison with the dreams of fevered imaginations; reality is therefore abandoned, but so too is possibility abandoned when it in turn becomes reality. A thirst arises for novelties, unfamiliar pleasures, nameless sensations, all of which lose their savor once known. (Durkheim, 1951: 256)

Merton also recognizes that the cause of crime stems from both the individual and social structure. Merton and subsequent strain theorists reflect this idea in their view that crime is one of a range of normal, albeit deviant, adaptions to

---

[9]Other commentators have variously interpreted the meaning of anomie. A good summary is provided by Masters and Roberson (1990: 137): "fragmentation or disassociation from one's center; atomization; the feeling of being a number, not a person; rootlessness; aimlessness; frustration; normlessness; hopelessness; collective sadness; social isolation; or social loneliness." Anomie is not, therefore, merely the absence of norms but a state in which normative guidelines cease to be meaningful and where the social order fragments. For an extended treatment of the anomie concept see Mestrovic and Brown (1985), Olsen (1965), and Horton (1964).

[10]For Merton, however, anomie is the *outcome,* not the cause, of a disjunction between aspirations and the opportunity for achieving these.

structural strain. In his 1938 work Merton aimed "to discover how some social structures *exert a definite pressure* on certain persons in the society to engage in non-conforming conduct rather than conformist conduct" (Merton, 1938: 672, our emphasis). Observers agree that for Merton and classical strain theorists the greater weight of the explanation for crime and deviance is to be seen in the structure, not the individual. As Young (1981: 281) asserts, strain theorists reject "the notion that crime arises from innate drives or instincts of the individual," while Empey and Stafford (1991: 228) say of Merton: "Humankind is not, by nature, inherently deviant. Deviant impulses are socially induced." Indeed, Bartollas and Dinitz (1989: 171) suggest that in Merton's theory "the drive to commit crime lies in culture rather than human nature." And for Adler et al. (1991: 110) strain theories "focus on the social forces that cause people to engage in criminal activity."

As we have said earlier, Merton's concept of anomie is somewhat different from Durkheim's and incorporates some aspects of Durkheim's concept of egoism. In general, Merton accepts the normality of crime and agrees with Durkheim, that modern industrial society creates the conditions that make both crime and a variety of other social ills possible. However,

> Merton shifts *his* meaning of anomie away from a Durkheimian position towards one which is peculiarly his own. Initially, Merton appears to be discussing the *emphasis on normative means* of achieving cultural goals ... However, later in his analysis, Merton appears to shift the focus of his attention away from an *emphasis on normative means to differential access to opportunity structures,* such as schools and employment organizations, through which cultural values can be properly and legally realized ... The emphasis upon normative means is Durkheimian because, by implication, it suggests that human aspirations have to be regulated and channelled ... the trick of social control was not to give people what they want ... but to persuade them that what they have is about all they morally deserve. When ... people were not persuaded about the priority of certain behaviors, then society could be conceptualized as anomic ... Merton needed to transform [Durkheim's] conception of anomie; he did this by shifting from an under-emphasis on normative means to a discussion on the differential access to legitimate opportunity structures ... Anomie was no longer a condition of deregulation or normlessness, but one of *relative deprivation.* Individual motivation behind deviant behavior emerged out of the frustration of such deprivations. (Box, 1981: 97–99)

According to Box, Merton's adaption of Durkheim's formulation of anomie enabled him to make it consistent with his beliefs about a modern democratically organized society, and especially about the distribution of crime in such a society, which he believed was a lower-class phenomenon.

Using the United States as his example, Merton points to an emphasis on common goals such as "material success" or "financial success" in a culture that induces all to aspire to them. This common cultural goal is promoted by societal institutions through parents, schools, government proclamations about the

"American Dream," and through advertisers and the media. Thus, he says, "A cardinal American virtue, "ambition," promotes a cardinal American vice, "deviant behavior" (Merton, 1957: 146). The primary emphasis of ambition in Merton's formulation are economic goals, particularly monetary success.

> It would of course be fanciful to assert that accumulated wealth stands alone as a symbol of success just as it would be fanciful to deny that Americans assign it a place high in their scale of values. In some large measure money has been consecrated as value in itself ... [however] acquired, fraudulently or institutionally, it can be used to purchase the same goods and services. (Merton, 1968: 190)

This is reflected in the popular culture, nowhere better perhaps than in the pop star Madonna's "material girl" living in a "material world." Indeed, the media, including television, billboards, movies, and magazines push the value of material wealth as a desirable goal and inculcate a "powerful emotional investment in that goal" (Conklin, 1989: 210). Conklin (ibid.: 209) explains how this occurs:

> Television commercials urge consumers to spend money on goods and services that will bring them happiness. Sometimes the message to consume is more subtle. For instance, the large kitchens that are shown in television commercials for dish soap, scouring pads, and floor wax can be found in homes that only a small proportion of Americans can afford. Television viewers may vaguely sense being disadvantaged because the kitchens they see in television commercials are so much better than their own; they may even begin to hope that they will someday have enough money to afford a home with such a kitchen, which seems to them to be "just an average American kitchen."

The reality, however, is that not everyone is so situated that they have the opportunity to attain such goals through legitimate routes, which traditionally involve hard work, deferred gratification, prudence, and personal sacrifice until such rewards have been saved up or earned via prescribed means such as education and occupational mobility. Sanders gives an excellent illustration of how, in Merton's reformulated concept of anomie, the structural source of this strain bears down differently on persons at different positions in the class structure:

> For example, if a wealthy man wants to start a new business, he has a variety of resources at his disposal in order to do so; the necessary financial backing, contacts, and the information required for a successful transaction. The poor man, on the other hand, will have difficulty in obtaining both the required financial means, and the necessary contacts to ensure success. This is not to say that it is

impossible for a poor man to start a new business and prosper in it, it is simply more difficult, and compared to the rich man, it entails a greater chance of failure. This has nothing to do with either's frame of reference, personalities or intelligence—it is simply a matter of their different situations via the social structure. (Sanders, 1983: 98)

One only has to add gender and race stratification together with child-care responsibilities to this picture to appreciate the structural difference in people's "available means" or opportunities. As Conklin (1989: 209) observes: "Racial discrimination in education and employment makes access to the institutional means of achieving success difficult for blacks and other minorities." Indeed, some feminist commentators have suggested that, because much of strain theory does not address these differences but only vaguely those of class, it does not apply to women and cannot explain their rule-breaking activity (Leonard, 1982).

The disjunction between the culturally induced aspirations and the structurally limited opportunities to attain them causes strain, and its resolution can lead to deviance (Merton, 1968). It is this strain which Merton refers to as anomie: "Contemporary American culture appears to approximate the polar type in which great emphasis upon certain success-goals occurs without equivalent emphasis upon institutional means" (Merton, 1968: 190). To Merton, then, the root cause of the strain leading to deviance lies not in the individual but in the disjunction between the culturally induced aspirations and the structurally available opportunities to attain them. Thus it is not only on occasions of societal upheaval that deviance occurs, as Durkheim asserted, but continually, as a result of disjunctions in society which affect individuals differentially at all times. In Merton's version of strain, this disjunction is experienced more prominently, though not exclusively, by those in the lower class, whose structural routes to opportunity are severely constrained. An additional complication affecting both aspirations and *perceived* opportunities is the institution of "credit," which deludes most people into believing that they do, in fact, have the means for immediate gratification. When the reality of "payments" consumes what little legitimate means they had previously possessed, the strain is intensified.

To resolve the strain-induced frustration Merton indicates five types of adaptation individuals can make, four of which are deviant. He emphasizes that these adaptations are the result of a limited set of choices made available by one's position in the social structure. After we consider Merton's five adaptions and point out how the collective and revised versions of strain theory differ from these, we shall discuss the variations and subdivisions of these types described by Dubin (1959) and Simon and Gagnon (1976).

Conformity is the first of Merton's modes of adaption to strain. It is the nondeviant adaptation that, he argues, is the most common since the stability and continuity of society could not otherwise be maintained. Here persons accept both the societal goals and the legitimate means to obtain them, even if the goals remain out of reach. As an example, this category includes those who strive to achieve the symbols of material success, such as cars, houses, stereos, VCRs, and so forth, who may not be successful but who do not deviate; instead such persons may take on second and third jobs to try to achieve their goals or to "make their payments." Alternatively, they may lower their expectations, distinguishing between ideal goals and realistic expectations (Agnew, 1991b). Importantly, the acceptable legitimate means to achieve these ends can be different, depending on gender, race, and ethnicity. A man might be expected to pursue a lucrative profession in order to obtain wealth, whereas, until recently a woman could only be expected to meet the same end through the pursuit of a potentially lucrative man (Leonard, 1982). In Cohen's (1955) interpretation of *collective* responses to strain, conformity is seen in the "college boy" subculture through which some working-class youth, although the odds are stacked against them, struggle to achieve the aspirations of middle-class economic and social status.

Innovation is the second and most discussed form of adaptation. Here persons have assimilated the emphasis on culturally defined goals but have not internalized them, or do not accept that they are limited only to the approved or institutionalized means to obtain these. This is the adaptation leading to most forms of economic crime. Merton sees this as largely, though not exclusively, a problem for the lower class.

> [I]ncentives for success are provided by the established values of the culture and second, the avenues available for moving toward this goal are largely limited by class structure to those of deviant behavior. It is the combination of the cultural emphasis and the social structure which produces intense pressure for deviation. (Merton, 1968: 199)

As Sanders (1983: 95) points out, those lower-class members who become innovators "started the race from far in the back, and by the time they neared the goals through legitimate channels, all of the positions were filled. However there was still emphasis on success, and so illegitimate routes were taken." Examples of the behaviors resulting from this deviant adaptation can include classic street crimes, such as theft, burglary, shoplifting, and urban drug dealing but such adaptation also accommodates the occupational embezzler; "stock frauds and tax evasion schemes of the rich" (Siegel, 1989: 169), the underground economy employer; as well as the corporate price fixer, who uses illegal means to maintain a competitive edge and increase corporate profits.[11] Moreover, Merton claims that the persistence of successful forms of innovation "enlarges the extent of anomie within the system" (Merton, 1968: 234), as others who originally conformed, abandon their adherence to conventional means and themselves resort to innovation (Siegel, 1989: 169).[12]

Merton's innovative adaption has largely been interpreted as an individual response to structural strain. But others, notably Cohen (1955), rejected it as applicable to what he saw as the largely nonutilitarian nature of juvenile crime and deviance. Similarly, Cloward and Ohlin (1960) saw innovation as highly relevant to some juvenile delinquency. But each also saw these modes of adaption as *collective* responses to structural strain. Cloward (1959), for example, points out that the subcultural collective definition of available means by those who perceive themselves defined as failures by the system is also dependent on the available *illegitimate* opportunities in a given area.

Ritualism is the third adaption identified by Merton. It refers to a deemphasis, scaling down, or relinquishment of the cultural goals of success and upward mobility and to an overemphasis on the institutionalized means. It is a reaction to severe competition or a realization that "lofty goals of great pecuniary success" (Merton, 1938: 273) may never eventuate and one's aspirations may have been unrealistic. "But though one rejects the cultural obligation to attempt to get ahead in the world," "though one draws in one's horizon, one continues to abide almost compulsively by institutional norms" (Merton, 1968: 204). In a society where considerable emphasis is placed on achievement and many fail, it is not surprising that ritualism is prevalent. Though it may be difficult to see that this in any way is deviant, Merton argues that since the culture demands a striving toward its goals such as material success, their relinquishment as in "getting by," "working just to survive," or "not taking chances," rather than striving to "get ahead," is a deviant adaptation. Examples would be those who "go by the book" and always "play it safe" in organizations or who in general consider the rules and routines more important than the goals the organization is supposed to meet. This might include the insistence on strict manners or customs that serve no purpose (Siegel, 1989: 169). An extremely mischievous version of this adaption might also include the law-abiding bureaucrat, such as a social security clerk or a state department transportation

---

[11]It is worth pointing out here that any particular crime can occur for a variety of reasons. Just because it has a common legal definition does not mean that the meaning structure of those who participate is the same. Thus only some of any one type of theft could be explained by innovative strain, just as only part of any one type of drug use may be explained by retreatism, discussed below (see Meier, 1989: 141–42). Holman and Quinn (1992: 219, 223), for example, suggest that Merton's approach is best equipped to explain instrumental crimes rather than expressive ones (e.g., theft rather than violence).

[12]This part of Merton's explanation has connections to social learning theory and particularly to Matza's (1964) neutralization (which we discuss in Chapter 8).

official who gains a perverse pleasure from forcing others to conform to the mindlessness of system rules. In its collective mode, ritualistic adaption might involve members of a labor union who "work strictly to rule," knowing that doing so cannot get them fired but neither will it maintain production levels.

Retreatism is a fourth mode of adaptation outlined by Merton. Retreatism refers to the abandoning of both the success goals of the culture and the institutionalized ways of achieving them. Persons in this category are the "dropouts" of society. The category includes *some* drug addicts, severe alcoholics, vagrants, psychotics, and others, who may have originally accepted the goals and means held out to them, but for a variety of circumstances have given up the struggle. Merton (1964) describes these types in the following manner:

> They are in society but not of it ... [They] piece out an existence by eating little, sleeping a lot, and abandoning the effort to create patterns of daily life they can respect ... Some finally succeed in annihilating the world by killing themselves. (Merton, 1964: 219)

The retreatist response may befall those who, for whatever reason, can neither make it in the legitimate opportunity structure, nor in the illegitimate. However, this does not preclude those failures from themselves joining together as a collective reaction to their situation. Cohen (1955), for example, describes the "corner boy" (and his subculture) who is defeatist and aware that he has failed or will fail to succeed by the standards of American culture and so retreats to his peer subculture. Here he finds emotional closeness, support, and activities, some of which may be marginally deviant but which are fatalistic rather than rational and goal oriented. Similar are Cloward and Ohlin's "retreatist" gangs who may adopt a drop-out drug culture lifestyle, indulging in promiscuous and risky sexual behavior, and in various unorganized survival activities such as hustling and pimping. Cloward and Ohlin argue that the membership of these gangs consists of those who either could not make it in the other two forms of gangs or who had an aversion to violence and theft. Affected by the disjunction between lack of opportunity and the mandate for achievement, they essentially "retreated" into drug use as a means of escape and solace.

Rebellion is the final mode of adaptation discussed by traditional strain theory. Here both the existing means and goals are rejected and replaced with new goals and means as attempts are made to build a new society within the existing social structure, but with a view to changing that structure. These attempts are typically collective, rather than individual. However, they may take several forms. In Merton's formulation the alternative form is that of the revolutionary or cult groups, characterized by deviance rather than crime, by symbolic but nonvictimizing acts of deviance. Examples might include the ecology movement, the sixties student movement, the seventies punk and new-wave movements, and the nineties rappers.

However, other theorists draw a more sinister picture of this form of adaption. According to Cohen (1955) delinquent subcultures form as a result of a hostile "reaction formation" to the strain experienced by lower-class youths. Unable to meet the standards set for them because of differences in their background, some lower-class youths experience "status frustration," which they resolve by turning middle-class standards upside down, forming a "delinquent subculture" that values instant gratification (short-term hedonism), fighting, and malicious, destructive delinquent behavior. He notes that "the delinquent's conduct is right by the standards of his subculture precisely because it is wrong by the norms of the larger culture" (Cohen, 1955: 28). Similar characteristics are also a feature of Cloward and Ohlin's "conflict gangs," whose members are angry at the humiliation they receive in the system. But unlike Cohen's delinquents, they blame the system rather than themselves for their failure. The result is a war against society through expressions of anger and fighting by whatever means are necessary to protect the gang's honor. Unlike the established illegitimate opportunity structure of the criminal gangs, conflict gangs are concerned with status through acts of violence, bravado, and the creation of a "hard and cool" image or reputation. The only means of achieving any self-worth is through the development of a macho "rep" through the threat and willingness to engage in violence; hence, the fighting gang.

It is important to recognize that, although Merton's concept of strain operates at the societal level and his idea of anomie "refers to a property of a social system" (Merton, 1964: 226), various renditions of strain conjure up different ideas of what it means, making the concept problematic. Perhaps the most dramatically different view sees strain as translating into a personal, psychological state; accordingly persons and groups can be in a state of "anomie." Here their members are seen as experiencing stress, tension, and frustration: "The strain is uncomfortable to the individual, who is likely to define it as a form of stress" (Holman and Quinn, 1992: 219). To distinguish this individual-level concept from Merton's structural-level one, Srole (1956) invented the term *anomia,* which refers to the personal experience of continually arriving at goals only to find these have moved or have, in the process of arriving, been replaced by new ones (Merton, 1964: 221; Martin et al., 1990: 223).

At the individual level, then, strain can be brought about by a failure to socialize adequately individuals to accept the legitimate means available to them, which facilitates their hedonism, for example, wanting instant gratification, "wanting it all now." Merton's theory also allows the possibility for the strain between means and goals to be the outcome of raised aspirations (without increased opportunity or with perceived increases in opportunity), which allows those with seemingly adequate means to experience strain. With these related concepts, middle- and upper-class deviance is also explainable, even though Merton was more concerned with the lower class. In either case the individual experience of structural strain is held to be frustration.

For several traditional strain theorists the major differences from Merton's ideas have to do with the nature of the response to strains in the structure. The response is seen as collective rather than individual. Thus for Cohen (1955) a key issue is the egalitarian ideology of meritocracy. This ideology claims that everyone regardless of class or status can compete for the same goals. However, because this clashes with the reality of inadequate means for certain sections of the population, it generates the conditions for delinquency among youth. The inadequate means are principally a lack of educational opportunity. This results from poor socialization, inadequate parental facilities and resources, excessive amounts of unstructured and unsupervised time, misunderstanding of what is required for adequate school preparation, and includes everything from impoverished community resources to the absence of books and educationally oriented toys in the home. This relatively impoverished socialization puts lower-class children at a disadvantage to their middle-class counterparts in the school system. The strain results when, expected to complete but unable to, lower-class individuals are defined as failures in school by standards that are not their own but those of the middle-class ("middle-class measuring rods"). These youths find themselves at the bottom of the legitimate educational status hierarchy. Since under the prevailing ideology of meritocracy everyone competes as individuals, it is they, as individuals, that have failed. Their failure is personal. The result is "status frustration," which is held to be a psychological state involving self-hatred, guilt, self-recrimination, loss of self-esteem, and anxiety. They resolve this personal crisis in various ways in conjunction with others by (1) redefining the values among similarly situated peers; (2) dismissing, disregarding, and discrediting "school knowledge;" and (3) by ridiculing those who possess such knowledge. In Cohen's view, then, the social structure and differential socialization produce status frustration, which forms the basis for a subculture, and the subculture becomes the solution to their frustration through its expression of delinquency. Empey and Stafford (1991: 231) capture the essence of Cohen's version of subcultural strain as a cause of deviance when they say:

> In short the delinquent subculture is a contra-culture, that is, a way of life opposed to everything conventional. As an alternative means of avoiding failure, achieving recognition and acquiring status, it rewards almost any behavior that attacks the morality of the middle class.

For Cloward and Ohlin (1960) the essence of the problem is that the opportunities to succeed in the legitimate system have been blocked and are seen by adolescents, not as their own fault but as the fault of the system. They know what is required to succeed in school but they know they cannot afford it and are ill equipped. Rather than internalizing their failure as personal, adolescents perceive this as an "injustice" and blame the system from which they with-hold their support (Box, 1981; Empey and Stafford, 1991: 232). Their collec-tive response, therefore, includes several ways of expressing or dealing with the frustration and anger stemming from their own analysis, one of which is proto-political protests aimed at correcting the situation. Differences in individual response stem from (1) differences in the kind of legitimate aspiration they hold, which may be for middle-class status and lifestyle and/or for increased eco-nomic success (Cloward and Ohlin, 1960: 90–94; Beirne and Messerschmidt, 1991: 403–404), and (2) from differences in the structure of existing illegiti-mate opportunities in their community. As Empey and Stafford (1991: 232) observe, "while Cohen's delinquents are irrational and malicious, the opposite of everything middle class, Cloward and Ohlin's law violators are rational and utilitarian." In *Delinquency and Opportunity* Cloward and Ohlin (1960), extend-ing Merton's conception, argued that the social structure is such that not only are the legitimate means to societal goals differentially distributed but that illegitimate means are equally unavailable to some.

In their research on youth gangs, Cloward and Ohlin were able to demon-strate that different types of gangs developed, depending on the type of neigh-borhood in which they arose. Thus, they referred to "criminal gangs," which arose in neighborhoods where there was a connection between theft-oriented gangs and various rackets through which successful gang members could pur-sue illegitimate careers. Only where an established and integrated stable crim-inal subculture existed would some juveniles be able to join this illegitimate opportunity structure. As Cloward and Ohlin (1960) argued, only through the "criminal subculture" would they be able to pursue rational criminal activ-ities to achieve the culturally defined success goals, and in this pursuit are steered away from "irrational" crimes such as violence which would threaten their success at illegal criminal enterprises.

Where these established criminal alternatives did not exist, their juvenile collective response to structural strain would take another form. Thus Cloward and Ohlin were able to demonstrate that not only are legitimate means differ-entially distributed through the social structure but also that *illegitimate* means are not available to everyone equally, either. A good illustration of this can be found in the differential resources people have to work in the underground or hidden economy, such that the "unemployed" are its least likely operatives (Henry, 1982; Pahl, 1984).

Finally, Agnew's recent revisions of strain theory also see anger and frus-tration as part of the causal chain leading to crime. Rather than being ratio-nally directed, however, this anger is more the outbursts of youth frustrated by the constraints of a wide range of painful constraining situations from which they may wish to escape but are only able to with peer support through delin-quent behavior.

It is worth briefly considering the theoretical extensions to Merton's original typology of adaptions, especially in the work of Dubin (1959) and Simon and Gagnon (1976). The latter is based on variation in commitment to cultural goals and the degree of progress toward achieving these. It results in nine types, which include: optimal conformist, detached conformist, compulsive achiever, conforming deviant, detached person, escapist, conventional reformer, missionary, and total rebel. Dubin's (1959) earlier extension begins with the argument that Merton does not allow for replacing the cultural goals while rejecting the means, nor for rejecting the goals while replacing the means. Thus he says the modes of adaption are underdeveloped by Merton. He argues that without acknowledging, for example, that innovators replace or substitute the means rather than simply rejecting them, it is not possible to see how they deviate. In addition Dubin distinguishes between norms and means, norms being the specifications of acceptable behavior in a particular situation, whereas means are the actual behaviors contained within the limits set by norms. These two distinctions allow for the possibility of six types of innovator, three of which are "behavioral innovators," who accept cultural goals but replace either or both the norms and means, as do three types of "value innovator," who also replace the goals. Likewise there are six types of ritualist, three of which are "behavior ritualists," who as well as rejecting the goals may accept both norms and means or accept either one while rejecting the other, as do three types of "value ritualist" who also accept rather than reject the culturally defined values. Together with the original retreatist and rebellion adaptions, Dubin's typology contains a total of fourteen types, which he claims account for a greater range of deviance. Most notable here is his category of constructive or positive deviance. However, the resulting complexity of Dubin's extension might account for the very limited attention it has received in the literature (but see Martin et al., 1990: 224–27).

Whether an individual reacts individually or collectively, the form of adaption that results is also affected by several factors other than those that emerge in research studies. It is not our purpose to evaluate the contribution of these factors here but simply to mention that the adolescent's individual skills and abilities, their degree of contact or isolation with delinquent others, the role of family and peers in providing approval, and the individual's intelligence and creativity and even appearance, all play a role. However, they are best considered as part of other theories such as differential association, social learning, and social control, which we discuss in the next chapter.

It is worth reiterating that each of these modes of adaption, whether individual or collective, are not mutually exclusive. Actual adolescents may respond in more than one of these ways simultaneously while being a member of several types of gang. Indeed, Agnew's revised strain theory is especially helpful here, pointing out that "adolescents may avoid strain by pursuing several goals at once so that, although they might not be able to achieve all their goals, they will be able to achieve some. And this may be enough to prevent serious strain and frustration" (Agnew, 1991b: 281). It follows that this pursuit may be facilitated by multiple gang or subcultural memberships, some of which might even include the "college" mode of conformity. Further such multiple memberships might facilitate pain–avoidance and thereby lessen frustration behavior that results from blocked opportunities in other arenas (legitimate or illegitimate).

CRIMINAL JUSTICE SYSTEM IMPLICATIONS

Overall strain theory is more concerned with changing the conditions in a society that lead to crime than with modifying or reforming the operation of the criminal justice system. It is enough that the criminal justice system is sensitive to the strains produced by the society leading to crime. While it cannot excuse or overlook criminal behavior, given the inequalities in society at large, the criminal justice system must be perceived as just and neutral in its dealing, especially with the lower-class offender. Thus strain theorists imply a relatively nonpunitive criminal justice system.

Criminal Justice Policy and Correctional Ideology

The correctional ideology is directed toward reforming the structure of society to reduce its strain, rather than toward individuals. It involves intervention to change the social structure. However, the kind of intervention required depends on whose analysis of the problem is adopted. The implications of Durkheimian theory are (1) that absent or weakened normative regulation must be reinstated through some form of moral community, and (2) steps should be taken to reduce or temper people's unlimited aspirations. As a result, Durkheim's theory is also appropriately classifiable as a version of control theory (considered in the next chapter).

The implications of Merton's analysis, in contrast, are that greater opportunities must be provided for people to employ legitimate mechanisms to reach the desired societal goals. This requires institutional changes to engender equal opportunities for those who find themselves in disadvantaged positions because of structural constraints. In the long run it requires the restructuring of society so that it becomes more egalitarian and "equal opportunity" becomes a reality. The theory lends itself to broad justice policy reform as a method to control crime (see discussion of crime control below). However, the scope of reform and change is limited by the implicit assumptions of the perspective that contemplates change only within the existing institutional relations.

The correctional ideology implied by Merton's strain theory embodies several justifications for intervention. Essentially it operates on two levels. Primarily it is preventative. Operating at the broader and intermediate levels of society, it aims to prevent the inequity in access to opportunity, by providing programs to better equip children to compete in the educational system to achieve societal goals. At the individual level it is treatment oriented: those who have deviated from society are to be subject to various programs designed to bring them back in and enable them to cope with the strain using legitimate rather than illegitimate means. As we shall see later, the resistance to change of the wider system, and the vulnerability of the powerless (both dimensions that are acknowledged components of the strain formulation) mean that individual programs to bring personal change received more attention than social programs to bring societal change.

Techniques of Crime Control

The preferred enforcement technique of strain theory is nonpunitive. The focus is on institutional- rather than personal-level intervention for those not yet involved in delinquency and training or retraining of those who have offended. In each case the object is to enable those most strained to have the skills needed to use the legitimate opportunities that may be available most profitably and allow them to compete on an equal footing. It is also important to demonstrate that gang behavior is counterproductive and that self-worth may be achieved through legitimate avenues once skills have been learned.

Several programs were developed during the 1960s' Kennedy–Johnson era to implement policy recommendations derived from Cloward and Ohlin's and Cohen's versions of subcultural strain theory. These also indirectly addressed some of Durkheim's concerns about the decline of community. Programs such as "Mobilization for Youth," the later "War on Poverty," and its associated initiatives "Head Start," "Job Corps," "Vista," "Neighborhood Legal Services," and the "Community Action Program" were designed to fulfill the largely preventative side of the policy. Mobilization for Youth, for example, addressed the lack of adequate family socialization by establishing Neighborhood Service Centers to provide counseling and other forms of assistance. It addressed the inadequacy of educational background by providing children with preschool programs and improved educational services. It encouraged adolescents who were already in gangs to participate in legitimate activities that were provided, such as Adventure Corps, and it addressed the fragmentation of communities by organizing through neighborhood councils and associations (Empey and Stafford, 1991: 235). Similarly, the Perry Preschool Project in Ypsilanti, Michigan, involved intensive teacher–student supervision aimed to develop skills among minorities which proved to double employment rates and college attendance, cut teen pregnancy in half, and reduce arrest rates by 40 percent.

EVALUATION

Strain theory found high acceptance initially, perhaps because of its intuitive appeal. Several commentators evaluated the theory positively. As Clinard expresses it, Merton's theory is "the most influential single formulation in the sociology of deviance in the last 25 years" and his original article is "possibly the most frequently quoted single paper in modern sociology" (Clinard, 1964: 10). It "has appeared more often in the footnotes and references of other works than any other" (Cole, 1975: 175) and is a work that "every sociologist has read"! (Livingston, 1992: 366). It has had "a tremendous impact" and has resulted in "numerous spin-offs" (Martin et al., 1990: 223).

However, theoretically there are several logical problems with strain analysis, not least those relating to imprecision and ambiguity. Major controversy has arisen, especially when the results of empirical research have been examined. Criticism focuses on strain theorists' use of an oversimplified class analysis from which they then deduce, based on official crime statistics, that the lower classes commit more offenses. Such a view omits middle-class crime or for that matter crimes of the powerful, regardless of their class. Moreover, Kornhauser (1978) claims that anomie is unnecessary to explain crime among the lower classes if, as Merton (and especially Cohen) argue, these sections of society are weakly socialized. Such persons are less likely to be constrained as a result of internalized social limits and therefore may deviate anyway, without feeling the strain that the more socialized experience. She concludes: "Merton's conception of cultural imbalance is neither viable nor true; it should be pruned from the causal structure of strain theory" (Kornhauser, 1978: 165).

As we have seen, some renditions of strain theory also assume that everyone strives for the same goals and shares common values. Lemert (1964) points out that pressure comes not by trying to conform to a consistent value order, but from the multiple allegiances to various groups which exert conflicting demands in a "value pluralistic" society. Similarly, Young (1981: 285) says the theory fails to recognize the "widespread existence of contradictions in value, cynicism, fatalism and disassociation from the major institutions—as well as outright rejection." Perhaps even more problematic is the failure of strain theory to consider the different situation of gender pressures. As Leonard (1982) enlightens us, women in our society have not traditionally been subject to cultural definitions to succeed at obtaining a well-paying job, but to marry and have a family.[13] Thus the consensus assumption that underlies all functional theories does not fit reality.

A related issue in the strain analysis has to do with understanding the key concepts of goals and means. Whereas most commentators agree that "goals" are the objects of rationally directed action toward an end, this determined by shared cultural values, they disagree about whether the goals are aspirations or expectations and whether they are long-term and general or short-term and specific. For example is a goal "money success" or is it the ambition to pursue that

---

[13]See further discussion of this point and other feminist issues in Chapter 11.

objective? There are also differences in the interpretation of "means." One view sees means as opportunities such as chances or options or offers; another describes them as resources, such as educational resources, or skills, and some see "means" as the "guidelines or rules they were to follow in their pursuit of the goals" (Sanders, 1983: 94). Further, some have argued that Merton's theory "is not logically adequate because steps are missing from his typology" (Bartollis and Dinitz, 1989: 173). Although Merton's original argument does not allow for replacing the cultural goals while rejecting the means, nor for rejecting the goals while replacing the means, these and other subcategories are apparent in later formulations that Merton subsequently accepted as an extension of his theory (Merton, 1959: 177–78). Thus we have seen, that the work of Dubin (1959) attempts to deal with this issue but at the cost of introducing considerable complexity.

A serious weakness of strain theory, especially the traditional version, is its underlying assumption that structural conditions *determine* human reaction to them without making allowance for human agency. Chapman (1977: 17) for example, taking a conflict approach, criticizes Merton for elevating culture to a place of permanent dominance over human agency in defining what is legitimate. This is dealt with more adequately, says Chapman, by distinguishing between types of goals and types of means, depending on whether these are personal, social, or cultural. Though Chapman's basic criticism is valid, his resulting nine-item typology has the same problems of complexity shown in Dubin (1959) and Simon and Gagnon (1976). Moreover, although the more recent revision of strain theory by Agnew (1992) seems to deal with the individual by its incorporation of social psychological concepts and individual inputs, it does this in such a narrow way that any notion of "agency" is reduced to a reactive response to stimuli. Any notion that meaning is socially constructed is displaced under the behaviorist pleasure–pain–reaction principles. More enlightened was Suchar's (1978: 90) observation that Merton's theory gives the actor "the appearance of a nonparticipating, acted-upon subject whose fate is a function of his position in the social structure" and that "anomie theory, in its various guises, has generally neglected the role of the actor in interpreting the meaningfulness of the constraints, pressures, and deprivations to which he is subject" (ibid.: 100).

Strain theory also sees deviance and normality as distinct categories, a view that overlooks the shifting boundaries between the two. Again Young's comments are instructive.

> Normality and deviance are not separate watertight categories of behaviour, nor does normal behaviour automatically precede ventures into deviance. Rather, at times, they blend together, are mistaken for each other or are irrevocably interwoven into the actual patterns of social behaviour. (Young, 1981: 285).

Although versions of the theory that emphasize the disjunction between aspirations and opportunities allow an explanation of white-collar and corporate crime, the emphasis in Mertonian versions of the theory remains on lower-class crime. This is because the theory contains little analysis of how crime is constructed by the powerful and is based on what is defined as legal rather than how some harm others, regardless of whether this is sanctioned in law.

In summarizing Merton's contribution to criminology, Gibbons (1992: 113) finds it "markedly long in the tooth":

> Merton put forth an abstract explanatory metaphor rather than a tightly reasoned, unambiguous set of propositions about deviance. The critics are surely correct in indicting him for failing to spell out the scope of the argument and for linking the categories of adaption to the social labels for deviance familiar in everyday life ... When we turn to the real world, we quickly discover that it is full of deviants whose activities fall outside the scope of the anomie formulation. (Ibid.)

Indeed, Gibbons says that although it has a "ring of plausibility" in explaining some property crimes, Merton's theory fairs poorly as an explanation for assaultive conduct and a myriad of other forms of crime and deviance. He concludes that on balance it is an incomplete theory of deviance whose critics have had the better of the exchange and "should be abandoned in favor of accounts that are free from the flaws plaguing his statement, but that continue to place economic influences at center stage" (ibid.: 114).

The major delinquent subcultural theories that were formulated within the strain framework have also received their share of criticism. Though many of the comments already mentioned apply equally to them, in turn these formulations have had their own critics. Spergel (1964) for example found a more complex system of gangs than Cloward and Ohlin presented. Kitsuse and Dietrick (1970), and Hirschi (1969), argued that it was difficult empirically to demonstrate Cohen's contention. Bordua (1961) and more recently Katz (1988) have made the argument that, contrary to Cohen's assertion about the nonutilitarian nature of delinquency, it can be exciting, thrilling, and nothing if not symbolically meaningful.

The policy implications of the social engineering program that emerged from the subcultural strain theories also demonstrated that there are severe limitations, given the existing economic structure, to providing long-term meaningful opportunities without making major societal changes (Young, 1981). Such reform, though perhaps achievable, is not readily accepted because it requires fundamental change that established sectors of the society are unwilling to accept. Efforts have focused on piecemeal solutions that concentrate on certain areas or neighborhoods without restructuring the whole. Some have argued that these efforts have largely failed because they did not go far enough in opening avenues for genuine success. Others, however, have argued that the wrong tactics have been used by people who lacked the political insight to anticipate the immense opposition to the activism many community action programs carried out: "One does not easily alter the basic structure of society—economically, politically, and socially—without incurring great opposition" (Empey and Stafford, 1991: 238). Moreover, too much was expected:

> Based on the romantic myth that members of delinquent gangs could transform the ghetto—from a place of misery, crime, and poverty to a place of enterprise, safety and economic well being—many of the nations newspapers, television networks, and fashionable leaders threw their support behind Youth Organizations United. They editorialized, idolized, and otherwise supported the notion that these uneducated, unskilled, even depredatory youths could lead the way in changing the slums. It was too much. (Ibid.: 237)

Perhaps the most illustrative of criticisms comes from Taylor (1971: 148):

> It is as though individuals in society are playing a gigantic fruit [i.e., slot] machine, but the machine is rigged and only some players are consistently rewarded. The deprived ones then either resort to using foreign coins or magnets to increase their chances of winning (innovation), or play on mindlessly (ritualism), give up the game (retreatism) or propose a new game altogether (rebellion). But in this analysis nobody appears to ask who put the machine there in the first place and who takes the profits. Criticism of the game is confined to changing the payout sequences so that the deprived can get a better deal (increasing the educational opportunities, poverty programs).

Finally, it is important to recognize a major failing of the policy implications drawn out by theorists is the concentration on the socioeconomic means or opportunity structure as a site of structural intervention. What has received almost no attention is the equally valid policy implication that deals with the cultural definition of societal goals or, more precisely, addresses *both* Durkheim's and Merton's ideas about raised aspirations. To do so would take the policy in a different direction since the site of intervention would be the cultural definitions of what is desirable, with the purpose of lowering unnecessary expectations of what is achievable. Crime control techniques in such a policy framework might involve limiting the extent to which corporations create demand for unnecessary consumption through advertising in the mass media. Controls might include laws minimizing advertising to informational claims, reducing the length of advertisements to one or two line announcements as currently occurs on Public Broadcasting Service sponsorship, and vigorously controlling *any* "hyping" of product that is not substantially supported by independent consumer research.

In spite of these and several other criticisms, strain theory remains a popular explanation. Soon after its abandonment in the late 1960s and 1970s, it was reintroduced, albeit as a weaker partner, in several "integrated" theories, such as those that combine strain with differential association and/or control theory (e.g., Elliott et al., 1985) or by those who sought to salvage aspects from Mertonian contamination (Cullen, 1984, 1988). As we have seen, however, it has recently undergone a revival and reassessment (Bernard, 1984) and now exists in a very new guise in the work of Agnew which some have suggested, "remove[s] the theory from its social structural context" (Farnworth and Leiber, 1989: 272). Indeed, some believe that Merton's theory has been "reborn" as "a viable and promising theory of delinquency and crime" (ibid: 273). Even accepting its limitations, strain theory at least can be commended for sensitizing us to structural conditions as a force in the genesis of certain forms of crime. It has dealt less well with the moral regulation aspect of Durkheim's analysis and its implications for social control. It is toward theory that draws out these dimensions that we turn in the next chapter.

CHAPTER EIGHT

Social Process Theories I: Learning, Bonding, and Social Control

In this chapter we turn to a group of theories whose focus is on social-psychological processes that develop over time in the course of social interaction. They are called "social process" theories because they explain the process by which crime occurs (Williams and McShane, 1988: 125). As Siegel (1989: 188) says,

> Social process theories hold that criminality is a function of individual social-ization and the socio-psychological interactions people have with the various organizations, institutions and processes of society ... all social process theorists share one basic concept: people in all walks of life have the potential to become delinquents or criminals ... Consequently, social process theorists focus their attention on the socialization of youths and attempt to identify the developmental factors—family relationships, peer influences, educational difficulties, self-image development—which lead them first into delinquent behavior then into adult criminality.

In this chapter we analyze those social process theories that take a relatively passive view of humans, seeing them as "social blanks" that can be shaped and influenced by the ways others treat them.[1]

Several theories are considered, including learning theories derived from operant conditioning; social learning theory, which claims that socialization takes place primarily among intimate groups; differential association, which suggests that learning to be criminal is no different from learning to conform; and the idea of becoming criminal through imitation and cognitive learning. (See Table 8-1.) We give particular emphasis to social control theory, which argues that learning is considerably affected by the strength of people's bonds to conventional role models. We contrast this with the position of neutralization theorists, who believe that bonds are present very early but that, subsequently, people learn how to erode them and free themselves from the moral inhibition not to break rules.

---

[1]In the next chapter we examine a group of social process theorists that take a more active view of human nature and who see humans as coproducers of their social worlds.

Table 8-1 RELATED THEORIES*

Social learning theory
Differential association theory
Reinforcement theory
Imitation theory
Neutralization theory
Drift theory
Social control theory
Containment theory
Bond theory

*Theories that take a perspective similar to or overlapping with the model that we develop in this chapter.

BASIC IDEA, CENTRAL MOTIF, AND MAJOR THEORISTS

Each of the different theorists considered here (see Table 8-2) argues that humans commit crime as a result of learning and socialization experiences with significant others. Learning is seen to be of two kinds. One kind refers to learning the range of ways that maintain an individual as conventional, rule-abiding, and conforming to society's laws. In its simplest behavioral version, based on Skinner's theory of operant conditioning (Skinner, 1953, 1971), humans are assumed to be rational responders to stimuli, avoiding pain and pursuing pleasure. As a result, they are said to be considerably affected by the consequences of their behavior. They can be conditioned through the manipulation of rewards and punishments, which reinforce conventional action and punish antisocial conduct. Criminologically this idea is reflected in Jeffery's (1965) theory of differential reinforcement, which recognized the differences in people's reinforcement history and the different meaning stimuli have to them. In the "socially oriented" learning approach of Akers (Burgess and Akers, 1966; Akers, 1985), social interaction in the social environment, particularly in subcultural groups,

Table 8-2 Theorists Using Social Learning and Control Explanations of Crime

THEORIST	MAJOR WORK[S]	DATE
	Social Learning	
Tarde	*The Laws of Imitation*	1890
Sutherland	*Principles of Criminology*	1939
Cressey	"The Differential Association Theory and Compulsive Crimes"	1954
	"The Theory of Differential Association: An Introduction"	1960

Jeffery	"Criminal Behavior and Learning Theory"	1965
Burgess and Akers	"A Differential Association-Reinforcement Theory of Criminal Behavior"	1966
Akers	*Deviant Behavior: A Social Learning Approach*	1985
Bandura	*Aggression: A Social Learning Analysis*	1973
	Social Learning Theory	1977

Neutralization

Mills	"Situated Actions and Vocabularies of Motive"	1940
Cressey	*Other People's Money*	1953
	"The Respectable Criminal"	1970
Sykes and Matza	"Techniques of Neutralization: A Theory of Delinquency"	1957
Matza and Sykes	"Juvenile Delinquency and Subterranean Values"	1961
	Delinquency and Drift	1964
Scott and Lyman	"Accounts, Deviance and the Social Order"	1970

Bonding and Social Control

Carr	*Delinquency Control*	1950
Reiss	"Delinquency as the Failure of Personal and Social Controls"	1951
Reckless	"Self-Concept as an Insulator against Delinquency"	1956
Dinitz and Murray	"A New Theory of Delinquency and Crime"	1961
Reckless	*The Crime Problem*	1955
Nye	*Family Relationships and Delinquent Behavior*	1958
Toby	"Social Disorganization and Stake in Conformity"	1957
Hirschi	*Causes of Delinquency*	1969
	"Crime and Family Policy"	1983
Gottfredson and Hirschi	*A General Theory of Crime*	1990
Krohn and Massey	"Social Control and Delinquent Behavior: An Examination of the Elements of the Social Bond"	1980
Krohn	"Control and Deterrence Theories"	1991

is seen as the major source of behavioral reinforcement. Akers's argument draws on and expands the earlier differential association theory of Sutherland (Sutherland, 1939; Cressey, 1954, 1960; Sutherland and Cressey, 1978). This theory describes the learning of knowledge, skills, rationalizations, and justifications that enable or facilitate rule-breaking activity by defining it as favorable and/or desirable.

More cognitive versions of social learning theory suggest that the mechanism of learning is strongly influenced by images and role models that are imitated and reproduced or played out (Tarde, 1890). Versions of this theory recognize the indirect nature of such role modeling through identification with images made through media presentations, especially those appearing on television and in film (Bandura, 1969, 1973, 1977). This debate over the media's role has recently been extended in both critical and postmodernist directions, in the course of which it has ceased to become the exclusive province of social learning theory (Surette, 1984; Barak, 1994).

Neutralization theory (Mills, 1940; Cressey, 1953; Sykes and Matza, 1957; Matza, 1964; Scott and Lyman, 1970) takes for granted that most people are socialized into conventional behavior. It assumes that what is learned is attitudes and devices, expressed in language and accounts, that temporarily free people from morality and conformity and that allow them to commit crime without moral qualms. Crime can thus become a behavioral option for people when their commitment to conventional values and norms is neutralized by excuses and justifications that render them morally free, but not compelled to break rules.

Control theory (Hirschi, 1969) makes the reverse assumptions to those made by both learning and neutralization theory. It assumes that most people are *already disposed* to nonconformity *unless* they receive protective socialization in the form of controls. Thus for control theorists what needs to be explained is not deviance and crime, but conformity. As in psychoanalytic personality theory discussed in Chapter 5,[2] social control theory argues that inadequate or ineffective external socialization can result in weak or absent internal controls over behavior. Moreover, we saw in the previous chapter that this idea was also implied in Durkheim's concept of anomie, whereby a sufficient level of moral integration through normative regulation is necessary for a society to contain its crime to "normal" levels. However, in the social process version of control theory the emphasis shifts to explaining how individuals' specific past patterns of social interaction protects them from their deviant inclinations. The theory is concerned with the ways in which relational ties between young people and adults result in some youths having respect for the values and norms of conventional adults. In an early version of social control theory, called containment theory (Reckless 1950; Reckless et al., 1956; Carr, 1950), it was argued that the formation of positive or negative "self-concepts" in young people could affect their "inner controls" over their personal biopsychological "pushes" and over

---

[2]Psychoanalytic theory and social disorganization theory are also classified as control theory by some criminologists. Thus Williams and McShane (1988: 110) say that Reiss's (1951) combination of psychoanalytic theory with Chicago School sociology to explain delinquency as the failure of internal and external controls "produced a social control theory which anticipated most of the later work." (See also Empey, 1982: 163, 263.)

universal environmental "pulls" toward rule-breaking behavior. However, Hirschi's (1969) version of social control through social bonding with conventional others has become the leading statement in the field. This theory focuses on the idea that social controls are learned through particular kinds of bonding processes in social relationships and that, were it not for these controls, we would all be lawbreakers. It implies that role modeling is important, especially of beliefs, values, and attitudes learned as a result of social bonds formed with conventional actors (e.g., parents, teachers, youth leaders) and conveyed through societal institutions. Control theorists see conformity as being induced in several different ways. We will consider some of these but will focus chiefly on the most cited and influential dimensions of bonding developed by Hirschi (1969) and by Gottfredson and Hirschi (1990). Finally, we shall examine the criminal justice implications of these theories which point to policies designed to recondition, reeducate, or rebond people to convention.

HUMANS, HUMAN NATURE, AND HUMAN BEHAVIOR

All learning theories assume a rational goal-seeking actor. However, there are three different assumptions about human nature made by these theorists that largely account for the different directions their theories have taken. Social learning and differential association theories assume that humans start out as social blanks *until* socialized into conforming social roles by primary groups such as families and friends. Beirne and Messerschmidt's (1991: 385) metaphor is illustrative: "The image of the social actor postulated by Sutherland is that of an empty vessel with no history, no beliefs, no preferences, and no capacity for choice." What people become is a product of social learning, of "tendencies poured into this human vessel" that lead it to engage in one type of action or another.

Learning can also occur in the same way in subcultural groups and peer groups, with a nonconforming (rule-breaking) outcome. However, learning theorists make no distinctions between offenders and nonoffenders in the process of learning. All are seen as following some kind of rules. Which rules they follow depends on which groups socialize them, what messages these groups send, and the methods they use. In addition to learning behaviors through intimate groups, people learn techniques and skills, motives, drives, attitudes, and rationalizations in interaction with others, that go beyond simple imitation or copying of others' behavior.

For neutralization theorists (e.g., Matza, 1964), people are assumed to have a considerable degree of self-determination, even willpower. Neutralization theory assumes that rational actors choose behavior out of moderately free will in a context of various degrees of commitment to established conventions. They may be influenced by a buildup of past experiences and be caught, for example, in a "mood of desperation" (wherein they experience some pressure), but they must choose to exercise their will in order to act. As a result of their ambivalent relation to conventional society, actors are believed to be capable of much moral ambiguity in their behavior. Rules and what is counted as acceptable behavior are open to interpretation and outcomes can be recast to suit the occasion at hand.

> Control theorists, in contrast, have an essentially Hobbesian view of human nature. They assume that human beings are born free to break the law, and will refrain from doing so only if special circumstances exist ... It is not part of control theory that humans are born wicked or evil ... instead they are perceived as being by nature morally neutral ... capable of engaging in a wide diversity of acts. (Box, 1981: 122)

Thus, like classicists, control theorists believe that humans are rationally calculating individuals who seek to satisfy their self-interests. They are motivated to commit deviant acts to obtain these interests, unless constrained. Indeed, referring to Bentham, the classical scholar, Gottfredson and Hirschi (1990: 5) state:

> all human conduct can be understood as self-interested pursuit of pleasure or the avoidance of pain ... It tells us that people behave rationally when they commit crimes and when they do not. It tells us that people are free to choose their course of conduct, whether it be legal or illegal. And it tells us that people think of and act first for themselves, that they are not naturally inclined to subordinate their interests to the interests of others.

Unlike classicists, however, control theorists assume that the diversity of behavior is limited by connections and bonds to others who are significant reference groups for them. This view of the importance of significant others they share with social learning theorists.

Within social learning and control theory, as with some other theories outlined in this text, human agency tends to be neglected in favor of a focus on a variety of means to keep humans in check to follow a prescribed societal course to conformity. Thus in their implied view of humankind there is little emphasis on human potential for *good* based on human action. Rather the emphasis is on the "evil" potential of human behavior that must be prevented from emerging.

VIEW OF SOCIETY AND THE SOCIAL ORDER

As in their treatment of human nature, the various theoretical strains make different assumptions about society. From the perspective of most social control theorists, society is based on a consensus of values and norms. It is also seen as a system of institutionalized conduct embodied in a dominant moral order that reflects this consensus. Institutions such as the family, the school, the justice system, and so forth, serve to inculcate the basic moral stance of the society and provide the mechanisms to control the individual. The family is given priority as the institution of choice to inculcate traditional social values through its socialization of children. The school is also considered an important institution and perhaps more expert in dealing with and implementing methods of discipline and control (Hirschi, 1983). Other social institutions come into play either to reinforce the family or provide formal controls where the family fails. Gottfredson and Hirschi (1990: 105), for example, believe that the school has certain advantages over the family in providing the kind of supervision and control necessary to those not properly socialized by the family.

> First it can more effectively monitor behavior than the family, with one teacher overseeing many children at a time. Second, as compared to most parents, teachers generally have no difficulty recognizing deviant or disruptive behavior. Third, as compared to the family, the school has such a clear interest in maintaining order and discipline that it can be expected to do what it can to control disruptive behavior. Finally, like the family, the school in theory has the authority and means to punish lapses in self control.

Society must insure that formal controls are in place for the moral order to survive should the socialization process fail to instill conformity in its members.

In contrast, differential association theorists, social learning theorists, and neutralization theorists assume a pluralist-conflict view of society. They see both mainstream or conventional values and traditions coexisting and conflicting with "subterranean values" (Matza and Sykes, 1961). Subterranean values are a hidden but ever-present underbelly of the dominant culture. These are not different, delinquent, or evil values but values "widely and diffusely held throughout society." (Box, 1981: 145). Although deviant by themselves, in that they violate accepted behavioral norms, as the unspoken context of conventional mainstream society they are ignored, hidden, and accommodated. As an example, consider the values of ambition, shrewdness, and ruthlessness valued in corporate executives that can result in a disregard for the rights of others in the interests of profit and power (Gross, 1978). For control theorists it is the undercurrent of subterranean values manifest through subcultures, gangs, and peer groups that provides a repository for the knowledge, skills, and rationalizations necessary for crime and deviance. Importantly, these theorists place more value on the primary group's role in the socialization process than on the larger, more anonymous structures of society. However, even when they acknowledge the plurality, as does Akers (1985), they still maintain a view that the overriding character of society is that of consensus (Williams and McShane, 1988: 125).

THE ROLE OF LAW, THE DEFINITION OF CRIME, AND THE VIEW OF THE CRIMINAL

Law is seen by control theorists as an expression of the mainstream culture's norms and values that reflects the moral consensus of conventional society. Law institutionalizes what is acknowledged to be the correct moral conduct and creates crimes out of what is considered to be reprehensible behavior. Law is thus nonproblematic to learning theorists generally, and control advocates in particular, since it represents the collective will of the people. The moral stance of the law must be inculcated in youth through the socialization process if crime is to be avoided. Barring that, the law's provisions for punishment are the outer perimeter providing constraints but only belatedly in the process.

Law as well as the criminal justice system is considered to be largely a symbolic edifice to control theorists. Thus the law, in the final analysis, is both the consolidation of conventional values to be held up as a symbol of morality, as well as the symbolic limit of what is acceptable in society.

For neutralization theorists, however, law reflects both the dominant mainstream culture *and* the subterranean values. As Matza (1964: 60) observed, "law contains the seeds of its own neutralization." Because of this, legal norms may be violated without the violator surrendering allegiance to them or without a person belonging to a distinct and separate delinquent subculture:

> The directives to action implicit in norms may be avoided intermittently rather than frontally assaulted. They may be evaded rather than radically rejected. Norms, especially legal norms, may be neutralized. Criminal law is especially susceptible of neutralization because the conditions of applicability, and thus inapplicability, are explicitly stated ... The criminal law, more than any comparable system of norms, acknowledges and states the principled grounds under which an actor may claim exemption. (Matza, 1964: 60)

From the neutralization perspective, the law, then, facilitates its own violation. Law is thus as ambiguous as the culture it represents.

The image of the criminal from these theorists' perspective is somewhat similar. Rule breakers are no different from conformists. From the perspective of neutralization theory all members of society are subject to neutralization by context and circumstance. On certain occasions, all humans excuse or justify their lawbreaking. The criminal might be someone with a highly developed ability for such neutralizing or someone who has learned words and phrases by which they can convince themselves that whatever they want to do is justified. In differential association theory the criminal is someone who learns that under certain circumstances law violation is acceptable.

Although control theorists see everyone as potential lawbreakers, with the same basic desires to deviate, they also see differences. For them the difference between criminal and conformist lies in the fact that criminals have not been bonded to society and have developed no "stake in conformity," so they have no reason not to deviate. Crimes, as Gottfredson and Hirschi (1990) allege, provide simple, immediate gratification. Crimes are exciting, risky, and thrilling. They provide little long-term benefit and require little skill and planning. For example, robberies are committed mostly by young males in their late adolescence when they feel that they can make a quick gain and escape the scene. Hirschi and Gottfredson point out, however, that delinquents and criminals do not engage in crimes all the time, but given the opportune moment, there is a greater likelihood that they will engage in criminal activity than others who are deemed conventional. Persons with low self-control are considered to be insensitive to the feelings of others. This facilitates their lack of empathy for suffering victims (Gottfredson and Hirschi, 1990: 88).

CAUSAL LOGIC

Sutherland's differential association theory argues that individuals participate in both conventional and criminal primary groups and use the same process to learn behavior in both. In these groups or "learning situations" they learn patterns of conventional and criminal behavior and the rationalizations that accompany them as well as the skills to carry them out. Learning "an excess of definitions favorable to committing crime over those unfavorable" results in a disposition to criminal behavior. Whether they commit this behavior depends on (a) *priority of learning*—how early criminal knowledge is learned in life: the earlier the contact, the more lasting the learning; (b) *frequency*—how often one participates in groups encouraging criminal behavior; (c) *duration*—length of exposure to particular patterns; (d) *intensity*—the higher the prestige or status of those manifesting a pattern, the greater its effect. Overall, if these factors are high, then the probability of choosing the behavior is also high.

Differential reinforcement (Jeffery, 1965) adds to this process the idea of being rewarded or punished for past deviations. Reward for deviance leads to crime, and punishment to restraint. However, if punishment is perceived as receiving attention, then it may indirectly be a reward. In this case the result would be that punishment leads to crime. Jeffery argues that once a criminal behavior pattern is learned it can be sustained because the person's own past experience of the behavior provides the reinforcement for its continuance in the future. Thus although a person may begin criminal activity in company and learn to experience its rewards with others, once learned, the activity can be sustained in isolation. This autonomous reinforcement, says Jeffery (1977) ultimately derives from the pain-pleasure centers of the brain, making social reinforcement a secondary form of learning. In Akers's (1985) version of this theory, however, it is the social environment through social interaction in subcultural groups that provides the primary reinforcement for criminal activity.

The imitation and role modeling theories (Tarde, 1890; Bandura, 1973, 1977) take a broader approach to social learning. These claim that learning can be indirect and that observation and experience of poor role models can produce self-reinforcement of observed deviant behavior, and that this can occur through imitation and copying. Violent behaviors can be learned as acceptable behavioral options, and such learning need not take place in small groups. Rather, imitation of others' criminal behavior options only requires that the person identify himself or herself with the image portrayed and that the medium can be impersonal, such as television and movies.

In contrast, in Matza's (1964) neutralization theory, key issues are the *content* and *timing* of what is learned, irrespective of the medium. What is learned are ways to neutralize moral constraints in the company of others. One excuses or justifies one's behavior through giving accounts to others after rehearsing these in one's mind (Scott and Lyman, 1970). But these are not words or phrases absent from the wider society, nor words unique to delinquent subcultures. Rather, they are an existing part of the subterranean values running through the whole society.

Invocation of words and phrases can occur in many circumstances. Timing is critical. Simply excusing or justifying after an act has been committed is not part of its cause, but merely rationalization, part of the "remedial work" people may practice in order to minimize the consequences for themselves of negative interpretations of their action (Goffman, 1971: 139). However, envisaging the possibility of successfully using such excuses and justifications *before* committing an act can act as a motivation, as in Mill's (1940) "vocabularies of motive." Mills points out that if such defensive account giving is seen as unlikely to be successful—if the actor sees that his account is unlikely to be "honored" (Scott and Lyman, 1970)—then this may serve as a mechanism of social control, inhibiting the person's participation in the activity. As in Cressey's (1953, 1970) related concept of "verbalization," the internal discussion a person has with himself or herself can be motivating through removal of inhibition. As he says of embezzlers, "I am convinced that the words and phrases that the potential embezzler uses in his conversations with himself are actually the most important elements in the process that gets him into trouble" (Cressey, 1970: 111).

For Matza (1964), learning words and phrases, and using these extensions and distortions of conventional values *unwittingly*, as excuses and justifications *before* not only committing the act but also prior to even contemplating it is the key to the process that results in commission of a crime (Taylor, 1972; Henry, 1976). Thus, for Matza words and phrases could be learned as part of the subterranean values of the wider culture, and when used in certain contexts, could invoke meanings that result in the unwitting neutralization of a person's commitment to morality. Henry (1976, 1978) showed that in some cases the words and phrases may even be part of the mainstream culture as in the case of sellers of stolen goods who use the language of consumer market economies, such as "bargain," "damaged stock," "bulk purchase," "manufacturers' overrun," to frame their sales. Moreover, the seller need not even make such a false claim but simply cue it, relying on the buyers to invoke the appropriate account and thereby inadvertently and unwittingly render themselves morally free to engage in an illegal purchase. Thus, behavior, albeit illegal, can simply appear morally justified. Once neutralization occurs and people are released on a "moral holiday," they are free to choose or drift into delinquency. Whether or not they do so depends upon their motivation and desire for the rewards of the activity, goods or service, just as it does for participation in any activity, legal or otherwise. The key is the moral release, says Matza, not the motivation.

According to Matza (1964) and Sykes and Matza (1957), neutralization occurs through several techniques, such as

1. denial of responsibility
2. denial of injury
3. denial of victim
4. condemnation of condemners
5. appeal to higher loyalties

Additional excuses and justifications have also been identified, such as Klockars's (1974) "metaphor of the ledger" (e.g., "In balancing up the good and the bad, I'll come out on the good side") and Henry's (1990) "claim of normality" (e.g., "Everyone does it"), "denial of negative intent" (e.g., "I was just joking"), and "claim of relative acceptability" (e.g., "There are others worse than me"). (See Pfuhl and Henry, 1993: 69–70; and Hollinger, 1991.) These neutralizations can also be adopted by governments to justify human rights violations in what Cohen (1993) has called a "culture of denial."

A fundamental disagreement exists between control theory and neutralization, as a result of their different starting assumptions. Control theorists argue that neutralization theory assumes effective socialization and a commitment to the moral bind of law from which the potential lawbreaker has to be released prior to committing an offense. Neutralization, therefore, omits to consider those cases where commitment to law, morality, and convention fails to form in the first place. This is the starting point for Hirschi's control theory.

The causal logic of control theory is both simple and complex. For Hirschi, crime is the result of a failure of people to be socialized into a bond with society. As a result, they fail to develop a "stake in conformity." Thus Hirschi (1969: 16) states: "Control theories assume that delinquent acts result when an individual's bond to society is weak or broken." The complexity of control theory arises with the definition and explanation of the nature of the social learning that produce elements of this social bond:

> To facilitate such social learning, society, through social interaction, attempts to seduce individuals with affection, trap them with physical and social possessions, and threaten them with sanctions. Rather than assume that this human miracle invariably works, control theorists view its outcome as extremely problematic, and even if "success" is achieved it is seen as tenuous and fragile rather than permanent and invulnerable. (Box, 1981: 122–23)

Before examining the nature of bonding and the conditions under which its absence leads to law violation, it is helpful to review how early social control theorists envisaged the socialization-into-conformity process.

Nye (1958) stressed the importance of the socialization process in the development of conscience as a feature of internalized control over errant behavior. To this he added the importance of affectional identification with others significant in one's life, such as parents. His focus was on the family as the origin of social control. If it were possible to fulfill all needs of the individual adequately and expeditiously, only minimal control would be necessary because there would be no need to violate the law to achieve one's needs. This psychological emphasis on individual internal dynamics as the basis of control was a continuation of earlier studies such as Reiss's (1951) argument about the offender's lack of personal controls.

Perhaps the most extensive attempt to develop a control theory was that of Reckless (1961, 1973), who advanced a theory of containment. Reckless proposed that there are both internal and external control mechanisms as well as internal and external forces that push or pull individuals to commit delinquent or criminal acts. He felt it was the dynamics involved in the interplay of these forces that determine delinquent or conventional outcomes. Reckless considered positive self-perception or self-concept as a strong protection against delinquent behavior. In order for the individual to have a positive view of self, argued Reckless, they must have the external community's (i.e., others') approval, which was achieved by behaving in the approved manner. This approved behavior, in turn, binds the person to the community and conventionalism. Influenced by the labeling perspective and symbolic interactionism (discussed in the next chapter), Reckless felt that if youth were seen and reacted to in a positive fashion, the results would be reciprocal respect and positive self-image. In contrast, negative reaction on the part of others of significance would likely result in negative self-image and loosening of ties to conventionalism.

In an earlier work, Toby (1957) argued that although everyone had a desire to commit some form of delinquency (thus placing Toby in the mainstream of control advocates), an important protection against law violation was that the potential offender have an investment in something that she or he does not wish to lose. The costs of possibly losing the fruits of this investment may not be worth the risk of discovery. For example, the investment in getting an education or training for a career may be lost if the person is apprehended for deviant activity. The fear of losing important relationships in a person's life may also be a barrier to acting out the impulse to violate. Thus the greater the stake in something of importance to the person, the less likely the urge to violate will be acted upon.

As indicated above, the most widely known theory of social control is Hirschi's (1969) social bonding theory, as well as his later work with Gottfredson that attempts to develop a general theory of crime based on control theory concepts. In the earlier work, Hirschi concentrates on elaborating the four elements of the social bond which he considers vital in the explanation of delinquency and, by extension, adult crime. These are (a) attachment—to teachers, parents, and friends and the desire not to lose them or hurt them; (b) commitment—to conventional behavior, which includes a willingness to do what you have said, expressed in trust; (c) involvement—in conventional activity, especially school related; and (d) belief—in the need to obey conventional rules, and belief in the institutions of society (Hirschi, 1969). Let us examine these in more detail.

Attachment refers to the sensitivity a person has to another's thoughts and feelings. "The essence of internalization of norms ... lies in the attachment of the individual to others" (Hirschi, 1969:18). Hirschi's attachment refers to the affective relations a person has with other people and their concern about others' feelings and expectations of their own behavior. A person with good affective ties does not wish to place them in jeopardy. A married person with a good relationship with his or her spouse will not wish to do anything that would negatively affect the relationship. A child who is affectionally attached to her or his parents will not wish to displease and anger them. Hence attachment is an element in the formation of the social bond, although by itself it is insufficient to stem deviance.

In explaining the second element, *commitment,* Hirschi approvingly quotes Thomas Hobbes ("Of all passions, that which inclineth men least to break the laws, is fear") as an indicator of what he calls commitment. By being committed, one avoids loss, the loss of someone or something held dear. Commitment, therefore, refers to the degree to which a person will persist in continuing his or her behavior along the lines of conformity. Hirschi argues that whenever anyone considers delinquent behavior he or she must consider the cost and risks of his or her stake in conforming behavior. Giving up conforming behavior is by its very nature a risky undertaking, which creates the potential status of an outcast. Hirschi implies this when he states, "Most people, simply by the process of living in an organized society, acquire goods, reputations, prospects that they do not want to risk losing (Hirschi, 1969: 21)." This also applies to future aspirations, and as a result most persons become committed to conforming behavior in most areas of endeavor.

A closely related third element is that of *involvement.* The basic premise here is that if people are committed to something or someone, they become involved in carrying out the commitment to the extent that it leaves little time to deviate. Put more colloquially: "The Devil makes work for idle hands." The more someone participates in conventional activities, the less time there is left over to engage in deviance. Hirschi indicates that this line of reasoning is often used in delinquency prevention programs and leads to the provision of recreational activities.

Finally, the fourth element, *belief,* rests on the assumption of a common value system and on the assumed human capacity to evaluate and take a position on moral issues (Box, 1981: 130). Hirschi conjectures that people vary in the extent to which they believe they should obey the rules of society engendered by this value system (Hirschi, 1969: 26). He argues that "delinquency is not caused by beliefs that require delinquency, but is rather made possible by the absence of (effective) beliefs that forbid delinquency" (ibid.). Belief, therefore, points to people's variability in their acceptance of the validity of moral rules. If a person's belief in the rules of society are not strong or are weakened, the chances of violation are thereby increased. Hence the strength of belief is a measure of the acceptance of conformity.

Hirschi does not indicate a causal order of these elements of his theory but does feel that attachment must come temporarily before the others. He develops a scheme of the logically possible combination of the elements in order to show the interrelationship among them. Attachment and commitment, Hirschi believes, vary together. This is in contrast to other research, which tends to show that too much attachment might hinder someone from becoming committed to accepted aspirations. Hirschi admits, with relation to the combination of commitment and involvement, that being free of them does not necessarily lead to delinquency: "To say a boy is free of bonds to conventional society is not to say that he will necessarily commit delinquent acts; he may and he may not" (Hirschi, 1969: 28). However, he asserts that commitment limits one's chances of becoming involved in delinquent activity. Attachment and belief have a straightforward connection as far as Hirschi (1969: 30) is concerned: "Insofar as the child respects (loves and fears) his parents, and adults in general, he will accept their rules. Conversely, insofar as this respect is undermined, the rules will tend to lose their obligatory character." Belief in mandatory rules is assumed to continue even if respect is lost, however, and attachment is assumed to lead to conformity, despite beliefs that harbor deviance. Thus the basic thrust of the theory is that complex social bonding mechanisms are the key to the unraveling of criminal conduct.

In developing their general theory, Gottfredson and Hirschi (1990) place emphasis on the desired result of an effective social bond: the establishment of self-control. If appropriate child rearing occurs and the elements of the bond are in place, proper self-control (high self-control) will also be in place and deviance and criminal behavior are minimized. It is low self-control or lack of self-control that is likely to result in crime and deviance. High self-control, on the other hand, argue Gottfredson and Hirschi (1990: 89), "effectively reduces the possibility of crime—that is, those possessing it will be substantially less likely at all periods of life to engage in criminal acts." They argue that other factors, such as peer groups, economic and structural factors, poverty, psychological conditions, strain, and so forth, are inconsequential as causes of delinquency and crime. What matters is the establishment of proper self-control early in the socialization process.

Low self-control is a negative manifestation. This is an important distinction for control theorists, and one that separates them from other social learning theorists. Thus they argue that low self-control is not something that is acquired because of association with others or through learning processes or socialization, or training. Rather, they allege, low self-control emerges "in the absence of nurturance, discipline, or training" (Gottfredson and Hirschi, 1990: 95). That is, the characteristics become manifest if constraints are not put in place. Put another way, lack of self-control is the "natural" condition that must be tempered by proper child-rearing practices. Low self-control is characterized by impulsivity, insensitivity, physical risk taking, short-sightedness, and lack of verbal skills (Gottfredson and Hirschi, 1990: 90). Low self-control persons operate in the here and now; they have little concept of deferred gratification and long-term future planning. Thus they act to gain immediate gratification of their wants. These are traits that are highly compatible with delinquent and criminal activity.

For Gottfredson and Hirschi self-control is the key concept in the explanation of all forms of crime as well as other types of behavior. Indeed, they believe that all current differences in rates of crime between groups and categories may be explained by differences in the management of self-control. For Box (1981), who has extended control theory's argument, whether people actually decide to break laws also depends on whether they have the *ability* to do so. Thus, Box (1981: 132–140) asserts that "whether or not an individual with the option to deviate decides to, depends to some extent on what she or he makes of the issues of secrecy, skills, supply and social and symbolic support."

Before leaving the causal analysis of the various social process theories it is important to point out that several theorists have combined them to form an integrated theory. For example, Glazer's (1978) differential anticipation theory combines differential association and control theory, arguing that whether someone engages in crime depends on the consequences that are expected from its commission, prior learning experience, and the quality of the bonds the person has with others. Other theorists such as Elliot et al. (1985) combine social learning, social control, and subcultural strain theory. We will not consider these integrated theories here, but will return to the integration issue in our concluding chapter.

CRIMINAL JUSTICE SYSTEM IMPLICATIONS

Most social learning theory is silent with regard to the criminal justice system, indicating an acceptance of the prevailing due process model. However, a bureaucratic version of due process justice is implied, containing the following elements and emphases:

1. advocates objectivity and neutrality
2. is rule-governed and independent of politics
3. is fast, efficient, and predictable
4. relies on the use of records, especially those of the background circumstances of offenders
5. favors a nonadversarial system of justice in order to minimize conflict
6. favors swift punishment

Thus King (1981: 22–23) states:

> The bureaucratic objective is to process defendants according to standard procedures, a closed system of rules which operate independently of political considerations and regardless of who is in the dock ... one would expect to find encouragement and rewards given to any procedures, strategies and decisions which save time and expedite the processing of cases; conversely, one would expect to see discouragements and sanctions applied to time-wasting and the prolongation of cases ... one would expect to find ... important status given to records ... a strong presumption may exist that anything that does not appear in the record is irrelevant, unreliable or otherwise unacceptable as evidence.

The essence of the bureaucratic approach, then, is to process as many people in the shortest possible time, to minimize the impact on their life and on the cost to the community. For example, control theorists believe that the criminal justice system should have a lower priority in a society's response to crime. They argue that the family is the first line of defense in prevention through creating conformist behavior. Should it and school fail as institutional attempts to bond the child to society, the state is the final arbiter. Hirschi, for example, believes that in this lesser role the criminal justice system must emphasize using enforcement in a stringent manner to promote near certainty of apprehension. Since adherence to conventional values is to be encouraged, laws reflecting these values must be created and supported. In other words, the justice system should lay stress on convention over innovation. Importance is placed on mechanisms that encourage respect for law and order. Moreover, Hirschi believes that a policy emphasizing punitive measures rather than rehabilitative or treatment alternatives is to be preferred since the criminal justice system comes too late in the process and is, by its very nature, ineffective in preventing crime. Thus the criminal justice system carries largely a symbolic function. As Gottfredson and Hirschi (1990: 255) put it: "Because low self control, [the cause of crime], arises in the absence of powerful inhibiting forces of early childhood, it is highly resistant to the less powerful inhibiting forces of later life, especially the relatively weak forces of the criminal justice system."

Criminal Justice Policy and Correctional Ideology

The social process theories examined here imply that since failed socialization or ineffective socialization has resulted in rule breaking, the policy solution is to be found in an ideology emphasizing some form of preventative socialization, resocialization, relearning or, in the case of control theory, recommitment to the moral order. Indeed, underlying control theory is an emphasis on the micro-management of human development to keep nascent deviancy in check. Thus their preventative policy is aimed at producing the maximum amount of conformity by ensuring that social bonding takes place. The different versions of learning and bonding theory differ, however, on how best to prevent the drift to delinquency and crime.

Techniques of Crime Control

Crime control practices vary somewhat depending on whether social learning theory or social control theory is being considered. Learning theorists believe that when people have already learned antisocial behaviors they should be rehabilitated through reeducation and resocialization programs. During this process there is strong support for the segregation of offenders so that developed offenders and their criminal subcultures do not contaminate and reinforce the unlawful behavior of the young.

Some neutralization theorists believe that publicly proclaiming the law, and elaborating the reasons for following it, serves a reinforcing, clarifying, and preventative function, as does challenging all the excuses and justifications for disobedience. Public exposure, and declaring rationalizations justifying harm as invalid, is seen as helpful, as is education in ethics and how we deceive ourselves into "honest dishonesty." For example, in his recommendations for dealing with embezzling and employee theft Cressey (1965) recommends that companies adopt programs to discuss emerging problems, especially financial ones, and that they introduce educational programs to emphasize how offenders use characteristic verbalizations. Such programs

> would make it very difficult for trusted employees who are potential embezzlers to think of themselves as "borrowers" rather than "thieves" when they take the boss's money ... What I am proposing is an educational program in which we say over and over again that the person who "pilfers" or "taps the till" or "borrows" or who is guilty of "defalcation," "peculation," or some other nice term is, in fact, a crook. And if a trusted employee rejects the notion of himself as a crook (and as

a "respectable" type he must) he will also reject the possibility of embezzling. (Cressey, 1987: 250)

Of course, whether a person becomes "respectable" in the first place depends on their values and socialization. This is why, unlike neutralization theorists, control theorists place particular emphasis on proper socialization and consistent child-rearing practices in families.

Control theorists believe that effective and efficient crime prevention that produces enduring consequences should be directed at parents or adults with responsibilities for child rearing. They believe that minimum standards of child rearing should be established to ensure proper self-control. According to Gottfredson and Hirschi (1990: 97) these should include

1. monitoring the child's behavior
2. recognizing deviant behavior when it occurs
3. punishing rule-breaking behavior

Hirschi (1983) considers a family's use of punishment as an essential tool of child rearing to prevent delinquent behavior. Although the meaning of punishment is never fully explicated, in their later work Gottfredson and Hirschi (1990: 101) explain that punishment "usually entails nothing more than explicit disap-proval of unwanted behavior." Showing "affection for or investment in the child" by correcting wayward behavior should result in the child's being able to delay gratification and develop high self-control.

The ability to accomplish adequate childhood socialization rests on a num-ber of conditions that may make it more difficult to achieve. For example, Hirschi believes that allowing adolescents to be employed may be contrary to good child-rearing practices, for it provides independence from family supervi-sion and undermines the family's ability to control and punish youths. As a con-sequence, Hirschi (1983: 6) asks:

> How, if at all, does the employment of the youth affect the family's ability to punish his deviant behavior? The power of the family in this situation will depend on the resources available to it relative to the resources available to the child ...
>
> If the child does not want to go to college, his family does not own a car, and the money he earns provides him a level of living equal or superior to that of his family, he is by definition no longer dependent on them. His parents no longer have the material means to punish him, and the entire system of family control is vulnerable to collapse. Henceforth, the adolescent is free to come and go as he pleases ... the "child rearing" days are over. It is time to hope for the best.

Large families may also present difficulties because sheer numbers may make supervision difficult. Single working parents have difficulty because of work schedules. The strategy here seems to imply a traditional mother who stays at home to rear children. However, according to Gottfredson and Hirschi, any "responsible adults committed to the training and welfare of the child" (Gottfredson and Hirschi 1990: 273) can carry out the child-rearing function, which can be accomplished in properly run day-care facilities where children are under supervision.

EVALUATION

Social learning theory, especially the differential association version, has earned considerable respect from critics, even if it has not been as strongly supported empirically. Siegel (1989: 195) says the theory makes "a significant contribution to our understanding of the onset of criminal behavior" and cites studies by Short (1960), Reiss and Rhodes (1961), Tittle (1980), Matsueda and Heimer (1987), and Paternoster and Triplett (1988) which tend to support the central concepts of the theory. Beirne and Messerschmidt (1991: 384) claim that the theory "continues to be one of the most fertile causal accounts of crime." They recount that its critics have often misunderstood the theory or taken it in too narrow a frame.

Critics have charged that the theory fails to account for crimes by individuals as opposed to those learned in groups or other association. Others argue that it fails to specify the conditions that motivate people to associate with established offenders to learn from them, and does not answer how it is that even with such association, some become criminals while others do not. Although social learning explains why some people in high-crime areas refrain from crime, it does not explain how behaviors originate or who started them. Sutherland's theory does not explain what appears to be an "excess of definitions" nor how irrational acts of violence or destruction occur. Perhaps most salient is Beirne and Messerschmidt's (1991: 385) tripartite criticism that:

1. The theory takes a nonproblematic stance on what counts as crime and its support, neglecting to consider for example the institutional harms promoted by law, and by implication the sometime benefits of its violation.

2. It does not account for the initial motivation to learn criminal behavior.

3. It ignores the interpretive qualities of what it is to be human.

Indeed, as we have seen, most versions of social learning assume a passive and unintentional actor who lacks individuality. Because of this limited conception of human nature, learning theories generally also ignore the differential receptivity of individuals to criminal messages. Because of these weaknesses, Beirne and Messerschmidt (ibid.: 396) believe that differential association theory is much better at explaining the transmission of criminal behavior than its origins, a point Sutherland acknowledges.

Akers modified version, differential reinforcement theory, is held by supporters to address some of these issues. However, although the theory is better able to explain the self-sustaining nature of crime, differential reinforcement fails to explain why those rewarded for conventional behavior, such as middle-class youths, commit crimes, and it fails to explain why some delinquent youths do not become adult criminals, despite being rewarded for crime (Siegel, 1989: 212).

Neutralization theory explains why most delinquents undergo maturational reform and how people can participate simultaneously in both conventional and unconventional illegal behavior (Henry, 1976, 1978), and this has been supported by some empirical research (Ball, 1966). However, as Ball argues, it is difficult to test empirically since it is not easy to establish whether neutralization occurs before or after law violation (see also Hindelang, 1970), nor why some people feel the need to neutralize and others do not. Many argue that if neutralization is used at all it is *after* the act has been committed, in the form of a rationalization (Hamlin, 1988). Indeed, Minor (1980: 115) goes so far as to say that in many cases, "neutralizations and rationalizations are simply unnecessary."

Social control theory has enjoyed considerable popularity but, like the other social learning theories, has also received considerable criticism. The theory, with its simple appeal and its straightforward focus on the relationship between individuals and their early upbringing, fits in with the popular developmental thinking about crime. Moreover, the theory is neither class, nor gender, nor race based, (except that in ignoring these divisions, it advantages those in power), and it is deemed to explain all varieties of crime without reference to special conditions. Thus it is both popularly as well as theoretically attractive. This is particularly true for the latest modification of control theory into a general theory of crime.

Control theory has spawned considerable empirical research, the majority of which has been supportive, but the theory has its critics. Empirical testing of the theory has focused essentially on delinquency rather than adult crime. Upon introducing the theory, Hirschi took the unusual step of also testing his ideas on social bonding empirically. He surveyed a large sample of 17,500 students entering public junior and senior high school to see whether the claims concerning the four elements of the bond were justified. Although there was support for the hypothesized outcome, it was at a low level of significance, thus inconclusive. Subsequent studies have found mixed results. A study by Hindelang (1973) seemed to support most of Hirschi's claims concerning the elements of the bond. What was not supported was Hirschi's contention that no matter with whom attachment occurs it is a delinquency preventative. Hindelang found that attachment to delinquent peers is related to delinquency. This finding supports the arguments of social learning rather than control theory.

Other studies critical of Hirschi have focused on methodological and conceptual problems. In a review of the literature of empirical studies related to

Hirschi's theory, Krohn (1991) for example, points out that some of the elements of the social bond are not individually distinctive. Thus it is difficult to distinguish involvement from commitment. Both are intercorrelated (Krohn and Massey, 1980, cited by Krohn, 1991: 302). Indeed, Box (1981) in his extension of the theory collapsed these two elements into one category.

Moreover, according to Krohn, Hirschi has been criticized for not indicating the causal order of the elements of the social bond (Massey and Krohn, 1986, cited by Krohn, 1991: 302). For example, in one study (Liska and Reed, 1985), it was found that the causal structure of delinquency related to the social bond was not unidirectional but reciprocal with regard to the element of attachment to parents and school. Just as parental attachment affected delinquency, delinquency affected school attachment.

In a survey of junior and senior high school students, Krohn and Massey (1980) show that Hirschi explains female delinquency better than male, and minor crimes better than more serious offenses. LaGrange and White (1985) point to differences in the age cycle in terms of the nature of the social bond. At different stages parents, teachers, and peers have greater influence on behavior, not solely parents. Other recent studies (Matsueda and Heimer, 1987; MacLeod, 1987; Cernkovich and Giordano, 1992), have focused on racial differences because blacks have been underrepresented in school delinquency studies. Though there is tentative support for the theory, Cernkovich and Giordano (1992: 284) caution: "[O]ur research has left unanswered some important questions and has raised additional ones that must be addressed before we can say with any degree of certainty that there are or are not race-specific differentials in the relationship between school bonding and delinquency."

Yet others, such as Wells and Rankin (1988), show that direct parental controls are more important than parental attachments. Foreshadowing Gottfredson and Hirschi (1990), their research indicates that normative regulation, monitoring, and punishment by parents has a significant effect on delinquency. However, this is not a simple relationship. Some kinds of control increase delinquency; others reduce it. They conclude that " 'direct control' over delinquent behavior is a complex, multidimensional set of processes in which distinct component dimensions of control operate in very different ways" (Wells and Rankin, 1988: 280). In later research Rankin and Wells (1990: 163) conclude that discipline is not a simple solution to teenage delinquency: "punishment that is too strict, frequent or severe can lead to a greater probability of delinquency *regardless* of parental attachments." Thus a strong parent–child bond need not lessen the impact of severe punishment. Likewise the simple conception of punishment that Gottfredson and Hirschi offer turns out to be much more complex than Hirschi initially maintained.

Thus, although there is general support for control theory, some research points to conceptual and methodological difficulties and challenges as well the operationalization of concepts. Ideologically the theory represents a conservative approach to the explanation of delinquency and crime. Its basis is one of acceptance of classical principles that the principal authors of control theory consider to have been abandoned prematurely. In this acceptance, a view of humans is projected that posits basically a greedy, noncooperative antisocial nature that must be contained through controlling child-rearing practices. With this negative emphasis there seems to be little room for change through human agency; if controls are insufficient there is little that can be accomplished. In fairness, the theory does incorporate maturation as a way of exiting a delinquent or criminal path. However, in its singular emphasis on the establishment of self-control as the barrier to deviance, it gives no credence to the context in which self-control and crime take place. In so doing it fails to examine the possibility that the inability to form high self-control and its resultant crime may both have a contextual basis (Sykes and Cullen, 1992: 309).

Finally and perhaps more importantly, control theory's very emphasis on control may impose a condition of powerlessness on the part of the maturing adolescent that, in turn, may foster the very alienation from conventionality that monitoring, control, and punishment are presumed to avert. Constant surveillance easily fosters a sense of distrust and discourages the need to explore, to create, and to make the mistakes from which to learn. Thus the road to a mature independent adult existence may be blocked for the sake of controlling prospective deviance. Further, the theory seemingly does not take into account the point of view of the adolescent. In its unidirectional emphasis (parent or responsible adult to child), little is said of interactional effects. The perception and meaning to the child of monitoring and punishment is not examined. As has been demonstrated, the type of punishment, how it is applied, and at what stage in the growth cycle it is implemented, are of major significance. Thus the process involved in the creation and maintenance of high self-control may not be as rudimentary as we are led to believe and the road to conventionality, as seen by Gottfredson and Hirschi, may be more of a complex interactive process than control theory implies. It is toward an examination of the social process theories that take this complexity into account that we now turn.

CHAPTER NINE

Social Process Theories II: Interactionism, Labeling, and Social Constructionism

Like the theories analyzed in the previous chapter, the ideas we shall now examine see human action as part of a process that develops over time through interaction with others. However, instead of assuming a relatively passive actor who learns information, values, or behavior patterns from others, the theories to which we now turn assume humans are *active agents* in the construction of their own biographies. They are *coproducers* of a dynamic interactive process that forms their social world.

These "interpretive" social process theories argue that existing positivistic social science explanations of crime and rule breaking fail to explain the meaning of crime and deviance and are ignorant of the way official government agencies construct crime statistics.[1] Static in its vision of human nature, the social order, and social change, sociological positivism is especially limited in its capacity to explain deviance as diversity. Phillipson's contrast of traditional positivistic criminologies with the interpretive approach is instructive:

> In simple terms the criminological positivist argues that there are underlying causes for every criminal act and that his job is to define, find and measure them ... the positivist perspective ... is based on mistaken and limiting assumptions about social behavior in general and criminal behavior in particular. The alternative perspective ... is based upon different assumptions, has different aims, has different methods and has a different subject matter to those of traditional criminology. The approach ... moves away from the narrow focus on the individual ... to the broader issues of situations, social processes and social structures ... [it] proposes that the amount and quality of deviance in society ... is the product of the interaction between deviants, potential deviants and the society's or group's social control mechanisms ... crime can only be understood by showing how intimately it is bound up with the non-criminal features of society. (Phillipson, 1971: 8–24)

Early interpretive criminologists took an anti-establishment stance. They found dissatisfaction with the use of official data, such as the government statistics on

---

[1]Interpretive social science believes that knowledge of the social world is discoverable only by using qualitative methods of research and analysis that enable us to understand the shared meaning of action to the participants.

crimes known and arrests made, claiming that these data were biased and that they distorted and "mystified" the reality of crime. As we shall see, this was especially true in the case of criminologists who favored the labeling perspective. Instead of the quantitative testing of hypotheses, these theorists took a humanistic stance that prioritized understanding and the naturalistic appreciation of crime and deviance (Matza, 1969). They argued that any attempt to explain rule-breaking behavior must involve an appreciation of the meaning of action from the actor's perspective. This relied on *qualitative* interpretation based on ethnographic methods (Douglas, 1972). Again, as Phillipson (1971: 8–28) comments:

> The deviance perspective ... would attempt to describe and interpret ... the actors' typical definitions of the situation ... this necessitates focusing on the meanings which individuals give to the multitude of situations faced in everyday life and describing the patterns which these social meanings form ... the goal of the perspective is not "the causes" but rather certain kinds of "understanding" or interpretation of social phenomenon. This understanding is qualitatively rather different from causal explanation; essentially it seeks to understand the processes by which actors arrive at their particular pattern of choices.

The theories we consider here, then, fit this broad interpretive framework and are known variously as symbolic interactionism, labeling or social reaction theory, ethnomethodology, and phenomenology (see Table 9–1). Although each has its own long tradition in philosophy, sociology, and social psychology, they emerged during the 1950s and 1960s as leading perspectives in criminology. These theories subsequently informed the social constructionism of the 1980s and also became influential in criminal justice, where they were responsible for attempts to decriminalize and divert juveniles before they became stereotyped as criminals. For our purposes, the intellectual foundation of these theories can be traced to George Herbert Mead's (1934) social behaviorism and to its interpretation and extension by his student, Herbert Blumer (1969), as "symbolic interactionism."

Table 9-1   RELATED THEORIES*

Interactionism
Symbolic interactionism
Ethnomethodology
Phenomenology
New deviancy theory
Labeling theory
Social reaction theory
Social constructionism

*Theories that take a perspective similar to or overlapping with the model that we develop in this chapter.

Other influences include William James's (1890) concept of "the self," his ideas of voluntarism and nominalism, and his pragmatic and experiential philosophy; John Dewey's (1886, 1922) pragmatism and his ideas of active learning; Charles Horton Cooley's (1902, 1909) social process and the concept of the "looking-glass self"; Alfred Schutz's (1932; 1971) phenomenological interactionism and his studies on experience, subjective meaning, and the commonsense construction of social reality; and George Kelly's (1955) cognitive phenomenology of "personal constructs." These later became amalgamated in the 1960s and 1970s ideas of Lemert, Goffman, Becker, Schur, Berger and Luckmann, Garfinkel, Cicourel, and Young and Cohen. (See Table 9-2.)

Table 9-2   Theorists Using Interpretive Social Process Explanations of Crime

THEORIST	MAJOR WORK[S]	DATE
	Interactionist	
Cooley	*Human Nature and the Social Order*	1902
	Social Organization: A Study of the Larger Mind	1909
Thomas	*The Unadjusted Girl*	1923
Mead	*Mind, Self and Society*	1934
Goffman	*The Presentation of Self in Everyday Life*	1959
	Interaction Ritual	1967
	Behavior in Public Places	1971
Blumer	*Symbolic Interactionism*	1969
	Social Constructionist	
Schutz	*The Phenomenology of the Social World*	1932
	Collected Papers	1964
Garfinkel	"Conditions of Successful Degradation Ceremonies"	1956
	Studies in Ethnomethodology	1967
Sudnow	"Normal Crimes"	1965
Berger and Luckmann	*The Social Construction of Reality*	1967
Cicourel	*The Social Organization of Juvenile Justice*	1968
Quinney	*The Social Reality of Crime*	1970
Douglas	*American Social Order*	1971
	"Observing Deviance"	1972

Rock	*Deviant Behaviour*	1973
Pfuhl	*The Deviance Process*	1980
Goffman	*Forms of Talk*	1981

Labeling and Social Reaction

Tannenbaum	*Crime and the Community*	1938
Lemert	*Social Pathology* *Human Deviance, Social Problems and Social Control*	1951 1967
Goffman	"The Moral Career of the Mental Patient" *Asylums* *Stigma: Notes on the Management of Spoiled Identity*	1959 1961 1963
Becker	*Outsiders*	1963
Kitsuse	"Societal Reaction to Deviant Behavior"	1964
Schur	*Crimes without Victims* *Labeling Deviant Behavior* *Radical Non-Intervention* *The Politics of Deviance*	1965 1971 1973 1980
Scheff	*Being Mentally Ill*	1966
Lofland	*Deviance and Identity*	1969
Matza	*Becoming Deviant*	1969
Sagarin	*Odd Man In*	1969
Scott	*The Making of Blind Men*	1969
Szasz	*The Manufacture of Madness* *The Myth of Mental Illness*	1970 1973
Duster	*The Legislation of Morality*	1970
Mankoff	*Societal Reaction and Career Deviance*	1970
Young	"The Role of Police as Amplifiers of Deviancy, Negotiators of Reality and Translators of Fantasy"	1970
Cohen	*Folk Devils and Moral Panics* "The Punitive City: Notes on the Dispersal of Social Control"	1972 1979
Rosenhan	"Being Sane in Insane Places"	1973
Plummer	"Misunderstanding Labelling Perspectives"	1979

It was Mead (1934) who first synthesized the early philosophical positions into a coherent whole "that linked the emergence of the human mind, the social self, and the structure of society to the process of social interaction" (Turner, 1986: 313). Mead rejected the divide between "nominalism" (the idea that the social world is created by humans who impose order on it through their labels and classificatory schemes) and "realism" (the idea that social reality determines who we are and is not affected by how we think). The central question for Mead was to grasp *both* the nominalist and realist elements as "dialectically" related (coproducing), and thereby to see individuals as creating social forms that in turn re-create individuals.

In this chapter we will examine the theoretical assumptions of the interactionist tradition in some detail and consider, albeit more briefly, the variations and contributions made by particular theorists.

BASIC IDEA, CENTRAL MOTIF, AND MAJOR THEORISTS

The key principle of the interactionist/labeling perspective is that people can adopt deviant or criminal identities as a result of cumulative negative social reaction in the course of official institutional processing by social control agencies, during which processing they are labeled as "outsiders" (Becker, 1963; Lofland, 1969). As Box (1981: 208) says, "Clearly the organizing assumption in labeling theory is that officially registered individuals sometimes undergo an identity change from *being normal* to being deviant."

Underlying this position is the assumption that humans are social beings who are creative and free to interact with others but in the process they become subject to others' controls. Although actively contributing to the development of their own identity, humans are seen as susceptible to identity transformations through their social interaction, based on how others see them (Lofland, 1969). As a result of its ongoing development through interactive relationships, human behavior is not fixed in its meaning but open to interpretation, negotiation, and reformulation (Blumer, 1969). From this position rule breaking is seen as no different from other human behavior. It is meaningful and purposeful action. As part of ongoing human activity, it is constantly emerging in different social contexts. These contexts both shape meaning and are the medium through which action makes sense.

Society is seen as a conflicting plurality of groups dominated by the most powerful, who use their power to stigmatize the less powerful (Quinney, 1969, 1970; Duster, 1970). This occurs in many ways, but ultimately it is brought about through law, which is the symbolic and coercive expression of the power of interest groups. "Moral entrepreneurs" and control agents reflecting these interests determine which behaviors are criminalized and which are not (Becker,

1963; Schur, 1980). In the public conflict over legal definitions of crime and deviance, some people's deviant behavior or "primary deviance" (Lemert, 1951) is banned as immoral, illegal, or both. Episodically, the generation of such bans is accompanied by media-generated "moral panics" and "crime waves" are then "discovered," with the ultimate "demonizing" of those accused for their non-conformity (Cohen, 1980; Ditton, 1979).

Primary deviance is "polygenic, arising out of a variety of social, cultural, psychological, and physical factors ... [it] has only marginal implications for the status and psychic structure of the person concerned" (Lemert, 1967: 40). For those whose primary deviance is banned, stereotyping begins through institutional processing by society's control agents (which include the police, psychiatrists, teachers, social workers, and the courts). Instead of simply breaking rules, selected and vulnerable people are defined and labeled as rule-breaking identities or social types, for example, thieves, robbers, and shoplifters, rather than people who have stolen. Anyone can become a labeled "criminal" if their deviance becomes subjected to the scrutiny of the criminal justice system, but typically this is the fate of the powerless (Duster, 1970).

Thus, because of bans on their behavior, some people wish to conceal their deviant activities. They are confronted with the problem of "transparency," whereby they conceal their secrets and present to others an image of themselves as ordinary and conventional (Matza, 1969). If in the course of this acting they recognize they are only acting at being normal, then they are open to the suggestion that they might in reality be deviant.

The selective application and enforcement of powerful groups' rules on some rule breakers can tip the balance, confirming those whose primary deviance has led them to question the nature of their true selves. This official processing produces stigma, a "spoiled identity" or "master status," which results in a deviant and negative self-image (Goffman, 1963). Initial attempts at stereotypical designation may be negotiated and bargained over, as in psychiatric assessments or through police discretion. But if the designation is pursued to formal processing, say through the courts, routine processing and classification confine the rule breaker into one of several "normal" criminal categories (Sudnow, 1965; Emerson, 1969). The outcome of such processing can be individual "role engulfment" and moral conversion into a deviant career (Schur, 1971). The person so labeled now deviates *because* he or she is a deviant, because he or she has a deviant identity. His or her behavior is now said to be qualitatively different than it was as primary deviance. It is now "secondary deviance," which refers to "responses people make to problems created by the societal reaction to their deviance ... [it] concerns processes which create, maintain, or intensify stigma" (Lemert, 1967: 40–41).

Through processes such as "retrospective interpretation," whereby "audiences" perceive a signified actor as having always been deviant, and whereby past behavior is reinterpreted for "signs" and "cues" of current status (Schur, 1971), a person's behavioral options are narrowed. An individual's conforming activity is subsequently limited by the actions of those who overreact to initial rule breaking or primary deviance and who subsequently embellish its formal classification, thereby "amplifying" the original deviant choices through a narrowing of the range of nondeviant behavioral possibilities. Deviance then becomes the repeated rule breaking that emanates from the belief that the person *is* now the identity type that has been labeled. Further "deviancy amplification" comes from expansion of deviant behavior as those labeled now engage in other deviance in order to conceal their deviant identity (Young, 1971).

In summary, labeling theory argues that *additional* crime and deviance (beyond that which would be normal in a society) is brought about as a self-fulfilling prophecy by some people's responses to the stigmatic effects of excessive overreaction by society's control agents to their expression of individuality and diversity. Thus, social control agents are seen as the cause of this excess crime.

The criminal justice policy of those sharing this perspective is to prevent the stigmatizing denunciation and degradation of those signified as deviant by reducing the range of banned behavior and by delaying the onset of any institutional processing of primary deviants. The former is achieved by decriminalizing "crimes without victims" (Schur, 1965) and thereby reducing the range of possibilities for which a person can be subject to institutional control. Moreover, by limiting institutional social reaction to their behavior, and by channeling some deviants away from formal agencies, the occasions for "status degradation" in public forums designed for "dressing down" offenders as morally inferior (Garfinkel, 1956) are considerably reduced. The preferred alternative policy is "radical nonintervention," in which tolerance replaces moral indignation (Schur, 1973). The correctional ideology underlying this policy comprises the philosophies of diversion, rehabilitation, restitution, and reparation. Thus a minimalist approach to enforcement is taken which seeks to enact diversion programs that avoid stigmatizing adolescents. The policy also attempts to reverse any future stigmatization by the following means: ceasing to build prisons; decarceration (letting out members of the existing prison population, especially nondangerous offenders); reserving prisons for only the most serious offenders; and by developing alternative programs that allow offenders to be rehabilitated from their label (Cohen, 1979).

HUMANS, HUMAN NATURE, AND HUMAN BEHAVIOR

In the interpretive social process perspective humans are seen as both active in the creation of their world and malleable, pliable, and plastic in their communication with others. They are inextricably social beings who are creative and relatively free to interact with others. However, they also become subject to the meanings others construct of them and with them through interaction with them. In this interaction people act in relation to the *meaning* others have of them, and in doing so they incorporate some of the others' definitions into their own definition of themselves (Cooley, 1902; Blumer, 1969). Human behavior therefore, is not fixed in its meaning but open to interpretation, definition, redefinition, and negotiation. Humans are not static types but dynamic and emerging social statuses.

This idea is found in Mead's (1934) concept of the "mind," which he sees as an ongoing social process, not fixed, but in the process of becoming. In interacting with others, people both remake themselves and transform themselves. However, in so far as interactive processes become institutionalized, formalized, and routine, there is a tendency for human creative energy to become channeled into remaking existing selves, rather than exploring their diversity and potential. It is this ultimate contradiction that leads the potential for change and growth to become self-limiting and stifled and to result in the ossification or "mortification of selves" (Goffman, 1961).

The emphasis within this framework, then, is on potential human agency and its ability to make a difference to self and others. Interpretive social process theorists understand human agency as the ability of human beings to act in a meaningful way, taking into account the meaning that others have of them, as well as to construct new meaning for the purpose of the situation at hand (Blumer, 1969). Thus interactionist and social constructionist theorists see humans as creative beings, acting according to meanings they impart to situations that confront them. Hence human activity is not simply the result of stimuli and reaction, or of learning information or values, but is a socially creative process whereby human beings take things, particularly other humans, into account before they act.

The process of meaning construction is possible because humans are seen as having social selves. Interactionist and social constructionist theorists consider the ability to develop a self the distinguishing feature that separates humans from the animal world. The concept of the "self," central to Mead's (1934) work, refers to the fact that humans have the ability to make objects of themselves. Mead said that this develops from the process of role-taking, whereby people place themselves in the position of others and look back on themselves as others do and become objects to themselves. Thus we can act toward ourselves in the same way that we can act toward others. We can take ourselves into account in formulating or constructing our action. For example, we can be happy with our performance of some task or chastise ourselves for having done poorly; we can "kick ourselves" or "pat ourselves on the back." When persons place themselves in the position of the collective view (the "generalized other"), then they are able to see themselves as a social status.[2]

---

[2]Mead's discussion of the child development process of play and games whereby this ability comes about is beyond the scope of our discussion here.

According to Mead (1934) the self is comprised of two subprocesses, the "I" and the "Me." Internalizing the attitudes of the "generalized other" forms the Me. This is the "social self." Erving Goffman (1959) showed that we can manipulate others' readings of this "Me" by presenting our social selves as a package of how we want others to see us. We can "manage impressions" or construct images of ourselves that we want others to believe is "really" us. We can keep the identity of ourselves, what we believe we really are, hidden in a "back stage." As Mead (1934) claimed, it is only by our responses to the experience of the community internalized as "Me," that the "I" becomes apparent, never entirely predictable or controllable, and partly autonomous. Indeed, it is through this response that the person can change the "Me." We can play roles, or distance ourselves from the roles others put us in, and we can generally engage in strategies and devices that affect the constructions and "typifications" constituting the commonsense knowledge that others have of us (Schutz, 1932).

This ability to be both a subject and an object in our activities is uniquely human. It is the ongoing interaction between the "I" and the "Me" that constitutes our social selves. As Herbert Blumer (1969: 12) pointed out, nothing esoteric is meant by "the self":

> It means merely that a human being can be an object of his own action. Thus, he can recognize himself, for instance, as being a man, young in age, a student, in debt, trying to become a doctor, coming from an undistinguished family and so forth. In all such instances he is an object to himself; and he acts toward himself and guides himself in his actions toward others on the basis of the kind of object he is to himself.

The reason humans are able to direct their action toward others is that they can relate to each other through the use of symbols. This refers to the human ability to make one thing stand for something else (hence the notion of symbolic interactionism). For example, the word *apple* stands for the real apple, a flag stands for a country, the ringing of a bell for the end of class, and so forth. In other words, we can symbolically represent anything—objects, ideas, virtually any phase of human experience.

Humans relate to each other through "significant symbols," which are gestures or language that arouse the same response in the communicator as it does in the person who receives it. The use of significant symbols invokes a set of meanings. Importantly, these symbols not only stand for an object but also indicate a course of action that is to be followed. For example, the "camcorder," an object, also indicates the related action of observing and recording the actions of others. Symbols, therefore, are frameworks through which meaning is conveyed.

Moreover, by virtue of having a self humans can communicate with others, not only by means of gestures and symbols, but as beings who are able to make indications to others and interpret whatever response they receive to shape their actions. According to Blumer, when a gesture has the same meaning to two persons, they understand each other. Schutz (1932) referred to people seeing the world as others see it as a "reciprocity of perspectives" and the "inter-changeability of standpoints." The meaning of the gesture has three components:

> It signifies what the person to whom it is directed is to do; it signifies what the person who is making the gesture plans to do; and it signifies the joint action that is to arise by the articulation of the acts of both. (Blumer, 1969: 9)

Blumer gives the example of a robber intent on robbing his victim.

> A robber's command to his victim to put up his hands is (a) an indication of what the victim is to do; (b) an indication of what the robber plans to do, that is, relieve the victim of his money; and (c) an indication of the joint act being formed, in this case a holdup.

Human action, therefore, is shaped by the interpretation of the anticipated response of others. It is facilitated by the ability of humans to take the role of other persons, as a way of understanding their meaning.

However, there is no assurance that we all interpret symbols and gestures in the same way. The mind is flexible enough to allow interaction even when shared meaning is not identical. Meaning can be brought closer together by "reciprocal interaction," whereby we are able to monitor reflexively our presentation of symbols and adjust these if they do not sound right or if, on reading the other person's response, they do not seem to understand. Schutz (1932) pointed out that people also rely on the commonsense assumption of the "et cetera clause" to close out an interaction. This means that in any communicative exchange people could go on and on elaborating what they mean but they do not. Rather they rely on the other person to "know what they mean."

Such communication of meaning, however, assumes relatively equal power between those engaged in interaction. Where this is not present, communication of meaning can become distorted, leading to misunderstanding. The likelihood of misunderstanding is particularly acute when we deal with entire systems of symbols, such as laws, ideologies, concepts of justice, and so forth, especially since there is typically a one-way communication between senders of messages and those receiving them. Under such circumstances the reality is created by the definitions made and imposed on others. This reality may be different from that experienced by persons who are labeled.

Whether definitions are accepted depends on the extent to which they are forcefully defined as real. The early interactionist William I. Thomas (1923) wrote that "facts" did not have an independent existence apart from the people who observe and interpret them, and depend for their existence on different people entering a situation and defining certain elements of it as real. This condition is summarized by his often quoted axiom: if a situation is defined as real it is real in its consequences. This means, for example, that a belief in mental illness is sufficient to induce the effects of mental illness, even though no mental disease may actually exist. In criminological matters, as in other areas of human conduct, we define a situation (i.e., create a reality) and then act toward the situation on the basis of the definition constructed, even though the meaning of the activity to the participants may be very different from the way it is presented.

The question of the nature of social reality, in relation to human action, is one that divides theorists who otherwise share the interpretive social process perspective. The major division is between, on the one hand, interactionists and labeling theorists, who share the view that there exists an objective reality to which humans attach meaning, and phenomenologists and social constructionists, who believe that there is no reality other than the meaning that people construct. (See Pfuhl and Henry, 1993, for an elaboration.)

When considering behavior, criminal or otherwise, it is important to distinguish between the action occurring in its meaningful context and the accounts for and about that activity, taking place in their own context with their own construction of meaning. This is illustrated very well by Matza's (1964) concept of neutralization discussed in the previous chapter.

In summary, humans are conscious, reflective beings continuously engaged in ongoing purposive activity in relation to others which is mediated by language and gesture through the use of symbols. Humans define their world of objects and events, socially constructing their meaning in relation to preexisting meanings by selecting, classifying, interpreting, signifying, and naming them and thereby objectifying them as social reality in the context of the situation and wider setting of which they are a part. In short, humans are both the script writers and the actors in the play of social life.

Just as interactionists and social constructionist theorists see human nature as the active construction of human beings interacting in a social world, so their view of society and the social order is one in which humans interact with one another in complex ways and construct meaning to shape social existence. Let us now examine the societal dimension of these theorists' perspective.

VIEW OF SOCIETY AND THE SOCIAL ORDER

According to symbolic interactionists, society is a social construction but it is not a total fiction. It is merely the appearance of consensus that warrants this description. Rather, society consists of "acting units" (Blumer, 1969). Acting units are individual persons acting together in a common or joint activity, such as a family, an organization, a police department, a gang, a church, and so forth. While interactionists would not deny other ways of perceiving society, through such concepts as class and institutions, they insist on the recognition that even classes and institutions consist of a core of acting human beings (Blumer, 1969) and comprise the social organization of the acts of different people.

Whatever action is staged, it always takes place in regard to some situation and occurs in a specific context. Contexts are the settings or situations (comprised of both meaningful physical places and flows of social action) in which the interpretation of action takes place. As Blumer (1969: 85) states:

> Whatever be the acting unit—an individual, a family, a school, a church, a business firm, a labor union, a legislature ... any particular action is formed in light of the situation in which it takes place.

This in turn

> leads to the recognition ... that the action is formed or constructed by interpreting the situation. The acting unit necessarily has to identify the things it has to take into account—tasks, opportunities, obstacles, means, demands, discomforts, dangers, and the like; it has to assess them in some fashion and it has to make decisions on the basis of the assessment.

From this perspective, society is merely a framework inside of which social action takes place in specific social contexts. Social structure, from this perspective, is the correspondence, aggregation, and alignment of the chains of meaningful interaction or "interaction rituals" (Collins, 1981) in which people engage. It is not fixed but dynamic and ever-changing.

The observation that society is composed of acting social units, with their own construction, interpretation, and view of social reality, suggests a conflict rather than consensus view of society in which classes, strata, or groups exist in a constant state of struggle. The nature of the relationship between these segments is transient, and agreement between them is felt to be through domination of one by another, rather than as a result of value agreement. But as Pfuhl and Henry (1993: 9) caution:

> the unity of "values" and "norms" assumed to exist by consensus theorists is said to be a fiction and should not be confused with expedient, short-term unity— as when groups are in more or less agreement with one another while pursuing shared goals. The appearance and taken-for-granted nature of such "small group" unity does not preclude the existence of widespread value disagreement. However,

such alliances quite often are matters of expedience and rest on the belief that they serve unique purposes for each group. Given its utilitarian basis, such "unity" should not be confused with "essential value consensus and stability".

Indeed, it is argued that any notion of societal consensus is largely an ideological construction resulting from social activity by agencies such as the media who voice the definitions of organized groups who make claims that "people in general" or the majority of people or the "moral majority" share their idea of what is real.

In addition, social constructionists present a variation of social order that, not surprisingly, depicts the society as a constructed representation of reality. They argue that the social world has no underlying objective character. Thus Pfuhl and Henry (1993) observe that "if people appear to be ordered and orderly it is the outcome of their own active concessions, their own contributions (unwitting or otherwise) to consensus." In this view society is an ongoing, constantly emerging outcome of human agents' interaction with one another that produces shared "representations" (Knorr-Cetina, 1981). These are composite mental pictures taken to represent a reality *assumed to exist and acted toward as though it does exist.* When people's mental pictures of reality approximately correspond to each other, as assessed by communicated cues and signs on which they share and agree, then they assume for practical purposes that a reality exists. Enough is held in common to produce patterns of behavior, whose very repetition serves to reinforce the original notion of reality and bolster the appearance of substance and structure. However, where the discrepancies that exist are not suspended for the time being, when they are challenged, conflict emerges. Through such challenges the idea of consensus is exposed as a fabrication:

> The social constructionist view regards society as a grand or ongoing social construction, the medium through which individuals constitute their social worlds. Unlike the bifurcated vision of earlier perspectives, they see *both* consensus and conflict as simultaneously present as co-contributors to the illusion of the whole. Indeed, without conflict, consensus would be meaningless, as would conflict without consensus. Neither represents the truth in any objective sense; each are exaggerations of integral aspects of the mental pictures people have of the world in which they live. (Pfuhl and Henry, 1993: 10)

One of the major battlegrounds where this contradictory vision of the nature of society is exposed is law.

THE ROLE OF LAW, THE DEFINITION OF CRIME, AND THE IMAGE OF THE CRIMINAL

From the interactionist, and particularly social constructionist, perspective, perceived differences that are negatively evaluated are the source of much banning of behavior and subsequent enactment as law. Identifying and defining a behavior are said to draw it out from the vast array of possible behaviors as a significant one—one about which something needs to be done.

Although banning may be accomplished in the course of asserting a particular positive direction and intention, it is more common for these theorists to discuss banning as a reactive, rather than proactive, behavior done by audiences against something real or imagined. Audiences may be made up of ordinary citizens or interest groups or others organized to lobby, which Becker (1963) eloquently describes as "moral entrepreneurs."

> The prototype of the rule creator, but not the only variety ... is the crusading reformer. He is interested in the content of rules. The existing rules do not satisfy him because there is some evil which profoundly disturbs him. He feels that nothing can be right in the world until rules are made to correct it. (Becker, 1963: 147–148)

While the moral crusader may be an ideal type, there are a large variety of moral entrepreneurs who do not reach the level of crusaders. Legislators, lobbyists, interest groups, political action committees, and other powerful blocks who either create laws or suggest that various behaviors be criminalized or not, all fall within the category. Advocates of the perspective stress that successful moral entrepreneurs are those that have the social power to have their version of morality imposed on the rest:

> Unfortunately within the pluralistic order of society certain groups—variously and vaguely termed "the powerful," "the bureaucracy," "the moral entrepreneur"—with more power than others, enforce their values upon the less powerful, labelling those who infringe their rules with stereotypical tags. (Young, 1981: 288)

A variety of studies have concentrated on the role of moral entrepreneurs in the creation of laws reflecting particular moral stances and the "discovery" of problems: alcohol use and temperance (Gusfield, 1955); sexual psychopathy (Sutherland, 1950); marijuana use (Becker, 1963); witchcraft (Erikson, 1966); delinquency as a category (Platt, 1969); child abuse (Pfuhl, 1977); smoking (Markle and Troyer, 1979); and wife abuse (Tierney, 1982). Each of these studies discusses the process of how certain behaviors came to be defined as social problems or as crime, and the role played by certain individuals, groups, or agencies as moral entrepreneurs. Such groups are no less social types than the social types their banning creates, but are simply people who feel threatened, powerless, offended, or unsettled. As Box (1971) has said, they become people who have the power, and sometimes the authority, to impose their judgments on others.

According to the interactionist/constructionist perspective, the process of banning and rule making may begin with fear but quickly moves to a shared sense of danger and a belief among the fearful that the behavior in question is not going to go away by itself. Moreover, it is seen as controllable, and its control can be implemented by creating new rules or by strengthening existing ones through extra enforcement. Alternatively, a more symbolic motive may be held to underlie rule-making activity, such as establishing or underpinning a particular social group's position in the society. Gusfield (1963) has forcefully demonstrated this in the case of the early twentieth-century Prohibition laws, the enactment of which he says was driven by downwardly mobile white Protestant Americans fearful of losing their dominance in society to Irish Catholic immigrants and using legislation to demonstrate symbolically that they could still define morality.

Whether it is instrumental or symbolic, the conversion of some groups' private moralities into public issues, according to the interactionist and social constructionists, is necessary if their concern is to gain sufficient legitimacy to warrant more formal rule making. In this process, a principal partner is seen to be the mass media. They can act either as a forum for the display of concern or as an instrument for agitating it.

According to these theorists, the range of strategies for mobilizing moral support is as wide as that available to candidates in a political campaign. Moral entrepreneurs are said to promote their case for a behavioral ban by associating their proposed rules with positive values or benefits to society. Particularly popular are bans claimed to increase health or freedom. A similarly powerful impact can be achieved by associating the continued existence of questioned behavior with negative values, pointing up its threat to the mental, physical, or moral fabric of organized society. Groups of moral entrepreneurs are said to draw respectability from the public by establishing alliances with respected members of society or by recruiting these people's testimonies, if not their person. Any endorsement by public officials takes the rule-making case toward a complete ban. Any myth making that can be employed to exaggerate aspects of the behavior or to help hang the activity on the backs of already recognized undesirable social types is seen to help their cause.

Ultimately, for those sharing this view, the goal of banning a behavior will be met if the state can be "captured," so that laws are passed. This, they say, will empower the major law enforcement agencies to act, in the name of the whole society, on behalf of those groups with immediate concerns. At this point, the interest group can be said to have established an official ban against the behavior (Quinney, 1970).

The chances of resisting the ban, say interactionists and constructionists, are considerably advanced if those engaged in the behavior, or those who wish to see us remain free to choose it, engage in a counter political campaign (Schur,

1980). In this context, controversy, rather than consensus, can be claimed. In such circumstances, the law, as Turk (1976) has argued, becomes a weapon in the battle between competing interest groups and can actually create conflict by being a resource to be won.

These bans are subsequently enforced by control agents who determine which behaviors are criminalized and which are not. Rule enforcers themselves become moral entrepreneurs when they seek to create rules to make their jobs easier or work to maintain laws and rules that justify their existence (Dickson, 1968).

In summary then, law is seen as the expression of the power of some people to defend their interpretation of reality over that of others. In one sense, law is part of what Henry (1987) describes as policing the boundaries of socially constructed definitions of reality. It is the formalization of the bans placed on some people's behavior by moral entrepreneurs.

According to interactionists and labeling theorists crime and deviance are some people's definitions of what they find offensive. There is nothing inherently criminal in behavior selected for banning. Rather crime is a category, defined in law, that is relative to cultures, historical period, group, social status, social context, and, importantly, those who hold the power to criminalize. People's standards as to what is ideal or acceptable behavior may be set in the face of real or imagined behavior that is feared or disliked. Acts may be banned because of a desire to promote a particular set of values or lifestyle. Standards can be precisely specified as rules or laws, or else they may be more loosely constructed as informal norms and expectation. The laws, rules, and norms take the form they do as a result of being shaped by individual personal biographies, by group pressures and processes, and by the wider societal context in which these individuals live. Sometimes, say these theorists, behaviors judged to be deviant are the product of precisely the same process of social construction as are the standards of those who are judging their behavior unacceptable; one group's standards are another group's deviance. For example, when a government enacts food and drug legislation, making the unhygienic preparation of carcass meat unlawful, it is promoting a particular set of values and making deviants out of those who prepare meat in ways deemed to be unhygienic. When a group of vegetarians declare any meat preparation and consumption to be "killing," they are making deviants of, among other people, the Food and Drug Administration. Both groups, however, are setting norms that are designed to promote a particular, albeit different, lifestyle.

These theorists point out that some crime is statistically deviant, such as murder, while other crime is statistically typical, such as tax evasion. Some activities that were formally crimes are now defined as legal, while others which were formerly legal, such as cocaine consumption, and more recently cigarette smoking, are now illegal in many contexts (Markle and Troyer, 1979). Critically, then, whether a particular activity is judged criminal or not depends upon the context or situation. Consider the following illustration:

The members of the jury were requested to complete claim forms for expenses they had incurred while fulfilling this civic duty. On filling these in, there was considerable discussion concerning which items could be inflated, such as mileage by car, and whether to risk the claim that by fulfilling their jury service they had lost their normal weekly wage. After payment had been made, there were comparative calculations on the amount of money that had been illegally obtained, or "spending money" as one of them called it. The money acquired in this fashion ranged from 3 ($6) to 25 ($50) pounds. No one condemned this practice or reported it to policemen on duty in the court; yet shortly before the same [jury] men had found an adolescent guilty of stealing items valued at 2 pounds 50p ($5), and had all morally condemned his behaviour by agreeing with the judge's sentencing of nine months in prison. (Box, 1971: 63)

In this example it can be seen that those who have the power can offend and not be subject to legal definitions, whereas those who do not have power become the subject of legal processing. Those whose behavior becomes defined as crimes are typically those whose offending takes place, visibly, in public places. Those whose behavior escapes this definition are able to mobilize the machinery of law in their defense, either to avoid becoming the subject of criminal processing or to ensure that the outcome of any trial is favorable. As Box (1981: 235) cynically observes, their route "is paved with enormous stones of profit and tree-lined for protection from the cold wind of law enforcement."

CAUSAL LOGIC

As we have seen, the theorists considered here believe human behavior to be an outcome of interactive relationships, whether or not the behavior is judged as conforming or deviant, conventional or criminal. In the production of crime two broad processes merge. One of these concerns the actor as a rule breaker, the other the audience as control agent.

The Intentional Actor

Interactionist and constructionist analysis start from the view that humans have some degree of choice over whether to break rules, but this varies depending on people's personal biography (Pfuhl and Henry, 1993). People's past experiences render some behaviors available while closing off others that have never been part of their behavioral scope. Choices are unequal because past experiences have been unique. Yet choices are patterned because the members of some social groups, such as blacks, the disabled, children of alcoholics, those raised in state homes, and so forth, have been subject to broadly similar conditions. Yet even within these categories patterns of behavior are variable.

Combining meanings from one's sociocultural environment with personal experiences shapes the way a situation is defined. People will have an "affinity" to some activities and an "aversion" to others (Matza, 1969). The decision to commit an act of deviance or break a law is arrived at with more or less openness, more or less willingness, and more or less affinity or aversion. People are relatively free to make choices but are neither certain nor compelled to act in a particular way. What tips the balance may depend, quite literally, on how open and willing they already are. It may depend as much on how they see the act furthering their self-identity, or how it adds to who they already see themselves as being. Alternatively, reluctance to commit a deviant act may be slowly worn away by the persistent requests from friends. Once it has been experimented with, deviant behavior is a source of its own motivation. If the experience was bad, the person may have been "turned off" by the behavior and may be unwilling to try it again. However, the experience may be sufficiently neutral or attractive that they are more willing to try the activity again. After a succession of increasingly favorable experiences, people may become "turned on" to the activity.

However, participating in rule-breaking activity, once or even repeatedly, is not sufficient to make a deviant or criminal identity. As we mentioned earlier, Lemert (1951) argues that there is a difference between acts of "primary deviance," which is rule breaking that occurs through the process described above and that almost everyone engages in at one time or another, and acts of deviance or crime committed as a result of the reaction to an original act of deviance or crime, which Lemert calls "secondary deviance." The primary deviant does not perceive himself or herself as criminal. The reasons for primary deviance are diverse, and much of it may be transitory and carried out in the nature of an exploration.

However, engaging in behavior that has been banned by those who wish to conceal the fact gives rise to problems of secrecy and "transparency" (Matza, 1969). In continuing primary deviant activities, some rule breakers will decide that their best option is to hide their deviance and they do this by playing conventional roles. However,

> The problem of transparency ... is that others may see through the subject's flimsy attempts to conceal the fact that he has misbehaved ... The subject has to appear conventional ... To do this, the subject has to be devious—he has to play at being ordinary. The irony is that, having exerted so much effort to appear ordinary, the subject performs a self-disservice by glimpsing the possibility that he is, after all, only playing at it ... This doubt is sufficient to prepare an individual to be slightly more compliant with the State's altercasting when, and if, he is apprehended for committing a further offence. (Box, 1981: 211)

Indeed, this self-doubt prepares the way for the identity transformation that produces secondary deviance.

Lemert says secondary deviance is the direct result of societal reaction to primary deviance. Secondary deviation comes about because of the process described earlier, whereby humans take on, as part of themselves, others' definitions of them. Thus, the public and official labeling of a person as criminal over time can result in an identity transformation (Lofland, 1969). Instead of the person breaking rules because the behavior is one of a vast array of options, they are now more likely to break rules because of who they have become. Secondary deviant behavior is part of their social self or criminal identity.

The Reactive Audience

For secondary deviation to occur the activities of the audience, especially negative evaluation, are particular important. Tannenbaum (1938) in his studies of delinquency first highlighted the significance of what later was described by Lemert as secondary deviation when he referred to the "dramatization of evil." By this he meant the impact the label of "delinquent" or "criminal" has on the person or persons concerned. The very fact of attributing a label, thereby stigmatizing the individual, he argued, may create more serious problems. By emphasizing the negative qualities of the person through the attribution of the label, the person may eventually become what he or she is described as being. In other words, a self-fulfilling prophecy is generated. The intention of the labeler does not seem to matter. The very fact of labeling is the source of the discord.

> The process of making the criminal ... is a process of tagging, identifying, segregating, describing, emphasizing, making conscious and self conscious; it becomes a way of stimulating, of suggesting, emphasizing and evoking the very traits that are complained of ... The person becomes the thing he is described as being. Nor does it seem to matter whether the valuation is made by those who would punish or by those who would reform ... The harder they work to reform the evil, the greater the evil grows under their hands. The persistent suggestion, with whatever good intentions, works mischief, because it leads to bringing the bad behavior it would suppress. The way out is through a refusal to dramatize the evil. (Tannenbaum, 1938: 19–20)

Labeling theorists point out that the roots of the process resulting in secondary deviation comes not so much from the actor but from the reactions to the actor by various audiences of others. They argue that all social groups have rules. Once these rules are enforced, the person who violated the rule tends to be seen as a special type of person, someone not to be trusted, an "outsider" (Becker, 1963). Labeling proponents argue that *society,* or at least *social groups* that form society, transform what is originally merely rule breaking behavior into a *commitment* to crime or deviance. According to Becker (1963: 9): "Social groups create deviance by making the rules whose infraction constitutes deviance, and by applying those rules to particular people and labeling them as outsiders." Therefore, who is called a deviant or criminal depends, not only on whether a person breaks rules, but also on whether or not a "label" is successfully applied. Hence crime and deviance *as a systematic or routine activity* is not something inherent in the person or act but something that is attributed to the person and his or her action. As Becker (1963: 9), in an often quoted passage, says: "Deviance is not a quality of the act a person commits, but rather a consequence of the application by others of rules and sanctions to an 'offender.'" The effect of this application of rules is that who is called an offender and what is called an offense—who is considered deviant or criminal—depends on the response of others, the audience to the person-in-question's behavior.

From this it follows that there is no necessary uniformity as to who and what becomes defined as deviant or criminal because the response to each act and actor may differ. Although the potential to break rules and laws may be universal, *criminality* is not lodged within the person as part of his or her personality but depends on what label is conferred by those doing the defining, the agents of social control. Thus what labeling theorists argue makes an act "criminal" is not necessarily the rule-breaking behavior itself, nor the harm or outrage it causes, but whether the definition of "crime," the label, is attributed to the act by agents of the state (or any social control agent, e.g., psychiatrist, social worker, etc.), and whether the action so defined is successfully attributed to a particular individual or group. Major implications follow from this simple but rather profound view.

Becker (1963) called attention to a sequential process of engaging in a criminal career which takes into account the crucial step of being publicly labeled as criminal or deviant. The process typically begins with law enforcers. Not all laws can be enforced equally, hence there are priorities and enforcement is selective. Enforcers develop "their own private evaluation of the importance of various kinds of rules and infractions of them" (Becker, 1963: 161), with the imputation of "ancillary qualities to the deviator" (Schur, 1971). Enforcement is never exact. Often the wrong persons are accused and labels are erroneously attributed, and only some of those who break the law are actually arrested and prosecuted. The point made by interactionists is that the enforcement of rules is not only based on the violation of rules but on extraneous factors that often are more important determinants than the violations themselves (Lilly et al., 1989). Often the demeanor of the person toward the police, the context in which the supposed violation occurs, and the social class and race of the suspect are factors that enter into the decision to make an arrest or not (Piliavin and Briar, 1964; Black and Reiss, 1970). Thus social reaction is not something objective and is not totally a function of some identified deviant act. It is arbitrary and, interactionists argue, as a result, who gets labeled as a deviant or criminal also is arbitrary. Therefore, no generalizations may be made about offenders as a class other than that they share having been labeled as such. This is so because we know nothing about those who have engaged in the same behavior but have not been officially labeled. Arrests are determined by the definition enforcement officials make of the situation, whether or not the definitions officials make are "correct."

Labeling theorists argue that whether a label is successfully applied depends on negotiation and that this process involves some power relations (Schur, 1971). Many instances occur in which the criminal status is negotiated during organizational processing and through "plea bargaining." From the initial arrest, to the courts, to probation, to prison and parole there are procedures designed to process and classify individuals into "criminal molds." This typification, classification, and use of case records create a seeming bureaucratic efficiency but have a negative impact on the status of the individual, as we have seen. Moreover, interactionists argue, that the system as presently constituted only adds fuel to the fire in creating more intractable criminal behavior. Again we see this in plea bargaining, which Schur (1971) says is an attempt to negotiate a particular type of label. Depending on the social resources and relative social power of the parties involved, different outcomes are the result. Obviously those who find themselves potentially labeled as criminal and who have considerable resources are in a better position to resist the label than those who lack those resources. Moreover, the type of label that is attached has other significant implications in the causal logic of the labeling tradition. Though there is no definitive method to predict if there is going to be a societal reaction or a particular label attached, Scheff (1966) indicates that a number of variables increase the likelihood of a reaction. These include the degree and amount of rule violation, how visible the violation is, how powerful the rule violator is, the social distance between violator and reactor, the level of tolerance in the community, and the degree to which legitimate roles are available in the group or culture to which the violator belongs. The variables do not act independently but must be considered as part of an interactional system.

Others have pointed to the consequences of this process in terms of both societal perceptions as well as self-perceptions. Garfinkel (1956) argues that the public accusation and labeling of the individual amounts to a moral degradation, which once attributed (even if false) is not easily removed. Criminal trials thus become "degradation ceremonies," where not only the criminal conduct is defined as wrong but the offender as a person is redefined as a criminal. Moreover, this redefinition is not just a simple labeling but a "reconstituting" of the person whereby the individual is perceived as being somehow qualitatively different from the beginning and any previous perceptions to the contrary is reassessed as erroneous (Garfinkel, 1956). Persons become in essence "a burglar," "a robber," "a thief," "a drug fiend." The behavior becomes a "master status" (Hughes, 1945; Becker, 1963; Goffman, 1963) wherein their deviancy role is deemed the person's total identity and the overriding basis on which judgments about the person are made. Thus, according to Becker:

One will be identified as a deviant first, before other identifications are made. The question is raised: "What kind of person would break such an important rule?" And the answer is given: "One who is different from the rest of us, who cannot and will not act as a moral human being and therefore might break other important rules." The deviant identification becomes the controlling one. (Becker, 1963: 33–34)

So, according to labeling theorists, when primary rule breakers are labeled they undergo an identity transformation and identify themselves as criminals. However, a second process may also operate to accentuate the likelihood of rule breaking and facilitate the firming of a deviant or criminal identity that is the source of secondary rule breaking. This occurs when the societal reaction to the original deviance is such that it limits or totally restricts the chances and opportunities of persons to engage in legitimate activities. As a result of these restrictions, the individual has few options other than to engage in further deviance and crime. As Mankoff (1971: 201) explains, "rule breakers become entrenched in deviant roles because they are labeled 'deviant' by others and are consequently excluded from resuming normal roles in the community." Young (1971) refers to this as "deviance amplification," wherein the reaction creates the very deviance the reactors wished to prevent (self-fulfilling prophecy), and as reactions become more severe the deviance and crime become more severe as well. Eventually he is perceived as a deviant or criminal and takes on that perception as a self-definition (Lemert, 1951, 1967). The classic example of deviancy amplification through the labeling process is the ex-convict who, because of his or her status (label) as "socially disabled," is unable to find legitimate opportunities and, as a result, engages in further crime as a criminal career (Irwin, 1970). Another example is the marijuana user's response to policing whereby secrecy and avoidance tactics result in further encounters with deviance in an increasing spiral of involvement in rule breaking and disengagement from conventional activity (Young, 1971).

Hence, secondary deviance comes about when the person's deviant or criminal behavior becomes, first, a response to the transparency problem of banning behavior; second, a part of their self-identity; and, third, a means of adjustment to the societal response. As Lemert (1967) has indicated, it is at this juncture that labeling and its stigmatization become "full blown." Partly as a means of accommodating to this, some rule breakers develop a commitment to a criminal career.

We may summarize the causal sequence of this perspective as follows. People can and do engage in a wide variety of acts. Some of these are banned by powerful groups as illegal. *Some* people's banned behavior is observed by audiences of others, identified as offensive, and interpreted as significant enough to do something about, such as, reporting it to social control agents. To avoid this some rule breakers conceal their behavior and play at being normal and conventional. But the problem of transparency allows them to glimpse the possibility that their secret behavior is a reflection of who they really are, and they become susceptible to an identity change. Control agents pick up some people who fall into the stereotypical category for that type of offender. These people are processed through the criminal justice system, whereby they undergo a status degradation ceremony that further defines their behavior as different and judges them to be morally inferior, as "bad persons." The label serves as a "master status," indicating a whole set of stereotypical behaviors associated with an identity that overrides all others. This is enhanced by others who react not to the person, but to the stereotype indicated by the label. These others engage in retrospective interpretation, redefining previous different behavior as indicative of the person's real identity. The force of the label and the stigma leads some of those labeled to question who they really are, to question their self-identity. Because of their interactive communication with the system and its labelers, some of these individuals undergo an identity transformation whereby they see themselves as criminals. Such labeled persons are channeled into acting and believing that they are governed by the identity that has been conferred upon them. Their criminal identity is further enhanced through deviancy amplification whereby others limit the possibilities to behave in conventional activity and the person tries to conceal their rule-breaking identity by engaging in secret rule breaking, which further marginalizes them. Eventually they adjust to their criminal status, especially through the normalization and positive redefinition that occur when they interact with similarly defined others. They are then on the path of developing a deviant career.

CRIMINAL JUSTICE SYSTEM IMPLICATIONS

Because of their causal analysis, which gives a central place to the role of the criminal justice system, labeling theorists offer two views of criminal justice. The first forms part of their critique and analyzes how criminal justice operates to stigmatize offenders. The second view of criminal justice forms the labeling theorists' policy for reforming criminal justice (see Criminal Justice Policy and Correctional Ideology below).

The critical analysis of the criminal justice system has been called the *status passage model*, since it presents criminal justice institutions as stages in a process through which a person's moral identity is transformed (Glazer and Strauss, 1971; King, 1978, 1981):

> This perspective stresses the function of the criminal courts as institutions for denouncing the defendant, reducing his social status and so promoting solidarity within the community ... Criminal courts may be regarded as places where the

moral standing of citizens is put at issue. In many cases then the social function of the court may be seen as that of moral condemnation and hence degradation of status ... The ceremony ... where the defendant pleads guilty and is sentenced, marks the culmination of the process of denunciation and degradation. The preceding steps in this process are seen as preparation for this moment. (King, 1981: 23–25)

King (ibid: 111) argues that the status passage model sees the central aims of the criminal justice system as imposing a new social status on all or most defendants and that all those involved in criminal justice are "engaged in the task of reducing the defendant to a symbol within a recurrent social ritual."

Criminal Justice Policy and Correctional Ideology

Given their analysis that social control causes crime, or at least that the existing practices of criminal justice exacerbate crime rather than diminishing it, it is not surprising that interactionists, labeling theorists, and social constructionists believe that the appropriate policy response is to limit social reaction to crime. They believe that instead of overreacting to instances of rule breaking, these must be accommodated to as instances of diversity, and in some instances even celebrated as expressions of the individuality of humanity. The policy broadly stated by Schur (1973) should be one of "radical nonintervention." Given their focus on the impact of reaction by the agents of control as being a crucial link in the causal chain of continued criminal behavior, interactionists prefer a minimalist approach to criminal justice processing. The least amount of intrusion necessary is considered the best policy.

A multipronged correctional ideology is adopted within this overall approach that involves four basic strategies:

1. decriminalization
2. diversion
3. decarceration
4. the philosophies of restitution or reparation

We will consider the meaning of each of these and their proposed implementation in the following section.

Techniques of Crime Control

Decriminalization means that some acts that are presently offenses should be legalized. Although seemingly a trite idea, the theorists supporting it believe that laws actually create crime (Morris and Hawkins, 1970; Schur, 1965, 1973; Schur and Bedau, 1974). There are a number of reasons for this. To begin with, the very fact that there is a law creates a category of potential offenders. Further, additional crimes are committed in order to engage in the banned activity. For example, drug users may commit burglaries to obtain money to buy drugs whose price is exorbitant because they are illegal. Of course the very fact that drugs are an illegal commodity for which there is a high demand sets up an illegal marketplace and creates problems of enforcement, which more often than not, are resolved by illegal means by the enforcers. In that event both substantive and procedural law are violated. With status offenses the issue becomes one of labeling and the consequences of such labeling, as we already discussed. It is, therefore, apparent that certain forms of criminalizing are criminogenic.

Accordingly, many labeling theorists believe that there is an overreach of the criminal law, through which too many behaviors are defined as crimes, particularly in those areas where there are "crimes without victims" (Schur, 1965; Schur and Bedau, 1974). Labeling theorists argue for decriminalizing those behaviors (a) that are voluntarily engaged in, (b) that have no victim (in the usual sense of the term), and (c) that may create a high demand for services even though these may be illegal. Hence, the idea is to decriminalize behavior that is against the law because it offends the state or public morality—such as public drunkenness, gambling, pornography, some kinds of prostitution, and the use of illegal drugs, as well as so-called status offenses (certain behaviors permitted to adults but against the law when engaged in by those under a certain age).

Clearly, legislative action is necessary to decriminalize certain offenses but that, in turn, requires the political action of interest groups to lobby for legislative change. Various groups, such as NORML (National Organization for Reform of Marijuana Laws, which is pro-legalization of marijuana) and ACT-UP (promoting homosexual rights), and COYOTE (Call Off Your Old Tired Ethics, a prostitutes' rights group) are seen as necessary and instrumental in bringing about legislative change.

A second component of radical noninterventionist ideology is *diversion.* From the labeling theorists' perspective it is vital that the reaction to any offense be kept within limits in order to lessen its impact and prevent the development of secondary deviance. To achieve this, the least amount of contact with the criminal justice system is considered desirable. Thus, in addition to cutting down on the number of ways someone can enter the criminal justice system, labeling theorists believe that many offenders should be redirected to other forms of institution to deal with the issue instead of forcing them through the stigmatizing process of the criminal justice system. This process of redirection, called diversion, must be accomplished through the application of various alternative methods to formal handling by the criminal justice system. For the most part, diversion from the criminal justice system has been used with juvenile offenders, diverting them from the juvenile court to other private or public agencies thought to be less stigmatizing. Such agencies and special treatment programs deal with specific problems such as substance abuse. Adult offenders have been similarly processed, particularly for such offenses as drunk driving or illicit drug use. Part of the reason for the popularity of diversion (Lemert, 1981) came because there was already in place a movement to deinstitutionalize the mentally ill, elderly, and the retarded (Warren, 1981; Shover and Einstadter, 1988).

A central aim of the diversionary alternatives is to divest the criminal justice system of its power to stigmatize, while at the same time rendering a resolution to the rule breaker's offense. These alternatives lean heavily on the idea of dispute settlement. Instead of offenders being seen as rule breakers, they are reconceived as persons in dispute, with society and the community at one level, and with particular individual representatives of it at another. Attempts are then made to resolve the "dispute," without incurring moral degradation, which is seen as wasteful and counterproductive. Instead, the informal community techniques of dispute resolution, such as mediation and conciliation, are used, which are geared to repairing the breached relations between the victim and the offender.

The third element of the noninterventionist policy is *decarceration.* Because incarceration is considered to have the most stigmatizing and criminogenic effect, it makes sense that the less people receive prison sentences for their offenses, the more rapidly they will be able to return to a life of convention. The less contact they have with a community of like offenders, the less their offending will be normalized.

To bring about the objective of decarceration, Cohen (1979) suggests attrition (wearing down the control system of prisons). He suggests a three-part program:

1. a moratorium on prison building
2. a release program, whereby 70 percent to 80 percent of the prisoners incarcerated for nonviolent property offenses be freed, and
3. excarceration, which stops putting people in prison for nonviolent, less serious offenses, such as drug use or sale

Finally, a combination of *restitution and reparation* should be used for those who offend. In other words, the aim should be to bring the offender and victim together to return the situation to how it was before the offense. The attention should be directed toward the consequences of the rule-breaking behavior, not the crime itself. The aim is to bring home to the offender the consequences of his or her action, and also to include victims into the system to enable them to understand why they were victimized. Both the offender and the victim should be actively involved in the determination of the amount of restitution.

To satisfy the restitutive philosophy, offenses against property might involve monetary payment over a period (especially in the case of offenders such as embezzlers whose job skills and employment possibilities are high). When the offense is against public or community property, reparation in the form of community service might be appropriately used. Indeed, this is perhaps the most widely used diversionary practice, especially when the victim is anonymous, unknown, or does not wish to participate. Increasingly, home incarceration in combination with the use of electronic-monitoring "tether" has become a popular disposition (Ball and Lilly 1985, 1987). For less serious offenses they recommend a variety of noncoercive or nonrestrictive sanctions. Intensive probation is one alternative that is also used as a substitute for prison.

Importantly, labeling theorists do not recommend the total abandonment of incarceration but argue rather that its use should be reserved for the most serious offenses, specifically those involving violence. Instead of a punitive and highly disciplined correctional system, prisoners would be encouraged to develop and run their own societies within prison, through a participative system with prison officers, along the lines of the "just community" attempted in the Connecticut women's prison in 1971 and the Barlinnie prison in Scotland (Scharf, 1977; Boyle, 1977). During 1971 inmates, guards, and prison administrators in a Connecticut prison met in a "constitutional convention" in which rules were proposed for a model democratic framework whereby "inmates would control internal discipline and define objectives and activities. All prison offenses, apart from major felonies would be referred to a 'cottage community meeting' " (Scharf, 1977: 104). A community member could call a meeting at any time and when a "cottage rule offence" was discovered. The meeting acts as a jury to determine guilt or innocence. If discipline is called for, it is referred to a discipline board, which includes two inmates and one staff member, chosen at random:

> Routine issues, involving matters like work assignments, love triangles or personal conflict, are dealt with through open discussion. The community occasionally deals with issues of contraband, assault and attempted escape. Cottage rules are redefined every twelve weeks in a marathon meeting. Here there are often further negotiations with administrators as to the kinds of issues that cottage democracy may deal with. (Scharf, 1977: 104)

Other suggested sanctions have included "banishment" or even a return of "transportation" (Douglas, 1971: 42–43). In this, as with the prison option, the form taken by social control is very different from the current system.

It is clear that the sanctioning system suggested by labeling theorists and some social constructionists is very different from that offered by the earlier perspectives that we have examined. Perhaps not surprisingly, in spite of the experimentation that has taken place at various levels with the system, the interactionist/constructionist framework has come under considerable criticism and is epitomized as being "soft on crime."

EVALUATION

The labeling perspective's contribution to criminology lies in its focus on the importance of the variability of human behavior and of social reaction to behavior and the resultant consequences for further criminality. The implicit assumption of the diversity of behavior and values serves as a counterpoint to the assumption of a moral consensus implied in earlier explanatory frameworks. In addition, the perspective's focus on *process* serves to sensitize us to the interpretive and interactional aspects of criminal definition and labeling. Particularly important is the recognition that more problems can come from a society's banning of behavior and stigmatization of those it defines as different, than from the "offense" created by the difference.

However, the theory is not without its critics, who reject the causal connection of reaction to deviance by pointing to the previous, temporarily independent existence of the deviant or criminal act (Gibbs, 1966). Mankoff (1971) points out that deviant careers can occur without the public labeling of offenders, as in the case of systematic employee theft, or marijuana users, many of whom have never been subject to the criminal justice system (see Ditton, 1977; Henry, 1978). Mankoff says that it is helpful to distinguish between "ascribed rule breaking," in which deviant status is acquired, irrespective of the rule breaker's wishes, and "achieved rule breaking," in which the individual will actively take part in an offensive activity regardless of the attachment of a deviant label.

A related criticism is that primary deviance is not readily explained, nor are the motivations to engage in crime or the precipitating events leading to the criminal activity. As Box (1981) argues: "Unfortunately the theoretical links between social control and further deviant behavior have never been completely forged" (p. 208) and "interactionists have been poetic, polemical and political, but unfortunately they have been rarely precise" (p. 210).

Moreover, the perspective deals little with the fact that some never perceive themselves as stigmatized even though they carry pejorative labels (e.g., Richard Nixon, Oliver North). Some even use the label in their interest (e.g., former drug users, ex-alcoholics, former inmates in rehabilitation programs; see Sagarin, 1969; Robinson and Henry, 1977; Katz and Bender, 1976; and Pfuhl and Henry, 1993). Differences between individuals and groups in the same stigmatized category are also not explained.

A paradox pointed out early on by Akers (1967) and subsequently by others (Taylor, Walton, and Young, 1973; Schervish, 1973; Quandagno and Antonio, 1975) is that a perspective that starts out with the assumption of an intentional creative human being, ends up with a passive actor locked into a stereotypical "oversocialized" role. As Akers (1967: 46) cynically observed, it is just as though "people go about minding their own business, and then—'wham'—bad society comes along and slaps them with a stigmatized label. Forced into the role of deviant, the individual has little choice but to be deviant."

Certain forms of crime that tend to be one-time affairs such as homicide are not as easily explained through labeling, nor are crimes such as incest, rape, and domestic violence (Schur, 1971: 21). As Schur points out, labeling lends itself best to low-consensus repetitive forms of deviance and crime but overlooks the harm caused by some so-called victimless offenses such as prostitution and drug abuse (Young, 1981).

Critics point out that labels are not permanent but are just coping mechanisms for those who offend to adjust to their institutional confinement (Gove, 1975). The label is soon abandoned upon a person's release, say, from incarceration.

There have also been mixed results in relation to the various attempts to change criminal justice policy and practice. Ironically, diversion has not resulted in the hoped-for lessening of control; the opposite has occurred. With the advent of increasing numbers of diversionary programs the control of the criminal justice system has not been lessened but has been increased. The nets of control have become wider (Austin and Krisberg, 1981; Cohen, 1985) and the actual confinement of offenders, the most stigmatizing disposition, has increased (Scull, 1984). The reason given for the expansion of control through diversion is that those selected for alternative programs have often been minor offenders who, prior to diversion, would have been dismissed or given some lenient disposition. These persons are now given some form of supervision and control while more severe dispositions have also increased (Frazier and Cochran, 1986; Shover and Einstadter, 1988). Even where programs have been implemented and successful, there seems to be a political unwillingness to accept them. For example, the possibilities inherent in decarceration were dramatically demonstrated in 1972 in Massachusetts when the juvenile institutions were closed and the inmates given community alternatives, with no harmful effects as a consequence (Miller and Ohlin, 1985). However, such alternatives are politically unpopular and ultimately have been rejected. Since the 1980s there has been no reduction in imprisonment; indeed the rate of imprisonment has increased to historical highs, and even parole has been scaled back.

Finally, and perhaps most significantly, especially in light of the theoretical perspectives to be discussed in the following chapters, the society's wider structural conditions are not considered in the labeling theorist's explanation. The early labeling perspective ignores the question of how control agents are allowed to exist as they do, and it ignores in whose interests they serve. It overlooks the stratified structure of society as *real in its consequences* and as a result fails to show the nature of the political economy which results in rules and enforcement agencies. In particular, says Young (1981), labeling theorists ignore the social structure that shapes the situations that lead to differences between offenders and nonoffenders. Some have argued that this places the labeling theorist in a comfortable liberal position in which attacks are made on society's caretakers, such as the police, prison warders, social workers, and so forth, while ignoring the organizational power of conflicting interests (Davis, 1975). In perhaps the most virulent version of this assessment, Liazos (1972) accused labeling theory of focusing on "the nuts, sluts and perverts" at the expense of covert institutional violence, which is ignored or underestimated.

Overall, the interactionist and social constructionist aspects of the interpretive social process perspective have fared much better than the more narrowly framed labeling theory. As Plummer (1979) has said, when it was first formulated in the 1960s, labeling theory was seen as a radical approach, attracting the "young turks" of sociology, perhaps as much for its irreverence of the system and for established knowledge as for any sound empirical basis. However, by the late 1960s it had been co-opted into the mainstream and had become *the* theory of deviance, if not of criminology (see, for example, Rubington and Weinberg, 1968, 1987; Filstead, 1972). However, between 1970 and 1975 there was, says Plummer (1979: 85), a "de-throning of its dominant position" whereby "In just ten years labeling theory has moved from being the radical critique of established orthodoxies to being the harbinger of new orthodoxies to be criticized." Such is the fate of criminological theories.

As we shall see, the social constructionist version of the perspective has survived (see Pfuhl and Henry, 1993), has been particularly influential in some radical feminist critiques (considered in Chapter 11), and has informed the constitutive version of postmodernist criminology (see Chapter 12).

CHAPTER TEN

Critical Criminologies I: Conflict, Anarchist, and Marxist Theories

Critical criminology is a broad term that applies to theories claiming crime is the outcome of conflict and domination. It assumes societies are more divided by conflict than they are integrated by consensus. It argues that groups having or claiming power define what counts as crime in order to preserve their dominant positions in the social order. These groups use the criminal justice system to enforce their definitions of reality on the powerless.

Critical criminologies are designated "critical" for several reasons. Like interactionism, labeling theory, and social constructionism, they are "critical" because they do not take for granted, nor limit themselves to, state definitions of crime. They prefer to define crime as social harm and/or as violations of human rights. Critical criminologies do not accept conventional analyses of causation that blame the individual offender without also considering how offenders have themselves been "victimized," first by society, and subsequently by the criminal justice system through its selective processing of the powerless. Critical criminologies are critical too, because they oppose the existing social order of power based on inequality, facilitated through the capitalist organization of society. They question the purpose and methods of the criminal justice system, which they see as a reflection of the dominant power structure rather than an instrument to correct injustice. Finally, they are critical because their policies usually demand a radical transformation, not just of criminal justice, but of the total social and political organization of society.

Believing that reformist tinkering with parts of the system, such as its institutions, will do little to change the causes of crime, critical criminologists' policies are concerned with broad societal-level changes. In other words, instead of seeing some people as inherently "bad apples" or as causing other apples to go bad, critical criminologists see the society as a "bad barrel" that will turn most of the apples bad that are put into it. From the perspective of this analogy the only solution is a new barrel.

In considering critical criminologies, we shall analyze several theoretical contributions in the next three chapters. In Chapter 11 we shall look at the critical criminology of feminist theory, which sees crime as the outcome of conflicts over gender inequality in a patriarchal society. We end our analysis of criminological theories by examining postmodernist theory, which sees crime as the outcome of human agents acting toward social constructions of power as though they were realities. Our exploration begins with the earlier theories of conflict-pluralism, instrumental and structural Marxism, anarchism, and the recent left (or radical) realism. (See Table 10–1.)[1]

BASIC IDEA, CENTRAL MOTIF, AND MAJOR THEORISTS

The predominant cause of crime according to this perspective is societally generated conflict fueled by a capitalist system of domination, inequality, alienation, and injustice. The perceived nature of conflict varies in different versions of critical theory. Pluralist conflict theorists (e.g., Vold, 1958) have been called "conservative conflict theorists" (e.g., Williams and McShane, 1988: 98). (See Table 10-2.) They base their criminology on notions of interest groups conflict found in the work of Simmel (1955), Coser (1956), Mills (1956, 1969), and Dahrendorf (1959). They see society divided on several dimensions and depict its structure as made up of numerous groups, each defining its own interests and struggling for the power to define and control public issues. Conflict theorists recognize that crime may stem from differences in economic wealth, a clash of cultures, or from the outcome of symbolic and instrumental struggles over status, ideology, morality, religion, race, and ethnicity. They argue that some groups, claiming an allegiance to mainstream culture, become dominant by gaining control of key resources. As a result these groups are able to criminalize the behavior of those deviating from their own cultural standards and behavioral norms (Sellin, 1938; Vold, 1958; Quinney, 1970). Conflict criminologists, therefore, see crime as having both instrumental and symbolic roots in a multidimensional, fragmented society, with struggles for control occurring at multiple sites of difference.

Other critical criminologists, however, believe that the status and symbolic dimensions of inequality are mere epiphenomena, consequences of a

Table 10-1 RELATED THEORIES*

Conflict theory
Critical criminology
Radical criminology
Instrumental Marxist theory
Structural Marxist theory
The new criminology
Left realism
Anarchist criminology

*Theory that takes a perspective similar to or overlapping with the model that we develop in this chapter.

---

[1]We shall also make reference to anarchist criminology (Tifft and Sullivan, 1980; Pepinsky, 1978; Ferrell, 1994) in Chapter 12 on postmodernism, since its philosophical assumptions straddle both theoretical frameworks.

Table 10-2   Theorists Using Conflict Explanations of Crime

THEORIST	MAJOR WORK[S]	DATE
Simmel	"The Sociology of Conflict" *Conflict and the Web of Group Affiliations*	1904 1908
Sutherland	"Crime and the Conflict Process"	1929
Sellin	*Culture, Conflict and Crime*	1938
Vold	*Theoretical Criminology*	1958
Turk	"Conflict and Criminality" *Criminality and the Legal Order* "Law as a Weapon in Social Conflict" "Class and Conflict and Criminology"	1966 1969 1976 1977
Quinney	*The Social Reality of Crime*	1970
Chambliss and Seidman	*Law, Order and Power*	1971
Box	*Deviance, Reality and Society* *Crime, Power and Mystification*	1971 1983
Hills	*Crime, Power and Morality*	1971
Krisberg	*Crime and Privilege: Towards a New Criminology*	1975
Pepinsky	*Crime and Conflict*	1976
Reiman	*The Rich Get Richer and the Poor Get Prison*	1979

deeper *economic* conflict (Taylor, Walton, and Young, 1973; Quinney, 1974). They see this conflict rooted in economic power and the appropriation and concentration of wealth by minority class interests in class-divided societies. (See Table 10–3.) These theorists draw on the sometimes divergent writings of Karl Marx (1868), Friedrich Engels (1845), and Willem Bonger (1916). They point to the structure of capitalism, based on the private ownership of property, which generates vast inequalities of wealth, as providing the conditions for crime. As Engels says, crime is rooted in the basic conflict between the bourgeoisie and the workers and is a consequence of the mechanism of free competition:

> In capitalist societies the basic class struggle is between the capitalist class (bourgeoisie) and the working class (proletariat). The economic site of this particular struggle is the productive process; it occurs over the distribution of the fruits

of this process. The capitalist class, on the one hand, strives to maximize profit from the unpaid labor of the working class. Its income lies in rent, interest, and industrial profit. The working class, on the other hand, strives to maximize wages. It attempts to do so by reducing the length of the working day, by compelling employers to pay higher wages, and by wresting such concessions from the capitalist class as health insurance, work-safety regulations, and job security. The goals

Table 10-3 Theorists Using Marxist Explanations of Crime

THEORIST	MAJOR WORK[S]	DATE
Engels	*The Condition of the Working Class in England*	1845
Bonger	*Criminality and Economic Conditions*	1916
Rusche and Kirchheimer	*Punishment and Social Structure*	1939
Gordon	"Class and the Economics of Crime" "Capitalism, Class and Crime in America"	1971 1973
Taylor, Walton, and Young	*The New Criminology* *Critical Criminology*	1973 1974
Quinney	*Critique of the Legal Order* "Crime Control in a Capitalist Society" *Class, State, and Crime* "The Production of a Marxist Criminology"	1974 1975 1977 1978
Platt	"Prospects for a Radical Criminology in the United States"	1974
Chambliss	"Toward a Political Economy of Crime" "On Lawmaking"	1975 1979
Block and Chambliss	*Organizing Crime*	1981
Chambliss and Seidman	*Law, Order and Power,* 2nd ed.	1982
Spitzer	"Towards a Marxian Theory of Deviance"	1975
Greenberg	*Crime and Capitalism*	1981
Melossi and Pavarini	*The Prison and the Factory*	1981
Schwendinger and Schwendinger	*Rape and Inequality*	1983
Michalowski	*Order, Law and Crime*	1985
Box	*Recession, Crime and Punishment*	1987

of the capitalist class and the working class are thus mutually exclusive. Typically, the one maximizes its return from the productive process at the expense of the other. (Beirne and Messerschmidt, 1991: 340–341)

Marxist criminologists differ among themselves over the structure of social order. They differ on the number and nature of classes, the priority given to powerful economic interests, and, importantly, the relationship of the state to class interests. Thus Bohm (1982) points out that theorists are divided over the issue of whether the state is manipulated by the interests of the ruling-class, who also mystify the system that sustains their domination, or whether the impersonal forces of capitalism are responsible for the maintenance and reproduction of that system. In conceptualizing this difference it has become conventional to distinguish between instrumental and structural Marxist criminologies (Sheley, 1985, 1991; Lynch and Groves, 1986).[2]

Instrumental Marxism (Chambliss, 1975; Quinney, 1973; Krisberg, 1975) holds a power model in which capitalist societies are presented as a monolithic system of inequality dominated by powerful ruling economic interests. They see power divided unequally between a dominant elite (comprising owners of wealth) and those whose only wealth is the power to sell their labor. The dominant elite use the state's law and criminal justice system as a coercive apparatus to criminalize those threatening or challenging their position in the social order.

In contrast, structuralist Marxist criminology (Spitzer, 1975; Greenberg, 1981; Chambliss and Seidman, 1982) conceptualizes a dual power structure in which the state serves a more dominant but semi-autonomous or independent role in relation to specific powerful economic interests. Through its mediating influence, the worst excesses of economic exploitation, and the crises these create, are controlled in the interests of legitimating the long-term maintenance of the system of inequality. As a result, the state, as an allegedly neutral element in the power structure, allows capitalist inequality to prevail without obvious challenge. From the structural Marxist perspective, it is the behavior of those threatening the *overall* system of capitalism that is criminalized. This threat can come as much from the very individuals and corporations that hold power (only if their behavior threatens to expose the system), as from the resistance and protests of the powerless.

As in the history of Marxism, so in critical criminology there is a division between Marxism and anarchism.[3] Whereas Marxists believe in the replacement of the class society by a socialist alternative, anarchists see all hierarchical systems

---

[2]We do not review "integrated" structural Marxist theories here (Colvin and Pauly, 1983; Hagan, Gillis, and Simpson, 1985; Hagan, 1989) but discuss these when considering other integrated theories in Chapter 13.

[3]Historically this is depicted by the split between Marx and Bakunin. (See Woodcock, 1963).

of power and authority, whatever their configuration, as flawed (Ferrell, 1994). (See Table 10-4.) Anarchist criminologists (Pepinsky, 1978; Tifft and Sullivan, 1980; Ferrell, 1994: 161–62) believe that hierarchical systems of authority and domination should be opposed and defied. They believe that existing systems of justice should be replaced by a decentralized system of negotiated justice in which all members of society participate and share their decisions (Wieck, 1978). Recent anarchist criminology is an "integration" of critical approaches which seeks to relate crime as a meaningful activity of resistance to both its construction in social interaction and "its larger construction through processes of political and economic authority" (Ferrell, 1994: 163).[4]

In a direction polar opposite to the idealism of anarchist criminology, a new critical perspective has recently developed known as "left realism" (see

Table 10-4 Theorists Using Anarchist Explanations of Crime

THEORIST	MAJOR WORK[S]	DATE
Godwin	*Political Justice*	1793
Pepinsky	"Communist Anarchism as an Alternative to the Rule of Criminal Law"	1978
Pepinsky and Jesilow	*The Myths that Cause Crime*	1984
Pepinsky and Quinney	*Criminology as Peacemaking*	1991
Wieck	"Anarchist Justice"	1978
Tifft	"The Coming Redefinitions of Crime: An Anarchist Perspective"	1979
Tifft and Sullivan	*The Struggle to be Human: Crime, Criminology and Anarchism*	1980
Ferrell	*Crimes of Style: Urban Graffiti and the Politics of Criminality*	1993
	"Confronting the Agenda of Authority: Critical Criminology, Anarchism, and Urban Graffiti"	1994

---

[4]In believing that existing structures of domination should be replaced by a "fragmented and decentered pluralism" that "celebrates multiple interpretations and styles" (ibid.), anarchist criminology has parallels with interactionism and social constructionism. Further, in believing that knowledge and information is a structure of domination to be discredited and replaced by embracing "particularity and disorder," anarchism has parallels with chaos theory, deconstructionism, and postmodernism (as we shall see in Chapter 12).

Table 10-5 Theorists Using a "Left Realist" Explanation of Crime

THEORIST	MAJOR WORK(S)	DATE
Young	"Left Idealism, Reformism and Beyond"	1979
	"The Failure of Criminology: The Need for a Radical Realism"	1986
	"The Tasks Facing a Realist Criminology"	1987
Lea and Young	*What Is to be Done About Law and Order?*	1984
Kinsey et al.	*Losing the Fight Against Crime*	1986
Matthews	"Taking Realist Criminology Seriously"	1987
Matthews and Young	*Confronting Crime*	1986
	Issues in Realist Criminology	1991
Young and Matthews	*Rethinking Criminology: The Realist Debate*	1991
MacLean	"In Partial Defense of Socialist Realism"	1991
Lowman and MacLean	*Realist Criminology*	1992

Table 10-5) (Young, 1979, 1986; Young and Matthews, 1992; Lea and Young, 1984; Matthews and Young, 1986, 1992; Kinsey et al., 1986; MacLean, 1991a, 1991b; Lowman and MacLean, 1992). Instead of romantic celebrations of the offender as a primitive revolutionary, left realists focus on the reality and seriousness of harm created by structurally powerless "street" offenders. Unlike critical perspectives, which focus on crimes of the powerful, definitions of crime, and "victimization" of powerless offenders by the state, left realism emphasizes the tripartite relationship between offenders, victims, and the criminal justice system. Thus, instead of ignoring the victims of "street crime," radical realism is based on an appreciation, not only of the state's victimization of offenders but also of offenders' victimization of those harmed. The perspective takes into account the fear of crime among powerless victims. In short, it takes the victims of crime seriously.

All five versions of critical/radical criminology considered in this chapter (conflict pluralists, instrumental and structural Marxism, anarchism and left realism) share some key themes. Typically these theories see individuals as products of hierarchical power structures. Though they variously recognize a degree of individual human agency, ultimately they see humans as repressed, co-opted, and manipulated for the benefit of dominant interests. Even left realists see offenders as relatively deprived by systems of inequality and injustice.

Crime in these perspectives is generally defined as the socially constructed categories of those with the power to impose their definitions on the powerless. However, for realists crime is no less harmful to its victims because of its socially constructed origins.

Criminal justice is, at best, an ideological system of legitimation and mystification which has to make some real concessions to maintain popular assent and, at worst, a means of coercive repression.

Each of these versions of critical theory has a position on the failure of criminal justice. Because of their total societal perspective, they see this failure stemming from the flawed organization of the wider societal structure. However, because of their diverging analyses, the various critical theories have differing views about what precise changes are necessary and what system of justice should replace that which exists. At one extreme is the anarchist call for its total replacement with a warm, living "face to face" justice (Tifft, 1979: 397), a system of "collective negotiation as a means of problem solving" (Ferrell, 1994: 162). At the other extreme, left realists want to strengthen and control the criminal justice system of capitalist society, believing that the law can provide the structurally powerless with real gains, if not ideal victories. In the following discussion we shall attempt to present the overall view of these critical positions within each of the dimensions of our analysis, noting any divergence between the various types.[5]

HUMANS, HUMAN NATURE, AND HUMAN BEHAVIOR

Critical theorists generally see humans as capable of making a difference to their social worlds and as subjects shaped by it. The form this takes varies. According to conflict theory humans are individuals who cooperate with others sharing their interests and collectively compete against those having different interests. Individual interests are partly shaped by the cultural context, and partly by individual perceptions. However, it is humans' joining together with like-minded others to further their group's interests that fuels social conflict.

For Marxist theorists, however, there is less emphasis on human individuality and more on social selves that have been fragmented by destructive societal forms. Jaggar (1983: 53) points out that in Marxist theory, although humans are seen as rational, they are closely related as a biological species to nonhumans. Their difference as a species lies in their intentional ability to make a

---

[5] A note about the work of Richard Quinney is in order here. The various critical perspectives reviewed in this chapter and the later postmodernist chapter refer to Quinney, as did the last chapter on social constructionism. This is because, unlike many theorists, Quinney's ideas have changed sequentially relatively rapidly during his life. As Martin et al. (1990) have noted, he began his intellectual life as a positivist, moved to becoming a functionalist, embraced social constructionism, then conflict theory, then instrumental Marxism, before transcending to a spiritual peacemaking position (which we consider under postmodernism). While many theorists shift positions marginally, or expand a position by incorporating some elements of others, Quinney has published books taking a stance in each of a series of positions. Therefore, it is important to remember *which* of the many "Quinneys" is referenced so as not to merge these differing and not always consistent ideas. For an autobiographical insight on Quinney's criminological metamorphosis see Quinney (1984, 1991).

difference in the world they inhabit rather than simply to use it. In other words they "transform the world" (ibid.: 52) by consciously contemplating it in advance in their imagination. Thus "human activity is conscious and purposeful"[6] (ibid.: 54). Moreover, human activity is fundamentally social in that it requires interdependence and cooperation from others. Human capacity for rational thought is not, therefore, a universal, as argued by classical theorists, but emerges during and is shaped by human productive activity.

Although human activity is originally directed toward satisfying biological needs, such as hunger, shelter, and procreation, in the course of this transformative process humans create new needs and are eventually themselves transformed. Thus in Marxist theory humans change

> not only the non-human world but also the human producers themselves. As new needs emerge, people develop new means of satisfying the needs; the new products, in turn, give rise to still further needs, until the original human nature is completely transformed. (Ibid.: 54)

It is the distinctive way that humans consciously act to transform the world in a given society "that determines the fundamental features of that society and the nature of its inhabitants"[7] (ibid: 55). For Marx, therefore, human nature is a product of a particular historical configuration of society, dependent on how people together transform their world at any particular time period. As Marx said: "The human essence is no abstraction inherent in each single individual. In its reality it is the ensemble of social relations" (Marx, 1968: 29).

Marx believed that humans are fundamentally social beings who create the world in which they live, but not under conditions they have chosen for themselves, "rather on terms immediately existing, given and handed down to them" (Marx, 1852: 115). As Young (1981: 295) summarizes the perspective: "Humans are both the producers and products of history; they create institutions and meaning within a particular historical period, which is in the last instance, determined by the mode of production of the time." On balance, however, Marx argued that humans are more shaped by the form of their society's economic organization ("mode of production") than by their own ideas, intellect, or reason: "It is not the consciousness of men that determines their being, but, on the contrary, their being that determines their consciousness" (Marx, 1859: 504).

---

[6] This is what Marx meant by "praxis." It is conscious social action such as labor, directed at transforming the material world for human purposes.

[7] The way humans cooperate with one another to transform their world for the purposes of satisfying their needs Marx called the "relations of production," whereas the way members of a society organize their productive activity was referred to by Marx as a society's "mode of production" (Jaggar, 1983: 55).

Weiss (1983) cautions about linking Marx exclusively with one view of human nature. He says Marx's view changed and has resulted in two versions of Marxist criminological theory:

> Scientific, materialistic Marxism emphasizes the importance of socioeconomic structures and therefore views people ("agents") as constrained by objective forces, while critical or humanistic Marxism, based on idealism, views humans as rational, purposeful, and potentially capable of removing unnecessary institutional constraints. (Weiss, 1983: 133)

Further aspects of this dual view of human nature in Marxist analysis derive from the depiction of humans as inherently both *cooperative* and *competitive.* However, their competitive characteristics are magnified and distorted by certain forms of productive organization, notably, capitalism. Depending on the theoretical emphasis, humans are either seen as directly shaped by the structural conditions of a particular historical period (instrumental Marxism) or are the indirect product of a historically specific structural context that provides the medium through which their agency must operate and that limits their potential (structural Marxism, radical realism). In either case it is the way a society is structured and organized, in a particular time period, in conjunction with its culture, that colors the framework of human propensities, and these propensities can only be described in relation to that broader context.

Most Marxists "strongly imply that human nature is inherently good" (Empey and Stafford, 1991: 415). For example, Quinney (1971: 52) admits he is assuming that man is "basically good rather than being evil" and that if left alone will cooperate. If humans appear otherwise, it is the structural-cultural matrix that, especially in capitalist societies, conceals and represses their cooperative spirit beneath an ideology of individualism. This individualism is incorporated into such notions as "freedom of the individual," and "individual rights." Such a system of production, say Marxist theorists, masks and denies the essential human interconnectedness of societal members as well as their common experiences and cooperative or collective interests. It does this by the intertwined process of dehumanization, alienation, and reification. This process stems from the way people are treated as objects or "commodities."

In the capitalistic production process people are available to be hired for the power of their labor in the service of others (entrepreneurs or corporations) for the pursuit of profit. Their creative capacities are confined to a narrow arena, as are their relations with others. They are narrowly defined by the productive system as specialized "occupational positions," (e.g., surgeon, factory worker, plumber, computer programmer, teacher, housewife, etc.), designated by material value (e.g., how much they earn, where they live, and what kind of car they drive), which in turn determines their social status. This false construction of humanity alienates (separates and isolates) humans in several ways. First, it alienates them from each other (their fellow species) by creating false barriers (differences) between them. Second, it alienates them from the products of their labor, since they rarely see the whole product through from start to finish, typically contributing an isolated small part to the whole. Third, it alienates them from their labor power, since their work is being done for a wage or salary rather than for its intrinsic or exchange value. Fourth, it alienates them from themselves, since, by becoming fragmented into occupational roles, they are separated from the other dimensions of their lives. Finally, by coming to believe that the institutions comprising their social organization have a reality apart from their own contribution, they "reify" their relationship to their world, losing sight of their own agency in its making (i.e., deny their own ability to make a difference to the world). This can result in a loss of self-worth and self-esteem and lack of care for other, equally "worthless," individuals. Thus capitalist production

> obscures the ways in which the members of society are interdependent; it sets individuals in competition with each other so that they learn to view one another as potential enemies and are unable to perceive their mutual dependence and the interests they have in common. They conceive of themselves as isolated individuals, rather than as beings who are necessarily social. (Jaggar, 1983: 58)

As a result of this structural distortion from true human nature, some have taken a very pessimistic view of the potential of humans to act cooperatively or to recover their true spirit. Others, more optimistically, believe that social cooperation is an essential human trait that only needs the right structural conditions to liberate it. Marx, for example, held that humans are potentially open to development and change under the right structural conditions (Geras, 1983). Thus, critical Marxist theorists believe that humans would not become truly bad, in spite of having some selfish tendencies, "if they were liberated from the evils of the class struggle," allowing their "cooperative instincts ... to become dominant and a humane, crime free society" to emerge (Empey and Stafford, 1991: 415). Similarly other Marxists have argued that we can imagine and create other lives and other futures that would be more fulfilling, but the very society in which we live places hurdles to achieving such goals. Therefore, society must be changed so as to establish the social conditions under which we can be what we want to be or can explore the myriad of ways that our life can be meaningful or purposive (Unger, 1976, 1986; Collins, 1987).

Perhaps most optimistic about the inherent human potential for creative goodness and cooperation are anarchist criminologists. They believe that the cooperative human spirit is secreted within a person, constituting his or her essence (Proudhon, 1876). Their humanity will be liberated through a spiritual awakening made possible by the struggle to dismantle the state and other hierarchies of authority (Tifft and Sullivan, 1980).

VIEW OF SOCIETY AND THE SOCIAL ORDER

One of the major differences between the varieties of critical criminology is its theorists' views of the structure of society. Though all consider capitalist society to be divided between conflicting interests, competing for scarce resources, they disagree over the nature and basis of the division. Conflict theory sees society comprised of numerous interest groups in a constant competitive struggle for the power to define events or control issues they consider important:

> These theories assume that conflict emerges between groups attempting to exercise control over particular situations or events ... almost as if social issues were fields of combat with opposing armies fighting to see who will prevail and rule the land. As with armies ... [i]t is the controlling of resources (money, land, political power) which provides the ability to successfully "fight" and to emerge victorious on a particular issue. (Williams and McShane, 1988: 98)

However, unlike world wars, in which there is typically a final victory, followed by periods of stability, in this conflict-pluralist vision of society the struggles are more akin to guerrilla warfare, ongoing, with no single group emerging as victorious for a long duration, and with most organized groups having sufficient power to destabilize complete dominance by any others. However, some conflict theorists, such as Turk (1969, 1976, 1982), disagree with this "balance of powers" notion and believe that particular groups do emerge as more powerful. These groups command an authority relationship over others who become subject to their control. Turk (1969) argues that people have to learn to deal with others having authority over them. This results in a permanent adjustment of the subordinate to those in authority. Over time this authority–subject relationship becomes less coercive and more autonomous as new generations are born into the existing structural arrangements containing preexisting laws, rules, and definitions of reality. Quinney's (1970) early work reflects this same conflict-pluralism. He talks in terms of a diversity of powerful interests and "segments of society ... in conflict with others" (Quinney, 1970: 17).

In contrast, the Marxist position shares much of Marx and Engels's view of society as narrowly based on the competition over scarce economic resources in systems of production that preserve hierarchical power structures (Greenberg, 1981). Competition is between powerful owners of economic wealth (capitalist entrepreneurs or bourgeoisie) and powerless wage-laborers (proletariat) who are exploited in ways that render them passive to resist the injustices of such inequality. Their economic and political powerlessness is assured by maintaining a class of relatively "surplus" labor. These persons are the unemployed or marginally employed, whose labor can be drawn on when business booms but can be readily cast off in times of economic slump. Keeping such a "surplus population" not only serves as a "reserve army" or pool to be drawn on in times of need, it also ensures that wage levels are maintained at their lowest possible levels. In addition, it minimizes internal conflict and discipline problems since workers fear that their situation could worsen; that if they protest they could be replaced (Spitzer, 1975; Quinney, 1977).

Marxist criminologists see all other conflicts as manifestations of this basic economic struggle. However, there are differing versions of the power hierarchy, depending on the number of classes envisioned. Instrumental Marxists see two major classes: a capitalist elite and the mass of the proletariat. Some instrumentalists, whose views are reflected in the mid-1970s' work of Quinney (1974, 1975a, 1975b, 1977), argue that there is a ruling economic elite that is itself divided into two major groups. At the top of the class structure is the more powerful "monopoly capitalists," who own major units of the economy and who head the most powerful corporate, banking, and financial institutions (Quinney, 1974: 53). Monopoly capitalists, says Quinney, totally control the state and orchestrate its every action through the legal system. They also delegate power to a subclass of elite that he calls "lieutenant capitalists." These subordinate groups own or manage less powerful companies. Together the lieutenant capitalists and the criminal justice apparatus of the state act to repress the subordinate classes on behalf of the ruling dominant elite.

Marxist critics of this crude instrumentalism (e.g., Greenberg, 1981) argue that if such a view of society were accurate, it would be unnecessary for powerful elites to legislate against their own interests and they would simply change the law to suit their interests rather than violate it. Further, this view ignores conflicts between capitalists and cannot explain conflicts over legislation on noneconomic issues such as abortion, drugs, and so forth. Though the instrumentalist position applies to early capitalist production, coercion becomes less necessary as the mode of domination "becomes supplanted by the silent compulsion of the market" (Young, 1981: 296). The capitalist system of production serves as its own system of regulation and autonomous discipline in which the reality of having to compete in situations of exploitation in order to survive is accepted by subordinate classes as natural. As a result, the state can take a less coercive role, reserving its repressive apparatus for use in exceptional cases of riot and collective protest (Kinsey, 1979; Geary, 1985). Indeed, Box and Hale (1986; Box, 1987) point out that repressive crime control in capitalist society occurs, not in relation to changing levels of crime, but in relation to the cycle of growth and recession in the economy. According to their analysis, imprisonment increases in capitalist societies during periods of economic crisis to control those classes who might prove "dangerous" and become a revolutionary threat in recessionary times.

As a result of these insights several Marxist critical theorists (Hirst, 1975; Chambliss, 1988; Chambliss and Seidman, 1982; Spitzer, 1975; Greenberg, 1981) take what has been called a "structuralist" position (Sheley, 1985, 1991).

They argue that the state is not simply a pawn of the dominant economic elite, but has a degree of autonomous power and the ability to curb the excesses of exploitation in the long-term interests of preserving the existing capitalist arrangements. Whether the controls they exercise over powerful economic interests are real or token, such as where laws protecting employees' health and safety contain built-in barriers to effective enforcement (Carson, 1971), they argue that a degree of real autonomy is necessary for effective legitimation. As Young (1981: 298) points out, this system of domination is not simply mystification or "false consciousness," as argued by labeling theorists, instrumental Marxists, and anarchists, but is based on the contradictory dualism within the capitalist system. This reflects (1) the real power of the state to limit particular excesses of exploitation while allowing the overall system of exploitation to remain; (2) the control of all the population while exercising greater control over some classes than others; and (3) "the *real* freedom and gains of capitalism that coexist and conceal coercion and exploitation; that is the 'double freedom' of the worker under capitalism": the freedom to sell labor and the "freedom from ownership of the means of production" (ibid.). Young (1981: 299) summarizes how the state and the economic system of capitalism work together and separately to ensure compliance of the exploited classes:

> (a) The "reserve army of labour," a relatively immiserised pool of people out of work, affects the market position of those in work by posing a constant potential competition for jobs.
> (b) The social conditions of the reserve army and the threat of those in work joining them allow the imposition of a rigorous discipline in the workplace.
> (c) Both workless and those in work are rewarded and punished in terms of the same principles of proportionality; there is a continuum of reward and punishment within society.
> (d) The prison's "failure," in that it well-nigh irrevocably stigmatizes the recalcitrant, serves as a first line of control for the workless and an important second line of control—after work itself—for those in work.
> (e) The state in acting against the criminal serves to legitimate itself as the protector of universal interests in society.

Thus for structural Marxists the state is supportive of *capitalism* rather than of individual capitalists.

Other structural Marxists claim that capitalist society is even more fragmented than is often admitted. Not only are capitalists said to exist in fierce competition with each other, supporting laws that force their smaller competitors out of business, but the state is itself fragmented. It is a composite of numerous competing agencies, each with their own interests (Spitzer, 1980; Jessop, 1982). Moreover, all working classes are not disorganized masses; some coalesce to form effective interest groups and unions that align with agencies of the state to improve their class position. Thus, a composite view of a class-divided society is modified by incorporation of elements of the pluralist interests model, in such a way that the basic dual hierarchy between the fragmented state and divided powerful corporations is left in place. These dominate and co-opt the most vociferous groups from the subordinated classes, leaving the disorganized, such as the inner-city unemployed and homeless, the single-parent family, among others, to suffer the worst ravages of the system of inequality, whose protests are contained through the penal system (Rusche and Kirchheimer, 1939; Melossi and Pavarini, 1981; Box, 1987).

Finally, it is worth pointing out that in the anarchist vision of society, nothing is more formidable than the unchallenged supremacy of centralized authority structures that feed off of divisions of class, gender, and race (Ferrell, 1994). Anything that fragments the state from its seamless hierarchies of authority and power is desirable.

THE ROLE OF LAW, THE DEFINITION OF CRIME, AND THE IMAGE OF THE CRIMINAL

Conflict and Marxist theorists see law as the socially constructed product of powerful interests. For some, these interests are primarily economic, impacting the legislative process to produce laws favorable to their economic and political position in society. For others they are ideological, religious, moral, and social. Law represents the power to control the social meaning of society's institutions and the dominant values in society.

For conflict-pluralist theory the assumed socially constructed nature of law implies that it can be made and redefined in ways that ultimately can transform society. In the early work of Quinney (1970: 35), for example, law is seen as the product of persons and groups who are able to impose their view of reality by influencing the criminal law. Therefore, it is in the interests of groups to gain access to various economic and political institutions, such as industry, government, education and particularly law, in order to exercise power and supremacy over other competing groups. The attempt to control various interests by controlling society's institutions is known as the "capture thesis." In Turk's (1976) rendition of conflict theory, for example, law is a weapon in social conflict, representing a resource to be won, the key to controlling other social institutions.

Similarly, according to the elite domination or instrumental Marxist theory, the law is seen primarily as an instrument that serves those more powerful at the expense of those less powerful (Chambliss, 1975). However, rather than being seen as a resource, or merely a construction reflecting relative definitions as in pluralism, here law is depicted as an instrument of class power, a repressive apparatus of government working on behalf of dominant economic elites to control the less privileged. Indeed, in a shift from his conflict stance referred to above, Quinney (1974, 1975b: 55) reconsiders the law as an instrument of *the state,* controlled by the economic elite in order to repress the subordinate classes for the purpose of maintaining and perpetuating the existing economic and social order.

However, for structural Marxists criminal law comprises an ideological[8] means of domination. Like the instrumentalists, structuralists believe that contradictions of capitalist society, which include the pronounced tendency for economic inequality to generate suffering for those in the lowest social classes, create a force of disturbance that needs to be contained. Unlike the instrumentalists, however, the structuralist version does not hold that criminal law exclusively represents the interests of the ruling elite, nor that it is used merely repressively. As Box (1983) says, there are times when laws are enacted that benefit the less powerful, particularly when there are organized efforts to bring this about, but these efforts are usually short-lived. These counterpower laws, ensuring, for example, health and safety at work, controls on price fixing, or environmental protection, reflect an ideological need to develop *consent* for the existing social order. Promoting the idea that no person or group is above the law, fostering the view that agencies of social control are protecting all of the public from offenders, and protecting private property in general, these laws generate consensus over the existing power arrangements.

Such consensus, and the legitimacy it brings, are especially pronounced when couched in terms of universal notions of justice, protection, and security for the general population, and equality before the law. Thus, it is important to show the population that law is not an instrument of the powerful, nor controlled by them, but is a neutral body serving all. This is why the state, through its government, must exercise a degree of *real* autonomy. In order to mask its connection and protection within powerful economic class interests and to free owners of wealth from the appearance of direct control, the state presents an image of itself through law as neutral, universal, and working in the common interest. This sometimes requires laws against the immediate interests of corporations or their practices, which serves to increase the state's sense of neutrality and legitimacy in the eyes of the oppressed and to placate its most vociferous organized critics. The contradictory role of capitalist law is such that it embodies some real protection against crimes of which the working classes are a victim and, in doing so, sustains the legitimacy of the very system of exploitation that gives rise to these crimes (Young, 1981: 300).

Chambliss (1979, 1988) and Carson (1971; 1979) see the ambivalent role of law resulting from the compromise of powerful interests, rather than an outright victory of one class over another. However, they do not believe a society's interest groups are equally powerful. As Chambliss (1979) argues:

---

[8]Although *ideological* has several meanings, the sense of the concept here is as "a process whereby beliefs, deriving from real social relationships, hide or mask the precise nature of such relationships ... masking from exploited classes the nature of their oppression and its precise source" (Beirne and Messerschmidt, 1991: 342).

> The single most important force behind criminal law creation is doubtless the economic interest and political power of those social classes which either (1) own or control the resources of society, or (2) occupy positions of authority in the state bureaucracies. (Chambliss, 1979: 154)

However, Chambliss (1988) also sees the continual presence of resistance from those exploited who force some concessions.

Some critical theorists have developed the idea of the dual role of law in capitalist society through a historical analysis that integrates the ideas of pluralists, instrumental Marxists, and structural Marxists into a grand theory of law. Unger (1976; Collins, 1987), for example, specifies the political, cultural, and economic conditions that are "formative contexts" for the development of three types of law. What others describe as different critical theories of law are, according to Unger, actually recurring forms or models, each corresponding to different turns in the cycle of law's development and each reflecting different stages of societal development. The patterned sequence is one in which new forms of legal domination emerge, have their legitimacy challenged, fragment, reform (making new concessions and new claims to legitimacy) and once again emerge as a prevalent mode of domination, before themselves succumbing to challenge and crisis as the pattern repeats.

Unger argues that the inherent inequalities of the capitalist system of production have ultimately resulted in one of several "legitimacy crises." The attempt to channel conflict through courts has led to a decline in people's belief that the legal system can deliver justice since judges' decisions systematically seem to support some groups over others. In time this practice has outstripped the ideology of equality. As a result, says Unger, we are now moving away from the liberal democratic law of the capitalist state, to a postindustrial society in which ideas of welfarism, corporatism, and communitarianism take precedence. Here the state, in the ideological role of protector of rights of individuals and autonomous administrator of fair justice, is subject to pressures from people to *actually* protect those rights. It is pressured into acting more forcefully against elite classes to protect certain groups in society based on a substantive form of justice oriented to results. However, although some lower-class groups have captured the state to work in their favor, a parallel development has occurred in which the economic elites have effectively formed themselves into their own "state governments," which merge with and look similar to the state: "corporatism means that people find themselves and their lives increasingly controlled by private governments which rival the power of the state" (Kidder, 1983).[9] A

---

[9]This may be seen in corporations' increasing use of public space, the burgeoning use of private security forces, and the ever-increasing encroachment into the privacy of citizens (Marx, 1988; Einstadter, 1992).

person is now a member of one or other special interest, corporate, or state group, or else is excluded from protection. As a result, many people feel an increasing loss of control over their own lives. They want and desire to get back to community, to a more personal and meaningful way of living. The result is a push for popular justice. Moreover, the clamor over special interests and private corporate governments is creating yet another legitimacy crisis that has not yet been resolved.

According to those sharing the critical perspective, what counts as crime is inconsistently defined in the capitalist society's system of law. Certain serious harms that are committed by powerful persons, particularly in the corporate area, are never defined as crimes (Michalowski and Bohlander, 1976; Michalowski, 1985). Those acts which challenge or threaten their interests are criminalized, whereas other acts harmful to the welfare of society, but in keeping with the powerful's economic interests, are either ignored or given lesser punishments (Spitzer, 1975; Reiman, 1979; Chambliss and Seidman, 1982). Thus robbery and homicide are always treated as serious criminal offenses, whereas defrauding small bank depositors, illegal loans, pollution of drinking water, or unhygienic food preparation processes affecting millions are dealt with less seriously by administrative regulatory agencies:

> Rather than being a fair reflection of those behaviours objectively causing us the most avoidable suffering, criminal law categories are artful, creative constructs designed to criminalize only some victimizing behaviours, usually those more frequently committed by the relatively powerless, and to exclude others, usually those frequently committed by the powerful against subordinates. (Box, 1983: 7)

Not surprisingly, critics believe that the basis of crime should shift to one based on social harm or human rights (Schwendinger and Schwendinger, 1970; Platt, 1974; Young, 1979; Tifft and Sullivan, 1980; Cohen, 1993; Barak, 1994a).

While conventional criminological theories see the criminal primarily as the economically marginal person, critical theorists, in contrast, see little difference between criminals and noncriminals. Both are rational in their response to the shared and uncertain economic circumstances of capitalist society (Gordon, 1971, 1973). Moreover, Gordon has argued that there is little difference between the street offender and the white-collar offender other than their differential access to illegal opportunities. In addition, the white-collar offender is more able to deal effectively with the criminal justice system or achieve similar ends through quasi-legal means (Chambliss, 1975). All those in capitalist society are affected by the wider conflict over accumulating wealth and the competition to achieve material success, social status, and respect. The criminal is an individual or group that acts without consideration against his or her fellow species in the pursuit of self-interests. This is why, according to critical theorists, corporations are guilty of crime when harms result not only from acts of deliberate negligence but also by "omission," whereby the consequences of business activity results in human suffering (Balkan et al., 1980; Box, 1983; Kramer, 1984). Moreover, as Balkan et al. (1983) argue, although in the state's prevailing dominant ideology offenders are criminalized as individual actors (e.g., as "a dishonest employee" or "a violent robber"), this is merely individualizing a collective issue. People strike out, neither because of their individual pathology nor from willful defiance but because of their common experience of an oppressive situation. So often in history, argue the critics, resistance such as riots, sabotage, and vandalism have been treated as individual issues instead of collective protests against further deprivation (Taylor and Walton, 1971; Brown, 1977). For example, Ferrell (1993, 1994: 172) argues that urban graffiti constitute a form of playful, direct, collective action against authority: a "visceral resistance to the constraints of private property, law, and corporate art." The act of writing graffiti "stands as a sort of decentralized and decentered insubordination, a mysterious resistance to conformity and control, a stylish counterpunch to the belly of authority" (ibid.: 175).

As a consequence, critical theorists see corporate and government crimes of the structurally powerful as the product of greed and systemic disregard for humanity in the interests of power and profit (Pearce, 1976; Barak, 1991b, 1994a). In this regard states, like corporations, are collective offenders. States are the "publicly powerful" and as such are "responsible for much of the global crime, injury, harm, violence and injustice" (Barak, 1994: 265). Moreover, the connection between some government activities and organized crime has been well documented (Pearce, 1976; Chambliss, 1988). In contrast, violent and property crimes of the structurally powerless are seen as misguided and random expressions of the anger and resistance to injustice and inequality and authority (Ferrell, 1994). Indeed, Krisberg (1975) and Quinney (1977) have argued that criminals are a potential revolutionary class, who may contribute, if only indirectly, to the "fiscal crisis of the state" (O'Conner, 1973), which could ultimately collapse through having to invest so much of its resources into welfare programs and crime control that little is available for future investment. Others, especially left realists, however, side with Marx, who believed that criminals were not revolutionary (Lea and Young, 1984) and was scornful of their contribution to social change (see Wenger and Bonomo, 1981). Indeed, some argue that they provide the arena in which the state can maintain its legitimacy through helping to resolve contradictions and effectively justifying its claim of protecting all (Hirst, 1972).

Moreover, while everyone wants to be protected against common street offenses that are typically crimes of the structurally powerless, such as murder, rape, robbery, assault, theft, and other forms of serious crime, some benefit more from the enforcement of laws against these offenses than others. Police protection will take crimes against the powerful more seriously than those against the powerless. As Chambliss notes: "Crime is a matter of who can pin the label on whom, and underlying this socio-political process is the structure of social relations determined by the political economy" (Chambliss, 1979: 165).

In an attempt to offer a more inclusive critical analysis of types of offender, Quinney (1977) distinguishes between (1) *crimes of domination and repression* by either the dominant economic elite or agencies of the state, and (2) *crimes of accommodation* and resistance by those subordinated in the capitalist class struggle. Through this analysis it is possible to see the state, its control agencies, and private corporations committing crimes of domination, while at the same time seeing more conventional crimes of robbery, assault, and rape as those committed by the working class as an adaptation to their oppression by the powerful.

The failure of capitalist systems either to criminalize equally or equally protect is an unacceptable position for those who believe that the law should criminalize behavior that is a violation of human rights (Schwendinger and Schwendinger, 1970; Platt, 1974) and that causes social harm (Young, 1979), irrespective of the status of its perpetrators. They believe that crime needs to be defined in much broader terms to include the activities of those creating conditions such as hunger, homelessness, joblessness, and other conditions of human suffering, especially violations of human rights created by state governments (Cohen, 1993; Barak, 1994a).

Given that these critics believe the total social structure is in need of change, it is important to ask what would count as crime in a decentralized collective system of the kind advocated by many of these critics. Some who have attempted to address the issue of discipline in collective systems suggest that what counts as "crime" and deviance is that which offends the collective interests, irrespective of whether a specific rule has been broken or not. At a general level, "the abuse of persons and anything that tends toward creating patterns of 'enslavement' or that hinders the realization and continuity of free cooperation is wrong in such a society" (Wieck, 1978: 232). Behavior that goes against the cooperative spirit of taking full responsibility for one's actions in a socially aware way is considered deviant. It includes any number of specific actions and can be called by any member of the collective; indeed, not to call attention to deviance would itself be seen as avoidance of responsibility and may invoke its own questions. Concrete examples of rule-breaking behavior under a collective decentralized community are failure to participate in activities of the collective such as meetings; unwillingness to help other members if asked; attempting to create personal advantage at the expense of other members; and failure to contribute an equal amount of effort (Henry, 1983, 1984). Indeed, as Taylor (1982: 120–23) states in his review of communes and other intentional communities, "a central problem was inequality of work effort." Free riding in any structure where benefits are available on the basis of need or on an equal basis, independent of contribution, is seen to be tantamount to theft (Olson, 1965).

CAUSAL LOGIC

Although Marx and Engels made little mention of crime in their writings, when they did do so it was explained as a product of the fundamental conditions of capitalist society. In part these conditions caused some people's behavior (the working class) to be criminalized. The conditions also led to a demoralization of the masses, which produced a lack of care for self or others. In some cases societal conditions even led to crimes as an expression of protest. Radical and critical scholars have concentrated on Marx's method of analysis, beginning with the total society to explain crime in its broader etiological context.

For all theorists who write in the critical tradition, capitalism, as an economic system of inequality, is considered "criminogenic." This means that there is something about the organization of the whole society that gives rise to crime. Capitalism sets the parameters within which criminality develops and is nurtured. "As crime does not exist in isolation, it must be analyzed in the context of its relationship to the character of the society as a whole" (Greenberg, 1981: 17). Thus Quinney (1980: 67) states:

> Crime control and criminality ... are understood in terms of the conditions resulting from capitalist appropriation of labor. Variations in the nature and amount of crime occur in the course of developing capitalism. Each stage is characterized by a particular pattern of crime. The meaning and changing meanings of crime are found in the development of capitalism.

The differences that exist in the various theoretical approaches reflect differences in the emphasis given to the direct impact of the capitalistic structure on criminality. For some, notably instrumental Marxists (Engels, 1845; Bonger, 1916; Chambliss, 1975; Quinney 1974, 1975b), capitalism is a direct determinant of crime since its system of production encourages destructive conflict through competition for wealth and power. Engels (1845) in his book on the condition of the working class in England, first explained the increase in crime with the advent of capitalist society as the product of their "brutalizing treatment" by the bourgeoisie. Crime was seen as a form of "demoralization" in which humanity and dignity were undermined by the system of production in which many were exploited by a few, in the interests of profit (Taylor, Walton, and Young, 1973: 209). Bonger (1916) saw the crime producing mechanism as the creation of "the criminal thought." Criminal thoughts result from the tendency of capitalism to emphasize "egoism" as opposed to "altruism," a tendency which in turn leads to exploitation, misery, and crime. From this perspective, it is the greed and self-centeredness fostered by the system of capitalist competitive production that creates the mental conditions for crime, not just in the working classes but throughout the social order.

Chambliss (1975), for example, argues that crime is no different from conformity in that both reflect the social class position and class opportunities.

Chambliss (1979) used empirical studies in an attempt to demonstrate this perspective. His investigation of crime in Seattle, Washington, and Ibadan, Nigeria shows that, in these cities, members of the ruling elite, "legal and political officials and racketeers [are linked] in joint ventures which involve them actively and passively in criminal activities as part of their way of life (ibid., 1979: 165)." He argues that everyone, not just the lower class, is involved in crime but that the crimes of the lower class are noted, while those of the elite are treated as normal ongoing activity. In short, the laws are differentially enforced. As Quinney (1977) says, the real harms committed are part of the domination by the powerful, which he calls crimes of control, crimes of government, and crimes of economic domination. Those harms institutionalized by society such as racism and sexism are not criminalized, whereas predatory and personal crimes and crimes of resistance committed by the working class are subject to the force of the criminal justice system.

Others, too, have directed attention to the inequalities that arise under a capitalist economic structure as important variables in generating crime. Blau and Blau (1982) show that basic economic inequalities generate violent crime. They show that inequality weakens social cohesion which in turn leads to social disorganization and crime. In their analysis it is not poverty as such, however, that is criminogenic, but the relative deprivation created in systems of inequality which is at the center in the genesis of crime.[10]

More recently, Chambliss (Chambliss and Seidman, 1982; Chambliss, 1988) has revised his earlier instrumental Marxist perspective and has adopted a structuralist Marxist theory of crime causation. In this he argues that the basic contradiction between capital and labor and the attempts at resolution of these conflicts culminate in crime. Rather than being linear, the struggle between capital and labor is a cyclical or a dialectical process.[11] First, the capitalist class gains an advantage through maximizing profits, which in turn reduces the income of workers and increases the levels of relative deprivation, suffering, and social problems. Resultant protest and industrial action bring increased wages and benefits to workers at a cost to employers, who seek to restore their maximum profits by replacing workers with machines, violating safety rules, or finding cheaper labor from marginalized classes or migrant labor whom they can employ off-the-books. In turn workers' wages and benefits go down, problems increase, again workers protest,

---

[10]Indeed, the same point was made by Bonger (see Weiss, 1983: 132) and has been elaborated recently in critical versions of revised strain theory that adapt the relative deprivation perspective to explain middle-class rather than just lower-class delinquency (Burton and Dunaway, 1994).

[11]*Dialectical* is a difficult concept to grasp and is variously defined in the literature. Here we take it to mean "the generation within systems of societal organization of opposing forces and ideas whose contradictions lead to a new organizational form different from both the original and its opposite," or, put simply: "the development of contradictions and their solutions, resulting in social change" (Balkan, Berger, and Schmidt, 1980: 336).

sometimes through internal theft and sabotage, drug use, and strikes or work "slow-downs." If employers concede to wage demands, their profits decline, with the recessionary result that some people are laid off temporarily or permanently. This body of "surplus labor" serves to keep wages down and reduces protest, with the result that profits again increase. But as the surplus population persists and grows, the state is blamed for ineffectively ameliorating the problems. To establish or to restore its legitimacy the state increases social programs and welfare benefits. However, it does this by levying taxes on capitalist businesses, whose relative profits again go down. This struggle continues until the state becomes fiscally overburdened and then begins to privatize its welfare programs, which causes another reduction for workers.

Chambliss (1988) says this continual struggle is ongoing, in part, to avoid slow growth. During recessions employees need sufficient wages to purchase commodities. But when they receive adequate compensation employers have less profit and cannot grow as rapidly. Chambliss calls this "the wages, profits, and consumption contradiction." At the same time, because of the "wages-labor supply contradiction" in which a "surplus labor force" is maintained to contain wage growth, an underclass is born whose final resolution to their dilemma is to resort to illegal sources of income.[12]

In addition to recent development in structural theory, some radical scholars have called for greater sensitivity to lower-class victimization in formulating causal explanations. This has been carried furthest by the development of "left realism," which accepts the notion of relative deprivation as the basic cause of crime but is critical of past radical romanticizing of lower-class crime, for it overlooks the suffering in inner-city communities (Lea and Young, 1984). This new variant of the perspective essentially argues that crime rates are a product of interacting factors involving the police, other agencies of social control, the public, the offender, and the victim. The crime rate is affected by change in the action of any of these components (Young, 1986, 1991).

The critical perspective, therefore, has a number of different and changing approaches to the understanding of crime. All accept that larger socioeconomic processes are the root cause but differ in their specific explanation of its manifestation.

CRIMINAL JUSTICE SYSTEM IMPLICATIONS

The current approach to criminal justice is seen by critical criminologists as largely repressive, representing the wealthy and powerful. It would be unnecessary

---

[12]We will examine Hagan's (1989, 1990) power-control "structural criminology" under the integrated theory in Chapter 13.

were it not for the structural conditions that ensure its need through perpetuating the conditions of conflict. Indeed, for some, the system operates as a class control enterprise that focuses primarily on the underclass and marginalized populations that are continually being created by the inherent contradictions of capitalism. The entire system is perceived to require restructuring. However, the major focus is not the criminal justice system itself because it "cannot be a meaningful avenue of social change, as changing criminal justice practices does little to alter the fundamental economic inequalities which structure social relationships" (Lynch and Groves, 1986: 108).

Criminal Justice Policy and Correctional Ideology

Since the basic cause of crime lies in the inequalities produced by the capitalist structure, policy efforts must be directed to reduce these inequalities toward a restructuring of society to close the gap between those who own wealth and those who do not. Particular stress must be laid on reducing "relative deprivation" by restructuring the distribution of wealth and ownership, thereby narrowing the vast chasms of inequality that now exist and that produce the propensity toward crime. Not surprisingly, most Marxist-informed critical theorists take the view that reforms of the social structure are not only inadequate to address the issue, but may even extend the historical period where this mode of production is dominant.[13]

To them reform is only patching up the problems and providing "another turn of the ideological screw" whereby workers and the powerless are co-opted (Abel, 1981). A good illustration of this is the attempt to focus on the management of conflict rather than the removal of its source. Attempts to introduce systems of conflict management or alternative dispute resolution that seem to be less authoritarian and more participatory are seen simply as ideological devices to conceal the existing power structure and maintain the existing arrangements. This is why even though such attempts may look radical, they are actually, more often, conservative (Abel, 1981, 1982; Harrington, 1985).

Criminal justice policy must be tied to the political economy. Until a political economy is introduced that recognizes diversity and minimizes material differences of property and wealth, these theorists believe, crime will remain. As Engels (1845: 248–49) argued, "where everyone receives what he needs to satisfy his natural and spiritual urges, where social gradations and distinctions cease to exist" and where "we eliminate the contradiction between individual man and all others, we counterpose social peace to social war, we put the axe to the *root* of crime" then "crimes against property cease of their own accord." In these

---

[13]As we shall see, left realists take a different view, arguing that reform brings real gains and should be pursued in the interim while more extensive social change is sought.

circumstances there will be less need for a criminal justice system, since the bulk of crime will be *prevented* through the socialist administration of society.

For left realists, in contrast, all the talk of revolution and collective systems of justice and control are part of the problems of radical criminology in failing to deal with the reality of crime today. Realists believe it is crucial to reintroduce the neglected victim into critical analysis. Left realism "starts from the problems as people experience them" (Young, 1986: 24), and so implies an accurate victimology that acknowledges the working class as a victim of crime from all sides. He proclaims:

> We must develop a realist theory which adequately encompasses the scope of the criminal act. That is it must deal with both macro- and micro-levels, with the causes of criminal action and social reaction, and with the triangular inter-relationship between offender, victim and the state. It must learn from past theory … It must stand for theory in a time when criminology has all but abandoned theory … On a research level we must develop theoretically grounded empirical work against the current of atheoretical empiricism … In terms of practical policy we must combat impossibilism … Let us state quite categorically that the major task of radical [realist] criminology is to seek a solution to the problem of crime and that of a socialist policy is to substantially reduce the crime rate. (Young, 1986: 27–28)

Indeed, Young sees crime as divisive of the working class and one of a number of potential unifiers for re-creating community.

Radical realists share a view that offenders harm their victims as a result of the conspiring forces of capitalism, patriarchy, and racism, mediated through a state social control apparatus that not only fails to protect those who are most vulnerable but that exacerbates crime and produces its own victims. The powerless and exploited social categories are victims of class inequality, and of sexual and racial differentiations in power, status, and wealth. Isolated from community, rendered objects of exploitation by commercialization, and frequently abandoned by a fickle productive process, these marginal categories are available for further victimization by individual perpetrators of crime. Yet even the perpetrators recruited from the ranks of the working classes are themselves victimized by a fearful and hungry criminal justice system. It is not just the entry into crime that is shaped by these forces, it is also the state criminal justice system. Radical realists show how aspects of the criminal justice system interplay with the capitalist economic structure to deliver their own casualties. It is neither individual responses nor societal revolution that left realists want. Rather their agenda is to promote democratic socialist change by affecting relations within capitalist society toward achieving greater social justice and reduced levels of crime. They are less inclined to overthrow the existing criminal justice apparatus than to restructure it, making it more accountable and more responsive to the needs of the powerless.

Techniques of Crime Control

Although considerable effort is given in the critical literature to document the failure of criminal justice policy and practice under capitalism, little attention has been paid by critical criminologists to what this policy and practice would look like under the decentralized collective system they envisage. However, anarchist critics (Wieck, 1978; Taylor, 1982) and those who have studied cooperatives have given some substance to the decentralized collective approach (Henry, 1983, 1985). First its philosophy is designed to bring the individual to accept responsibility for his or her own behavior by reminding the offender of his or her connectedness to other members of the collective. The major sanctions used are collective persuasion through approval or disapproval. This can be expressed through public opinion, personal appeals, withdrawal of cooperation, ostracism, shaming, and expulsion. The aim of these techniques of control is to restore the wholeness of social existence to the collective after it has been breached by a person's failure to accept responsibility and connectedness. Informal procedure operates as a continuous control on each member's behavior. (Henry, 1983, 1985).

Collective persuasion can either work to correct an individual's behavior so that the connections are reestablished positively, or else they can lead to the member deciding that she or he does not want to take the responsibility, in which case she or he may voluntarily leave the cooperative. As Godwin astutely observes, "Under the unequivocal disapprobation and observant eye of public judgment," individuals are "inevitably obliged ... either to reform or emigrate" (Godwin, 1946: 211; 340).

However, it is rarely the individual alone who takes responsibility for breaking the cooperative spirit of responsibility and connectedness to others. The other members also share this responsibility. Wieck (1978: 234) recognizes this when he says that "reparation would not always be exclusively a demand made on a guilty person, but a task for the community concurrently." Indeed, this approach has been described as "celebrative" (Henry, 1983: 94–95; 179–219) to reflect the view that crime and deviance, rather than being seen necessarily as a negative experience, may sometimes, and ideally often, contribute positively toward a society's need to revise its relationships in order to adapt to changing circumstances. In this view crime and deviance may be no more than indicators of a new direction and the offender, a kind of functional rebel. Such a view, therefore, demands an "antiauthoritarian justice" that "would entail respect for alternative interpretations of reality" but would oppose "any attempt to destroy, suppress, or impose particular realities" (Ryan and Ferrell, 1986: 193) and would encourage "unresolved ambiguities of meaning" (Ferrell, 1994: 163).

Melville (1972: 130) has pointed out that where there is no general agreement about a problematic behavior, it is "a sign that part of the group should leave and form another community." This is a process Taylor (1982: 92) describes as "fissioning," which he says may occur "when there is persistent internal conflict."

In short, then, the collective philosophy of sanctioning is often one of turning negative connectedness into positive by reminding individuals of their responsibilities. As such, it is a *celebration* of human agency over negative structures that necessarily involves "acts of imagination ... to rectify injustice, to resolve conflict, just as acts of imagination are called for in the normal creation of ongoing life" (Wieck, 1978: 235).

EVALUATION

Early formulations of critical criminology, such as instrumental Marxism, lend themselves readily to criticism. They either tend toward romanticism, as in anarchism and left idealism, or to the dogmatic and doctrinal. In either case they embody an unrealistic and untestable air of "conspiracy theory." Mainstream criminologists such as Inciardi (1980), and Klockars (1979) have been foremost in criticism. They argue that critical criminology is facing its own crisis of confidence, and even supporters (e.g., Bohm, 1982) acknowledge that some of its theoretical contradictions, such as whether the real villains are the dominant classes or the system itself, still have not been resolved. Some critics have pointed out that critical criminology's revelations are rather unremarkable, merely a restatement of the old Robin Hood adage that the poor steal from the rich to survive (Toby, 1979). But Toby says this does not justify an offender's actions, nor recognize that, like crimes of the rich, they are driven by greed. Toby also objects to expanding the definition of crime to include the broader concept of social harm.

Klockars (1979), like others (Sparks, 1980; Mankoff, 1978; Turk, 1980), attacks the weak empirical base of much Marxist criminology, and he argues that radicals misrepresent capitalist societies as destructively class divided, when in reality class divisions can be beneficial and that many divisions are by interest group and unite people across class boundaries. Chambliss and Seidman (1982), in developing their structural Marxist position, criticize the instrumental Marxist view for obscuring the diversity and conflict within both the state and corporate elites. They (like Greenberg, 1981) argue that not all law is designed to protect ruling capitalist class interests but is intended to protect the overall system of capitalism. Perhaps most important, and anticipating left realism's position, Klockars asserts that the state's actual empowering of oppressed people's rights is genuine, not a sham or a mystification. Klockars points out further that critical theorists demonstrate the obvious greed of some of those in society with power while ignoring the contradictory facts, such as crime in socialist societies (see also Kennedy, 1976; Greenberg, 1979) and the apparent low crime rate in some very capitalistic societies like Switzerland and Japan.

To be fair, this latter criticism is overplayed, if not distorted. Few critical criminologists would accept that the kind of state socialism operative in the party-run authoritarian regimes of Eastern Europe for much of the twentieth century represents the kind of decentralized, democratic socialist society that they, or for that matter Marx, envisaged (Quinney, 1977: 40). Indeed, the collapse of these state-run systems and the adoption of variations on capitalist free-market production has resulted in dramatic increases in crime. Further, recent revelations of the political corruption and collapse of Japanese governments reinvigorates the critical criminologists' charge that whether a society has "crime" depends very much on how it is defined and on who controls the legal definitions and the criminal justice system. However, it is also true that some aspects of critical criminology stand in need of revision and this has been recognized by radicals themselves. Critical theorists following Marxist principles by focusing exclusively on how the capitalist system generates crime have overlooked the deprivations created through the harsher collective systems of production in socialist societies. By romanticizing socialism, critical theorists failed to take into account the known dehumanizing conditions that socialism produced. Moreover, the implicit deterministic character of their analysis minimizes the self-generated uncooperative behavior of humans. Thus critical theorists were unprepared for the wholesale rejection of socialist practice and adoption of the principles and practices of capitalism by former socialist states.

The most meaningful and constructive criticism has come from "the critically introspective debate waged by radical criminologists themselves" (Curran and Renzetti, 1994: 285) in their attempt to make their theorizing relevant to changing conditions (e.g., Greenberg, 1981). Indeed, Taylor et al. (1974) have criticized conflict criminologies for being limited to the exposé and demystifying of ruling-class bias in the criminal justice system, and ignoring how the crimes of both the poor and the wealthy are related to the structural elements of capitalist systems of production. Subsequently radicals have been their own severest critics. Weiss (1983: 140) provides an excellent summary of these criticisms. He argues that early critical criminologies

> failed to provide a convincing understanding either of the etiology of criminal behavior or the state's function in the maintenance of capitalism. Materialist accounts, which see the function of the criminal law as buttressing the "free" labor market by deterrence, training and discipline, seem cogent ... However, by concentrating on the functional pre-requisites of the capitalist system, some of these studies have ignored the complexity of politics and ideology. Instrumentalist versions of materialism have attempted to provide social mechanisms by which the capitalist class determines state policy, but structuralists maintain that this requires the imputation of motives and largely ignores the issue of legitimacy. Moreover they argue that capitalists are not able to act in their own long-term interest. Structuralism in turn has been criticized on the grounds that it represents a

"structural super determinism," almost completely devoid of human agency. While critical criminology assumed class consciousness, structuralists deny its usefulness to social change ... The matter of voluntarism, determinism, or dialectics ... remains unresolved.

Most recently critical and radical criminologists have been forced to acknowledge that other dimensions of social inequality such as race and gender are also important (Beirne and Messerschmidt, 1991: 350).

The challenge from within known as "left realism"—as opposed to "left idealism," in its characterization of earlier radical criminology (see Kinsey and Young, 1982; Lea and Young, 1984; Matthews and Young, 1986; Kinsey et al., 1986; MacLean, 1991a)—offers five criticisms and alternatives. First, left realists criticize much of radical criminology for being overly idealistic in their depiction of criminals as politically motivated (Young, 1979, 1987). Young (1986: 16) says radical criminology's left idealism has abandoned its original agenda in favor of a voluntaristic, rational law breaker who is temporarily dreaming but will awake when "left-wing intellectuals ... click their fingers."

Second, left realists say radical criminology has ignored the seriousness of crime and the disproportionate harm suffered by working-class victims of crime (Matthews, 1987). As Young (1986: 16) says, the radical view somewhat simplistically theorizes about the state but purges criminology of crime. And when it does acknowledge crime, it "ignores the fact that most working class crime is directed at working class people and that the 'challenge to property relations' is more often the appropriation of working-class property than any threat to capitalism."

Third, radical criminology is indicted for ignoring that law and criminal justice have made real gains for the powerless over the powerful. The powerless are not well served by radicals who side with those on the right who want to do away with rehabilitation approaches to crime control.

Fourth, in its broad focus on societal conditions, radical theory has prematurely abandoned the search for causality. And finally, fifth, left realists assert that radical criminology fails to make a difference to policy because their ideology prevents them engaging in policy debate for fear of being co-opted by the capitalist state. The result, says Young, is a convergence between neo-classicism and left idealism, both ignoring crime, both agreeing that social rehabilitation programs are impossible or impractical; both explaining crime control but devoid of a causal analysis of crime.

The left realist agenda that follows from this analysis is more active and reformist and has been well summarized by Cohen (1990), a sympathetic but critical supporter. Left realists agree on the following five assertions:

1. Crime is a real problem for the marginal weak and powerless: the working class, the elderly, ethnic minorities, and women, who are the most severely victimized.

2. The rule of law represents the history of victories of the powerless over the arbitrary powerful and must be expanded to deal with street crime, suite crime, and crimes of gender; and its enforcement arm, the police, should be retained but democratized.

3. Treatment, rehabilitation, and welfare must be defended against attacks from the right.

4. Causal analysis is important to analyze the multicausal features of crime in a modern capitalist society.

5. There is a need to engage the political and policy debate and to construct the socialist vision of law and order from the inside, more as a reformist than a utopian agenda, to influence government on what works and what is cost-effective.

Cohen (1990) rejects the notion of left realism as merely radical criminology "come of age." Instead he sees its reformist turn as a reflection of both the aging of radical criminologists, who have now become tenured and tempered their ideas in response to broader social developments such as stable conservative governments, growing awareness of the relevance of feminism and the ecology movements, and the collapse of state socialism. Cohen (1990: 19) expresses his uneasiness:

> Now as someone whose values come from the same socialist or communitarian liberal vision ... I should be satisfied with the realist solution. And indeed I respect their political stance and their attempt to stake out a clearly radical opposition to today's grim coalition between enterprise capitalism and neutered administrative criminology. Unlike their harsh critics from the Left, I see no reason to question their continued commitment to socialist theory and practice. But why does their sociology leave me uneasy? With a sense that this is a premature closure of debate, a denial of the tension between intellectual doubt and political action? Have not some important theoretical problems, insights been forgotten in order to respond to a particular set of political contingencies?

Certainly Cohen's concerns are not quelled by left realists' ambivalent notions of the role of the state, nor by their support of increased state powers which serve to strengthen the existing structure, not least that part that is its bureaucratic apparatus. Left realists have not reconciled the central contradictions between the call for increased powers of the state to control crime, and their preferences for a minimalist state, subject to public scrutiny and accountability, a point that some advocates have acknowledged (Matthews, 1987). Moreover, although not intended, the focus on working-class victims of working-class crime, while long overdue, has taken the spotlight off crimes of the economically powerful outside the state. Certainly it is true that "while the Left realist position is provocative, its empirical validity has yet to be established" (Curran and Renzetti, 1994: 284), and its neither new nor novel reformism leaves some suggesting it is little different from mainstream criminology (Gibbons, 1994: 170). However, perhaps the most damning criticism comes from feminist scholars, who have argued that, although the impact of left realism on critical criminology "has been profound ... the construction of the realism/idealism debate has been diversionary, regressive and purposefully misrepresentative of the advances within critical criminology since the mid-1970s" (Scraton, 1990: 20). The feminist claim has been that left realism, like radical criminology generally, has remained gender blind and as such remains part of the "malestream" ignoring activism, research, and theory drawn from women's experiences (Kelly and Radford, 1987; Edwards, 1989, cited in Scraton, 1990).

Indeed, this criticism has been made by Jaggar (1983), who finds Marxism generally wanting in its conception of human nature, which is both gender blind and gender biased: "It is not a conception of humans as genderless but rather a conception of humans as male" (Jaggar, 1983: 78), a conception that "excludes much women's work, and especially procreative work, from the category of labor and construes it more as biological processes. So women are excluded from history and even full humanity" (ibid., 79). Thus Marxism, says Jaggar, and by implication any criminology based on its premises, mystifies social reality, legitimates the continued oppression of women, and is "another ideology of male domination" (Jaggar, 1983: 78).

Overall radical/critical theorists have faced considerable criticism over the years from their more traditional rivals and now from within their own critical ranks. However, as Barlow (1990: 66) says "despite predictions of its demise, it has remained viable for the past twenty years." Indeed, Adler et al. (1991: 193) correctly observe that as long as there are substantial population groups excluded from the economic and political system, radical criminology "will continue to be heard."

The most important challenge facing critical theorists is the implementation in practical terms of their theoretical challenge. How does one realistically bring about the necessary broader changes that critical theories about crime imply? The early emphasis on revolution is not a likely nor a feasible alternative given recent world changes and the move toward a global capitalist economy. The dilemma is that internal system tinkering has always been rejected as a viable means of addressing the basic contradictions leading to crime. Thus the challenge of realism lies in creating conditions that will modify or sensitize the emerging system to create the equalities needed for a less criminogenic society. How this is to be done, without strengthening the very system of inequality and oppression along its existing class, gender, and racially segmented lines, remains a challenge and one that is perhaps better addressed by the new directions in critical criminology to which we turn in the remaining chapters.

CHAPTER ELEVEN

Critical Criminologies II: Feminist Theories

Feminism in criminology entails more than simply adding women as a subject in the study of crime. It argues for the inclusion of feminist theoretical analysis. Feminist criminology includes the recognition that most criminological theory has been based on studies of male offenders. It demands an acknowledgment that most victims of hidden or unreported crime are women victims of male violence. It contends that women's contribution to society has been limited in legal definitions by a focus on their stereotypical gender characteristics. It claims that law and criminal justice are used to contain women through control over their sexuality and procreation in the alleged interests of health and humanity. In this chapter we analyze the various contributions of feminist criminology, paying particular attention to feminist theorizing about the etiology of crime.[1]

BASIC IDEA, CENTRAL MOTIF, AND MAJOR THEORISTS

A major claim of feminism is that social science in general, and criminology in particular, is shaped by a male view of the social world. There are two facets to this charge. First, it is argued that the study of crime has focused almost exclusively on male offenders. Thus Morris (1987: 1) asserts it is quite typical "for criminology textbooks, even critical reviews, to contain nothing at all on women … Criminology, like most academic disciplines, has been concerned with the activities and interests of men." Studies largely use male subjects in their samples but then generalize from their findings to explain all criminal behavior, regardless of gender. Insofar as theories of crime have been formulated on these results, they are biased toward male experiences and activities. Moreover, much research demonstrates that, compared to men, women do not commit serious crime and

---

[1]We shall omit our table of related theories from this chapter since all of the theories we consider here are contained under the grouping "feminist," as in "liberal feminist," "radical feminist," "Marxist feminist," and "socialist feminist," and more recently "postmodernist feminist" (which we consider under postmodernism), and black feminist or "women of color" feminism (Simpson, 1989). Moreover, for some, each of these classifications is considered "exclusionary" of someone else's differences and so there has recently been a move to dissolve distinctions that violate the differences of others (Currie, personal communication, 1993) as well as a move to emphasize the "commonalities" among feminist pluralisms, rather than their divisions (Caulfield and Wonders, 1994).

are not often arrested or convicted for crime. Indeed, this most remarkable finding of the difference between male and female crime is never dealt with in any
consistent theoretical manner. As Cain (1989: 3) has said, although it is well
known that "the most significant criminological finding historically and world-
wide is that most offenders are male," most criminological theories fail to take
this gender difference into account.[2] This failure presents great difficulty in the
ability to generalize (Daly and Chesney-Lind, 1988). All mainstream criminological explanatory models implicitly assume that those variables used to explain
male criminality are similarly applicable to explain female criminality. As
Leonard (1982: 182) puts it: "Simply predicting female behavior by reference to
male behavior is unlikely to work. This is precisely the problem confronting all
our theories—they barely acknowledge let alone incorporate existing differences between men and women." To ignore the roots of women's relative *conformity* is myopic. As a result, criminology's theories are unlikely to explain female
crime (Morris, 1987) and may even miss what is crucial to explaining male crime,
that is, the social construction of masculinity (Edwards, 1989: 165–66;
Messerschmidt, 1993; Caulfield and Wonders, 1994: 217).

A second facet of the feminist critique concerns the exclusion of a feminist
perspective in the construction of criminological theories. This means that a
criminology informed by gender experience has not been allowed to develop.
Even where women have become criminologists, their ways of thinking, presenting criminological analysis, organizing their research, and relating to its professional culture have, until recently, been constrained by the predominant male
framework (Menzies and Chunn, 1991). Consequently, feminist criminology is,
by definition, "marginal and oppositional, deconstructive and progressive, dangerous and endangered" (Menzies and Chunn, 1991: 7; see also Renzetti, 1993).
Thus the development of a gender-sensitive criminology has been precluded. Put
simply, there has been a failure by mainstream criminology and even critical
criminology to incorporate gender into the criminological enterprise (Gelsthorpe
and Morris, 1988: 231–33). With the exception of feminist criminology texts by
Smart (1976), Leonard (1982), Naffine (1987), and Messerschmidt (1993), virtually all textbook discussions of criminological theory have disregarded its
gender dimension and have ignored feminist theories of crime.[3] As a result of this

---

[2] One exception here is Hagan's (1989, 1990; Hagan et al., 1985, 1987) power-control theory,
which we discuss in Chapter 13.

[3] Gibbons's (1992) sixth edition of his text does include a discussion of feminist theorizing, as
does his treatise on the problems and issues of theory development (Gibbons, 1994). Likewise,
Beirne and Messerschmidt (1991) and Curran and Renzetti (1994) devote significant space to the
subject, but these are rare exceptions. The standard criminological theory text (Vold and Bernard,
1986) does not even mention it as a perspective.

avoidance, several feminist writers have labeled criminology as "malestream," embodying a "structured silencing of women's voices in virtually every corner of the criminological landscape," rendering it both "gender-blind and gender biased" (Menzies and Chunn, 1991: 7, 14). In this chapter, in contrast, we are concerned solely with the attempt to construct a feminist criminology.[4]

A central issue confronting feminist criminologists is how to deal with the omission of any consideration of gender in both research and theorizing. Many have asserted that rather than simply adding "women" to theories of crime, gender should pervade all theoretical explanations of crime. They argue that male criminological accounts of "reality," "need to be de-centered in order for women, not men, to be able to describe and name their experiences" (Ahluwalia, 1991: 5).[5] However, for Menzies and Chunn (1991: 14) feminist criminologies cannot simply be an add-on, "the point is *to become* the mainstream."

In recent years, as an outgrowth of the general feminist movement, several approaches have emerged which seek to establish a place for gender-aware explanations in the criminological enterprise (see Table 11-1). Initially feminists attempted to engage directly criminological discourse for its deficiencies in covering gender issues (Simpson, 1989). However, one of the founders of feminist criminology, Smart (1976), now takes the position that feminist theory is basically incompatible with criminology and that feminism has more to offer criminology than the reverse (Smart, 1990). A significant reason for the feminist shift away from crime and criminology is that these arenas are framed by the state, which is male dominated. Moreover, criminology, by definition, is exclusionary and marginalizes some people's experiences; typically those of powerless women, who are subject to victimization by males both inside the privacy of domestic environments *and* in the public arena of justice institutions where they are denied protection. In examining women's experiences, feminists feel that criminology's gender-blind theorizing is unlikely to liberate women from their oppression. Thus, following Daly and Chesney-Lind's (1988) framework, feminist criminologists believe that it is necessary to take a more inclusive perspective than offered

---

[4] Where feminism adopts similar analyses to other theoretical perspectives, such as in postmodernist deconstructionism, we have discussed its contribution in the relevant chapter. Where theories are about women's crime but not necessarily feminist, we have included them in the appropriate theoretical chapter. Finally, where there is a developed feminist critique of an existing theoretical framework, we have included this in the evaluation of the appropriate theoretical framework.

[5] According to Rosenau (1992: xi) "de-centering" is part of the discourse of postmodern deconstructionist critique (see Chapter 12), where it refers to the "absence of anything at the center or any overriding truth," with the injunction to concentrate attention on the margins. (See also Gagnier, 1990.)

Table 11-1 Theorists Using Feminist Explanations of Crime

THEORIST	MAJOR WORK(S)	DATE
Klein	"The Etiology of Female Crime"	1973
Adler	"Sisters in Crime: The Rise of the New Female Criminal"	1975
Simon	*Women and Crime*	1975
Brownmiller	*Against Our Will: Men, Women and Rape*	1975
Smart	*Women, Crime and Criminology: A Feminist Critique*	1976
	"The New Female Criminal: Reality or Myth?"	1979
	The Ties that Bind: Law, Marriage and the Reproduction of Patriarchal Relations	1984
	Feminism and the Power of Law	1989
	"Feminist Approaches to Criminology or Postmodern Woman Meets Atavistic Man"	1990
	"The Women of Legal Discourse"	1992
Edwards	*Female Sexuality and the Law*	1981
	"Violence against Women: Feminism and the Law"	1990
Leonard	*Women Crime and Society: A Critique of Criminology Theory*	1982
MacKinnon	"Feminism, Marxism, Method, and the State: Toward Feminist Jurisprudence"	1983
	Feminism Unmodified: Discourses on Life and Law	1987
	Toward a Feminist Theory of the State	1989
Carlen	*Women's Imprisonment: A Study in Social Control*	1983
	Women Crime and Poverty	1985
Carlen and Worrall	*Criminal Women: Autobiographical Accounts*	1988
	Gender, Crime and Justice	1987
Stanko	*Intimate Intrusions*	1985
	Everyday Violence	1990
Naffine	*Female Crime: The Construction of Women in Criminology*	1985
Cain	"Realism, Feminism, Methodology and Law"	1986
	Growing Up Good: Policing the Behaviour of Girls in Europe	1989
	"Toward Transgressions: New Directions in Feminist Criminology"	1990
Heidensohn	"Models of Justice"	1986
	"Women and Crime: Questions for Criminology"	1987
Messerschmidt	*Capitalism, Patriarchy, and Crime: Toward a Socialist Feminist Criminology*	1986
	Masculinities and Crime: Critique and Reconceptualization of Theory	1993

Morris	*Women, Crime and Criminal Justice*	1987
Gelsthorpe	*Sexism and the Female Offender*	1989
Gelsthorpe and	"Feminism and Criminology in Britain"	1988
Morris	*Feminist Perspectives in Criminology*	1990
Daly	"The Social Control of Sexuality"	1988
	"Gender and Varieties of White-Collar Crime"	1989
	"Reflections on Feminist Legal Thought"	1990
Chesney-Lind	"Girl's Crime and Woman's Place:	
	Toward a Feminist Model of Female Delinquency"	1989
Daly and	"Feminism and Criminology"	1988
Chesney-Lind		
Chesney-Lind		
and Shelden	*Girls, Delinquency and Juvenile Justice*	1992
Simpson	"Feminist Theory, Crime, and Justice"	1989
Currie	"Women and the State: A Statement	
	on Feminist Theory"	1989
	"Battered Women and the State"	1990
	"Feminist Encounters with Postmodernism:	
	Exploring the Impasse of the Debates	
	on Patriarchy and Law"	1992

by traditional criminology. In such a perspective feminism is "a world view and a social movement that encompasses assumptions and beliefs about the origins and consequences of gendered social organization as well as strategic directions and actions for social change" (Simpson, 1989: 606). Only with such a vision is it possible for women to "transgress" the limits of criminology and the very structures and gender constructions that subordinate them (Cain, 1990).

Those who prefer the broader "feminist oriented" criminology (Caulfield and Wonders, 1994) as a perspective attempt to understand and explain crime in general as part of the wider configuration of social arrangements. Though women are presently the major proponents of this theoretical stance, its content and development are not restricted by gender and are not generally intended to exclude others employing a gender-aware analysis (e.g., Messerschmidt, 1986; 1993).

As in each of the theoretical perspectives we have analyzed, there are diverse strands and "competing conceptions of the origins and mechanisms of gender inequality/oppression, and divergent strategies for its eradication" that inform the different feminist criminologies (Simpson, 1989: 606). Although several currents of feminism have been recognized, four major approaches have been identified within the criminological literature: liberal, radical, Marxist, and socialist (Jaggar, 1983). However, it should be pointed out that this classification has recently been replaced by more inclusive approaches, which, as we shall see later, do not "subjugate other subjectivities" such as those of black feminists, lesbian feminists, Third World feminists, and aboriginal or Native American feminists, among others, but incorporates their differences and experiences (Smart, 1990: 82).[6]

Liberal feminism is concerned with gender discrimination as an issue of equal rights between men and women. It takes a noncritical stance on gender. It seeks to end discrimination by institutional changes. These are sought through legal reform, aimed at increasing women's opportunities (Hoffman-Bustamente, 1973; Adler, 1975; Simon, 1975; Edwards, 1990), rather than through challenges to the construction and existence of gender categories. Castro (1990), for example, depicts liberal feminists viewing the society as seriously flawed but correctable. They "have generally located the enemy as being masculinity" and are satisfied to work within the system, demanding "state action and intervention to remove this threat from women's lives" (Schwartz, 1989: 2).

In contrast, critical feminisms challenge a gender-structured world. For example, *radical feminism* sees the problem of gender inequality and the subordination of women to male power as a systemic problem of "patriarchy."[7] Patriarchy is rooted in male aggression and male domination in public and private domains, through the control of women's sexuality. Part of the radical agenda involves the liberation of women from male definitions of women's roles, and their "place" in male society, especially in relation to the nuclear family and child care (Simpson, 1989; Castro, 1990).

Marxist feminism recognizes gender relations and patriarchal structure but sees these rooted in class relations of production. Historically these class relations have created and used gender differences to control and subordinate women. As a result women are in weak positions of economic power, and like other minorities, are vulnerable to exploitation.

---

[6] Each of these positions also has its own subgroupings. Delmar (1986: 9) has added cultural feminism and material feminism to the "plurality of feminisms," and Tong (1989) argues that psychoanalytic, existentialist, and postmodern feminism also exist. However, there is controversy across divisions in terms of emphasis, approach, method, and whether the divisions should be mentioned at all (Caulfield and Wonders, 1994). As explained earlier, we have included feminist contributions in the extensions and evaluations of the relevant chapters. Postmodernist feminism and its criticism (see Nicholson, 1990; Smart, 1989, 1990, 1992, Gagnier, 1990) are included in the next chapter. We shall briefly outline liberal feminist criminology here for the purpose of comparison.

[7] *Patriarchy,* or the "law of the father," is the system of male domination that permeates all aspects of social life (Balkan et al., 1980: 208, 338; Messerschmidt, 1986). It is a sex/gender system of stratified production in the interests of men, "in which men dominate women" and where "that which is considered masculine is typically more highly valued than that which is considered feminine" (Curran and Renzetti, 1994: 272). By way of contrast, a *matriarchy* is "a society in which production serves the interests of reproduction; that is, the production of goods is regulated to support the nurturance of life" (Love and Shanklin, 1978: 186).

Socialist feminism "unites the primary concepts in radical and Marxist feminism to identify women's oppression as based in capitalist patriarchy" (Danner, 1991: 52). Socialist feminism says that it is important to recognize *both* the technology and class relations used in the production of goods and services (derived from Marxist feminism) *and* the construction of gender categories in labor, child care, and domestic care (derived from radical feminism), without prioritizing the one over the other, as the interrelated source of gender inequality and male domination over women (Eisenstein, 1979; Hartmann, 1979, 1981; Messerschmidt, 1986; Currie, 1989; 1991). As Danner (1991: 53) explains: "The crux of socialist feminist concern with the intersection of gender, class, and race is the recognition of difference ... Patriarchy cannot be separated from capitalism, neither can racism, imperialism, or any oppression based on 'otherness.' " The socialist feminist agenda believes that inequality and gender oppression can only be overcome by constructing a noncapitalist, nonpatriarchal society. Merely replacing or tinkering with parts of the system perpetuates the subordination of women in a different form.

In spite of their differences the varieties of feminisms share several core assumptions that they have contributed to criminology. Caulfield and Wonders (1994) have identified five of these "commonalities" as gender, power, context, social process, and social change. They argue that gender, power, and social context shape human relations along gendered lines through a social process. They believe all feminists share a commitment to develop methods to understand this process and to change the way it currently operates. In this regard they do not see feminism as focused exclusively on women but "concerned with the social construction of difference, particularly the construction of masculinity and femininity as meaningful social categories" (Caulfield and Wonders, 1994: 215).

HUMANS, HUMAN NATURE, AND HUMAN BEHAVIOR

Feminist criminology's view of human nature stems from the criticism that the prevailing view of human beings in the social sciences is fundamentally flawed, being based on an exclusively male perspective that reflects men's experiences of the social world. As a result, women's reality is either overlooked or seriously distorted. Moreover, the ability to create the world in one's own image is to use power and domination, a male practice that has produced a view of humanity giving females a secondary or marginal role as human beings. The agenda of feminism as stated by Faludi (1991: xxiii) "asks that women be free to define themselves—instead of having their identity defined for them."

Most feminists insist that alleged differences between men and women are socially constructed in order to maintain male dominance. These constructions are bolstered by institutions of society, not least of which are those of law and justice, which support male supremacy (Smart, 1989). Thus there is a common view among most feminist criminologists that humans are the product of socialization in gendered historical and cultural contexts. Although there are differences between the varieties of feminists on human nature, one of the most comprehensive views is that of socialist feminism, which sees humans as having their "inner lives," their bodies, and their behavior structured by a socially imposed gender that "occurs when we are very young and that is reinforced throughout our lives in a variety of different spheres; ... these relatively rigid masculine and feminine character structures are a very important element in maintaining male dominance" (Jaggar, 1983: 127).

Instead of the "passive" image of women in the face of patriarchal dominance or control, a gendered criminology portrays women as individuals who "possess their own subjective qualities and logics of rationality" and as "active participants in the social construction of their identities" (Schwendinger and Schwendinger, 1991: 40). From the socialist-feminist perspective women's gendered identity is negotiable in a context of "their shared interests with men who are also affected partly by similar gendered, class, racial, national and global relationships" (ibid.).

Because of an appreciation of the shared subjection to gender identity construction, some argue that it is not enough simply to look at constructions of femininity. It is also necessary to explore constructions of masculinity. Theorists such as Liddle (1989), Layland (1990), Ahluwalia (1991), Smart (1990), and Messerschmidt (1993), prefer a broader approach that does not so exclusively focus on women's lives. This approach argues that male lives are caricatured and the range and diversity of "masculinities" is overlooked. Thus, Layland argues: "We must demystify power and its components, one of which is the production of 'masculinity' and 'masculine' behaviour" (Layland, 1990: 129). It is for this reason that some urge a revision of the concept of patriarchy so that it can be "informed about how men vary in regard to women. It needs to be informed concretely about what kinds of males, interest groups and structures promote patriarchal relations or undermine them" (Schwendinger and Schwendinger, 1991: 42).

In this regard, Messerschmidt (1993: 58) has revised his earlier view of patriarchy. He now believes that the concept obscures "real variations in the construction of masculinity within a particular society and, consequently, encourages the theorization of one type of masculinity, the 'typical (patriarchal) male.'" He argues that there are differing "masculinities" that need to be considered. Indeed, he claims that gender does not have a prior independent existence but is constructed in social action. Hence for some males, committing crimes is a way of building particular kinds of masculinity and, depending on class, age, and situation, other forms of masculinity are also constructed.

Other feminists have similarly acknowledged that the initial polemical focus on "woman," as an unproblematic category presumed to represent all women, is an "exclusionary strategy" (Spelman, 1988; Minow, 1990; Smart, 1990). As Danner (1991: 52) says: "The weakness in radical feminism is its assumption of gender as a sex-caste. It assumes a universality and commonality of women's subordination that does not exist. Important power differentials among women are ignored." This, however, does not deny the existence of many commonalities among women's experiences. Clearly feminists have moved to a position on human nature that recognizes both commonality *and* difference, without one absorbing the other.

VIEW OF SOCIETY AND THE SOCIAL ORDER

Like other theoretical perspectives that take society and the social order seriously, feminist criminologists do not have a unitary view of the social order. A major division appears between radical feminists, who take an instrumental perspective of the state as a neutral resource to be captured in order to advance the interests of the powerful (e.g., MacKinnon, 1989), and feminists (Marxist and socialist) who take a structuralist view of the state as a relatively autonomous entity operating in the broad interests of capitalism and patriarchy (e.g., Messerschmidt, 1986).

According to Currie (1989: 4), those taking the instrumental approach envision the state as currently reflecting the interests of men. This equates state control of women's sexuality and their capacities for reproduction to the legal regulation of women as male property. Thus, both research on prostitution and on juvenile delinquency attest to the severe control exercised over female sexual activities. The instrumentalist solution to this inequity is to displace male dominance as the controlling interest in the state, by including women who have feminist concerns. But radical feminists such as MacKinnon (1987), while recognizing both law and the state as bastions of male dominance, nonetheless see the state as an instrument to power. This contradictory position can lead to an ambivalence whereby the state is actually strengthened, allegedly in the interests of women, but ultimately for their continued repression, and indeed, the repression of others subordinated by different categories of exclusion. For example, Edwards (1990: 149) has called for "more intensive policing, stricter laws, more control of men's power and the regulation of men's violence." This agenda is justified on the grounds that it provides equality and consistency for all victims, and serves to raise women's dignity and political awareness. Others agree that the long-term objectives of feminism should not deny the means of protecting "those who are harmed *today,* by whatever means are currently available" (Caulfield and Wonders, 1994: 226). Several feminist critics point out, however, that an alliance with the state, born of the struggle against the patriarchal control of women through male use of sexual and domestic violence, has involved increasing the power of the state against women (Pitch, 1985; Currie, 1989; Smart, 1989).

Not surprisingly, therefore, many radical and socialist feminist criminologists "have been extremely wary of calling on the capitalist state to intervene." (Schwartz, 1989: 2).

In contrast, for these feminists, the inclusion of women in the state apparatus cannot produce long-term radical change (Currie, 1989). In their alternative perspective, the state and the social system are the "incarnation of sexism with everything being organized around intersexual relations established on the basis of power" (Castro, 1990: 67).

For some feminists the state is a relatively autonomous entity that institutionalizes women's oppression (Eisenstein, 1979). They see the state operating in the long term, to maintain the patriarchal-class power structure. Consequently, the state episodically supports instances favoring women's interests over those of men without changing its overall patriarchal structure. Others see the state as the bastion of patriarchy. The state controls women through the welfare system in an era when capitalism no longer champions patriarchy (Ursel, 1986; Currie, 1989).

Whatever the differences in interpretation between feminist theorists, they are in accord that the state–society relationship is a male construction. However society is described, it represents male experiences and fails to reflect the reality of a gendered society as experienced by women. Female experiences are overlooked in the construction of viable theories that accurately reflect the interactive reality of the social order. The essential questions remain: (1) Is the state "male"? (2) Is the state the best focus for feminists who desire to bring structural change? and, perhaps most importantly, (3) If the state is the source of change, how can it be effectively harnessed without reproducing oppressive forms of control that in turn create new categories of exclusion? To date feminist theorists have not resolved these issues, but to be fair, nor have any others.

THE ROLE OF LAW, THE DEFINITION OF CRIME, AND THE IMAGE OF THE CRIMINAL

There are certain issues common to all feminist analyses of the law. It is clear that an important goal of feminist theory is to "challenge the reconstitution of patriarchy through law" with a view to removing women's oppression (Currie, 1991: 10; Smart, 1989) and to eliminate "relations of domination and subordination" (Daly, 1990: 10). However, the problem is how this can be achieved. According to Daly (ibid.), there is a core dilemma that consists of two components: (1) "If the law is fashioned from men's experiences and viewpoints, then where are the entry points for women? Can women's experiences and viewpoints be heard?" and (2) "If the law reinforces gender hierarchies and women's oppression, how, then, can women's demands for equality and justice be addressed in any significant way?" Daly points out that some feminist legal scholars see the goal accomplished by transforming legal reasoning. Such change is made difficult by the equality doctrine. This doctrine allegedly assures equal treatment of all who are subject to legal proceedings but often fails to provide substantive equality where women are involved. One reason for this, according to Daly, is the fact that although class is reflected in the prevailing model of law, gender is not. Thus law does not take into account disparities in wealth and poverty that affect women more than men. As a result, the equality standard does little for women and may even work to their detriment. As Daly (1990: 11) says, virtually all feminists writing on law "acknowledge that formal legal equality of women with respect to men cannot provide substantive equality ... [The] traditional equality approach can result in a worsening of women's situation." This is because notions of equality are based on men's lives, which form the standard, while women remain the exception. Because of this the equality doctrine cannot transform gender relations (Daly, personal communication, 1993). Daly gives an example from civil law in which, after a divorce with presumptive joint custody of children, some women find themselves in a much worse position than men because they are given responsibility for the major portion of child care and supervision but are denied supportive resources. Even where assets are divided equally, because law embodies an uncritical view of gender, there is an inequitable outcome. Without compensating for inherent gender inequalities in the social structure, women remain at a disadvantage.

Though some feminists accept the idea of equal treatment before the law, and despite the differences that exist in the way equality is sought, theorists agree that biological and social differences between men and women need to be addressed (Daly, 1990). A number of authors have dealt with this issue. According to Daly, writers such as Taub and Williams (1985) argue for laws that are neutral with regard to gender. However, where this neutrality has a negative effect on women they suggest a "disparate impact" approach, whereby the negative effect of the law is counteracted. Daly (1990: 13) states that other writers, such as MacKinnon (1982, 1983), make the case for gender-based analysis of power relations in the construction of difference, rather than the difference itself, arguing that if a law or practice places women in subordinate positions, legal action should be taken.

Most of these arguments center on the law generally and primarily on civil law rather than specifically on criminal law. It must be remembered that here, as with the role of the state, there is considerable difference of opinion among feminist scholars about whether law can be effective for women and how much the law should be used for women's concerns. For violence in the family, Edwards (1990: 149), for example, suggests that feminist demands for more law are largely symbolic:

> Feminists argue that it is the absence of law, the lack of application of the law or the selective enforcement of law which has created a cultural climate in which

particular behaviours, including violence against women, is condoned. The law then serves symbolically to support a climate of violence against women and sets the scene for that climate.

Edwards further observes that some feminists have taken extreme positions as to the role of the law in eliminating certain behaviors, such as the production and use of pornography (Dworkin, 1981). Others (Brants and Kok, 1986), however, consider the criminal law's effect doubtful in restraining such behavior.

Whether effective or not, the feminist challenge has introduced significant innovations in legal definition. Schwendinger and Schwendinger (1991: 39–40) argue that feminists have helped to universalize rape laws so that they are more inclusive, have redefined gender crimes based on the criteria of harm, proposing for example "that rape of a woman should be defined as a civil liberties violation (as well as a violent crime) and that international law should distinguish crimes against women as human rights violations."

However, feminists have found it difficult to affect the "male logic" embedded in jurisprudence and legal practice (Smart, 1992). Indeed, Currie (1991: 10) says a number of writers have argued that the notion of abstract objective rules within an adversarial format is based on hierarchical thinking and male rationality that "must be superseded by a system of justice based upon what are the specifically feminine principles of care, connection and community." Thus, although some success has been achieved in the struggle to change criminal law regarding rape and spouse abuse by challenging the basic premises that shaped the definition of these crimes in the past (Schwendinger and Schwendinger, 1982; Clark and Lewis, 1977; Brownmiller, 1975; Goldsmith-Kasinsky, 1978; Smart, 1984; Smart and Smart, 1978; Schwartz and Clear, 1980; Snider, 1985; Los, 1990), this has been accomplished with limitations and problems and disappointment (Currie, 1991).

Currie (1991) observes that among socialist feminist critics an explanation for the failure of law reform stems from the exclusive analysis of law without relating it to other political and economic institutions of capitalist society and without incorporating a theory of the state. Those who do incorporate such an analysis, says Currie (1991: 11), have tended to argue that legal reforms championed by women have become subsumed as part of "a totalitarian process of political, economic, and ideological control through which the dominated accept and actively participate in their subordination."

The role of law in feminist analysis, like the role of the state, raises difficult questions for theorists and activists alike. For example, should criminal law be extended or enlarged to take account of gender issues or will this further reinforce the law's support for patriarchal relations as Smart (1989) has argued? On the other hand, as Edwards (1990: 148) argues, the law does play a powerful symbolic function in the struggle for change.

A further problem for feminists in developing a feminist criminology is how women are defined and represented in law and crime. According to Daly (1992) there is some question about whether arrested women are to be seen as criminals, offenders, or victims who have become criminalized. There are several possibilities. Arrested women are either (1) victims who have become criminalized by a male-biased state and/or law, (2) people who have committed acts that are criminalized, or (3) people who break the law to survive or to resist oppressive relationships. Which of these definitions applies depends on whose account of the event is believed and accepted (women's? officials'?) and on whether the resulting generalizations apply to all women.

Daly (1992) also raises problems with the important concept of "blurred boundaries," which has been used to connect women's prior victimization and their offending. The concept refers to the argument that women are often victims either presently or that they offend because of past abuse and oppression. Given these conditions, when women are committing crimes, are they acting as initiating offenders or are they reacting as victims? Hence the notion of unclear demarcation of responsibility. However, as Daly (1992: 48) states: "by joining victimization and criminalization, feminist scholars evade core questions about the conceptual status of 'crime offender' and 'crime victim.'" This type of conceptualization by itself leaves little room for human agency and responsibility for offending. Without some notion of responsibility there is no way to deal with those women who do harm others. Indeed, Daly (1991) warns feminists against explanations of women's harm of other women that "romanticize or excuse too much," as when women's lawbreaking is politicized as resistance against oppressive people or institutional structures.

Further, the notion of blurred boundaries may also be used to explain and exonerate men's abuse of women if such men had been victimized and abused while growing up. To resolve this issue Daly suggests that "we abandon the implied gender-based overlay on victimization and criminalization (i.e., woman/victim; man/lawbreaker)" (Daly, 1992: 49). Not only does this overlay reinforce the notion of woman as passive object and man as active subject, but it obscures our ability to assess the genuine underlying conditions that generate crime.

CAUSAL LOGIC

According to feminist scholars, late-nineteenth-century to mid-twentieth-century studies that attempt to explain female criminality have serious flaws. Most are based either on moralisms, physical differences, male conjecture, social and biological influences, or a combination of all these factors (e.g., see Lombroso and Ferrero, 1900; Pike, 1876; Adam, 1914; Pollak, 1950), making them examples of male-dominated biases but not much else (Klein, 1973). More recent analyses have attempted to correct these errors by challenging the earlier assumptions but have serious flaws of their own (Adler, 1975; Simon, 1975). In one example of such an attempt to correct the errors of these earlier studies, Adler (1975) showed that rather than resulting from, say, mental illness, female crime had instead increased as a result of changing economic roles and increased opportunities for women. Adler's explanation was expressed in the concept of "the new female criminal," and was reinforced by the almost simultaneous publication of Simon's (1975) work on the alleged breakdown of gender distinctions. Simon claimed that this breakdown would cause an increase in female crime as a result of criminal opportunities related to increased labor-force participation. Adler (1975) said that women's increasing involvement in crime was the result of the "rising tide of female assertiveness" in which "determined women are forcing their way into major crimes ... pushing into—and succeeding at—crimes that were formerly committed by males only" (Adler, 1975: 1, 13–14). This was further distorted in the media and in some textbook accounts to suggest that the Women's Liberation Movement had caused the increase in female crime (see Faith, 1993: 6). Others countered that the Liberation Movement was not even established when women's crime began to rise (Steffensmeier, 1978) and that changing capitalist merchandising strategies have provided greater crime opportunities for the traditional female role (such as shopping), rather than these resulting from women's greater presence in the workforce (Steffensmeier and Cobb, 1981). Indeed, it has been argued by some feminist theorists that women's freedom has actually *decreased* as societal expectations of their role expand to include everything from child care, elder care, health care, and contribution to domestic income—that is, the "double burden" of wage labor and management of the domestic economy (Messerschmidt, 1986). Simpson's (1989: 611) review of relevant studies also shows the Women's Movement thesis to have been false and that its emphasis "diverted attention from the material and structural forces that shape women's lives and experiences."

Gender has emerged in the causal analysis of feminist criminology to be "the central organizing principle of contemporary life, shaping human actions in every sphere, including the criminal justice system" (Caulfield and Wonders, 1994: 215). This goes beyond what was formally termed rather simply "sex role" factors and beyond the social construction of women: "Rather, crime by men is a form of social practice invoked as a resource, when other resources are unavailable, for accomplishing masculinity" (Messerschmidt, 1993: 85). As indicated earlier, these constructions of masculinity differ in terms of different contexts requiring different demonstrations and constructions of gender depending on what is at stake. Thus the workplace may require a divergent masculinity from that in the home. Still another form may be required for the teenage gang member in public engaging in violent crime to demonstrate prowess in the company of his peers.

Messerschmidt advances a similar process for female criminality. Commenting on Daly's (1989: 788) conclusion that the rare involvement of women in white-collar crime was due to either their aversion to abusing positions of power or their being excluded from corporate crime groups, Messerschmidt (1993: 196–97) gives a gender explanation:

> Yet a woman who does engage in corporate crime is not simply doing masculinity. Although her very position is a protest against conventional femininity, she is still gender accountable ... In other avenues of everyday life, she most likely engages in stereotypical femininity. Thus ... women who participate in corporate crime are constructing a specific type of femininity that consists of conventional and unorthodox gendered practices.

Feminists' analysis of causality, consistent with its assumptions of human nature and society, has moved beyond explaining gender difference in the incidence and seriousness of criminal offenses as a product of a gender-biased system of criminal justice that "denies women their criminality" (Smart, 1976). Such analysis now has parallels with analyses of the social construction of deviant categories (e.g., Pfuhl and Henry, 1993) in that it concentrates on the processes whereby "difference" is generated and whereby some people's difference is controlled, marginalized, and dominated by the power conveyed and expressed through the gender construction and reconstruction process.[8]

CRIMINAL JUSTICE SYSTEM IMPLICATIONS

From a feminist point of view the justice system, as all other institutions, reflects a male bias. Much of the discussion concerning criminal justice by feminist criminologists focuses on gender discrimination in processing without addressing the construction of an alternative system of justice. However, the feminist criminological frameworks discussed earlier have certain implications for justice policy and intervention.

Policy Implications and Correctional Ideology

Liberal feminists are explicit in their demand that the ideals of liberty and equality in the process of justice be applied equally to women. They believe that women should have the same rights and receive the same opportunities as men. As Beirne and Messerschmidt (1991: 516) summarize their position: "The liberal feminist program calls for state reform to bring about those changes necessary

---

[8]Interestingly, there may also be emerging parallels with the "sociology of acceptance," whereby being different is acceptable (Bogdan and Taylor, 1987).

to promote women's rapid integration into the backbone of society." Part of this integration to bring about legal equality involves equal application of the social control apparatus. This means correcting the differentially severe treatment that women receive for minor deviances, (for example, status offenses, sexual misconduct (Gold, 1971; Chesney-Lind, 1973); providing equal protection against violence and coercion, (for example, rape, harassment, assault; see LeGrand, 1973); providing equal access to legal representation and due process; and furnishing equal correctional treatment in comparably equipped facilities (Rafter, 1983, 1985; Heffernan, 1972; Burkhart, 1976; Mahan, 1984; Baunach, 1985).

Radical feminists, in contrast, reject these kinds of system modifications as failing to address the core problem of male-dominated justice. Merely making women's rights equal to men's rights in law and justice does little to change women's subjugation by gender in the wider social structure. In some ways such equalization may reinforce women's subjugation by giving the symbolic appearance of equality without the substantive change. The radical feminist position on criminal justice policy, although not yet fully articulated, implies a total revamping of the system whereby male control over women's lives would be eliminated. This would require women to take over positions of power and decision making within the criminal justice system and would include the courts, law enforcement, and corrections.

For both Marxist and socialist feminists, however, replacing men in positions of power in the criminal justice system with women is insufficient because it does not change the underlying structural cause of the problem. As we saw in the previous chapter on critical criminology, Marxists believe that to change law and criminal justice we must first change the existing capitalist social order to one based on an equitable distribution of wealth, in which decision making is collectively shared. This would eliminate the power differentials between men and women, as well as between ethnic and racial groups. A system of justice based on such principles of equality would be nonhierarchical, populist, communal, and involve shared decisions about what counts as harm and how to respond to it. This might involve such control techniques as shaming and ostracism.

While socialist feminists also wish to replace capitalism with a collective political and legal order, in addition they want to expose and eliminate male-dominated power hierarchies and their fostering of male attitudes and behaviors. But their collective order requires more than an absence of hierarchy. It requires an equality based on the recognition of *differences of experience,* while at the same time not discriminating on the basis of these differences. This may imply the creation of what we might refer to as courts of experience, whose deliberations would acknowledge the significant different life situations or circumstances of those excluded by divisions of gender, ethnicity, race, age, and physical and mental disability. Such courts would have to be comprised of representatives of these social categories.

EVALUATION

Given the relatively recent history of feminist work in criminology, it may be premature to undertake an evaluation of its theoretical contribution. However, in the emerging debate so far, it is apparent that some of the initial positions have certain weaknesses. Not the least of these stems from the very notion that gender is the central organizing theme, a stance some theorists have accused of both essentialism, exclusionism, and implicit racism (Spelman, 1988; Rice, 1990). For example, a significant criticism has come from women of color who argue that not enough attention has been paid to the experiences of black women in feminist theorizing and that black women's experience is different from that of white women (Mama, 1989; Rice, 1990). They charge that "the sexism of deducing the experience of all from the experience of men is rivaled only by the racism of asserting white middle class experience as normal, and designating black people's experience to the category of 'other'" (Ahluwalia, 1991: 12). Despite recognition of the socially constructed nature of "femininity" and "sexuality," says Ahluwalia, there is a failure to reference black women's different cultural experience, socialization patterns, and experiences in the labor market and criminal justice system:

> Understanding men as the bearers of power and the perpetrators of all evil denies the privilege that white women have over black men and also neglects to implicate white women in perpetuating racism and using violence against black people. (Ahluwalia, 1991: 12)

Such criticism does not deny the essential validity of gender analysis but requires that gender include sensitivity to racial and ethnic differences (Kline, 1989). Such a sensitivity would also need to overcome the simplistic black/white distinction within a gender analysis. Different cultural experiences, such as those of Latino women, Asian women, American Indian women, and women with disabilities, would also benefit from such a broadened feminist analysis.

A related issue, says Ahluwalia (1991: 13) concerns some feminists' call for more intensive policing of men which, if the racial application of law is not taken into account, will simply result in more policing of minority males and more harassment of minority females, who will likely be subject to more mandatory arrests for a variety of trivial offenses. For these kinds of reasons, Ahluwalia and others have concluded that race and gender must be considered together.

Two recurring issues facing feminist theory are (1) the notion of "the new woman" and (2) the relation of law and feminism. The first of these refers to the dilemma of recognizing that including diverse women's experiences, black experiences, ethnic experiences, gay experiences, disabled experiences, even male experiences, into the gender analysis weakens the common experience of "women's oppression as women" (Currie, 1991: 12; see Minow, 1990). Some feminist writers, such as Currie (1991) and Smart (1989), have objected to theorizing that fragments women's common oppression. The second issue concerning the relation of law and feminism has been addressed by Smart (1989), who argues that in employing law as a vehicle for change, feminists may "cede to law the very power which is then deployed against women's claims. In accepting law's terms in order to challenge law, feminism concedes too much" (Smart, 1989: 5). Smart prefers instead to deconstruct the power of law to demonstrate how it systematically excludes women's experience of reality. As opposed to law, Smart wants to establish feminism as a source of power and resistance, but she acknowledges that law also "provides a forum for articulating alternative visions and accounts" (Smart, 1989: 88).

This admittedly is a brief review and assessment of feminists' criminological work in which only a limited number of representative works have been cited. A burgeoning literature in this area explores exciting new avenues of inquiry, long passed over by the established criminologies. This has had an impact at least on the complacent smugness of traditional criminological theorizing, so that any serious new theoretical developments in the discipline must now of necessity take the feminist perspective into account. Though a sophisticated feminist criminology is slowly emerging, it is still in its early stages of refinement. Given that criminology tends to accommodate new developments into its existing theoretical discourse, it is unlikely that a total restructuring of criminological theory will take place. The reality of criminological theorizing is that the more particular theoretical strains strive to prioritize their contribution over others, the more they tend to perpetuate the existing scheme of things. Despite this inertia, Caulfield and Wonders (1994: 213, 229) believe that feminist contributions "have already begun to influence criminology in lasting ways" and "we celebrate the fact that feminism has already moved us appreciably closer to a more just world." Ironically, to continue to have this impact the feminist contribution to the overarching criminological enterprise must develop from its own roots and with women's voice at the center or else it risks being absorbed.

CHAPTER TWELVE

Critical Criminologies III: Postmodernist Theories

Postmodernism is a broad philosophical movement with intellectual roots in France and Germany that was born out of early twentieth-century misgivings (historical *avant garde*) about the surge of modernism. It challenges the assumptions in social science, and especially in the arts and humanities, that a high-low distinction can be drawn between scientific knowledge and common sense or vernacular knowledge, between high art and mass or popular culture (Huyssen, 1986). Postmodernism is a reaction to modernism and its reliance on reason and realism as central concepts to predict and control the world (Borgmann, 1992).

Modernism refers to the historical period that followed the middle ages of feudalism and that continued until the mid-twentieth century. Modernism is characterized by an *opposition* both to traditional society and to its faith in divine constitution, cosmic centeredness, the supernatural, subjectivity, and local boundedness (Borgmann, 1992: 5). In modernism this faith was replaced by a belief in the values of innovation, rationality, and objective analysis, directed toward progress and the discovery of truth. It was in the modern era that science developed as the dominant mode of understanding, predicting and controlling the world. Its application in technology and economy worked the modern project "into a social order characterized by aggressive realism, methodical universalism, and ambiguous individualism" (ibid.).

However, modernity, by its use of strategies of exclusion, and ultimately dogma, produced considerable hardship in its pursuit of progress. As Best and Kellner (1991:3) state:

> The construction of modernity produced untold suffering and misery for its victims, ranging from the peasantry, proletariat, and artisans oppressed by capitalist industrialization to the exclusion of women from the public sphere, to the genocide of imperialist colonization. Modernity also produced a set of disciplinary institutions, practices, and discourses which legitimate its modes of domination and control.

As a result, the modern project "lost its theoretical confidence and credibility" (Borgmann, 1992: 5). Postmodernism attempts to address these negative outcomes, reflecting a disenchantment with, and questioning of, all claims to truth, knowledge, power, and progress, especially those based upon the assumed superiority of rational logic (Hunt, 1991).[1]

In the social sciences, postmodernism is an attempt to reconceptualize the way we experience relationships and social structure, and a method to work through how the world around us appears real, thereby questioning that it is real in truth or fact or that there is any way of making such judgments.[2] Indeed, postmodernism challenges the whole idea of how reality is conceived. It questions the superiority of "science" as a mode of analysis and explanation (just as it questions high art). It questions all attempts to reduce life to essences or causes. It questions any attempt by communities or individuals as "experts" to prioritize their knowledge over the knowledge of others, and it asserts that no one can claim their knowledge is privileged.

Because subordinated knowledge has often been the knowledge of subordinated classes and peoples, postmodernism lends itself to social and political movements, most recently to feminism (see Smart, 1990, 1992; Gagnier, 1990; Flax, 1990).[3] Postmodernism has been a challenge to different established disciplines at different periods and only was introduced to law and criminology during the late 1980s.

The attack on and destabilization of the high-low distinction has often been accomplished by showing the ways that "superior" knowledge and culture are constructed and by a critique of "privileged" knowledge and discourses, through what is referred to as "deconstructionism." It might be useful here to explain deconstructionism, since this term pervades and in many ways is central to the postmodern critique. In his review of the challenge of postmodernism to criminology, Cohen (1990: 11–12) enlightens us on the meaning of this often misunderstood term. He says deconstruction involves the breaking up of something that has been built, as in "demolition," and exposing the way in which it is built. Similarly, Rosenau (1992: xi) defines the deconstructionist method of analysis as seeking to "undo" all constructions: "Deconstruction tears a text

---

[1] It is important to distinguish postmodernism as a perspective from the postmodern historical period. Writers on the postmodernist period depict it as characterized by both a materialist culture and materialist products, containing new modes of communication, advances in information technology, and a shift away from the producer/manufacturer society to a consumer/service/information society. Various interpretations of this development see it positively (Etizoni, 1968), negatively (Bell, 1976), or as a higher stage of capitalism (Jameson, 1984; Harvey, 1989). Within postmodernism there is a difference between assumptions about human nature, society, and so forth, and the image that postmodernists present of postmodern woman and the social order. Here we are largely concerned with the postmodernist criminologists' assumptions but will draw on images presented by other postmodernists where we find this relevant or helpful. Note that some believe that any such postmodern "cultural interrelation" is a futile spinning of wheels (Balkin, 1992).

[2] This is the substance of Derrida's (1970) analysis of traditional distinctions in Western thought, wherein he points out that acknowledging the value or existence of the marginalized half of any distinction makes the issue of that distinction more valuable, undecidable.

[all phenomena, all events, are texts] apart, reveals its contradictions and assumptions; its intent, however, is not to improve, revise or offer a better version of the text." Thus, some postmodernists reject unitary realities, referring instead to "subjugated knowledges, which tell different stories and have different specificities" and which aim at "the deconstruction of truth" and the power effects of claims to truth (Smart, 1990: 82). Instead of replacing one truth with another, as had earlier "standpoint feminism," postmodernist feminists value feminist knowledge as a "multiplicity of resistances" to the ubiquity of power (ibid.). Perhaps reflecting a lingering modernism, other postmodernist criminologists (Henry and Milovanovic, 1991, 1994), in contrast, use deconstructionist exposure as the basis toward *reconstructing* a replacement text and in this regard attempt to depart from the nihilism of deconstructionism.

BASIC IDEA, CENTRAL MOTIF, AND MAJOR THEORISTS[4]

The relationship between postmodern thought and criminology is complex and indirect but could have considerable consequences for redirecting critical criminology, although this might depend on how readily communicable it becomes (see Schwartz, 1989; 1991). For some, the question is not postmodernism's place in critical criminology, but critical criminology's place in postmodernism. Thus Cohen (1990: 22) sees critical criminology, in general, as "part of the wider postmodern scepticism about the faith that with good will, scientific knowledge, and rationality, human problems could be solved." He argues that central to this critique of objectivity and reason is a linguistic challenge to "the relationship between the word and the world" (ibid.). For postmodernists, what is said in accounts, observations, reports, commentaries, analyses, and so forth, has no necessary connection to past, present, or future action, and no capability to reveal

---

[3]However, this has not been without considerable controversy and several feminist writers feel there are dangers, particularly for women, in abandoning the struggle for power on a global level in favor of an embrace with the denial of truth, the local, customary, and parochial, whereby, as Lovibond (1989) argues, men's voices will speak loudest and women's will remain silent. See also Soper (1991) and Jackson (1992) for similar arguments.

[4]The relatively recent introduction of postmodernism in criminology (since 1987) means that there has been insufficient development of the perspective for divergent forms of the theoretical position to emerge and for this reason we have omitted our chart of "related theories." For the same reason it is premature to list "key theorists," so this chart is also omitted. Important ideas expressing postmodernist thought, which are drawn on by criminologists are to be found in the works of Foucault, Derrida, Barthes, Lacan, Baudrillard, and Lyotard. Recent theoretical contributions by Manning (1988), Henry and Milovanovic (1991, 1994; Milovanovic and Henry, 1991; Henry, 1989, 1991; Milovanovic, 1989, 1992, 1994), Pfuhl (1993a, 1993b, 1992), Santos (1987), Smart (1989, 1990, 1992), and Goodrich (1987, 1990), take a criminological or sociolegal perspective informed by postmodernism, whereas the work by Hunt (1990, 1991, 1993) and Teubner (1992) is critical of the perspective, and especially of its value to criminology and law.

this. In critical criminology this idea takes the form of exposing established areas of *knowledge,* such as traditional criminology, for using flawed categories and methods of inquiry, and challenging the exclusionary and failed dominant *power* structures of crime control. Cohen says that early (idealist) "deconstructionist" criminologies, such as labeling theory and radical criminology, confused demolition, "taking the elements apart to make the structure collapse," with the second, postmodernist meaning of deconstruction: "showing that despite its anomalies and inconsistencies, the building goes on standing" (Cohen, 1990: 23).

As a result of its deconstructionist analysis postmodernism has been criticized for not valuing anything, and for a belief that "anything goes." In short, it is criticized for being an anarchy of knowledge. This idea taken to its extreme, by many critics of postmodernism and deconstructionism (e.g., Hunt, 1990), results in the charges of subjectivism, plural relativism, and nihilism. Put simply, if truth is not possible, how can we decide anything? As Cohen (1990: 23) expresses it:

> Deconstructionism proper is the culmination of this challenge to the Enlightenment faith in reason, progress and objective knowledge. It denies the possibility of rational discourse ... is so bizarre and irrelevant to a subject like criminology ... [and] offers little more than an impotent gesture of defiance. It becomes impossible to defend this version of "sceptical theory."

While this may apply to extreme forms of the literary version, it is a misreading of postmodernism and especially deconstruction, as it is being incorporated into criminology. To say that there is no single, stable meaning structure is not the same as saying everything is meaningless, or everything is relative. Nor does it deny social action, or imply that "no moral, political, practical or policy lines follow," as Cohen (1990: 24) claims. Many postmodernists recognize that meaning is very much present, not in the abstract or in general, but in historically situated local sites or in specific contexts. Thus it is not so much that judgments cannot be made that characterizes the postmodern project. Rather postmodernists take the anti-essentialist position that there is no single general framework of analysis from which everything can be judged and that any judgments made are only valid in the context of meaning wherein they are generated.[5] They believe that an appreciation of deconstruction also implies an appreciation of construction, and reconstruction. Thus exposing how an edifice is built, and how it stands, in spite of opposition (deconstruction), also implies how it can be rebuilt or built

---

[5] This means that discourse transgresses contexts. Indeed, "the same" words and phrases are operative in multiple contexts but they are reconstructed for each situation wherein they embody both meaning from other situations, as well as meaning constructed for the immediate purpose.

differently (constitutive replacement). Thus postmodernist work that has developed outside of critical criminology is informing a distinctive policy-oriented, postmodernist "constitutive" criminology that has crucial differences from the extreme versions of postmodernism's literary form.

Although classifying postmodernist criminology is contradictory to the postmodernist project, recent criminological work draws on several sometimes contradictory insights from the postmodernist perspective. Indeed, Milovanovic (1989, 1992, 1994) claims that postmodernism is a combination of poststructuralism, deconstruction, and semiotics. All more or less embrace the deconstructionist critique (Foucault, 1977, 1980; Derrida, 1970, 1981). However, some imply that at its core is a constant critique of truth claims via struggles at local sites, whereas others (Henry, 1987; Henry and Milovanovic, 1994; Henry, 1994; Garza, 1992) wish not only to deconstruct crime and the dominant sociopolitical order as a reality but to replace that construction with an alternative positive discourse.[6] This latter position contradicts extreme postmodernism, but in doing so it does not fall into the trap of "postmodern realism," as have some postmodern philosophers (e.g., Borgmann, 1992).

Moreover, different weight is given to different postmodernist influences by different criminological theorists. Manning (1988, 1989) takes up the semiotic dimension influenced by sociologist Baudrillard (1981). More recently Milovanovic (1992) has begun to incorporate chaos theory[7] into his Lacanian psychoanalytical-semiotic approach. In contrast, Henry and Milovanovic's "constitutive criminology"[8] (Henry and Milovanovic's 1991, 1994; Milovanovic and Henry, 1991; Henry, 1987, 1989, 1991) is also influenced by Schutz's (1932) phenomenological sociology, Blumer's (1969) symbolic interactionism, Berger and Luckmann's (1966) social constructionism, and Giddens (1984) structuration theory. The various postmodern criminologists have disagreements beyond the

---

[6] We use the term *discourse* in an inclusive way to refer to anything that is communicated, whether written, spoken on or represented by depictions in images, such as in film or television. This also includes nonverbal communication, such as gestures.

[7] The relatively new approach of chaos theory is attractive to some scholars because, unlike the more established postmodern positions, chaos provides a liberating discourse that acknowledges humans' capacity to make a difference on a global scale through local community action (see Garza, 1992). For discussion of chaos theory generally see Holden (1986), Gleick (1987), Briggs and Peat (1989), and Hayles (1990). In addition to Milovanovic's work, see Pepinsky (1991) and T. R. Young (1991) for the potential application of chaos theory to criminology.

[8] Constitutive criminology, broadly defined, is a theory proposing that human beings are responsible for the construction of categories of meaning within which they act. During this process the categories of meaning shape the individual actors into social beings. One consequence of this process is that humans create criminology (in a popular as well as an academic sense), which, in turn, shapes the way we think about crime and how we respond.

scope of our discussion here, but one important difference concerns the extent to which they see humans in their relationship to society. Although postmodernist criminologists generally recognize the coproduction of humans and society by agency and structure, they disagree about the relative weight agency has in this coproduction and thereby on the potential for social change. The issue revolves around the extent to which humans are determined by their discursive use of language or by the discursive structures that humans create and through which they communicate. The vagueness of precisely what shapes what, and to what extent, bothers some critics. For example, in a recent review of the postmodernist contribution to law Hunt (1990: 539) accurately describes the aspiration of the "constitutive" version of postmodernism as being "to grasp both discourse and practice ... to hang on to the coexistence and mutual determination of practices and discourses, structure and agency." Referring to some founding theoretical traces of constitutive theory (Fitzpatrick, 1984; Giddens, 1984; Harrington, 1988; Henry, 1987; and Hunt, 1987), Hunt (1990: 539) says:

> Perhaps this project has not been sufficiently developed to merit the slightly grand description "theory" ... This sense of "theory" is not one of a complete or formal model as a condensation or concentration of reality; rather it is a sense of theory as a provisional metaphor, as a potentially useful way of thinking and saying something new. Such a view of theory makes no claims to Truth or truths ... it involves a conception of theory without guarantees.

He further argues that though there is much of value to the approach, the deeper problem remains of the inherent pessimism and relativistic tendencies that carry over in their deconstructionist critique (see, for example, Derrida's 1981 "antifoundationalist" position).

Because postmodern theorists see human subjects and society as interrelated, we will not separate them in our discussion. Indeed, ideas about the creation of the human subject necessarily mean intersubjectivity (shared meaning of the interconnectedness of social life), since from this perspective human subjects cannot exist outside the socially constructed meaning in which they are constituted.

HUMANS, HUMAN NATURE, VIEW OF SOCIETY, AND THE SOCIAL ORDER

From the postmodernist criminological perspective of Henry and Milovanovic (1992), humans are seen as actively constructing their social world while at the same time being constructed by it. People are typically unaware that they are involved in this construction and tend to see themselves more acted upon than acting, only rarely being cognizant of their part in creating that world. However, although there is freedom to act, there is also constraint from the social medium through which they interact. As with the Marxist view of human nature, humans create their action but not necessarily under conditions or through discourse that they might have chosen for themselves. Indeed, their action is mediated by the preexisting structure of language and meaning. This does not mean that they are unable to create new meaning while re-creating the old, though when they do, it is also done in interaction with others. For example, the postmodernist feminist Carol Smart (1992: 40), while seeing women as resistant and active in the construction of gender, also sees the power of law as a technology of gender "productive of gender difference and identity." Goodrich (1987) even denies that human subjects are capable of generating meaning, arguing that human subjects themselves are constructed in the organized discourses of rationality that are part of the constitution of the state and its institutions, such as law (Goodrich, 1987). However, as Henry and Milovanovic (1994) point out with regard to human nature, there is a *duality* of freedom and constraint with which individuals must deal.

Though agreeing on the socially constructed nature of the human subject, postmodernism presents differing images of what this subject looks like and how it is recursively constructed. Some postmodernists see the human being as "conscious, purposeful and feeling," as a "decentered" and "emergent" subject with no specific identity (Megill, 1985: 203, cited by Rosenau, 1992). This emergent subject resists definitions imposed by others, struggles for autonomy and creativity, embraces personal freedom from general rules, inequality, and community constraints, and struggles for the freedom to have a fulfilling, satisfying, and self-actualizing life (Giddens, 1984, 1990; Touraine, 1988; Garza, 1992). For others, however, the image of humans in a postmodern society is

> relaxed and flexible, oriented toward feelings and emotions, interiorization, and holding a "be-yourself" attitude. S/he is an active human being constituting his/her own social reality, pursuing a personal quest for meaning but making no truth claims for what results. S/he looks to fantasy, humor, the culture of desire, and immediate gratification. Preferring the temporary over the permanent, s/he is contented with a "live and let live" (in the present) attitude. More comfortable with the spontaneous than the planned, the post-modern individual is also fascinated with tradition, the antiquated (the past in general), the exotic, the sacred, the unusual, and the place of the local rather than the general or the universal. Post-modern individuals are concerned with their own lives, their personal satisfaction, and self-promotion. Less concerned with old loyalties and modern affiliations such as marriage, family, church, and nation, they are more oriented toward their own needs. (Rosenau, 1992: 53-54)

Nor are postmodern professionals and academics immune from this decidedly "yuppie" depiction. One commentator calls them "Default Intellectuals," who don't value thought for its own sake. They are more interested in having private professional careers and secure salaries than scholarship or improving public education. Fearful of their own yawning mediocrity, armed with a self-serving relativism in which the value of any intellectual pursuit is relative to the C.V. [curriculum vitae] points it provides ... this generation of academic careerists are technologists rather than investigators ... [who] revere language ... but use it merely as a multifaceted tool capable of creating phenomenal realities independent from sensible material and mass reality, about which they make it a virtue of knowing as little as possible beyond investment portfolios and pension plans. (Fawcett, 1991: 22–23)

Contained within these images of the postmodern socially constituted human subject are some of the assumptions held by postmodern criminologists. For example, Henry and Milovanovic (1994) say humans are considered social projects in the process of continually creating themselves through the wider social context and in doing so recreate that context. They are "unique, with a multiplicity of needs, drives, desires, and abilities and [are] intersubjectively constituted" (ibid.: 2). Unlike traditional criminological interpretations, postmodernist criminologists see needs, drives desires, and abilities as socially constructed, culturally shaped images, toward which human agents act *as though* they were real and separable from themselves and/or their social world. For example, the need for immediate gratification is presented continually in popular cultural imagery and is the basis of much consumer product advertising. Products, ranging from cars to chocolate, that are unnecessary for basic existence are presented as desirable needs—as "sweet dreams you cannot resist" (Nestlē's ad for chocolate). These images are actively accepted and energized as "real" needs by human subjects who orient their lives toward obtaining them in order to have a "normal" identity. These same images are also creatively translated by some into the need for immediate gratification and feelings of well-being that are perceived to be satiable through "sex, drugs, and rock'n'roll." But also implied is a more general tendency to satisfy perceived needs through criminal activity such as shoplifting, fraud, price fixing, and so forth.

　　In the postmodern vision social structures are also inseparable from the humans that make them and are based on the categories of classification of the events that they allegedly represent (Knorr-Cetina, 1981). As such they are strengthened by routine construction in everyday life and by activity organized in relation to them, as though they were concrete entities (which they appear to be as a result of this routine action). The principal means through which social structures are constituted is language use and the discursive practice of making conceptual distinctions through the play of differences (Derrida, 1973, 1981; Lacan, 1977). In other words, humans use discursive practices to produce texts (narrative constructions), imaginary constructions, that produce a particular image claiming to be the reality.[9] Once social structures are constituted as images, their ongoing existence depends on their continued and often unwitting reconstruction in everyday discourse, a discourse replete with tacit understandings and preconstructed meanings that form part of our common "stock of knowledge" (Manning, 1988; Schutz, 1932).

A good illustration of the society–structure–human agency interrelationship can be found in the postmodern feminist analysis of the ongoing creation of the human subject and its structural oppression through discourse. Smart's (1992) sociolegal analysis of women and law, for example, focuses on the power of legal discourse as a "gendering strategy" in the human subject's construction (Smart, 1992). Smart distinguishes between the discursive construction of (a) a type of woman and (b) Woman. In defining certain behaviors as illegal, a type of woman is created as criminal, for example, a prostitute, female criminal, unmarried mother, "bad mother," and so forth. This definition sets women apart both as a criminal and as being a Woman. Unlike men, who may be criminal or not, in law the category of woman is constructed twice. This "double move" first constructs Woman as criminal woman and second simultaneously constructs "Woman in contradistinction to Man." As Smart says, "the very foundation of the discursive construct of modern Woman is mired in this double strategy" (ibid.: 36).

Whereas Smart tends to attribute more agency to discourse than to those using it (hence is somewhat discursively deterministic), other postmodernist feminists do the reverse. Garza (1992) integrates the structural concepts of race, class, gender, and sexuality into the postmodernist analysis. She sees this as helpful in showing how the dynamics of oppression contained in the discourse of the dominant culture exclude, deny, and subordinate the Chicana and other persons of color, refusing them an identity, a value, or attributes of their own. Unless they use the dominant discourse, she says, they are illegitimate and marginal to the dominant culture, but when they do use it, they deny themselves, fracture themselves, lose themselves. Echoing Foucault and drawing on chaos theory, she says that to speak in the existing discourse merely reproduces and remakes the very structures that oppress. Thus she urges Chicana women to embrace and exalt the difference they represent "as a tool of creativity and to question the multiple forms of repression and dominance" to which they are subjected, for therein lies their source of power, emerging out of the "instances of disequilibrium" (Garza, 1992: 11, 12). She asserts that "Chicanas must separate from the dominant discourse and continue to formulate their own space and

---

[9]Postmodernists consider any narrative construction to be a text, be it a book, a manuscript, all of history, a discipline. In other words all discourse of any kind is a text in postmodernist terms, as are, in the broadest sense, all phenomena and events (Rosenau, 1992: xiv).

language, always conscious of multiple differences" (ibid.: 13). Thus Garza (1992: 1) glimpses the possibility that humans can develop a "replacement discourse" (Henry, 1987, 1994; Henry and Milovanovic, 1991, 1994).

The postmodern feminist contribution, then, shows us how social forms are constituted and reconstituted in dominant discourse and how human identities are tied closely to the structures in which they are produced unless definite attempts are made to disengage from that production. The concept of replacement discourse shows us how to be self-reflexively aware and how human agency can be active in its own subordination *or liberation.*

THE ROLE OF LAW, THE DEFINITION OF CRIME, AND THE IMAGE OF THE CRIMINAL

The modernist view of law celebrated ideals of a society made up of diverse atomic individuals and private interests having formal equality, whose individual freedoms are guaranteed by formal procedure, universal principles, impartiality, rationality, and precise definitions of rights. This view began to be challenged in the post–World War II era of bureaucratic administrative law accompanying the rise of sociological positivism. During this period differences were recognized and embodied in various exceptional social categories, as in the civil rights legislation, women's rights, minority rights, disability rights, worker rights, and various other victim rights. However, by the late 1970s, disenchantment with both the liberal and bureaucratic visions of law saw the emergence of a new postmodernist vision of law and social order. This was captured by some adherents to the old modern liberal legal order who feared and ridiculed the development as marking a return to pre-industrial society and creating a crisis in legal ideology:

> Objectivity has now become … a dirty word, a synonym for the unfeeling and inhuman. The emphasis is on personalisation … the belief that only the sufferer can provide the remedy, that only the worm can know the heal, or … that all knowledge is shot through with subjectivity and that only the irrational, inexplicable action is truly free action … Much of the revulsion … presents itself as a conscious demand for a return to the face-to-face society, the organic community of living social bonds and commonly shared ideologies and interests … as an elevation of the non-commercial, pre-industrial organic community, Gemeinschaft … People are much happier talking about "community" than about the state, about participation than administration and planning, about "self-expression" than about emulation. There is a remarkable longing for the personalisation of law and legal proceedings, for the restoration of man to a place in the organic community that recognises him as a total person, and that makes justice, at least in principle, the work of the whole community and not a specialised branch of learning and experience. There is a parallel enthusiasm for a "situational ethic" to replace general impersonal principles of conduct … people's courts and people's judges seem more

human than the bewigged and begowned representatives of a complex and learned art, which still believes that men must be judged by universal principles grounded in and shaped by long-mulled-over and carefully recorded experience and that hard cases make bad law. (Kamenka and Tay, 1978: 52, 54–55)[10]

A number of postmodernists have provided a general analysis and critique of law consistent with this position and have done so by deconstructing modern law's basic premises (Santos, 1985; Henry, 1983, 1985, 1987; Goodrich, 1987, 1990; Seidman, 1989, 1990; Agger, 1989; Smart, 1989, 1992). From their work it can be deduced, consistent with the general position of postmodernism, that meaning in law is considered so subjective that no truth claims can be made. Rather than being a neutral body of principles, law is considered political and subject to personal interpretation. Indeed, for some, law is, and can only be, incoherent because its language has no definitive meaning. The view that there is only one true interpretation of a law or for that matter the U.S. Constitution, or that the text means what the authors of the Constitution intended it to mean, is rejected by postmodernists (Rosenau, 1992: 125).

Part of the deconstruction of law involves demonstrating that it is no more than a mythological appearance sustained through "a mixture of image, myth, oral memory and written text, custom and judicial legislation" (Goodrich, 1992: 8). Instead of being the authoritative basis for the state, says Goodrich (1987) "the law is principally a discourse of power which conceals its conditions of production through a series of rhetorical techniques" (McCahery, 1993: 414, summarizing Goodrich, 1987). The location of law's power is in extra-legal sources, a fact that "the rhetoric of law systematically denies" (ibid.).

Thus, one of the main ways that the deconstructive critique is achieved is by showing the interrelatedness between law and social structure, and via the central recognition of a plurality of legal orders, that is, legal pluralism rather than one law. As one postmodern protagonist says:

> Legal pluralism is the key concept in a post-modern view of law. Not legal pluralism ... in which different legal orders are conceived as separate entities coexisting in the same political space, but rather the conception of different legal spaces superimposed, interpenetrated and mixed in our minds as much as our actions. (Santos, 1985: 279).

---

[10]Kamenka and Tay are actually highly critical of the postmodern position on law that they so well capture. They are also critical of bureaucratic administrative developments in law which they see tied to the growth of totalitarian socialism. They believe that together with calls for community law and justice, bureaucratic administrative law is creating a crisis for bourgeois liberal law. As its supporters and, indeed, as defenders of modernism, Kamenka and Tay wish to see this challenge defeated, the crises defused, and bourgeois law regain its former prominence.

Though himself critical of postmodernism, Teubner (1992: 1443) begins to capture the essence of its views about law and explains how the view differs from views of the liberal legal order:

> Postmodern jurists love legal pluralism. They do not care about the law of the centralized state with its universalist aspirations. It is the "asphalt law" of the Brazilian *fevelas,* the informal counter-rules of the patchwork of minorities, the quasi-laws of dispersed ethnic, religious, and cultural groups, the disciplinary techniques of "private justice," the plurality of non-State laws in associations, formal organizations, and informal networks where they find the ingredients of postmodernity: the local, the plural, the subversive. The multitude of "fragmented discourses" which are hermetically closed to each other can be identified in numerous informal kinds of law that are generated quite independent of the State and that operate at various levels of formality.

Of course postmodernists would not accept the distinction between the plurality of legal orders and state law, but rather argue that these spheres are mutually constituting.[11] Indeed, what is challenged in all their critique is the basic assumptions law makes about its independence and priority over other legal orders.

In the postmodern view law, then, is not conceptualized as a separate body of rules that stands over and above society and its normative orders, but rather "is, in part, social relations and social relations are, in part, law." This means that law is influenced by informal normative orders and in turn influences the creation and workings of informal rules. State law, therefore, is not an autonomous edifice of rules but rather a flexible structure that is interpenetrated by other social forms that have rules and their own informal codes. For example, unions, work groups, corporations, and so forth, all have rules or informal "laws" that are both shaped by the "law" and in turn shape it (Henry, 1983). This is an idea developed by Fitzpatrick (1984) which he terms "integral plurality." While law brings in other forms and changes them into its own image, it thereby transforms itself and becomes part of other forms of rules in the process. According to Henry and Milovanovic (1992: 6, citing Fitzpatrick, 1984), "this demonstrates that there is not so much a unilinear relationship with other social forms ... [but] law's identity is constantly and inherently subject to challenge and change."

In summary, a postmodern stance argues that law is mutually constituted through social relations. The processes of nonstate normative orders, such as

---

[11]They do not, however, reduce state law to just another normative order but rather see it as comprised of numerous constitutive orders, some of which are the social forms with which law is interrelated (Fitzpatrick, 1984).

workplace rules, organizational procedures, group norms, and so forth, with which state law is interrelated provide a significant context of projects wherein old power is molded into new forms. This new postmodern legal pluralism displays a "discursive interwoveness" between the legal and social arenas whereby law is now seen as "a multiplicity of diverse communicative processes" (Teubner, 1992: 1451).

Some of the postmodern theorists have attempted a reconstruction of law that does away with the negative character of the postmodern critique. Thus Santos (1987: 299), implying a replacement discourse, hopes that a postmodern law will "become an edifying knowledge that, by enlarging and deepening our legal vistas, will contribute towards a radical democratisation of social and personal life ..." More to the point, with regard to criminal law, Henry and Milovanovic (1992) suggest a changed discourse in the way the crime is defined. Crime is considered a "socially constructed category," with legal definition giving closure where in actuality the discussion should begin.

> [Crime] is a categorization of the diversity of human conflicts and transgressions into a single category "crime," as though these were somehow all the same. It is a melting of differences reflecting the multitude of variously motivated acts of personal injury into a single entity. (Henry and Milovanovic, 1994: 118)

But crime is not considered to be something abstract. Rather the reality of pain and harm is acknowledged. Albeit a constructed category, crime is defined as the "expression of some people's energy to make a difference over others and is the exclusion of those others who in the instant are rendered powerless ... Crime then is the power to deny others (ibid.: 119)."

CAUSAL LOGIC

An extensive literature concerning postmodernism has arisen, but its presence in criminology is only just emerging. Though postmodernism's adherents are not in accord on how the theory should be applied, not least because they reject the separation of theory/practice, pure/applied, and they harbor different versions of what informs postmodernism, they do agree that there is no ultimate truth about anything. Postmodern scholars reject any notion of an authoritative text. By this they mean that all versions of truth seeking are valid and that no appeal to expertise or authority on any subject is to be tolerated since this subordinates other forms of knowledge that might enlighten. From a postmodernist view, then, there can be no unified or consistent representation of the world, rather there are multiple realities to be considered. Hence postmodernists would never consider themselves theorists of a single viewpoint. Central theorizing is rejected in favor of an appreciative relativism.

By its rejection of giving privileged status to any theory or point of view, postmodernists assume the creation of a kind of egalitarianism in which all points of view or accounts can be represented and no voice has any more authority or privilege than any other. In the more extreme versions of postmodernism any linear explanation of anything is rejected in favor of a total orientation to the present. Anything in the past is considered an interpretation or representation and no single explanation is better than another; therefore, conventional history is rejected, and any accumulation of knowledge in the traditional meaning of the term is unacceptable. Given this view, causal statements in the usual sense are impossible to make.

This implied relativism is not accepted by all postmodernists, however. Some are more flexible in their exposition of postmodern thought. Yet even for these more moderate interpreters, whom we take to include postmodern criminologists, there is a limit to how much the authority of the author and text are to be accepted. The moderate postmodernists tend to look at the social sciences in terms of process and are not as quick to reject the historical record. However, they view history in terms of the local situation. History is seen as form of storytelling (Rosenau, 1992: 171). We can observe this in the works of Foucault (1977) when he focuses on the local scene to describe the changes in the nature of punishment.

Though moderate postmodernists accept little of contemporary positivistic social science, their stance leaves some room for explanatory statements but in a much changed form. As Rosenau (1992: 171) explains: "One of their main goals is to expose the oppressive dimensions of modern temporal assumptions. They substitute an emphasis on local space and respect for the space-of-the-other for modern views of space." They tend to listen to the voices on the "margin" for creditable accounts. For criminology this means a renewed emphasis on listening to the accounts of offenders and victims, those who often are excluded from consideration:

> Their goal [postmodernists'] is to speak for those who have never been the subject (active, human), but who are rather so often assumed to be the objects (observed, studied). They would include new voices and new forms of local narrative but not in an attempt to impose discipline or responsibility. (Rosenau, 1992: 173)

For example, Henry describes the positive insights of various discredited deviants and the value of their nonprofessional knowledge of their lives (Robinson and Henry, 1977; Henry, 1990; Pfuhl and Henry, 1993); highlighting the importance of illegal, unofficial, hidden, or informal economic activity (Henry, 1978; Ferman, Hoyman, and Henry, 1987; Ferman, Berndt, and Henry, 1993; Cantor, Henry, and Rayner, 1992) and the centrality of informal and private forms of social control and justice (Henry, 1983), as well as documenting a wide range of other alternative informal institutions (Henry, 1981).

The attempt in all this description is not to find causes but rather to use narratives to give accounts, to explain without the usual claim to authority of an expert analysis or in the promotion of a grand theory, and to declare the relevance of these ordinary people's lives and knowledge. The reader in this approach must become an active interpreter of the text that is presented. There is no assumption of a controlling or overriding account although an author's interpretation is also given. It is for this reason that these approaches to crime and deviant behavior rely on extensive use of quotes of the original "authors" of texts. This, of course, flies in the face of much positivistic criminological work, or social science in general, where accounts or other data are organized to fit into preconstructed categories in order to "test" the hypotheses drawn from one or more theoretical perspectives. In the postmodern project, accounts would be left open to different interpretations.

Implied in this, therefore, is a rejection of the established methodology of science and its deterministic, positivistic foundation. Whereas some postmodern advocates seek total abandonment of scientific methodology, others seek modification. However, these more moderate advocates seek a methodology that avoids prediction and positivism but "emphasizes faith, emotion, and personal fulfillment" (Rosenau, 1992: 172). This fits in with feminist criminology in that feminists also seek a different methodology that is more inclusive of a feminist perspective and reflects qualitative rather than quantitative research techniques. This new emphasis does not focus on generalization nor attempt synthesis of criminological knowledge, but stresses "complexity, interrelationships, a focus on difference in the absolute sense, the unique, and the local" (Rosenau, 1992: 173).

For example, Henry and Milovanovic (1994) not only suggest a different view of crime, its creation, and continuance, but with regard to cause, they abandon the usual causal logic. The search for cause or causes of crime is considered to be futile because the standard approaches consider crime to be a separate reality and thus fail to address how crime is an integral part of society. From this perspective crime is seen to be the culmination of certain processes that allow persons to believe that they are somehow not connected to other humans and society. These processes place others into categories or stereotypes and make them different or alien, denying them their humanity. These processes result in the denial of responsibility for other people and to other people.

To illustrate their argument Henry and Milovanovic (1994) cite the work of Clinard (1983) concerning corporate crime. In his study Clinard found that middle managers of corporations tended to blame top management for corporate crime. Middle managers denied responsibility by stating that those at the top of the organization "set the tone" and they were the ones who gave the orders to do what they considered necessary. Hence, middle managers were "innocent" of any wrongdoing:

> Crime is contrived by the discursive construction of differences that allow peo-
> ple … the delusion that they are unconnected to those with whom they interre-
> late and are divorced from their own species. (Henry and Milovanovic, 1994: 124)

It is this process that allows persons to be detached from the consequences of
their actions and that creates crime. Often these discursive constructions (rationales) are part of an institutional structure and can be used as justifications for
any harmful activity. Thus "obeying orders," "only doing my job," "they are not
one of us," "they are taking over our jobs," racial and ethnic stereotypes, all are
examples of harmful discursive constructions of exclusion used as rationales to act
against a person or a group.

> What "causes" the crime … the structure, ideology and invocation of discursive
> practices that divide human relations into categories, that divide responsibility
> for others and to others into hierarchy and authority relations. (Ibid.: 125)

The most heinous crimes are committed when these discursive practices are part
of the ongoing system of rationales used by persons, groups, and nations to formulate their conduct. "Cause" in that sense is the rationale connected to action
"that allows individuals to fuse observation of difference with evaluations of
worth, structured by a power hierarchy that manifests in the denial of others as
human beings" (Henry and Milovanovic, 1994: 125).

CRIMINAL JUSTICE SYSTEM IMPLICATIONS

In the traditional view, criminal justice policies and practice are set in opposition to crime. Little thought is given to the contribution criminal justice
makes to crime. Moreover, criminal justice is not one single entity or policy
but rather the imposition of different strategies that supposedly are geared to
control crime. This fails to take into account the dialectic nature of control
schemes whereby attempts to control crime often result in increased amounts
of that which is to be controlled (Milovanovic and Henry, 1992). A good example has been the criminalization of certain drugs on the national and international level. At each juncture of increased control, the drug trade has shown
greater vitality.

Although agents of control such as the police, the courts, and correctional personnel purportedly represent and carry out some vague societal mandate and equally indistinct criminal justice policy, the reality is different.
According to the work of Henry and Milovanovic (Henry, 1991; Milovanovic
and Henry, 1991) criminal justice policy as it is currently constructed involves
the generation of an ideology supported by a series of strategies that ostensibly
are designed to "remove" the behavior allegedly represented by the category

"crime." These strategies are episodically implemented by members of a hierarchically divided power structure (government), through its varied semi-autonomous agencies, "control forms" (e.g., disciplinary regimes and gendered discourse—see previous chapter) or "control institutions" (police, courts, probation, etc.) (Henry and Milovanovic, 1994). From this perspective control institutions are the relations among human agents, acting to police the conceptual distinctions among discursively constructed social structures. Once constituted, these relations, expressed in symbolic form, themselves become structures and, as agencies and institutions, have relative autonomy. In turn, they too are policed by further "private" or internal relations of control.

Seen in this way, then, criminal justice policy is the ideology and the plan for the organized acting out of "control thoughts," whose very action reflects on the reality of that which they are organized to defend. Control institutions are rooted in control discourse and in their own parent social structures and cannot be divorced from them. Nor can the structures exist, however, without their control forms, since each implies the other.

Criminal justice agencies are engaged in administrative structures whose professionals define, hierarchize, and categorize others, concentrating that which is done more diffusely in the wider society. In this way they repress and constrain those that they classify, thereby violating them in the same ways these persons had earlier violated others. As a result, say the postmodernist criminologists, criminal justice policy and practice is itself a crime over others (through its expression of the power to deny others that follows from the definition of crime). Moreover, while administering control through disciplinary technology, criminal justice practice also partially constitutes the very crime it seeks to control. The ideology and practice of criminal justice become "criminal," for example, when offenders use the criminal justice system as a status-conferring institution, through which they can "rise" with prestige among peers. The criminal justice system is also co-opted as a resource and used principally as an educational and training ground for the relations of power by those who subsequently refine and reproduce offending behavior as recidivists.

The duality of criminal justice policy and practice as constitutive of crime can be illustrated through critical discussions on the notion of "fighting crime" and most recently fighting "the war on drugs" (Johns, 1992). Similarly, the undercover work of policing in the 1980s has produced the new "maximum-security society" (Marx, 1988; Weiss, 1987), in which there is an increasing tendency on the part of control agents to develop dossiers in computerized form; an increasing use of instruments that focus on producing predictive statements about persons in particular created categories; and an obsession to find the "predisposed" criminal. This has led to an extreme manipulation of the environment, inducing the very criminality that control agents seek to control: criminality becomes the controler's own creation.

From the postmodern perspective, therefore, criminal justice practices embrace the informational form, which places a high premium on collecting, filtering, categorizing, and disseminating increasingly complex data (Jackson, 1988; Manning, 1988; Thomas, 1988). One may conclude that the resultant new transparent society has seen the erosion of traditional notions of privacy, whereby even the citizenry has been recruited to monitor others as well as themselves for deviance or deviant proclivities (Marx, 1988; Einstadter and Henry, 1991; Einstadter, 1992; Pfuhl, 1992).

The process of constructing meaning is usurped by the agents of organizations who use these informational constructions as the criteria by which to further survey, control, and act on subjects, particularly those in predicted high-risk categories in the existing social arrangements. Simultaneously, such agents are given inadvertent ideological support through attacks on the automation of social control instruments. These are attacks by critical theorists and reformers alike, who take, as given, many of the concepts, presuppositions, or working hypotheses of these same agents of control. In so doing, critics and reformers produce the recursive machine.

The observation that power begets crime and is itself crime, manifest (among other arenas of "civil" society) as criminal justice policy, suggests that criminal justice as a separate institution can only increase crime (Henry and Milovanovic, 1991, 1993, 1994). Indeed, this is borne out by Adler's (1983) research on "societies not obsessed with crime," which were those having the lowest crime rate. Consistent with the expectations of the postmodern critique, societies such as Japan, Bulgaria, Peru, Switzerland, Nepal, and Saudi Arabia were found to have in common

> a very heavy informal social control system operating in each country ... people-to-people contact ... Not formal, not criminal justice ... Our study demonstrated that one cannot depend upon longer prison sentences and the criminal justice system to solve problems. Crime problems have to be solved elsewhere ... in many of these societies, people make decisions about each other. Dispute resolution is often used in place of formal criminal justice. (Adler interview: Faith, 1993: 8)

Postmodern analysis proposes the resurrection of informal social controls; the criminal justice system of postmodernism would be one in which those functions currently exercised by the separated formal justice system would be handled by local groups and local communities. At the same time, a societal-level disinvestment in the crimes of hierarchy and division would form a replacement discourse whereby those being newly socialized would emerge in a world not obsessed with crime, acquisition, and power. Thus instead of concentrating social control in informational and coercive arenas of the state, postmodernist criminology encourages the instigation of a *replacement discourse.* This discourse is directed toward positive, nondiscriminatory developments of human action. Criminologists, like others, are encouraged to contribute through avenues such as "newsmaking criminology" (Barak, 1988, 1994b; Henry, 1994). They are invited, as are journalists, to produce and communicate both corrective and positive accounts of crime data, substituting for example, victim support stories for repetitions of the imagery of guns, blood, and body-bag violence.[12] Feminist postmodernists such as Smart (1989) see replacement discourse directed at the heart of the law-making process. Rather than seeking to reform law, she believes feminists should focus on the law's power to define and disqualify. She argues that at the point at which law asserts its definitions, feminism should assert its alternative discourse, transforming, say, "harmless flirtation" into "sexual harassment," thereby directly challenging the power of law to construct reality. Whether changes in legal discourse such as these will serve to deconstruct crime or serve merely to raise the level of symbolic violence, is questionable and directs our attention to the importance of content.

The idea to develop a nonviolent replacement discourse has emerged in a movement that collectively has been termed "peacemaking." It is a perspective that has a variety of roots, not the least of which are in anarchist criminology. It is characterized by approaches and proposals that stress mediation, conflict resolution, and reconciliation with and emphasis on community (Pepinsky and Quinney, 1991). According to Pepinsky and Quinney, peacemaking criminology assumes that human transformation takes place when we change the actions that comprise our social, political, and economic structure. This is based on the assumption that human agents are constituted through their actions—you are what you do (see the discussion on Humans, Human Nature, Society, and the Social Order, above). Changing who we are can be brought about by changing what we do (as many 12-step self-help groups, such as Alcoholics Anonymous, know well). Since "doing" is discursively constituted (i.e., structured through language use, speech communication, etc.), a necessary requirement for such change is the development of discourse that describes what we do in nonviolent, nonexclusionary language.

Peacemaking criminology, as a form of replacement discourse, draws on a number of intellectual strands, such as the religious humanist tradition, feminism, and anarchism. Like postmodernist theory generally, it takes a stand that rejects power over others, violence to counter violence, and retribution and punishment as strategies to deal with crime. Focusing on reconciliation, peacemaking criminology steps outside "conventional wisdom" and traditional models of

---

[12]Some journalists, politicians, and media representatives have themselves recognized the importance of this.

thinking to confront the reality of crime. Like left realism (discussed in Chapter 10), it is an effort to understand the suffering of the victim and the offender who perpetrates the harm in a framework of community. The perspective rejects the trend toward increasingly severe punishments as counterproductive and points to the historical failure of its use to deal with crime. Indeed, the war metaphor in the "war on crime" and the "war on drugs" has only resulted in counterviolence and increased the toll of suffering. Johns (1992), for example, has argued that the metaphor has effectively masked a whole range of government and corporate crimes against the powerless, not only in the United States but globally, especially in Latin America.

According to peacemaking advocates, the task is to step away from conventional, rational, positivistic Western logic in the failed methods of the past and move into more global, nonviolent ways of thought and discourse. Drawing on the philosophical and nondoctrinal roots of spiritual thought, as well as feminist theory, humanism, and critical theory, peacemaking has a broad sweep that attempts to deal with human suffering whenever it reveals itself. Though how this change in the way of thinking about crime and suffering can manifest itself in action is complex, the following examples serve to illustrate current attempts to implement peacemaking alternatives.

Carringella-MacDonald and Humphries (1991) argue that despite reform in rape laws, it has not affected the coping options available to women who are victims of rape. The criminal justice response has been, and continues to be, ineffective in dealing with this problem of male violence. The authors suggest that community organizing against sexual assault, modeled after a program in Michigan, has potential for dealing with sexual assault in a more constructive manner.

In a similar vein Knopp (1991) points to the complete failure of the current system of punishment and lays out an abolitionist agenda. She argues for a new system of "restorative justice," founded "on social and economic justice and on concern and respect for all its victims and victimizers, a new system based on remedies and restoration rather than on prison, punishment and victim neglect, a system rooted in the concept of a caring community" (Knopp, 1991: 183).

Barak (1991a, 1991c) examines homelessness and describes a community-centered effort, based on compassion as a short-term aid in the crisis of low-cost housing. He contrasts the inhumane treatment the homeless received in Tucson, Arizona, where a typical criminal justice response was implemented using police harassment, arrest, and expulsion, with the humane and compassionate treatment in Aurora, Illinois. There, through community effort a homeless shelter, the Hesed House, and a soup kitchen, clothes closet, and day shelter were developed for those in need. Whereas the response in Arizona was violent, the response in Illinois was nonrepressive and humane. According to Barak (1991a: 55):

This non-violent alternative response to the homeless of Aurora reflects the twentieth century ideological values, the Judeo-Christian ethic as expressed in the welfare state and the notion of social security for all. The Auroran response also foreshadowed the possibility of developing a post-bourgeois future of greater community: corporate and state responsibility for victims of structural problems.

The point to be made by these few examples is that the peacemaking approach in criminology is not new but, as Pepinsky (1991) points out, "millennia old." It is a rejection of what peacemakers consider an unjust, wasteful, violent, and destructive system of criminal justice that itself is part of the problem of crime. Peacemaking as replacement discourse offers a different means of framing and thinking about crime that breaks out of the current punitive context. At the same time it brings into its discourse the voice of the victim, currently the mostly neglected element in the established justice system.

EVALUATION

It is still too early to evaluate the impact of postmodernism on criminology. Yet its influence is being felt in the increased questioning of traditional criminological concepts. In the forging of explanatory concepts, increased interest has also been shown in the voices of victims and offenders. As currently developed, however, postmodern contributions suffer from some internal inconsistencies that affect their challenge to existing social sciences such as criminology. First, as Rosenau (1992) points out, though postmodernism eschews any theory building, by its premises it develops its own theory. Second, though postmodern advocates place stress on "the importance of the irrational," they employ rational logic in their critique. Third, though postmodern advocates claim not to evaluate or judge accounts as either good or bad, their endeavors demonstrate otherwise: "Does their suggestion that social science focus on the excluded, the neglected, the marginal, and the silenced not indicate an internal value structure ... ?" (Rosenau, 1992: 176).

As presently written, postmodernist criminology has some serious questions to answer. It has been formulated as a theory when, as Hunt (1990: 539) says, it is merely a provisional metaphor, insufficiently developed to merit the grand description "theory." It is, he says, a conception of theory without guarantees. Indeed, even its own advocates caution against the "dangers of discourse" (Henry, 1991: 77), pointing out that although its greatest asset might be the "debunking of ideology and culture," postmodernism's "greatest danger is to be consumed by its own discourse." Moreover, the crucial role of nonverbal communication is seemingly left out of the postmodern script, an omission that ironically gives a privileged status to narrative text!

For others, it is the discourse itself that is a problem. Thus Schwartz (1991: 121–22) admits that if people cannot write so that he can understand the material, he has trouble maintaining an enthusiasm for it. He says that reading postmodernists is often "like reading Cervantes in the original when you cannot read Spanish" and that after reading postmodernist writers several times "I really do not know what the hell they are talking about." Also, like Hunt (1990) and Melichar (1988), he worries about the nihilism of the position that denies us the ability to make judgments about which philosophies are liberating, about a deconstruction that may lead to greater losses than gains. He offers this sobering reflection:

> [W]hen I think about theories which problematize and deny meaning to concepts of crime, I have flashbacks of survivors I have met in shelter houses. There are many types of "crime," to be sure, but to someone who has just been beaten or raped and received 75 stitches, the idea that crime only exists because we affirm the reality of existence, sounds a lot like victim-blaming, or at least, as Hunt points out, an ethical relativism that can be very scary. The absence of presence, so to speak. (Schwartz, 1991: 122)

For Cohen (1990, 1993) this is not only true for the victims of individual offenders but extends globally to victims of state violations of human rights. He argues that postmodernism's denial of values and standards feeds the "culture of denial" of oppressive state regimes while simultaneously subverting the basis of international standards of human rights, the sustenance for those who struggle for justice on a local level. He questions the sense of postmodernist declarations that there is no history "for those still living between death squads, famine, disease and violence," whose *history* is a daily event (Cohen, 1993: 111), and he points to the paucity of any theory that "denies any way of knowing what really happened" (ibid.: 112). Baudrillard's (1991) denial of the reality of the Gulf War, in the face of thousands lying dead and maimed in Iraq, marks a disturbing stage in this "emergent epistemological circus," chastises Cohen (1993: 112). The danger is not only that some academics are finding justification for their lack of desire to make political judgments and to take action, but that the postmodern project feeds state terror:

> If the Turkish government can deny that the Armenian genocide happened; if revisionist historians and neo-Nazis deny that the Holocaust took place; if powerful states all around the world today can systematically deny the systemic violations of human rights they are carrying out—then we know we're in bad shape. But we're in even worse shape when the intellectual *avant garde* invent a form of denial so profound, that serious people—including progressives—will have to debate whether the Gulf War actually took place or not. (Ibid.: 113)

This appears to take us back to the new directions in critical criminology offered by left realism (discussed in Chapter 10), and to the feminist criticism of postmodernists. For example, Jackson (1992) points out that whereas post-modernism denies the existence of any groups or social structures independent of our understanding of them, feminists recognize that while gender categories may be cultural constructs they are not merely fictional. She says that women's lives are *materially* bounded by gender categories and that by deconstructing them women may be denied a position from which to speak. Similarly, Lovibond (1989) says that feminism is endangered by postmodernism, which allows men to maintain their dominance through control over the local, customary, and parochial. Instead, she says, feminism should persist in seeing itself as a modernist project, a daughter of the enlightenment, moving toward global abolition of the sex-class system. Currie (1992), too, claims that postmodernism deprives feminists of the conceptual tools necessary to examine relations of domination and to deal with practice. Indeed, like Cohen and like Jackson, she suggests that the relevance of postmodernism is primarily as a critique (Currie, 1991). She says the perspective is largely theoretical, pointing out that "decentering the power of law in discourse, is not the same as decentering law in real life." She calls for feminist criminologists to engage actively in real political struggles rather than theoretical closeted intellectual debates. As we have seen, however, others, Cohen included, are also "uneasy" about the realist narrative.

Ironically, a way out of the postmodernist-realist dilemma is offered by Cohen (1990, 1991, 1993) and is consistent with the constitutive version of postmodernism presented earlier. Cohen (1990: 28–31) argues for criminology to maintain a connection and tension between both the demands of theoretical skepticism as articulated by postmodernist deconstructionism *and* the realists' activist construction of concrete policy. Thus he exhorts criminologists to be "sceptical and ironical at the level of theory, yet at the level of policy and politics, to be firmly committed," to "recognize the contingency of your values, language and conscience—yet remain wholly faithful to them," proposing "an honest deconstruction (which is not denial) of the facts plus an intuitive sense of the values." Both messages are important, says Cohen, but one without the other can be disastrous.[13] However, he points out that it is vital to guard against "false symmetry" or the "alchemists' stone of 'integration'" since such a position omits the tension, the reflexive doubt that allows each message to be revised in light of developments in the other. Cohen (1990: 29) concludes that "all we can do, is find the best guide to each one—then confront the tension that results," which

---

[13]Superficially Cohen's argument has some parallels with the call by Borgmann (1992) for a "postmodern realism," but differs in its sustained critique, which is ultimately lost in Borgmann to the new uncritical reality of "communal celebration."

he admits is "hard going." The seemingly impossible task is "to combine detachment with commitment ... not to use intellectual scepticism as a guide for political inaction" (ibid.: 32).

How criminological theory may address this "impossible task" is the subject of our final chapter, in which we examine the problematic nature of theoretical integration, before suggesting possible directions for development of the kind of criminology our analysis implies.

Fission or Fusion?

In this chapter we draw together our own thoughts on criminological theorizing. Though we have tried to remain faithful to the logic of each of the various perspectives presented, in some areas our biases may have colored our judgment. Now we wish to be quite explicit about our own stance. We will employ the same analytical framework used throughout the text and try to bring some closure to our admittedly abstract enterprise. We make no claims about the priority of our approach over others. Indeed, our position might be seen as simply another tool in the analysis of crime. As with each of the chapters, we try to present enough of our key ideas that readers can make their own judgments.

Before we state our position on the various analytical dimensions it might be helpful to clarify our views on the central issue addressed in the title to this chapter: Fission or fusion? Asked another way: is there merit in "integrating" some or all of the various approaches or are they best left as "separate and equal"? In the following section we address the integration issue. Mindful of Cohen's (1990) reflections on "the alchemist's stone of integration," we examine whether what is gained through integration offsets what is lost by the blending of important differences between the approaches. We explore attempts that have been made by certain theorists, by combining two or more theories, to overcome the limitations of relying on any single "grand" theoretical framework. We point out that integration may be little more than a shake of the kaleidoscope of theory construction, resulting in a mere rearrangement of old assumptions. Ultimately, a new series of tensions may emerge as different integration theorists struggle for a new "consensus" over whose "theoretical mix" is superior. Finally, we touch on whether criminological theory fares best as a fusion of interdisciplinarity or as a fission of multidisciplinarity.

THEORETICAL INTEGRATION

As Gibbons (1994: 176) has argued, criminology remains active in "theory work." Whereas some theorists are in the business of generating new theoretical paradigms and formulating the central concepts around which these should be focused, such as "control" (Gibbs, 1989) or "constitutive interrelation" (Henry and Milovanovic, 1991), others are engaged in integrating the theories that already exist (see especially Elliott et al., 1979, 1985; Colvin and Pauly, 1983; Hawkins and Weis, 1985; Pearson and Weiner, 1985; Messner et al., 1989; Akers, 1993). We are concerned with exploring adventures in integration, synthesis, or amalgamation that attempt to produce a "comprehensive" explanation of crime.

Integrating diverse theories involves drawing together various assumptions of theory to produce a comprehensive or even cohesive approach to understanding and explanation. Many teachers of criminological theory likely have experienced students' complete puzzlement at why, having demonstrated that flaws can be found in any particular theory, criminologists do not simply combine the best elements of all theories into a single grand theory which would cover all possibilities and in which one theory's strengths would compensate for another's inadequacies. Some criminologists agree, suggesting that criminology should draw together the most useful and empirically viable parts of theories into a coherent whole (Johnson, 1979). The solution seems simple: take the best of each and leave the rest.

However, certain assumptions implicit in this seductive proposition need further analysis. First, it is assumed that the theoretical perspectives we classify as separate and conflicting are themselves discrete and incompatible. This is a false assumption. Very few theories contain such a narrow range of assumptions that they could not be integrated. While this is not the place to embark on a sociology of knowledge, it must be acknowledged that most theories bring together a range of ideas prevailing in a particular historical period. Whether or not theories are explicit about this concurrence does not belie it. When Sutherland formulated his theory of differential association he did not exclude all that was not social learning theory. He simply enhanced the place of social learning in attempting to explain crime and delinquency. Some years later, Cohen and Cloward and Ohlin, whom we considered under subcultural strain theory, "integrated Chicago School approaches with the anomie tradition" (Williams and McShane, 1988: 133; Cullen, 1984). And who could deny that Quinney's work has progressed in a series of "paradigm shifts," each on the cutting edge of current thinking, while absorbing and building on what has gone before?

As we have tried to demonstrate throughout, theories are rarely exclusive of each other. Consider biological theory. Only in extremely simplistic textbooks and tabloid headlines will statements be found such as "genes cause crime." As we saw in Chapter 4, biological theorists do not believe this. They go to great lengths to point out that genes are a factor in a gene–brain–environment interaction that makes some people more likely candidates to offend under certain conditions.

What is different about the recent wave of integrated theories (since the 1970s) is the emergence of *explicit* rather than implied integration; theorists state that they are integrating specific sets of theories. The key to demystifying these new integration attempts is to recognize that the *emphasis* of different perspectives gives greater weight to some features than to others in the attempt to understand, explain, and respond to harmful behavior. It is our view that rather than merge the different emphases, we should respect their differences, retaining their integrity as part of the array of approaches instead of meshing them together with the risk of losing what is unique about their contribution. But we are getting a little ahead of ourselves here.

We have seen throughout this text enough of what constitutes different approaches that the concept of approach, or framework, need not be reexamined. What is worth drawing out, however, is (1) the derivation of the new integrated theories from the other broad frameworks, and (2) the range of questions or issues which confront theorists predisposed to integrate theory and against which we can judge whether their integrated approach is adequate.

Integrational Derivation

Table 13-1 shows some examples of the more prominent integrated criminological theories and their derivation. Even though this is an indicative rather than

Table 13-1 Integrated Theories and their Derivations

	CONGER, 1976	GLAZER, 1978	ELLIOTT ET AL., 1979; ELLIOTT ET AL., 1985	WEIS AND SEDERSTROM, 1981; WEIS AND HAWKINS, 1981	COLVIN AND PAULY, 1983	PEARSON AND WEINER, 1985	WILSON AND HERRNSTEIN, 1985	THORNBERRY, 1987	HAGAN ET AL., 1985; HAGAN, 1989, 1990	BRAITHWAITE, 1989
Classical						X	X		X	
Rational		X				X				
Biological							X			
Psychological/Personality							X			
Learning	X	X	X	X	X	X	X	X		X
Control	X	X	X	X	X	X		X	X	X
Labeling						X				X
Ecology						X		X		
Cultural										X
Subcultural				X	X	X				
Strain			X	X	X	X				X
Conflict					X	X			X	
Marxist					X	X			X	
Feminist									X	
Postmodern										

a representative chart, it can be seen that learning and control theories are more often part of the integrative mix than any other of the theories. Also it can be seen that most of the component theories drawn on are individual-level (micro) theories rather than societal-level (macro) theories. Let us take a close look at one of the more sophisticated of these integrational theories, Hagan's power control theory, otherwise known as structural criminology (Hagan, 1989).

Hagan's (1989, 1990; Hagan et al., 1985, 1987) power control theory is an integrated theory combining a Marxist, conflict, gender-analysis, control theory with classicist assumptions about human nature. It explains female criminality, or the relative lack of it, in terms of both patriarchy and the class structure, and how these translate into control over young women in the family. The power position of adult family members in the workplace shapes the social or relational power that they possess in the family. Hagan argues that "work relations structure family relations, particularly relations between fathers and mothers and, in turn, relations between parents and their children, especially mothers and their daughters" (Hagan, 1989: 13). Hagan considers two dimensions of power that are interrelated, although in explaining delinquency differences he has recently (Hagan, 1990) given more weight to patriarchy than previously (Hagan et al.,1985). Class power derived from Marxist theory is defined in terms of a person's position in the workplace. People are in relational positions of control, either as owners controlling the production process, as managers and supervisors controlling the work of employees, or as workers who have no control of anything other than the power to sell their labor. The unemployed (or surplus population) and those who work at home have no control over others and do not even have the power to sell their labor (Hagan et al., 1985). Those who have control over others are members of the "command" class while those who do not are members of the "obey" class (Hagan et al., 1987). These class-power positions translate to family life. Those in relatively powerful economic positions of ownership and/or authority outside the home compared with other members of their family have more power in the domestic context than those in less economically powerful positions. They have power based on access to a greater amount of class-structured resources than those who are underemployed, the unemployed, or those who work in the home, who lack the access to independent means.

In Hagan's second dimension, gender stratification derived from feminist theory, makes a distinction between patriarchal family structures and egalitarian ones. In typical paternalistic families with a high division of labor between men and women, where a man is working in the class-power structure and a woman is working in the household, mothers and daughters are the medium and the outcome of domestic social control by men. Mothers have the role of socializing their daughters and in the process replicating the gendered division of labor. Here girls are relatively more likely than boys to be the object of control and supervision, in the name of protecting their vulnerability to crime. Here Hagan brings in control theory. Girls are socialized by their parents into domestic roles, in order to limit their risk taking, restrict their sexual activity, and reduce any inclination to look for deviant role exits from their family structures. Girls, therefore, are controlled rela-tionally, both by male domination and by female role modeling and supervision and, therefore, are less likely to engage in crime than boys. In contrast boys are given greater freedom to take risks and are socialized to control others. As a result boys are relatively free to deviate.

However, in families with low domestic division of labor, such as in middle-class families, in which both parents work, the social power in the family is less gender structured. As a result there is less gender socialization and less maternal supervision of girls, and because they are more likely to take the same risks as boys, delinquency between boys and girls does not reflect a significant gender difference. Because of the lack of comparative gender difference in the single-parent family household, the same pattern occurs. When the gender dimension is combined with the class-power dimension (see Table 13-2) four ideal-type possibilities exist. Higher class-power, egalitarian families, such as dual-career professional families are likely to show the least difference in delinquency among their sons and daughters;

Table 13-2 Hagan's Integrated Power-Control Theory

| | PATRIARCHY | |
	Low Division of Labor Egalitarian Family	High Division of Labor Patriarchal Family
High Class-Power (Command Class)	EGALITARIAN-COMMAND E.g., dual-career professional Lowest control over daughters' risk-taking behavior Least difference between sons' and daughters' delinquency	PATRIARCHAL-COMMAND E.g., single-career professionals, owners, and managers Medium control over daughters' risk-taking behavior Medium difference between sons' and daughters' delinquency
Low Class-Power (Obey Class)	EGALITARIAN-OBEY E.g., dual-career working-class and single-parent families Relatively low control over daughters risk-taking Low difference between son's and daughters' delinquency	PATRIARCHAL-OBEY E.g., Single-career working-class families High control over daughters' risk-taking behavior High difference between sons' and daughters' families

dual-career working-class egalitarian families a higher difference, but lower than the difference in delinquency between sons and daughters of higher-class patriarchal families, since patriarchy is more differentiating than class power. All these types of families can be expected to show a lower difference than traditional working-class patriarchal families, experiencing as they do the combined negative effects of both class and gender.

Importantly, Hagan (1989) also argues that the greater access to power and resources liberates those in the highest economic positions to commit (white-collar and corporate) crime using either the corporation or occupational resources, and the same people are the most able to afford the means to separate and protect themselves from prosecution.

Hagan's integrated theory is one of the few to combine different critical structural (macro) theories with individual-level (micro) theories and specify how they interrelate and how the theory may be tested.[1] As a result, it has received more attention than most. However, to date the research evidence has been mixed. Moreover, some of the most ardent criticisms have come from advocates of the specific constituent theories, such as feminism. This is in part because the theory is similar to emancipation-causes-crime arguments in that it suggests that a mother's absence from the home reduces control over girls and increases their chances of delinquency. It is argued that the theory predicts that increased women's participation in the workforce should have led to higher aggregate crime rates for young girls, but in fact these have remained stable or declined (Chesney-Lind, 1989; Chesney-Lind and Sheldon, 1992). In addition, Messerschmidt (1993) argues that we cannot assume that those in authority at work translate that authority to the home. The notion of egalitarianism ignores the role of gender power separate from class, although Hagan has moved closer to Messerschmidt's position in giving greater weight to patriarchy than class power. Curran and Renzetti (1994: 274), however, argue that "the theory actually overlooks important class differences among types of family structure," especially differences of race and ethnicity and the quality of the child–parent relationship. For example, Jensen and Thompson (1990) found no greater differences in male-female delinquency in higher classes than lower classes, but differences between white and black. Hill and Atkinson (1988) found the kind of parental control more important than the degree, though they confirmed that familial control over children was stratified by gender, with girls more often the objects of maternal support and curfew rules. Singer and Levine (1988) found greater differences in parental controls, risk taking, and delinquency among boys and girls in egalitarian households than in the patriarchal, which is contrary to Hagan's hypotheses; further the researchers found that mothers in egalitarian households exerted

---

[1]See also Colvin and Pauly (1983) for a similar approach that relies less on the classicist perspective for its assumptions about human nature.

more control than those in patriarchal households.[2] As with the other theories we have examined, we are less concerned with the empirical findings than with the arguments exposing theoretical assumptions. Thus, significant, given our arguments below, is Naffine's criticism of Hagan for his "demolition" of female agency resulting in a model of the young female as a conforming, "grey and lifeless creature ... passive, compliant and dependent ... biddable rather than responsible ... unable to construct complex and caring relationships even with her mother who subjects her to her control" (Naffine, 1987: 69). Thus, while Hagan is to be commended for his attempts to operationalize the intertwining structural forces, his integration of micro-level assumptions about human agency is somewhat deficient, especially given the range of possibilities about human agency that we have identified throughout this book. Let us now turn to these broader theoretical issues that affect all attempts at integrated theory.

Evaluating Integration

First is the issue of what is being integrated. Here it is important to ask whether an integrated theory primarily combines theories oriented to the individual level of analysis (micro-level) and/or whether it draws on those oriented to the societal level (macro-level). Some theorists explicitly address this issue (e.g., Friday and Hage, 1976) but most do not. A related issue is whether theories that are combined are predominantly those emphasizing human agency, social action, and process (as in Wilson and Herrnstein, 1985), and/or whether they represent social structures or cultures (as we saw above with Hagan). In other words, do they address the widest possible unit or organization, for example, society or the global community? Put another way, are the theories used more representative of those taking a total picture of society or of those taking a partial view? Alternatively, do they endeavor to capture both the levels of agency and structure as in O'Malley and Mugford's (1994) synthesis of Katz's (1988) phenomenology of criminal experience with Mertonian-type analyses of structured opportunity?

A further consideration is the weight given to theories emphasizing a fixed or changing picture of social life. Do most of the theories combined assume a static or dynamic state? The "static state" theories would include those emphasizing organized structures and objectively measurable social roles, containing individuals with limited internal attributes and a limited capacity for spontaneity, as in biological, early personality theories or theories based on rational choice. The "dynamic state" theories would include those giving more weight to subjective interpretation, negotiated and spontaneous interaction, informal and

---

[2]In contrast, however, others have begun to find more support for Hagan's ideas (on theft but not violence) than did initial evaluations (Grasmick et al., 1993).

creative process, and conflicts between differences, such as labeling theory, social constructionism, and anarchist criminology.

Clearly, then, integrated theories may have a bias that is reflected in which theories they combine. In considering an integrated theory we must assess this bias and decide at least whether the overall integration is conservative, liberal, or radical/critical.

The second major issue concerns the basis on which theories are included in an integrated package. Some believe this is simply at the whim or preference of the theorist: "All too often the choice of theories to be integrated depends on the theories with which the researcher has developed an allegiance" (Adler et al., 1991: 168). Alternatively, is some objective measure used to determine which is best? Is "best" what the empirical evidence shows is supported and, if so, by what criteria or methods? To apply positivist research methods to assess interactionist theory (as many have, e.g., Gove, 1975) is perhaps as unacceptable as is applying interpretive methods to assess the efficacy of control theory. The reliance on "evidence" simply shifts the debate from which theory to include to which methods to use, with similar conflicts likely over differently held assumptions. In assessing integrated theory, therefore, we need to know the basis for inclusion and exclusion.

A third important consideration is whose version of a particular theory is to be included. As we have seen repeatedly, different theorists have different conceptions of the underlying assumptions. If, for example, an interactionist or feminist view of human nature were included by Hagan, instead of the limited classicist one he assumes, the overall integrated theory would be different. Power control theory would also be different if, say, Messerschmidt's conception of patriarchy were used. Moreover, even if a version of one theory is selected, how much of that theory is incorporated and how representative is it of the theorist? Some integrationists, such as Pearson and Weiner (1985), attempt to include such a wide range of theories (twelve), that they end up being very selective in their extraction of the core elements. As a result their representations, for example, of Hirschi's control theory and Sutherland's differential association theory are so restrictive that one commentator has seriously questioned whether this "integration" preserves the sense of the original theories (Gibbons, 1994: 187). Moreover, even with their wide range of theories Pearson and Weiner focus on those having learning as a main component.

The fourth major issue concerns to which population of offenders the integrated theory is meant to apply. Some integration theories, like Braithwaite's (1989), claim to apply to all types of crime; others, like Wilson and Herrnstein's (1985), also claim this degree of comprehensiveness, but in fact they simply focus on theories formulated to explain the violent street offender, to the exclusion of the violent corporate or white-collar property offender (Gibbons, 1994: 188). Yet others, such as Baron and Straus (1990), combine feminism and ecology theory to explain rape, whereas Hagan's seeks to explain both juvenile delinquency and corporate crime.

Finally, a very important issue concerns what integrated theorists understand as integration and by what mechanism they see the selected theories interrelating. For example, is one grand theory used, as in Hagan's (1989) power control theory, or does integration assume a sequential "end to end" process in which various theories kick in at different stages, as in Elliott et al.'s (1979, 1985) and Colvin and Pauly's (1983) theories? Does the mechanism of integration seek to provide a transcending approach, leaving the individual theories to deal with specifics, or does it have the more imperialistic designs of displacing existing theory? Does the mechanism used for integration discuss the interrelationship between the component theories, showing how each of the dimensions emerge from or imply the other, or are these mechanistically inserted as cafeteria options, depending on which crime/offender/situation is being analyzed?

These are just some of the issues that can be raised in considering integrated theories. It is clear from this brief presentation that integrated theory can result not so much in a solution to the problems of diversity but an intensification of the problem. Since each integration theorist may use different criteria to construct his or her own comprehensive approach, what emerges is integrational chaos. So what starts out as a recognition that there are competing theoretical perspectives in criminology, ends up in a battle for who has the best collection of theories in their integrated framework. We now no longer bob from theory to theory in our failure to transcend one-sided interpretations of reality (Young, 1981: 306–307) but scamper from one integrated theory to another.

The plain fact is that integrated theorizing does not lead to a more comprehensive understanding of crime or criminal etiology. Not only does the approach leave gaps between integrated theories through which vital nuggets of the total reality of criminological explanation slip, but by presenting a range of theories as an integrated package, it tricks us into believing that a comprehensive coverage of criminological theory has been achieved. The problem with integration is that we are so deluded by the appearance of diversity that we lose sight of what is missing and can even be mislead into thinking that because several of the key theoretical positions are included, that the integration theory is politically neutral. This sense of neutrality is dangerous not only because it legitimates leaving out particular approaches but also because it legitimates what is presented. Each one of the theories within the integrated package somehow acquires a false equality with its neighbors. Such leveling has the disarming effect of allowing dominant theories (such as control theory and learning theory) and, more crucially, the processes whereby their dominance is created and sustained, to go unchallenged. As a result, the danger exists that integration itself can become part of the process of ideological mystification, contributing to the obscurity of obtaining a complete understanding of the phenomenon of crime. If integration is not the answer, how do we go beyond the familiar sequential trashing and replacement of theories that is so much a part of "theory work"?

Suppose we broach the question of integration another way. A sometimes useful, though somewhat functionalist, analogy is to consider theory to be like a tool box. Each of the different theories represent different tools. In this approach to integration the criterion shifts to which theory, or parts of the theory, can be used to best explain and solve the problem. Just as a construction or maintenance worker might arrive at a job with a tool box containing several specialized tools, each designed and refined for a different job, so a criminologist might come analytically prepared with several different theories to explain and deal with crime. Just as the worker might decide that a job or a repair needs a saw to cut wood, glue or a hammer and nails to attach the wood to the existing structure, and a screwdriver and screws to secure it, so a criminologist might find that a type of crime or harm requires classical theory to analyze the offender's motives, strain theory to analyze the opportunity structure that shapes these motives, and Marxist theory to analyze why differences of opportunity exist. Alternatively, just as the worker might decide that in some cases a whole building is of such poor design that its structure is faulty and in need of a new design, so the criminologist might decide the same is true for society or some of its subsystems and look to the critical theories of postmodernism, feminism, and Marxism in formulating a cogent theory.

All analogies have their limitations. The point here is simply to illustrate the observation that retaining the individual integrity of theories whose differences and applications are refined and specialized may be more important than developing the grand explanatory tool. In this we agree with Hirschi's (1979) concept of "separate and equal," in which he argued that theories should be placed in opposition to each other rather than be integrated. As Gibbons summarizes Hirschi's position:

> The thrust of Hirschi's comments was that theoretical integrations muddy the empirical waters and make it more, rather than less, difficult to disentangle causal influences and to identify the differential contribution that each of them makes to the behavioral outcome, delinquency. (Gibbons, 1994: 185)

In regard to the tool box analogy, our own position might best be considered as the development of another new and specialized tool of analysis, rather than an approach that displaces all the others. However, our analysis throughout this book tries to provide the reader with a consistent set of criteria to compare and contrast each of the other theoretical contributions. Let us then return to our analytical framework to clarify where we stand and from where we draw our influences.

HUMAN NATURE AND THE SOCIAL ORDER

We see human beings as active agents in forming their own destiny. Humans construct and constitute their action, but they do so in the framework of their existing culture, with images and symbolic referents, as reflected in the language that is available to them. Humans act and react in terms of meanings that they construct and reconstruct in their ongoing activity and in turn are constructed themselves through this process. Thus we gain our self-identities in interactive reflexive action with others. Through this interaction we are in a continuing process of becoming. At the same time, by means of this process, we also build the structure of society, which, ongoingly shapes our very action and places limits and possibilities on the range of choice in our activity. The structure of our action, that is, the ongoing outcome of our action, simultaneously channels our action and amplifies it in certain directions. An important implication of these processes is that we have the capacity to bring about change by being aware of them and by reconstituting, reshaping, and redefining the institutions and the wider social order that we create and that shapes us.

In the process of becoming a social human being, biology is but one facet of the building block of life, and not among the most prominent in explaining why we behave similarly to or differently from others. Though each person is unique, much of this uniqueness comes from interaction with others. Whatever gender or racial behavioral differences emerge, these are created through the interactive process, structured by the larger social and cultural forces that are themselves constituted by channeled human action. There are no "natural" behaviors, in terms of behavior significant to social life, only behaviors *taken* to be natural and responded to *as if they were* natural.

Borrowing from classicism, we believe that humans, for the most part, act with reason. The reasoned part of our action, however, *follows* events and shapes its reality for us by conferring on it a rationale that we as humans find acceptable. In other words, there may be more rationality in making sense of action after an event than rational motivation leading to our participation in it. Moreover, even though humans perceive that they are living individual lives, they are never entirely "free" because they are interconnected to others in a myriad of linkages, not least of which is the shared language of culture that shapes the meaning of what we communicate and construct as a reality. Thus humans are always and foremost *social beings* working within a dynamic social context.

Thus, from our point of view, human beings, society, and the social order are part of the same process, each shaping the other and being ongoingly shaped by it. In this interplay, social institutions are fashioned out of discourse over time as recurrent patterns or ideas that we react to as if they were real. They are collective constructions sustained by our individual action. Social order, therefore, is a reality we create for ourselves, not an absolute that is "in the nature of things." By implication, society can be recreated differently as part of the ongoing process of sustaining its appearance of stable existence. How much we can make changes depends on how aware we are of our contribution to society's ongoing reproduction.

THE ROLE OF LAW AND THE DEFINITION OF CRIME

From our point of view, law is not a neutral instrument or institution that represents a consensus of shared values, nor do we conceptualize it as a distinct body of rules. Rather we see law as the outcome of social interactions and the interpenetration of various normative orders. The enactment of criminal law is a process that is influenced and guided by social relations, by images and discourse specifying its own past existence, and by the existence of other informal systems of rules that both influence lawmaking and law-sustaining processes and are themselves influenced by them. Thus the image of the law as an overarching edifice neglects the ever-changing nature of legal discourse and how this is consumed in the fire of legal reality. It neglects how law orders that which is not itself, to reproduce itself again. It neglects that law does not do these things but that we do them in the name of law and in the name of order.

We take crime to be a socially constructed, universalizing category that obfuscates the variety of harms that are encompassed by the term. We see crime in terms other than those provided by a purely legal definition. Rather we see it, as was stated in Chapter 11, as a multitude of differently motivated acts that produce personal or social harm for others, and not infrequently for ourselves. It comes about whenever power is used to subjugate others regardless of their will. This may occur in a simple robbery from a person, to stealing property in a burglary, to a corporation using their economic power to produce and sell dangerous products or dump toxins in the environment, to a husband forcing his wife to have sexual intercourse, to the state using its delegated power to gather information on citizens it deems disloyal, to the Central Intelligence Agency's support of pariah regimes, to a state's lack of provision for the relative poverty that systems of inequality inevitably impose on some of their members. In each of these examples power, either physical, emotional, social, economic, or political, is used to deny others certain human prerogatives—or, in other words, basic human rights and self-determination. Such denial is crime. In its most fundamental sense, crime is the expression and use of power to deny others their right to be human. Crime occurs thus when another's humanity is denied and the person is redefined as an object to be acted upon. Once this process is set in motion any atrocity becomes a possibility. Moreover, its force can extend to people collaborating in their own human demise, turning their energies against themselves in moments of painful self-denial.

CAUSAL LOGIC

It follows from our view of humans, society, and crime, that our concept of causality differs from traditional assumptions. Crime is not something separate from the ongoing social reality, it is part of it. Crime is created in various social contexts of human interaction. It occurs, as we indicated above, whenever power is used to dominate and is founded on constructions of meaning that write off the humanity of others. It results from the action of agents of institutions who through their political and economic roles create first in discourse, then in practice, the political and economic conditions and differentials in power and its use that become the breeding ground to deny others their humanity. Those who hold a claim to legitimate power but use it in ways that deny others the possibility to make their difference, epitomize the misuse of power that is in turn used by the powerless in denying others. When the powerless become the powerful and use their newly gained power in ways that oppress others, the pattern of crime is reproduced; albeit different players sing, but they all sing the same song.

At another level of analysis, crime is generated by the type of political economy that is the life blood of society. We believe, however, that it is not the abstract *system* per se that is responsible for crime as harm. Rather it is the invocation of certain discourses (attitudes, ways of thinking, language, and the meaning structures these invoke) generated in interaction by *people* acting in their institutional capacity to create and sustain the ideology of domination and with it the conditions wherein crime is inherent. This discursive construction of reality is the major pillar of criminogenic societies. By developing discourses that rest on exploitation and that create and give sustenance to conditions of inequality (differences of power), the conditions for crime as harm are also created. Such discourses permeate and structure the political and economic relations that make up our society. They constitute the common ways of thinking and the developed attitudes and accepted behavioral rationales of daily conduct.

Crime is the actions of individuals mediated by culturally generated discourse invoking particular meaning structures. It is within these discursively created contexts that individuals construct their harmful acts and find appropriate rationales to carry them out. In our schema, individuals, because of the existence of human agency, have responsibility for their action; they are not driven but are both constrained and liberated by the very discourses they create and respond to in their institutionalized forms and in which daily interactions are embedded. Thus criminal outcomes are the result of numerous contexts of interaction.

In other words, it is the interplay of discourses by human agents in various social matrices that create crime. In each the use of power for subjugation is present. Whether it is the media's use of power to create a useless "need," the power of the thief to deprive another, or the state's use of power to categorize and repress, all reflect a denial of the other. Crime is part of the process whereby some people believe it possible and acceptable to act on the differences they create to deny others their freedom to make their own difference (Henry and Milovanovic, 1993). This means that many persons become at least manipulatively aware of their role in the reproduction of the use of power that forfeits another's chances to a self-determined existence. Likewise, a considerable reflexive awareness is necessary if people are to resist those that will impose harm on them.

CRIMINAL JUSTICE IMPLICATIONS

Though the basic effort in a society should be, in our opinion, to empower individuals so that people may make a difference, this power must not be used to dominate or subjugate but rather to enable and to free. Criminal justice policy has increasingly become more repressive. There has been a staggering increase in the use of prisons and jails with a concomitant increase in the networks of formal social control and a simultaneous reliance on technologies of informal surveillance. The exponential increase in confinement has made the United States the nation with the largest number of persons under correctional restraint. This has resulted because the use of confinement and incapacitation has become the method of policy choice rather than a last resort. The rehabilitation and treatment ideology and policy of the 1950s and 1960s has been replaced by a policy of punishment and retribution harking back to former punitive eras.

It is all too evident that this policy has not resulted in any decrease in harmful activity; on the contrary, harm in the sense we define it above has reached greater levels. Following the logic of the theoretical position we present, a change in policy to one that relies more on reconciliation and restitution rather than retribution and punishment could have a more positive impact in reducing harm, if this policy were combined with a parallel transformation at the level of the political economy. At the most basic level it is necessary to eliminate the domination that denies people their humanity. The focus must be to incorporate rather than exclude so that people become a part of society and are acknowledged for their contribution.

As certain people persist in seeking to resurrect discourses of domination, denial, and control, the means must be found to resist their influence, not only for self-preservation but to prevent the pestilence of self-doubt and social demoralization such discourses create. Society must aim to use power to respond in a constructive manner rather than to reproduce the negative impact of a purely punitive reaction. However, alternatives must truly be constructive, replacing rather than augmenting the current repressive practices, or else they only add to the network of harmful control. A revised approach to criminal justice would place less emphasis on imprisonment, with a view toward eventual elimination of confinement altogether except in extreme cases. It would focus on reparation to the community and restitution to the victim. If direct restitution were not feasible, significant service to the community would be substituted. The main purpose would be to eliminate harm or meaningfully compensate it. Where possible, reconciliation should be attempted.

It is necessary also to think in terms of a changed dispositional discourse in dealing with offenders; one that focuses on a positive reconciliatory stance that does not deny the humanity of the victim(s) or the offender(s) and one that removes us from what has become the punitive trap. Retributive and punitive responses to crime may give a quick "fix" to the emotions aroused by crime and the subjugation of its victims but only result in the repetition of subjugation and the denial of the other in the long run. Thus, as history demonstrates, these responses do little to reduce social harm. It must be kept in mind, as Harris (1991: 90) emphasizes, "penal sanctions, like crimes, are intended harms." And harms do not bring social wholeness and security but simply add to the crimes against humanity already under way.

Nor are liberal rehabilitation approaches the viable alternative. Whatever their intended aim, they are wide open to abuse and symbolically harm both crime's victims and those who live their lives without harming others and who see rehabilitation as a reward for the harmful behavior they struggle to avoid. Moreover, these approaches are often a veiled strategy for manipulation, which is no less a perpetration of the very denial of human agency they are supposed to prevent.

The question becomes one of how to break out of the counterproductive cycle of denial–subjugation–repression–subjugation–denial. We suggest that it will require a different mind set, one that will not be achieved in the near future but that has promise for the long term. We would favor some of the elements encompassed in *peacemaking* that we briefly referred to in a previous chapter. On another level we would argue that the overriding approach might follow what we have termed the *judo metaphor.*

By the judo metaphor we refer to the philosophy behind judo and other martial arts. Judo means "gentle way" and is based on the seeming paradox that the best defense is nonfighting and that one gains victory over an opponent by yielding—gentle turns away the sturdy opponent (Kim and Shin, 1983). It is a method whereby the energy of the violent is redirected against the opponent to diffuse their violence. In a metaphorical sense this is a model stance that might release the United States from the punitive trap. A recent dramatic example of this model was demonstrated in the highly emotionally charged trial of the accused assaulters of Reginald Denny, a white truck driver, who had been viciously beaten by a group of blacks in the wake of the Los Angeles riots of 1991. After testifying, Denny went to the mother of the accused and hugged her in the courtroom. This powerful symbolic gesture did much to defuse the antagonistic and racially hostile atmosphere that had permeated the trial. It demonstrated the victim's humanity and recognized that of his tormentors' kin. Though admittedly a special case, it illustrates the principle of "judo responses," which must be developed to create social awareness, at the individual and collective levels, of the power used to harm.

How can harmony best be achieved by nonviolent or nonrepressive means? We are suggesting that we create criminal justice policies that reflect values other than those that result in the use of coercion and subjugation as instruments of those policies. These are values that reject the current stress on coercive power and place greater emphasis on compassionate responses that defuse the energy of violence and harm. They are values that recognize human interdependence. As Harris (1991: 93) proposes:

> We need to struggle against the tendency toward objectification, of talking and thinking about crime and criminals as if they were distinct entities ... We also need to reject the idea that those who cause injury or harm to others should suffer severance of the common bonds of respect and concern that bind members of a community. We should relinquish the notion that it is acceptable to try to "get rid of" another person, whether through execution, banishment, or caging away people about whom we do not care. We should no longer pretend that conflicts can be resolved by the pounding of a gavel or the locking of a cell door.

In the most fundamental sense, we envisage the giving up of power to deny others and developing policies that reenforce the integration of people with their social context, that is, with each other. This may seem naive given current methods and approaches, but that may be so only "because we have lost confidence in our capacity to choose, to recreate relations, and to realign priorities" (Harris, 1991: 95).

The greatest stress must be laid on preventive measures, in recognition of the fact that crime is not something that is separate from the various institutional discourses that create the condition for its emergence. Such a radical shift in perspective and policy will not easily be achieved, but incremental changes in this direction have already occurred as demonstrated in Chapter 11.

A major emphasis of such a redirected policy would be on methods and tactics that do not objectify the victim or the offender but focus on the mutual humanity of both. Such tactics will take courage and imagination as well as abandoning the popular attitude of revenge/retribution and the images of war and violence that now dominate our policies of viewing and dealing with crime. In working toward this goal we must not be sidetracked by the extraordinary case. We must begin to operate on a principle of least restraint to accomplish the purpose of reducing crime.

This principle will become clearer when we recognize the crime-generating energy of the ideology of criminal justice. Often an offender's journey through the system confers status and prestige among his or her peers and provides the justification for his or her acts as well (Henry and Milovanovic, 1994). By stripping away this energy and redirecting it, much recursive-crime-producing potential and negative power creation will be neutralized. The adverse educational influence of confinement is well known but is never seriously taken into account in the discourse of crime prevention.

Ultimately crime prevention on a macro level will rest on a reduction of the discourses that are invested with energy to both create and perpetuate the rationales that serve as the justificatory reservoir for social harm. Such justification resides in the messages, images, and symbols that equate humanity with its products: messages that tie material goods to self-worth and deny the individual by reducing life's worth to materiality; we-versus-they images in the presentation of crime to the public; crime myths that undergird an ideology of revenge and retribution. Finally, such justification resides in the crime control rhetoric that Cohen (1985) has referred to as "control talk," the discourse that both shapes and reconstitutes the view we have of what is crime, who is the criminal.

So what kind of strategy might our approach employ? An alternative to the confinement program that has been implemented is illustrative. For the past several years the University of Massachusetts in concert with a district judge has been holding literature seminars with so-called "hardcore" felons as an alternative to imprisonment. Participants work in the community but attend the seminar weekly and discuss the characters in the novels they are required to read. The idea is that, because literature mirrors aspects of individuals' lives, problems, and dilemmas, through its study, the participants could indirectly examine parts of their own selves. The discussion of literature could give empowerment and a sense of self-esteem to these offenders that criminal activity could not. Preliminary evaluations show that the program has had the anticipated effect of reducing these offenders' participation in criminal activity to a remarkable extent. Although this is a limited effort that includes only those who have a certain level of literacy, it is an undertaking that avoids the punitive trap and produces reintegration instead of exclusion.

Perhaps the best example of an approach with the features we see as important—and one that has been successfully operated for over two decades—is San Francisco's Delancy Street Project. Founded by Mimi Silbert, a Berkeley criminologist, this program has gained national attention. A self-supporting project, it has helped 10,000 former prisoners to become productive contributing members of society. The focus is on deconstructing stereotypical public beliefs about offenders as well as stereotypes former prisoners believe about themselves. The program teaches ex-offenders to be self-reliant, stressing each individual's responsibility for behavior and capacity to make a difference. Through group critiques and group support, the program accomplishes self-transformation from destructive behavior to constructive living. Skills and latent talents are developed for positive social ends.

Thus Delancy members have built a multi-million dollar commercial center on San Francisco's Embarcadero, run an upscale restaurant (in a city with high restaurant standards), and operate a moving company and several other enterprises. These are accomplishments by persons who had hit bottom and become total social outcasts. The success of Delancy Street rests in no small measure on an approach that is the reverse of the standard punishment rationale. Rather than the continual casting out of the convicted, it recognizes the importance of an integrative focus to reverse the destructive criminal patterns of offenders. Membes are responsible for themselves as well as the progress of othes, and, as such, learn the importance of community. They learn by working on productive projects and are thereby transformed. Within their community, member activities are organized to emphasize constructive approaches and de-emphasize what was negative and destructive in their past. Given the opportunity through their work within and for the community to *act* responsibly, they *become* responsible.

Delancy Street is a model of the positive effects to be gained from translating discourses related to crime into action. Interestingly, this effort has gained a measure of political support and perhaps may be a harbinger of reconstructive criminological work to come.

Practical efforts of this kind that reduce social violence with a gentle touch are the pragmatic consequence of the theoretical model we have outlined. These are minor steps in a long journey but, nevertheless, vital if the theoretical position we have outlined is to be realized in practice.

CONCLUDING THOUGHTS

Our suggestions will strike some readers as naively idealistic and politically absurd, but they are hard realities if we are serious in bringing needed reform to our attempts to cope with crime. Crime, like financial insolvency, does not get solved by the quick fix. It requires a slow and painful relearning of how to behave, a replacement discourse that signifies a new way of connecting to the world and others in it. It is a step-by-step process to generate words, meanings, and thoughts that heal instead of exacerbate harm-producing conditions. Crime being the complex and varied phenomenon it is, there will always be different explanations of it, depending on inherent theoretical assumptions and the meaning of crime to the theorist. There are no simple explanations; there are no simple solutions. Complexity is in the nature of social life. The challenge remains to capture the complexity and, in countering crime, to avoid reproducing the problem in our attempts to solve it.

References

Abel, Richard. 1981. "Conservative Conflict and the Reproduction of Capitalism: The Role of Informal Justice." *International Journal of the Sociology of Law* 9: 245–67.

Abel, Richard. 1982. *The Politics of Informal Justice.* 2 vols. New York: Academic Press.

Abrahamsen, David. 1944. *Crime and the Human Mind.* New York: Columbia University Press.

Abrahamsen, David. 1960. *The Psychology of Crime.* New York: Columbia University Press.

Ackerman, Nathan W. 1958. *The Psychodynamics of Family Life: Diagnosis and Treatment of Family Relationships.* New York: Basic Books.

Adam, Hargrave L. 1914. *Woman and Crime.* London: T. Werner Laurie.

Adler, Alfred. 1960 [1931]. *What Life Should Mean to You.* London: Allen and Unwin.

Adler, Freda. 1975. *Sisters in Crime: The Rise of the New Female Criminal.* New York: McGraw-Hill.

Adler, Freda. 1983. *Nations Not Obsessed with Crime.* Colorado: Rothman.

Adler, Freda, Gerhard O. W. Mueller, and William S. Laufer. 1991. *Criminology.* New York: McGraw-Hill.

Adler, M. J. 1967. *The Difference of Man and the Difference It Makes.* New York: Holt, Rinehart and Winston.

Agger, Ben. 1989. *Socio(ont)logy.* Urbana: University of Illinois Press.

Agnew, Robert S. 1985. "A Revised Strain Theory of Delinquency." *Social Forces* 64: 151–167.

Agnew, Robert. 1991a. "The interactive effect of peer variables on delinquency." *Criminology* 29: 47–72.

Agnew, Robert S. 1991b. "Strain and Subcultural Crime Theories." In *Criminology: A Contemporary Handbook,* ed. Joseph F. Sheley, 273–94. Belmont, CA: Wadsworth.

Agnew, Robert. 1992. "Foundation for a General Strain Theory of Crime and Delinquency." *Criminology* 30: 47–87.

Agnew, Robert, and Helene Raskin White. 1992. "An Empirical Test of General Strain Theory." *Criminology* 30(4): 475–99.

Ahluwalia, Seema. 1991. "Currents in British Feminist Thought: The Study of Male Violence." *Critical Criminologist* 3(1): 5–6, 12–14.

Aichhorn, August. 1935. *Wayward Youth.* New York: Viking Press.

Akers, Ronald L. 1967. "Problems in the Sociology of Deviance: Social Definitions and Behavior." *Social Forces* 46: 455–65.

Akers, Ronald L. 1985. *Deviant Behavior: A Social Learning Approach.* Belmont, CA: Sage.

Akers, Ronald L. 1993. *Criminological Theories: Introduction and Evaluation.* Los Angeles: Roxbury.

Alihan, M. A. 1938. *Social Ecology: A Critical Analysis.* New York: Columbia University Press.

American Friends Service Committee. 1971. *Struggle for Justice.* New York: Hill and Wang.

Anderson, Nels. 1923. *The Hobo.* Chicago: University of Chicago Press.

Armstrong, Gail, and Mary Wilson. 1973. "City Politics and Deviancy Amplification." In *Politics and Deviance,* ed. Ian Taylor and Laurie Taylor, 61–89. Harmondsworth, England: Penguin.

Asch, Stuart S. 1985. "Depression and Demonic Possession: The Analyst as an Exorcist." *Hillside Journal of Clinical Psychiatry* 7(2): 149–64.

Austin, James, and Barry Krisberg. 1981. "Wider, Stronger, and Different Nets: The Dialectics of Criminal Justice Reform." *Journal Research in Crime and Delinquency* 18: 165–96.

Bach, Paul J. 1979. "Demon Possession and Psychopathology: A Theological Relationship." *Journal of Psychology and Theology* 7(1): 22–26.

Baker, Laura A., Wendy Mack, Terry E. Moffitt, and Sarnoff A. Mednick. 1989. "Sex Differences in Property Crime in a Danish Adoption Cohort." *Behavior Genetics* 19: 355–70.

Baker, Roger. 1974. *Binding the Devil: Exorcism Past and Present.* New York: Hawthorn Books.

Baldwin, John. 1979. "Ecological and Areal Studies in Great Britain and the United States." In *Crime and Justice: An Annual Review of Research,* Vol. 1, ed. Norval Morris and Michael Tonry, 29–66. Chicago: University of Chicago Press.

Balkan, Sheila, Ronald Berger, and Janet Schmidt. 1980. *Crime and Deviance in America: A Critical Approach.* Belmont, CA: Wadsworth.

Balkin, J. M. 1992. "What Is Postmodern Constitutionalism?" *Michigan Law Review* 90: 1966–90.

Ball, Robert. 1966. "An Empirical Investigation of Neutralization Theory." *Criminologica* 4: 22–32.

Ball, Richard A., and J. Robert Lilly. 1985. "Home Incarceration: An International Alternative to Institutional Incarceration." *International Journal of Comparative and Applied Criminal Justice* 9: 85–97.

Ball, Richard A., and J. Robert Lilly. 1987. "The Phenomenology of Privacy and the Power of the State: Home Incarceration with Electronic Monitoring." In *Critical Issues in Criminology and Criminal Justice,* ed. J. E. Scott and T. Hirschi. Beverly Hills, CA: Sage.

Banay, Ralph S. 1948. *Youth in Despair.* New York: Coward-McGann.

Bandura, Albert. 1969. *Principles of Behavior Modification.* New York: Holt, Rinehart and Winston.

Bandura, Albert. 1973. *Aggression: A Social Learning Analysis.* Engelwood Cliffs, NJ: Prentice-Hall.

Bandura, Albert. 1977. *Social Learning Theory.* Engelwood Cliffs, NJ: Prentice-Hall.

Barak, Gregg. 1988. "Newsmaking Criminology: Reflections on the Media, Intellectuals, and Crime." *Justice Quarterly* 5: 565–87.

Barak, Gregg. 1991a. "Homelessness and the Case for Community-based Initiatives: The Emergence of a Model Shelter as a Short-term Response to the Deepening Crisis in Housing." In *Criminology as Peacemaking,* ed. Harold Pepinsky and Richard Quinney, 47–68. Bloomington: Indiana University Press.

Barak, Gregg, ed. 1991b. *Crimes by the Capitalist State: An Introduction to State Criminality.* Albany, NY: State University of New York Press.

Barak, Gregg. 1991c. *Gimmie Shelter: A Social History of Homelessness in America.* Westport, CT: Praeger.

Barak, Gregg. 1994a. "Crime, Criminology, and Human Rights: Toward an Understanding of State Criminality." In *Varieties of Criminology: Readings from a Dynamic Discipline,* ed. Gregg Barak, 253–67. Westport, CT: Praeger.

Barak, Gregg, ed. 1994b. *Media, Process and the Social Construction of Crime: Studies in Newsmaking Criminology.* New York: Garland Press.

Barlow, Hugh. 1990. *Introduction to Criminology.* 5th ed. Glenview, IL: Scott Foresman/Little, Brown.

Barnes, Barry. 1981. *T. S. Kuhn and Social Science.* New York: Columbia University Press.

Barnes, Harry Elmer, and Negley K. Teeters. 1943. *New Horizons in Criminology: The American Crime Problem.* New York: Prentice-Hall.

Baron, Larry, and Murray A. Straus. 1990. *Four Theories of Rape in American Society.* New Haven: Yale University Press.

Bartol, Curt R. 1991. *Criminal Behavior: A Psychological Approach.* 3rd ed. Englewood Cliffs, NJ: Prentice-Hall.

Bartollas, Clemmens, and Simon Dinitz. 1989. *Introduction to Criminology: Order and Disorder.* New York: Harper and Row.

Baudrillard, Jean. 1981. *For a Critique of the Political Economy of the Sign.* St. Louis, MO: Telos Press.

Baudrillard, Jean. 1991. "La Guerre du Golfe n'a pas eu lieu." *Liberation* (March 29).

Baunach, Phyllis Jo. 1985. *Mothers in Prison.* New Brunswick, NJ: Transaction Books.

Beccaria, Cesare. 1764a. *On Crimes and Punishments.* Trans. Henry Paolucci. Indianapolis, IN: Bobbs-Merrill, 1964.

Beccaria, Cesare. 1764b. *On Crimes and Punishments.* Trans. David Yound. Indianapolis, IN: Hackett, 1986.

Beccaria, Cesare. 1776. *An Essay on Crimes and Punishments.* Stanford, CA: Stanford University Press, 1953.

Becker, Gary S. 1968. "Crime and Punishment: An Economic Approach." *Journal of Political Economy* 76(2): 169–217.

Becker, Howard. 1963. *Outsiders: Studies in the Sociology of Deviance.* Revised Edition. New York: Free Press, 1966.

Beirne, Piers. 1991. "Inventing Criminology: The 'Science of Man' in Cesare Beccaria's Dei Delitti E Delle Pene (1764)." *Criminology* 29(4): 777–820.

Beirne, Piers. 1993. *Inventing Criminology: Essays on the Rise of 'Homo Criminalis.'* Albany, NY: SUNY Press.

Beirne, Piers, and James Messerschmidt. 1991. *Criminology.* New York: Harcourt Brace Jovanovich.

Bell, Daniel. 1976. *The Cultural Contradictions of Capitalism.* New York: Basic Books.

Bell, Robert R. 1971. *Social Deviance.* Homewood, IL: Dorsey Press.

Bentham, Jeremy. 1970a [1765a]. *An Introduction to the Principles of Morals and Legislation.* Ed. J. H. Burns and H. L. A. Hart. London: Athlone Press, University of London.

Bentham, Jeremy. 1970b [1765b]. *The Limits of Jurisprudence Defined, Being Part Two of An Introduction to the Principles of Morals and Legislation.* Westport, CT: Greenwood Press.

Bentham, Jeremy. 1789. *An Introduction to the Principles of Morals and Legislation.* London: Pickering.

Berger, Peter, and Thomas Luckmann. 1966. *The Social Construction of Reality.* Garden City, NY: Doubleday.

Berman, Louis. 1928. *The Glands Regulating Personality.* New York: Macmillan.

Bernard, Thomas J. 1984. "Control Criticisms of Strain Theories: An Assessment of Theoretical and Empirical Adequacy." *Journal of Research in Crime and Delinquency* 21: 353–72.

Best, Steven, and Douglas Kellner. 1991. *Postmodern Theory: Critical Interrogations.* Basingstoke, Hants., England: Macmillan.

Bischof, Ledford. 1964. *Interpreting Personality Theories.* New York: Harper and Row.

Black, Donald J. 1976. *The Behavior of Law.* New York: Academic Press.

Black, Donald J., and Albert J. Reiss. 1970. "Police Control of Juveniles." *American Sociological Review* 35: 63–77.

Blau, Judith, and Peter Blau. 1982. "The Cost of Inequality: Metropolitan Structure and Violent Crime." *American Sociological Review* 47: 114–29.

Block, Alan, and William J. Chambliss. 1981. *Organizing Crime.* New York: Elsevier.

Blumer, Herbert. 1969. *Symbolic Interactionism: Perspective and Method.* Englewood Cliffs, NJ: Prentice-Hall.

Bogdan, Robert, and S. Taylor. 1987. "Toward a Sociology of Acceptance: The Other Side of the Study of Deviance." *Social Policy* 18: 34–39.

Bohm, Robert M. 1982. "Radical Criminology: An Explication." *Criminology* 19: 565–89.

Bohman, Michael. 1978. "Some Genetic Aspects of Alcoholism and Criminality." *Archives of General Psychiatry* 35(3): 269–76.

Bonger, Willem. 1916. *Criminality and Economic Conditions.* Boston: Little, Brown.

Bonn, Robert L. 1984. *Criminology.* New York: McGraw-Hill.

Booth, Charles. 1891. *Life and Labour of the People in London.* 17 vols. London: Macmillan.

Bordua, David J. 1961. "Delinquent Subcultures: Sociological Interpretations of Gang Delinquency." *Annals of the American Academy of Political and Social Science* 338: 119–36.

Borgmann, Albert. 1992. *Crossing the Postmodern Divide.* Chicago: University of Chicago Press.

Bottomley, A. Keith. 1979. *Criminology in Focus.* London: Martin Robertson.

Bowker, Lee. 1978. *Women, Crime, and the Criminal Justice System.* Lexington, MA: D.C. Heath.

Bowlby, John. 1946. *Forty-Four Juvenile Thieves: Their Characters and Home-Life.* [Originally published in *International Journal of Psychoanalysis,* Vol. 25 (London: Bailliere, Tindall and Cox, 1944.)]

Box, Steven. 1977. "Hyperactivity: The Scandalous Silence." *New Society* 42(December 1): 458–60.

Box, Steven. 1971. *Deviance, Reality, and Society.* New York: Holt, Rinehart and Winston.

Box, Steven. 1981. *Deviance, Reality and Society.* 2nd ed. New York: Holt, Rinehart and Winston.

Box, Steven. 1983. *Power, Crime, and Mystification.* London: Tavistock.

Box, Steven. 1987. *Recession, Crime and Punishment.* London: Macmillan.

Box, Steven, and Chris Hale. 1986. "Unemployment, Crime, and Imprisonment and the Enduring Problem of Prison Overcrowding." In *Confronting Crime,* ed. Roger Matthews and Jock Young. London: Sage.

Boyd, Susan, and Elizabeth Sheehy. 1986. "Feminist Perspectives on Law: Canadian Theory and Practice." *Canadian Journal of Women and the Law* 2: 1–52.

Boyle, James. 1977. *A Sense of Freedom.* London: Pan Books.

Braithwaite, John. 1989. *Crime, Shame and Reintegration.* Cambridge: Cambridge University Press.

Brantingham, Paul J., and Patricia L. Brantingham. 1978. "Notes on the Geometry of Crime." Paper presented at the International Symposium on Selected Criminological Topics. Stockholm, Sweden.

Brantingham, Paul J., and Patricia L. Brantingham. 1981. "Introduction: The Dimension of Crime." In *Environmental Criminology*, ed. Paul J. Brantingham and Patricia L. Brantingham, 7–26. Beverly Hills, CA: Sage.

Brantingham, Paul J., and Patricia L. Brantingham. 1984. *Patterns of Crime.* New York: Macmillan.

Brants, C., and E. Kok. 1986. "Penal Sanctions as a Feminist Strategy: A Contradiction in Terms? Pornography and Criminal Law in the Netherlands." *International Journal of the Sociology of Law* 14(3): 269–86.

Briggs, John, and David F. Peat. 1989. *Turbulent Mirror: An Illustrated Guide to Chaos Theory and the Science of Wholeness.* New York: Harper and Row.

Brower, George D., and Isaac Ehrlich. 1987. "On the Issue of Causality in the Economic Model of Crime and Law Enforcement: Some Theoretical Considerations and Experimental Evidence." *The American Economic Review*, 77: 99–106.

Brown, Geoff. 1977. *Sabotage: A Study in Industrial Conflict.* Nottingham, England: Spokesman Books.

Brownmiller, Susan. 1975. *Against Our Will: Men, Women and Rape.* New York: Simon and Schuster.

Bufford, Rodger K. 1989. "Demonic Influence and Mental Disorders." *Journal of Psychology and Christianity* 8(2): 35–48.

Bullough, Vern, and Bonnie Bullough. 1977. *Sin, Sickness and Sanity: A History of Sexual Attitudes.* New York: Meridan.

Burgess, Ernest W. 1925. "The Growth of the City." In *The City*, ed. Robert E. Park, E. W. Burgess, and R. D. McKenzie. Chicago: University of Chicago Press.

Burgess, P. K. 1972. "Eysenck's Theory of Criminality: A New Approach." *British Journal of Criminology* 12(1): 74–82.

Burgess, Robert L., and Ronald L. Akers. 1966. "A Differential Association-Reinforcement Theory of Criminal Behavior." *Social Problems* 14: 128–47.

Burkhart, Kathryn. 1976. *Women in Prison.* Garden City, NY: Doubleday.

Bursik, Robert J. 1984. "Urban Dynamics and Ecological Studies of Delinquency." *Social Forces* 63: 393–413.

Bursik, Robert J., Jr. 1986. "Ecological Stability and the Dynamics of Delinquency." In *Communities and Crime.* Series in Crime and Justice: An Annual Review of Research, Vol. 8, ed. Albert J. Reiss, Jr., and Michael Tonry, 35–66. Chicago: University of Chicago Press.

Bursik, Robert J., Jr. 1988. "Social Disorganization and Theories of Crime and Delinquency: Problems and Prospects." *Criminology* 26: 519–51.

Bursik, Robert J., Jr. 1989. "Political Decision-making and Ecological Models of Delinquency: Conflict and Consensus." In *Theoretical Integration in the Study of Deviance and Crime*, ed. S. F. Messner, M. D. Krohn, and A. E. Liska. Albany: SUNY Press.

Bursik, Robert J., Jr., and Harold G. Grasmick. 1993a. *Neighborhoods and Crime: The Dimensions of Effective Community Control.* New York: Lexington Books.

Bursik, Robert J., Jr., and Harold G. Grasmick. 1993b. "Economic Deprivation and Neighborhood Crime Rates, 1960–1980." *Law and Society Review* 27(2): 263–83.

Bursik, Robert J., Jr., and Jim Webb. 1982. "Community Change and Patterns of Delinquency." *Social Forces* 88: 24–42.

Burton, Velmer S., Jr., and R. Gregory Dunaway. 1994. "Strain, Relative Deprivation, and Middle-Class Delinquency." In *Varieties of Criminology: Readings from a Dynamic Discipline*, ed. Gregg Barak, 79–95. Westport, CT: Praeger.

Cadoret, Remi J., Collen Cain, and Raymond Crowe. 1983. "Evidence for a Gene Environment Interaction in the Development of Adolescent Anti-social Behavior." *Behavior Genetics* 13: 301–310.

Cadoret, Remi J., Thomas O'Gorman, Ed Troughton, and Ellen Heywood. 1985. "Alcoholism and Anti-social Personality: Interrelationships, Genetic and Environmental Factors." *Archives of General Psychiatry* 42: 161–67.

Cain, Maureen. 1986. "Realism, Feminism, Methodology and Law." *International Journal of the Sociology of Law* 14(3/4): 255–67.

Cain, Maureen. 1989a. "New Directions in Feminist Criminology." *Critical Criminologist* 1(4): 3–4.

Cain, Maureen. 1989b. *Growing Up Good: Policing the Behavior of Girls in Europe.* London: Sage.

Cain, Maureen. 1990. "Toward Transgressions: New Directions in Feminist Criminology." *International Journal of the Sociology of Law* 18(1): 1–18.

Cantor, Robin, Stuart Henry, and Steve Rayner. 1993. *Making Markets: An Interdisciplinary Perspective on Economic Exchange.* Foreward by Amitai Etzioni. New York: Greenwood Press.

Carey, Gregory. 1992. "Twin Imitation for Antisocial Behavior: Implications for Genetic and Family Research." *Journal of Abnormal Psychology* 101(1): 18–25.

Carlen, Pat. 1983. *Women's Imprisonment: A Study in Social Control.* London: Routledge and Kegan Paul.

Carlen, Pat. 1985. *Criminal Women: Autobiographical Accounts.* Cambridge: Polity Press.

Carlen, Pat, and Ann Worrall, eds. 1987. *Gender, Crime and Justice.* Milton Keynes, England: Open University Press.

Carr, Lowell J. 1950. *Delinquency Control.* New York: Harper and Row.

Carringella-MacDonald, Susan, and Drew Humphries. 1991. "Sexual Assault, Women, and Community Organizing to Prevent Sexual Violence. In *Criminology as Peacemaking*, ed. Harold Pepinsky and Richard Quinney, 98–113. Bloomington: Indiana University Press.

Carson, W. G. 1971. "White-Collar Crime and the Enforcement of Factory Legislation." In *The Sociology of Crime and Delinquency in Britain,* Vol. 1, *The British Tradition*, ed. W. G. Carson and Paul Wiles, 220–36. London: Martin Robertson.

Carson, W. G. 1979. "The Conventionalization of Early Factory Crime." *International Journal of the Sociology of Law* 76: 746–63.

Castro, Ginette. 1990. *American Feminism—A Contemporary History.* Trans. from the French by Elizabeth Loverde-Bagwell. New York: New York University Press.

Caulfield, Susan, and Nancy Wonders. 1994. "Gender and Justice: Feminist Contributions to Criminology." In *Varieties of Criminology: Readings from a Dynamic Discipline*, ed. Gregg Barak, 213–29. Westport, CT: Praeger.

Cernkovich, Stephen A., and Peggy C. Giordano. 1992. "School Bonding, Race and Delinquency." *Criminology* 30: 261–91.

Cesaro, Grazia. 1988. "Il modello implicitio di personalita' nel codice penale." *Ricerche di Psicologia* 12(3–4): 53–67.

Chambliss, William. 1975. "Toward a Political Economy of Crime." *Theory and Society* 2: 149–70.

Chambliss, William. 1979. "On Lawmaking." *British Journal of Law and Society* 6: 149–71.
Chambliss, William. 1988. *On the Take: From Petty Crooks to Presidents*. 2nd ed. Bloomington: Indiana University Press.
Chambliss, William, and Robert B. Seidman. 1982 [1971]. *Law, Order and Power*. 2nd ed. Reading, MA: Addison-Wesley.
Chapman, Ivan. 1977. "A Critique of Merton's Typology of Modes of Individual Adaption." *Quarterly Journal of Ideology* 1: 13–18.
Chesney-Lind, Meda. 1973. "Judicial Enforcement of the Female Sex Role: The Family Court and the Female Delinquent." *Issues in Criminology* 8: 51–69.
Chesney-Lind, Meda. 1989. "Girl's Crime and Woman's Place: Toward a Feminist Model of Female Delinquency." *Crime and Delinquency* 35(1): 5–29.
Chesney-Lind, Meda, and Randall G. Sheldon. 1992. *Girls, Delinquency and Juvenile Justice*. Pacific Grove, CA: Brooks/Cole.
Christiansen, Karl O. 1974. "Seriousness of Criminality and Concordance among Danish Twins." In *Crime Criminology and Public Policy*, ed. Roger Hood. London: Heinemann.
Christiansen, Karl O. 1977a. "A Review of Criminality among Twins." In *Biosocial Bases of Criminal Behavior*, ed. Sarnoff A. Mednick and Karl O. Christiansen. New York: Gardiner Press.
Christiansen, Karl O. 1977b. "A Preliminary Study of Criminality among Twins." In *Biosocial Bases of Criminal Behavior*, ed. Sarnoff A. Mednick and Karl O. Christiansen. New York: Gardiner Press.
Clark, Gerald, et al. 1970. "Sex Chromosomes, Crime and Psychosis." *American Journal of Psychiatry* 126(11): 1659–63.
Clark, L., and D. Lewis. 1977. *Rape: The Price of Coercive Sexuality*. Toronto: Women's Press.
Clarke, Ronald V. 1983. "Situational Crime Prevention: Its Theoretical Basis and Practical Scope." In *Crime and Justice: An Annual Review of Research*, Vol. 4, ed. Michael Tonry and Norval Morris, 225–256. Chicago: University of Chicago Press.
Clarke, Ronald V., and Ronald V. Cornish, eds. 1983. *Crime Control in Britain: A Review of Policy and Research*. Albany: SUNY Press.
Clarke, Ronald V., and Derek B. Cornish. 1985. "Modeling Offenders' Decisions: A Framework for Research and Policy." In *Crime and Justice: An Annual Review of Research*, Vol. 6, ed. Michael Tonry and Norval Morris, 147–185. Chicago: University of Chicago Press.
Clarke, Ronald V., and Patricia Mayhew. 1980. *Designing Out Crime*. London: Her Majesty's Printing Office.
Cleckley, Hervey. 1955. *The Mask of Sanity*. St Louis, MO: Mosby.
Clinard, Marshall B. 1964. "The Theoretical Implications of Anomie and Deviant Behavior." In *Anomie and Deviant Behavior: A Discussion and Critique*, ed. Marshall B. Clinard. New York: Free Press.
Clinard, Marshall B. 1983. *Corporate Ethics and Crime: The Role of Middle Management*. Beverly Hills, CA: Sage.
Cloward, Richard. 1959. "Illegitimate Means, Anomie and Deviant Behavior." *American Sociological Review* 24: 164–76.
Cloward, Richard A., and Lloyd E. Ohlin. 1960. *Delinquency and Opportunity—A Theory of Delinquent Gangs*. New York: Free Press.
Cochrane, Raymond. 1974. "Crime and Personality: Theory and Evidence." *Bulletin of the British Psychological Society* 27(94): 19–22.
Cohen, Albert K. 1955. *Delinquent Boys: The Culture of the Gang*. Glencoe, IL: Free Press.
Cohen, Albert K. 1966. *Deviance and Control*. Englewood Cliffs, NJ: Prentice-Hall.
Cohen, Joseph. 1941. "The Geography of Crime." *The Annals of the American Academy of Political and Social Science* 217: 29–37.
Cohen, Lawrence E., and Marcus Felson. 1979. "Social Change and Crime Rate Trends: A Routine Activities Approach." *American Sociological Review* 44: 588–608.
Cohen, Lawrence E., and Richard Machalek. 1988. "A General Theory of Expropriative Crime: An Evolutionary Ecological Approach." *American Journal of Sociology* 94: 465–501.

Cohen, Stanley. 1980 [1972]. *Folk Devils and Moral Panics: The Creation of Mods and Rockers*. New York: St. Martin's Press.

Cohen, Stanley. 1979. "The Punitive City: Notes on the Dispersal of Social Control." *Contemporary Crisis* 3: 339–63.

Cohen, Stanley. 1985. *Visions of Social Control*. Cambridge: Polity Press.

Cohen, Stanley. 1990. "Intellectual Scepticism and Political Commitment: The Case of Radical Criminology." Bonger Memorial Lecture (May 14), University of Amsterdam.

Cohen, Stanley. 1991. "Talking About Torture in Israel." *Tikkun* 6(6): 23–30, 89–90.

Cohen, Stanley. 1993. "Human Rights and Crimes of the State: The Culture of Denial." *Australian and New Zealand Journal of Criminology* 26: 97–115.

Cole, Stephen. 1975. "The Growth of Scientific Knowledge." In *The Idea of Social Structure*, ed. Lewis A. Coser. New York: Harcourt Brace Jovanovich.

Collins, Hugh. 1987. "Roberto Unger and the Critical Legal Studies Movement." *Journal of Law and Society* 14: 387–410.

Collins, Randall. 1981. "On the Microfoundations of Macrosociology." *American Journal of Sociology* 86: 984–1014.

Colson, Charles. 1980. "Toward an Understanding of the Origins of Crime." In *Crime and the Responsible Community*, ed. John Stott and Nick Miller. London: Hodder and Stoughton.

Colvin, Mark, and John Pauly. 1983. "A Critique of Criminology: Toward an Integrated Structural-Marxist Theory of Delinquency Production." *American Journal of Sociology* 89: 513–51.

Conger, Rand. 1976. "Social Control and Social Learning Models of Delinquent Behavior: A Synthesis." *Criminology* 14: 17–40.

Conklin, John E. 1989. *Criminology*. 3rd ed. New York: Macmillan.

Cooley, Charles Horton. 1902. *Human Nature and the Social Order*. New York: Scribner's.

Cooley, Charles Horton. 1909. *Social Organization: A Study of the Larger Mind*. New York: Scribner's.

Cornish, Derek B., and Ronald V. Clarke., eds. 1986. *The Reasoning Criminal*. New York: Springer Verlag.

Cornish, Derek B., and Ronald V. Clarke. 1987. "Understanding Crime Displacement: An Application of Rational Choice Theory." *Criminology* 25(4): 933–47.

Corsini, Raymond. 1949. "Criminal Psychology." In *Encyclopedia of Criminology*, ed. Vernon C. Branham and Samuel B. Kutash, 108–115. New York: Philosophical Library.

Cortes, J. B., and F. M. Gatti. 1972. *Delinquency and Crime: A Biopsychsocial Approach*. New York: Seminar Press.

Coser, Lewis. 1956. *The Functions of Social Conflict*. New York: Macmillan.

Coughlin, Ellen K. 1993. "Miami a Unique Sociological Laboratory, Researchers on Immigration Find." *The Chronicle of Higher Education* (September 1): 6–7, 10–11.

Crabtree, Adam. 1985. *Multiple Man: Explorations in Possession*. New York: Praeger.

Craig, Maude M., and Selma J. Glick. 1963. "Ten Years of Experience with the Glueck Prediction Table." *Crime and Delinquency* 9: 249–61.

Cressey, Donald R. 1953. *Other People's Money*. Glencoe, IL: Free Press.

Cressey, Donald R. 1954. "The Differential Association Theory and Compulsive Crimes." *Journal of Criminal Law and Criminology* 45: 49–64.

Cressey, Donald R. 1960. "The Theory of Differential Association: An Introduction." *Social Problems* 8: 2–6.

Cressey, Donald R. 1987 [1965]. "The Respectable Criminal." In *Social Problems: A Critical Thinking Approach*, ed. Paul J. Baker and Louis E. Anderson, 246–51. Belmont, CA: Wadsworth.

Cressey, Donald R. 1970. "The Respectable Criminal." In *Modern Criminals*, ed. James Short 105–16. New York: Transaction-Aldine.

Cullen, Francis T. 1984. *Rethinking Crime and Deviance Theory: The Emergence of a Structuring Tradition*. Totowa, NJ: Rowman and Allanheld.

Cullen, Francis T. 1988. "Were Cloward and Ohlin Strain Theorists? Delinquency and Opportunity Revisited." *Journal of Research in Crime and Delinquency* 25: 214–41.

Curran, Daniel J., and Claire M. Renzetti. 1994. *Theories of Crime*. Boston: Allyn and Bacon.

Currie, Dawn H. 1989. "Women and the State: A Statement on Feminist Theory." *Critical Criminologist* 1(2): 4–5.

Currie, Dawn H. 1990. "Battered Women and the State: From the Failure of Theory to a Theory of Failure." *Journal of Human Justice* 1(2): 77–96.

Currie, Dawn H. 1991. "Challenging Privilege: Feminist Struggles in the Canadian Context." *Critical Criminologist* 3(1): 1–2, 10–13.

Currie, Dawn H. 1992. "Feminist Encounters with Postmodernism: Exploring the Impasse of the Debates on Patriarchy and Law." *Canadian Journal of Women and the Law* 5(1): 63–86.

Currie, Dawn H., and Marlee Kline. 1991. "Challenging Privilege: Women, Knowledge and Feminist Struggles." *Journal of Human Justice* 2: 1–36.

Currie, Elliot P. 1968. "Crime Without Criminals: Witchcraft and Its Control in Renaissance Europe." *Law and Society Review* 3: 7–32.

Dahrendorf, Ralf. 1959. *Class and Class Conflict in an Industrial Society*. London: Routledge and Kegan Paul.

Dalgard, Odd S., and Einar Kringlen. 1976. "A Norwegian Twin Study of Criminology." *British Journal of Criminology* 16: 213–32.

Dallos, Rudi. 1981. "Moral Development and Crime: The Development of the Family." In *Crime and Society*, ed. Mike Fitzgerald, Gregor McLennan, and Jennie Pawson, 371–402. London: Routledge and Kegan Paul/Open University Press.

Dalton, Katherine. 1961. "Menstruation and Crime." *British Medical Journal* 3: 1752–53.

Daly, Kathleen. 1989. "Gender and Varieties of White-Collar Crime." *Criminology* 27(4): 769–93.

Daly, Kathleen. 1990. "Reflections on Feminist Legal Thought." *Social Justice* 17(3): 7–24.

Daly, Kathleen. 1991. "Feminists Working Within and Against Criminology." *Critical Criminologist* 3(1): 5–6, 11.

Daly, Kathleen. 1992. "Women's Pathways to Felony Court: Feminist Theories of Lawbreaking and Problems of Representation." *Review of Law and Women's Studies* 2(1):1–42.

Daly, Kathleen, and Meda Chesney-Lind. 1988. "Feminism and Criminology." *Justice Quarterly* 5(4): 497–538.

Danner, Mona J. E. 1991. "Socialist Feminism: A Brief Introduction." In *New Directions in Critical Criminology*, ed. Brian D. MacLean and Dragan Milovanovic, 51–54. Vancouver: Collective Press.

Davidson, R. N. 1981. *Crime and Environment*. London: Croom Helm.

Davie, Maurice R. 1937. "The Pattern of Urban Growth." In *Studies in the Science of Society*, ed. George P. Murdock. New Haven: Yale University Press.

Davis, Nanette J. 1975. *Sociological Constructions of Deviance: Perspectives and Issues in the Field*. Dubuque, IA: Wm. C. Brown.

Dawley, David. 1992. *A Nation of Lords*. 2nd ed. Prospect Heights, IL: Waveland Press.

Delmar, Rosalind. 1986. "What Is Feminism?" In *What Is Feminism*, ed. Juliet Mitchell and Ann Oakley, 8–83. New York: Pantheon.

Derrida, Jacques. 1970. "Structure, Sign and Play in the Discourse of Human Sciences." In *The Languages of Criticism and the Sciences of Man*, 247–65. Baltimore: Johns Hopkins University Press.

Derrida, Jacques. 1973. *Speech and Phenomena*. Evanston, IL: Northwestern University Press.

Derrida, Jacques. 1981. *Positions*. Chicago: University of Chicago Press.

Dewey, John. 1886. *Psychology*. New York: Harper and Row.

Dewey, John. 1922. *Human Nature and Human Conduct*. New York: Henry Holt.

Dickson, Donald T. 1968. "Bureaucracy and Morality: An Organizational Perspective on a Moral Crusade." *Social Problems* 16: 143–56.

DiLalla, Lisbath F., and Irving I. Gottesman. 1989. "Heterogeneity of Causes for Delinquency and Criminality: Lifespan Perspectives." *Development and Psychopathology* 1(4): 339–49.

Ditton, Jason. 1977. *Part-Time Crime: An Ethnography of Fiddling and Pilferage*. London: Macmillan.

Ditton, Jason. 1979. *Controlology*. London: Macmillan.

Di Tullio, Benigno. 1969a. "Personality and Clinical Criminology." *Monographs of the Criminal Law Education and Research Center* 3: 13–36.

Di Tullio, Benigno. 1969b. "The Causes of Criminality." *Monographs of the Criminal Law Education and Research Center* 3: 53–79.

Dorfman, Andrea. 1984. "The Criminal Mind: Body Chemistry and Nutrition May Lie at the Root of Crime." *Science Digest* 92 (October): 44–47.

Douglas, Jack, ed. 1971. *Crime and Justice in American Society.* Indianapolis, IN: Bobbs-Merrill.

Douglas, Jack D., ed. 1972. *Research on Deviance.* New York: Random House.

Downes, David, and Paul Rock. 1982. *Understanding Deviance: A Guide to the Sociology of Crime and Rule Breaking.* Oxford: Clarendon Press.

Dubin, Robert. 1959. "Deviant Behavior and Social Structure: Continuities in Social Theory." *American Sociological Review* 24: 147–64.

Dugdale, Richard L. 1877. *The Jukes: A Study in Crime, Pauperism, Disease and Heredity.* New York: Putnam.

Durkheim, Emile. 1933 [1893]. *The Division of Labor in Society.* New York: Free Press.

Durkheim, Emile. 1938. *The Rules of Sociological Method.* 8th ed., trans. Sarah A. Solovay and John H. Mueller, ed. G. E. G. Catlin. New York: Free Press.

Durkheim, Emile. 1950 [1895]. *The Rules of Sociological Method*, ed. G. E. G. Catlin, trans. S. A. Solovay and J. H. Mueller. Glencoe, IL: Free Press.

Durkheim, Emile. 1982. *The Rules of Sociological Method and Selected Texts on Sociology and Its Method*, ed. Steven Lukes, trans. W. D. Halls. London: Macmillan.

Durkheim, Emile. 1951 [1897]. *Suicide: A Study in Sociology.* New York: Free Press.

Duster, Troy. 1970. *The Legislation of Morality.* New York: Free Press.

Dworkin, Andrea 1981. *Men Possessing Women.* London: Women's Press.

Earle, Alice Morse. 1896. *Curious Punishments of Bygone Days.* Chicago: Herbert S. Stone.

Edwards, Susan. 1981. *Female Sexuality and the Law.* London: Sage.

Edwards, Susan. 1989. "Sex/Gender, Sexism and Criminal Justices, Some Theoretical Considerations." *International Journal of the Sociology of Law* 17(2): 165–84.

Edwards, Susan. 1990. "Violence Against Women: Feminism and the Law." In *Feminist Perspectives in Criminology*, ed. Loraine Gelsthorpe and Allison Morris, 144–159. Milton Keynes, England: Open University Press.

Ehrlich, Isaac. 1973. "Participation in Illegitimate Activities: An Economic Analysis." *Journal of Political Economy* 81: 521–67.

Ehrlich, Isaac. 1982. "The Market for Offences and the Public Enforcement of Laws: An Equilibrium Analysis." *British Journal of Social Psychology* 21(2): 107–20.

Eisenberg, L. 1972. "The Human Nature of Human Nature." *Science* 176: 123–28.

Einstadter, Werner. 1992. "Asymmetries of Control: Surveillance, Intrusion, and Corporate Theft of Privacy." *Justice Quarterly* 9(2): 285–98.

Einstadter, Werner, and Stuart Henry. 1991. "The Inversion of the Invasion of Privacy." *The Critical Criminologist* 3(4): 5–6.

Eisenstein, Zillah. 1979. *Capitalist Patriarchy and the Case for Socialist Feminism.* New York: Monthly Review Press.

Ellis, Havelock. 1901. *The Criminal.* 3rd ed. London: Walter Scott.

Ellis, Lee. 1987. "Criminal Behavior and r/K Selection: An Extension of Gene Based Evolutionary Theory." *Deviant Behavior* 8(2): 149–76.

Ellis, Lee. 1988. "Neurohormonal Bases of Varying Tendencies to Learn Delinquent and Criminal Behavior." In *Behavioral Approaches to Crime and Delinquency*, ed. E. Morris and C. Braukmann. New York: Plenum.

Ellis, Lee. 1989. "Sex Differences in Criminality: An Explanation Based on the Concept of r/K Selection." *Mankind Quarterly* 30(1–2): 17–37.

Elliott, Delbert, Susan Agerton, and R. Canter. 1979. "An Integrated Theoretical Perspective on Delinquent Behavior." *Journal of Research on Crime and Delinquency* 16: 3–27.

Elliott, Delbert, David Huizinga, and Susan Ageton. 1985. *Explaining Delinquency and Drug Use.* Beverly Hills, CA: Sage.

Emerson, Robert M. 1969. *Judging Delinquents, Context and Process in Juvenile Court*. Chicago: Aldine.

Empey, LaMar T. 1982. *American Delinquency, Its Meaning and Construction*. 2nd ed. Homewood: Dorsey Press.

Empey, LaMar T., and Mark C. Stafford. 1991. *American Delinquency, Its Meaning and Construction*. 3rd ed. Belmont: Wadsworth.

Engels, Fredrich. 1845. *The Condition of the Working Class in England*. New York: International.

Erikson, E. 1950. *Childhood and Society*. Harmondsworth, England: Penguin.

Erikson, Kai T. 1966. *Wayward Puritans: A Study in Sociology of Deviance*. New York: Wiley.

Erlanger, Howard S. 1979. "Estrangement, Machismo, and Gang Violence." *Social Science Quarterly* 60(2): 235–48.

Estabrook, Arthur H. 1916. *The Jukes in 1915*. New York: Washington, DC: Carnegie Institute.

Etzioni, Amitai. 1968. *The Active Society*. New York: Free Press.

Evan, William M. 1990. *Social Structure and Law: Theoretical and Empirical Perspectives*. Newbury Park, CA: Sage.

Everett, Warren. 1970. "Introduction." In Jeremy Bentham's *The Limits of Jurisprudence Defined, Being Part Two of An Introduction to the Principles of Morals and Legislation*. Westport, CT: Greenwood Press.

Eysenck, Hans J. 1977 [1964]. *Crime and Personality*. London: Routledge and Kegan Paul.

Eysenck, Hans J. 1983. "Personality, Conditioning and Anti-social Behavior." In *Personality Theory, Moral Development and Criminal Behavior*, ed. S. Laufer and J. M. Day. Lexington, MA: Lexington Books.

Eysenck, H. J., and G. H. Gudjonsson. 1989. *The Causes and Cures of Criminality*. New York: Plenum.

Fadiman, James, and Donald Kewman. 1973. *Exploring Madness: Experience, Theory and Research*. Montery, CA: Brooks/Cole.

Faith, Karlene. 1993. "An Interview with Freda Adler." *The Critical Criminologist* 5(1): 3–4, 6–10.

Faludi, Susan. 1991. *Backlash: The Undeclared War Against American Women*. New York: Crown.

Faris, Ellsworth. 1944. "Robert E. Park: 1864–1944." *American Sociological Review* 9: 322–25.

Farnworth, Margaret, and Michael J. Leiber. 1989. "Strain Theory Revisited: Educational Goals, Educational Means and Delinquency." *American Sociological Review* 54: 263–74.

Fawcett, Brian. 1991. *Unusual Circumstances, Interesting Times and Impolite Interventions*. Vancouver: New Star Books.

Feldman, M. P. 1977. *Criminal Behavior: A Psychological Analysis*. London: Wiley.

Felson, Marcus. 1986. "Routine Activities and Crime Prevention in the Developing Metropolis." In *The Reasoning Criminal*, ed. Derek B. Cornish and Ronald V. Clarke. York: Springer Verlag.

Felson, Marcus. 1987. "Routine Activities, Social Controls, Rational Decisions and Criminal Outcomes." *Criminology* 25: 911–31.

Felson, Marcus, and Lawrence E. Cohen. 1980. "Human Ecology and Crime: A Routine Activities Approach." *Human Ecology* 8(4): 389–406.

Felson, Marcus, and Lawrence E. Cohen. 1981. "Molding Crime Rate Trends—A Criminal Opportunity Perspective." *Journal of Research in Crime and Delinquency* 18: 138–64.

Ferman, A. Louis, Stuart Henry, and Michele Hoyman, eds. 1987. *The Informal Economy: The Annals of the American Academy of Political and Social Science,* Vol. 493. Newbury Park, CA: Sage.

Ferman, Louis A., Louise E. Berndt, and Stuart Henry, eds. 1993. *Work Beyond Employment in Advanced Capitalist Countries: Classic and Contemporary Perspectives on the Informal Economy*. Vol. I, *Concepts, Evidence and Measurement*. Vol. II, *Revisions and Criticism*. Lewiston: Edwin Mellen Press.

Ferrell, Jeff. 1993. *Crimes of Style: Urban Graffiti and the Politics of Criminality*. New York: Garland.

Ferrell, Jeff. 1994. "Confronting the Agenda of Authority: Critical Criminology, Anarchism." In *Varieties of Criminology: Readings from a Dynamic Discipline*, ed. Gregg Barak, 161–78. Westport, CT: Praeger.

Ferri, Enrico. 1886. 1917. *Criminal Sociology*. Boston: Little, Brown.

Ferri, Enrico. 1897. *Criminal Sociology*. New York: Appleton.

Filstead, William J. 1972. *An Introduction to Deviance: Readings in the Process of Making Deviants*. Chicago: Markham.

Fink, Arthur. 1938. *Causes of Crime*. Philadelphia: University of Pennsylvania Press.

Fishbein, Diana. H. 1990. "Biological Perspective in Criminology." *Criminology* 28: 27–72.

Fishbein, Diana. H., and Robert W. Thatcher. 1986. "New Diagnostic Methods in Criminology: Assessing Organic Sources of Behavioral Disorders." *Journal of Research in Crime and Delinquency* 23(3): 240–67.

Fisher, Seymour, and Roger Greenberg. 1981 [1977]. *The Scientific Credibility of Freud's Theories and Therapy*. New York: Basic Books.

Fitzpatrick, Peter. 1984. "Law and Societies." *Osgoode Hall Law Journal* 22: 115–38.

Flax, Jane. 1990. "Postmodernism and Gender Relations in Feminist Theory." In *Feminism/Postmodernism*, ed. Linda J. Nicholson. New York: Routledge, Chapman and Hall.

Fletcher, J. 1848. "Moral and Educational Statistics of England." *Journal of the Statistical Society* 10: 193; 11: 344; 12: 151.

Fogel, David. 1975. *We Are the Living Proof: The Justice Model for Corrections*. Cincinnati: Anderson.

Fogel, David. 1977. "Pursuing Justice in Corrections." In *Justice and Punishment*, ed. J. Cederblom and W. Blizek. Cambridge, MA: Ballinger.

Forefreedom, Ann. 1992. "Feminist Witchcraft in Today's World." *On the Issues* 23: 22–27.

Foucault, Michel. 1977. *Discipline and Punish*. Harmondsworth, England: Allen Lane.

Foucault, Michel. 1980. *Power/Knowledge: Selected Interviews and Other Writings 1972–1977*, ed. Colin Gordon. Brighton, England: Harvester Press.

Fox, Richard G. 1971. "The XYY Offender: A Modern Myth." *Journal of Criminal Law Criminology and Police Science* 62: 59–73.

Fox, Vernon. 1976. *Introduction to Criminology*. Englewod Cliffs, NJ: Prentice-Hall.

Frazier, Charles E., and John K. Cochran. 1986. "Official Intervention, Diversion from the Juvenile Justice System, and Dynamics of Human Service Work." *Crime and Delinquency* 32: 147–76.

Freud, Sigmund. 1954 [1895]. *The Origins of Psychoanalysis*. New York: Basic Books.

Freud, Sigmund. 1915. *Der Verbrecher aus Schuldbewusstsein. Gesammelte Schriften*, Vol. 10. Vienna: Internationaler. Psychoanalytsischer Verlag.

Freud, Sigmund. 1923. *The Ego and the Id*. Trans. J. Riviere. London: Hogarth Press.

Freud, Sigmund. 1930. *Civilization and Its Discontents*. Garden City, NY: Doubleday.

Freud, Sigmund. 1940–52. *Gesammelte Werke*. 18 vols. London: Imago.

Freud, Sigmund. 1946. *The Ego and the Mechanisms of Defence*. Trans. C. Baines. New York: International Universities Press.

Freud, Sigmund. 1950. "Criminals from a Sense of Guilt." In *Gesammelte Werke*, Vol. 14, 332–33. London: Imago.

Friday, Paul, and Jerald Hage. 1976. "Youth Crime in Post-Industrial Societies: An Integrated Perspective." *Criminology* 14(3): 347–68.

Friedlander, Kate. 1947. *The Psychoanalytical Approach to Juvenile Delinquency*. London: International Universities Press.

Gabor, Thomas M., and Julian V. Roberts. 1990a. "New Wine in Old Bottles: Research on Crime and Race." *Canadian Journal of Criminology* 32(2): 291–313.

Gabor, Thomas M., and Julian V. Roberts. 1990b. "Rushton on Race and Crime. The Evidence Remains Unconvincing." *Canadian Journal of Criminology* 32(2): 335–43.

Gabrielli, William F., and Sarnoff Mednick. 1983. "Genetic Correlates of Criminal Behavior." *American Behavioral Scientist* 27: 59–74.

Gabrielli, William F., and Sarnoff Mednick. 1984. "Urban Environment, Genetics and Crime." *Criminology* 22(4): 645–52.

Gagnier, Regena. 1990. "Feminist Post-modernism: The End of Feminism or the Ends of Theory." In *Theoretical Perspectives on Sexual Difference*, ed. Deborah L. Rhode. New Haven, CT: Yale University Press.

Galliher, John F. 1989. *Criminology: Human Rights, Criminal Law and Crime*. Englewood Cliffs, NJ: Prentice-Hall.

Garafalo, Raffaelle. 1914. *Criminology*. Boston: Little, Brown.

Gardiner, Richard A. 1978. *Design for Safe Neighborhoods: The Environmental Security Planning and Design Process*. Washington, DC: LEAA-U.S. Department of Justice.

Garfinkel, Harold. 1956. "Conditions of Successful Degradation Ceremonies." *American Journal of Sociology* 61: 420–24.

Garza, Christine. 1992. "Postmodern Paradigms and Chicana Feminist Thought: Creating a Space and Language." *Critical Criminologist* 4 (3/4): 1–2, 11–13.

Geary, Roger. 1985. *Policing Industrial Disputes 1893 to 1985*. New York: Cambridge University Press.

Geis, Gilbert. 1960. "Jeremy Bentham 1748–1832." In *Pioneers in Criminology*, 2nd ed., ed. Herman Mannheim, 51–68. Montclair, NJ: Patterson Smith.

Gelsthorpe, Loraine. 1989. *Sexism and the Female Offender*. Aldershot: Gower Press.

Gelsthorpe, Loraine, and Allison Morris. 1988. "Feminism and Criminology in Britain." In *A History of British Criminology*, ed. Paul Rock. Oxford: Clarendon Press.

Gelsthorpe, Loraine, and Allison Morris, eds. 1990. *Feminist Perspectives in Criminology*. Philadelphia: Open University Press.

Georges-Abeyie, Daniel E. 1981. "Studying Black Crime: A Realistic Approach." In *Environmental Criminology*, ed. Paul J. Brantingham and Patricia L. Brantingham, 97–109. Beverly Hills, CA: Sage.

Georges-Abeyie, Daniel E., and Keith D. Harries, eds. 1980. *Crime: A Spatial Perspective*. New York: Columbia University Press.

Geras, N. 1983. *Marx and Human Nature: Refutation of a Legend*. London: New Left Books.

Gettis, Alan. 1976. "Psychotherapy as Exorcism." *Journal of Religion and Health* 15(3): 188–90.

Gibbons, Don C. 1992. *Society, Crime and Criminal Behavior*. 6th ed. Englewood Cliffs, NJ: Prentice-Hall.

Gibbons, Don C. 1994. *Talking About Crime and Criminals: Problems and Issues in Theory Development in Criminology*. Englewood Cliffs, NJ: Prentice-Hall.

Gibbs, Jack P. 1966. "Conceptions of Deviant Behavior: The Old and the New." *Pacific Sociological Review* 14: 20–37.

Gibbs, Jack P. 1989. *Control: Sociology's Central Notion*. Urbana, IL: University of Illinois Press.

Giddens, Anthony. 1984. *The Constitution of Society: Outline of the Theory of Structuration*. Oxford: Polity Press.

Giddens, Anthony. 1987. *Sociology: A Brief but Critical Introduction*. 2nd ed. San Diego, CA: Harcourt Brace Jovanovich.

Giddens, Anthony. 1990. *Consequences of Modernity*. Stanford, CA: Stanford University Press.

Gill, O. 1977. *Luke Street: Housing Policy, Conflict and the Creation of the Delinquency Area*. London: Macmillan.

Glazer, Barney, and Anslem Strauss. 1971. *Status Passage*. London: Routledge and Kegan Paul.

Glazer, Daniel. 1978. *Crime in Our Changing Society*. New York: Holt, Rinehart and Winston.

Gleick, James. 1987. *Chaos*. New York: Viking.

Glueck, Sheldon, and Elinor Glueck. 1950. *Unraveling Juvenile Delinquency*. New York: Commonwealth Fund.

Glyde, J. 1856. "Localities of Crime in Suffolk." *Journal of the Statistical Society* 19: 102ff.

Goddard, Henry H. 1912. *The Kallikak Family: A Study in the Heredity of Feeblemindedness*. London: Macmillan.

Godwin, William. 1946 [1793]. *Political Justice*. 3rd ed. Toronto: University of Toronto Press.

Goffman, Erving. 1959. *The Presentation of Self in Everyday Life*. Harmondsworth, England: Penguin.

Goffman, Erving. 1961. *Asylums*. New York: Doubleday Anchor.

Goffman, Erving. 1963. *Stigma, Notes on the Management of Spoiled Identity*. Englewood Cliffs, NJ: Prentice-Hall.

Goffman, Erving. 1971. *Relations in Public*. Harmondsworth, England: Penguin.

Gold, Sarah. 1971. "Equal Protection for Juvenile Girls in Need of Supervision in New York State." *New York Law Forum* 17(2): 570–598.

Goldsmith-Kasinsky, R. 1978. "Rape, the Social Control of Women." In *Law and Social Control in Canada*, ed. W. Greenaway and S. Brinkley. Scarborough, Canada: Prentice-Hall.

Goldstein, Abraham S. 1967. *The Insanity Defence*. New Haven: Yale University Press.

Goodman, Felicitas D. 1988. *How About Demons? Possession and Exorcism in the Modern World*. Bloomington: Indiana University Press.

Goodrich, Peter. 1987. *Legal Discourse*. London: Macmillan.

Goodrich, Peter. 1990. *Languages of Law*. London: Weidenfeld and Nicolson.

Goodrich, Peter. 1992. "Poor Illiterate Reason: History, Nationalism and Common Law." *Social and Legal Studies* 1(1): 7–28.

Gordon, David. 1971. "Class and the Economics of Crime." *Review of Radical Political Economy* 3: 51–75.

Gordon, David. 1973. "Capitalism, Class and Crime in America." *Crime and Delinquency* 19: 163–86.

Goring, Charles. 1913. *The English Convict: A Statistical Study*. London: His Majesty's Stationary Office.

Gottfredson, Michael R., and Travis Hirschi. 1987. "The Positive Tradition." In *Positive Criminology*, ed. Michael R. Gottfriedson and Travis Hirschi, 9–22. Newbury Park, CA: Sage.

Gottfredson, Michael F., and Travis Hirschi. 1990. *A General Theory of Crime*. Stanford: Stanford University Press.

Gove, Walter, ed. 1975. *The Labeling of Deviance: Evaluating a Perspective*. New York: Wiley.

Grasmick, Harold G., Brenda Sims Blackwell, and Robert J. Bursik, Jr. 1993. "Changes in the Sex Patterning of Perceived Threats of Sanctions." *Law and Society Review* 27(4): 679–705.

Greenberg, David F., ed. 1993 [1981]. *Crime and Capitalism: Readings in Marxist Criminology*. Palo Alto, CA: Mayfield.

Greenberg, David F. 1979. "Book Review of Quinney's Class, State and Crime." *Crime and Delinquency* 25(1): 110–13.

Griffiths, A. W. 1971. "Prisoners of XYY Constitution: Psychological Aspects." *British Journal of Psychiatry* 119 (549): 193–94.

Gross, Edward. 1978. "Organizational Sources of Crime: A Theoretical Perspective." In *Studies in Symbolic Interaction*, ed. Norman K. Denzin. Greenwich, CT: JAI Press.

Guerry, A. M. 1833. *Essai sur la Statistique Morale de la France*. Paris: Crochard.

Gusfield, Joseph R. 1955. "Social Structure and Moral Reform: A Study of the Woman's Christian Temperance Union." *American Journal of Sociology* 61: 221–32.

Gusfield, Joseph R. 1963. *Symbolic Crusade*. Urbana, IL: University of Illinois Press.

Hagan, Frank. 1986. *Introduction to Criminology: Theories, Methods, and Criminal Behavior*. Chicago: Nelson-Hall.

Hagan, John. 1989. *Structural Criminology*. New Brunswick, NJ: Rutgers University Press.

Hagan, John. 1990. "The Structuration of Gender and Deviance: A Power-Control Theory of Vulnerability to Crime and the Search for Deviant Role Exits." *Canadian Review of Sociology and Anthropology* 27(2): 137–56.

Hagan, John. 1993. "Introduction: Crime in Social and Legal Context." *Law and Society Review* 27(2): 255–62.

Hagan, John, A. R. Gillis, and John Simpson. 1985. "The Class Structure and Delinquency: Toward a Power-Control Theory of Common Delinquent Behavior." *American Journal of Sociology* 90: 1151–78.

Hagan, John, John Simpson, and A. R. Gillis. 1987. "Class in the Household: A Power-Control Theory of Gender and Delinquency." *American Journal of Sociology* 92: 788–816.

Haggett, Peter. 1977. "Human ecology." In *The Fontana Dictionary of Modern Social Thought*, ed. Alan Bullock and Oliver Stallybrass, 187. London: Fontana.

Hall-Williams, J. E. 1982. *Criminology and Criminal Justice*. London: Butterworths.

Halleck, Seymour. 1971. *Psychiatry and the Dilemmas of Crime*. Berkeley, CA: University of California Press.

Hamlin, John E. 1988. "The Misplaced Role of Rational Choice in Neutralization Theory." *Criminology* 26: 425–38.

Hare, R. D. 1970. *Psychopathy: Theory and Research*. New York: Wiley.

Hare, R. D., and J. F. Connolly. 1987. "Perceptual Asymmetries and Information Processing in Psychopaths." In *The Causes of Crime: New Biological Approaches*, ed. S. Mednick, T. Moffitt, and S. Stack. Cambridge: Cambridge University Press.

Harries, Keith D. 1980. *Crime and the Environment*. Springfield, MA: Charles Thomas.

Harrington, Christine. 1985. *Shadow Justice: The Ideology and Institutionalization of Alternatives to Court*. Westport, CT: Greenwood Press.

Harrington, Christine. 1988. "Moving from Integrative to Constitutive Theories of Law: Comments on Itzkowitz." *Law and Society* 22(5): 963–67.

Harris, Kay M. 1991. "Moving into the New Millennium—Toward a Feminist View of Justice." In *Criminology as Peacemaking*, ed. Harold E. Pepinsky and Richard Quinney, 83–97. Bloomington: Indiana University Press.

Harris, Marvin. 1974. *Cows, Pigs, Wars and Witches: The Riddles of Culture*. New York: Random House.

Hartmann, H. 1958. *Ego Psychology and the Problem of Adaption*. Trans. D. Rapaport. New York: International Universities Press.

Hartmann, Heidi. 1979. "Capitalism, Patriarchy and Job Segregation by Sex." In *Capitalist Patriarchy and the Case for Socialist Feminism*, ed. Zillah Eisenstein. New York: Monthly Review Press.

Hartmann, Heidi. 1981. "The Unhappy Marriage of Marxism and Feminism: Towards a More Progressive Union." In *Women and Revolution*, ed. Lydia Sargent, 1–41. Boston: South End Press.

Harvey, D. 1974. *Social Justice and the City*. London: Edward Arnold.

Harvey, David. 1989. *The Coalition of Postmodernity*. London: Blackwell.

Hawkins, J. David, and Joseph G. Weis. 1985. "The Social Development Model: An Integrated Approach to Delinquency Prevention." *Journal of Primary Prevention* 6(2): 73–97.

Hawley, Amos H. 1950. *Human Ecology: A Theory of Community Structure*. New York: Ronald Press.

Hawley, Amos H. 1968. "Human Ecology." In *International Encyclopedia of the Social Sciences*, Vol. 4, ed. David Sills, 328–37. New York: Macmillan/Free Press.

Hayles, K. 1990. *Chaos Bound*. New York: Cornell University Press.

Hayner, Norman S. 1933. "The Delinquency Areas in the Puget Sound Region." *American Journal of Sociology* 39: 314–28.

Healy, William. 1915. *The Individual Delinquent*. Boston: Little, Brown.

Healy, William, and Augusta Bronner. 1926. *Delinquents and Criminals: Their Making and Unmaking*. New York: Macmillan.

Healy, William, and Augusta Bronner. 1936. *New Light on Delinquency and its Treatment*. New Haven, CT: Yale University Press.

Heathcote, Frank. 1981. "Social Disorganization Theories." In *Crime and Society: Readings in History and Theory*, ed. Mike Fitzgerald, Gregor McLennan, and Jennie Pawson 341–70. London: Routledge and Kegan Paul.

Heffernan, Esther. 1972. *Making It in Prison*. New York: Wiley.

Heidensohn, Frances. 1985. *Women and Crime*. Basingstoke: Macmillan.

Heidensohn, Frances. 1987. "Women and Crime: Questions for Criminology." In *Gender, Crime and Justice*, ed. Pat Carlen and Ann Worrell. Milton Keynes, England: Open University Press.

Heineke, John M., ed. 1978. *Economic Models of Criminal Behavior*. New York: North-Holland.

Heineke, John M. 1988. "Crime, Deterrence and Choice: Testing the Rational Behavior Hypothesis." *American Sociological Review* 53: 303–305.

Henderson, Charles R. 1893. *An Introduction to the Dependent Defective Delinquent Classes*. Boston: D.C. Heath.

Henderson, D. James. 1976. "Exorcism, Possession, and the Dracula Cult: A Synopsis of Object-Relations Psychology." *Bulletin of the Menninger Clinic* 40(6): 603–28.

Henderson, James. 1982. "Exorcism and Possession in Psychotherapy Practice." *Canadian Journal of Psychiatry*, 27(2): 129–34.

Henry, Stuart. 1976. "Fencing with Accounts: The Language of Moral Bridging." *British Journal of Law and Society* 3: 91–100.

Henry, Stuart. 1977. "On the Fence." *British Journal of Law and Society* 4(1): 124–33.

Henry, Stuart. 1988 [1978]. *The Hidden Economy: The Context and Control of Borderline Crime*. Oxford: Martin Robertson; republished by Loompanics Unlimited, Port Townsend, Washington.

Henry, Stuart, ed. 1981. *Informal Institutions: Alternative Networks in the Corporate State*, New York: St. Martin's Press. Also published as *Can I Have It in Cash?* London: Astragal Books.

Henry, Stuart. 1982. "The Working Unemployed." *Sociological Review* 30(3): 460–73.

Henry, Stuart. 1983. *Private Justice*. London: Routledge and Kegan Paul.

Henry, Stuart. 1984. "Contradictions of Collective Justice: The Case of the Co-op Cops." *Howard Journal of Criminal Justice* 23: 158–69.

Henry, Stuart. 1985. "Community Justice, Capitalist Society and Human Agency: The Dialectics of Collective Law in the Co-operative." *Law and Society Review* 19: 303–27.

Henry, Stuart. 1987. "The Construction and Deconstruction of Social Control: Thoughts on the Discursive Production of State Law and Private Justice." In *Transcarceration: Essays in the Sociology of Social Control*, ed. John Lowman, Robert Menzies, and Ted Palys. Aldershot: Gower Press.

Henry, Stuart. 1989. "Constitutive Criminology: The Missing Paradigm." *Critical Criminologist* 1(3): 9, 12.

Henry, Stuart. ed. 1990. *Degrees of Deviance: Student Accounts of their Deviant Behavior*. Salem, Wisconsin: Sheffield. [First published in Aldershot, England, by Avebury Press.]

Henry, Stuart. 1991. "The Postmodernist Perspective in Criminology." In *New Directions in Critical Criminology,* ed. Brian MacLean and Dragan Milovanovic, 71–78. Vancouver: Collective Press.

Henry, Stuart. 1994. "Newsmaking Criminology as Replacement Discourse." In *Media, Process and the Social Construction of Crime: Studies in Newsmaking Criminology*, ed. Gregg Barak. New York: Garland Press.

Henry, Stuart, and Dragan Milovanovic. 1991. "Constitutive Criminology." *Criminology* 29: 293–316.

Henry, Stuart, and Dragan Milovanovic. 1993. "Back to Basics: A Postmodern Redefinition of Crime." *Critical Criminologist* 5(2/3): 1–2, 12.

Henry, Stuart, and Dragan Milovanovic. In press. "The Constitution of Constitutive Criminology: A Postmodern Approach to Criminological Theory." In *The Futures of Criminology,* ed. David Nelken. London: Sage.

Hibbert, Christopher. 1966. *The Roots of Evil: A Social History of Crime and Punishment*. London: Weidenfeld and Nicolson.

Higgins, Paul C., and Richard C. Butler. 1982. *Understanding Deviance*. New York: McGraw-Hill.

Hill, Gary D., and Maxine P. Atkinson. 1988. "Gender, Familial Control, and Delinquency." *Criminology* 26: 127–49.

Hills, Stuart L. 1971. *Crime, Power and Morality*. Scranton, PA: Chandler.

Hindelang, Michael J. 1970. "The Commitment of Delinquents to Their Misdeeds: Do Delinquents Drift?" *Social Problems* 17: 502–509.

Hindelang, Michael J. 1973. "Causes of Delinquency: A Partial Replication and Extension." *Social Problems* 20: 471–87.

Hippchen, Leonard J., ed. 1978. *Ecologic-Biochemical Approaches to the Treatment of Delinquents and Criminals*. New York: Van Nostrand Reinhold.

Hirschi, Travis. 1969. *The Causes of Delinquency*. Berkeley, CA: University of California Press.

Hirschi, Travis. 1979. "Separate and Equal Is Better." *Journal of Research in Crime and Delinquency* (January): 34–38.

Hirschi, Travis, and Michael J. Hindelang. 1977. "Intelligence and Delinquency: A Revisionist Review." *American Sociological Review* 42(4): 571–87.

Hirschi, Travis, and Hanan C. Selvin. 1967. *Delinquency Research: An Appraisal of Analytic Methods*. New York: Free Press.

Hirschi, Travis. 1983. "Crime and Family Policy." *Journal of Contemporary Studies* 4: 3–16.

Hirst, Paul Q. 1972. "Marx and Engels on Law, Crime, and Morality." *Economy and Society* 1(1): 28–56.

Hirst, Paul Q. 1975. "Marx and Engels on Law, Crime, and Morality." In *Critical Criminology,* ed. Ian Taylor, Paul Walton, and Jock Young, 203–232. London: Routledge and Kegan Paul.

Hobbes, Thomas. 1950 [1651]. *Leviathan*. New York: Dutton.

Hoffer, A. 1978. "Some Theoretical Principles Basic to Orthomolecular Psychiatric Treatment." In *Ecologic-Biochemical Approaches to the Treatment of Delinquents and Criminals*, ed. L. Hippchen. New York: Van Nostrand Reinhold.

Hoffman-Bustamente, Dale. 1973. "The Nature of Female Criminality." *Issues in Criminology* 8: 117–36.

Hoghughi, M. S., and A. R. Forrest. 1970. "Eysenck's Theory of Criminality: An Examination with Approved School Boys." *British Journal of Criminology* 10: 240–52.

Hollinger, Richard, C. 1991. "Neutralizing in the Workplace: An Empirical Analysis of Property Theft and Production Deviance." *Deviant Behavior* 12: 169–202.

Holden, Arun V., ed. 1986. *Chaos*. Princeton, NJ: Princeton University Press.

Holman, John E., and James F. Quinn. 1992. *Criminology: Applying Theory*. St. Paul, MN: West.

Holt, Robert, R. 1968. "Freud, Sigmund." In *International Encyclopedia of the Social Sciences,* Vol. 6, 1–12. New York: Macmillan/Free Press.

Hooton, Earnest Albert. 1939a. *Crime and the Man*. Cambridge, MA: Harvard University Press.

Hooton, Earnest Albert. 1939b. *The American Criminal: An Anthropological Study*. Cambridge, MA: Harvard University Press.

Horton, John. 1964. "The Dehumanization of Anomie and Alienation: A Problem in the Ideology of Sociology." *British Journal of Sociology* 15: 283–300.

Hughes, Everett C. 1945. "Dilemmas and Contradictions of Statuses." *American Journal of Sociology* 50: 353–59.

Hunt, Alan. 1987. "The Critique of Law: What Is Critical About Critical Legal Theory?" *Journal of Law and Society* 14: 5–19.

Hunt, Alan. 1990. "The Big Fear: Law Confronts Postmodernism." *McGill Law Journal* 35: 507–540.

Hunt, Alan. 1991. "Postmodernism and Critical Criminology." In *New Directions in Critical Criminology*, ed. Brian D. MacLean and Dragan Milovanovic, 79–85. Vancouver: Collective Press.

Hunt, Alan. 1993. *A Constitutive Theory of Law*. London: Routledge.

Hurwitz, Stephan, and Karl O. Christiansen. 1983. *Criminology*. London: Allen and Unwin.

Hutchings, Barry, and Sarnoff A. Mednick. 1975. "Registered Criminality in the Adoptive and Biological Parents of Registered Male Criminal Adoptees." In *Genetic Research in Psychiatry*, ed. R. R. Fieve, D. Rosenthal, and H. Brill. Baltimore: Johns Hopkins University Press.

Huyssen, Andreas. 1986. *After the Great Divide: Modernism, Mass Culture, Postmodernism*. Bloomington: Indiana University Press.

Ignatieff, Michael. 1978. *A Just Measure of Pain: The Penitentiary in the Industrial Revolution*. New York: Pantheon.

Inciardi, James A., ed. 1980. *Radical Criminology the Coming Crisis*. Beverly Hills, CA: Sage.

Irwin, John. 1970. *The Felon*. New Jersey: Prentice-Hall.

Jacobs, Patricia A., et al. 1965. "Aggressive Behavior Mental Subnormality and the XYY Male." *Nature* 208: 1351–52.

Jacoby, Joseph E. 1979. *Classics of Criminology.* Prospect Heights, IL: Waveland Press.

Jacoby, Joseph E. 1994. *Classics of Criminology.* 2nd ed. Prospect Heights, IL: Waveland Press.

Jackson, Bernard. 1988. *Law, Fact and Narrative Coherence.* Merseyside, England: Deborah Charles.

Jackson, Stevi. 1992. "The Amazing Deconstructing Woman Suggests Some Problems with Postmodern Feminism." *Trouble and Strife* 25: 25–31.

Jaggar, Alison. 1983. *Feminist Politics and Human Nature.* Totowa, NJ: Roman and Allanheld.

James, William. 1890. *The Principles of Psychology.* New York: Henry Holt.

Jameson, Fredrick. 1984. "Postmodernism, or the Cultural Logic of Late Capitalism." *New Left Review* 146 (July/August): 53–92.

Jeffery, C. Ray. 1956. "The Structure of American Criminological Thinking." *The Journal of Criminal Law, Criminology and Police Science* 46: 658–72.

Jeffery, C. Ray. 1965. "Criminal Behavior and Learning Theory." *Journal of Criminal Law, Criminology and Police Science* 56: 294–300.

Jeffery, C. Ray. 1971. *Crime Prevention Through Environmental Design.* Beverly Hills, CA: Sage.

Jeffery, C. Ray. 1977. *Crime Prevention Through Environmental Design.* 2nd ed. Beverly Hills, CA: Sage.

Jeffery, C. Ray. 1978. "Criminology as an Interdisciplinary Behavioral Science." *Criminology* 16(2): 149–69.

Jeffery, C. Ray. 1993. "Genetics, Crime and the Cancelled Conference." *Criminologist* 18(1): 1, 6–8.

Jeffery, C. Ray. 1994. "Biological and Neuropsychiatric Approaches to Criminal Behavior." In *Varieties of Criminology: Readings from a Dynamic Discipline,* ed. Gregg Barak, 15–28. Westport, CT: Praeger.

Jenkins, Philip. 1984. "Varieties of Enlightenment Criminology." *British Journal of Criminology* 24(2): 112–31.

Jensen, Gary F., and Kevin Thompson. 1990. "What's Class Got to Do with It? A Further Examination of Power-Control Theory." *American Journal of Sociology* 95: 1009–1023.

Jessop, Bob. 1982. *The Capitalist State.* New York: New York University Press.

Jessor, Richard, and S. Jessor. 1977. *Problem Behavior and Psychosocial Development: A Longitudinal Study of Youth.* New York: Academic Press.

Johns, Christina. 1992. *The War on Drugs.* Westport, CT: Greenwood Press.

Johnson, Richard E. 1979. *Juvenile Delinquency and Its Origins.* Cambridge: Cambridge University Press.

Jones, David A. 1986. *History of Criminology: A Philosophical Perspective.* New York: Greenwood Press.

Jones, Ernest. 1953. *The Life and Work of Sigmund Freud.* New York: H. Wolf.

Kamenka, Eugene, and Alice E. S. Tay. 1978. "Socialism, Anarchism and Law." In *Law and Society: The Crisis in Legal Ideals,* ed. Eugene Kamenka et al., 48–80. London: Edward Arnold.

Kamin, L. J. 1985. "Criminality and Adoption." *Science* 227: 982.

Katz, Alfred H., and Eugene I. Bender. 1976. *The Strength in Us: Self-help Groups in the Modern World.* New York: New Viewpoints.

Katz, Jack. 1988. *Seductions of Crime: Moral and Sensual Attractions of Doing Evil.* New York: Basic Books.

Katz, Janet, and C. Abel. 1984. "The Medicalization of Repression." *Contemporary Crises* 8: 227–41.

Katz, Janet, and William J. Chambliss. 1991. "Biology and Crime." In *Criminology: A Contemporary Handbook,* ed. Joseph F. Sheley, 245–71. Belmont, CA: Wadsworth.

Katz, Janet, and Frank H. Marsh. 1984. *Biology, Crime and Ethics: A Study of Biological Explanations for Criminal Behavior.* Cincinnati: Anderson.

Katz, Nancie L. 1993. "Books Instead of Bars: Jail-for-Literature Program Is Deliverance for Some Lawbreakers." Sunday Punch Section, *San Francisco Chronicle* (September 19): 5.

Keller, Evelyn Fox. 1982. "Feminism and Science." In *Feminist Theory*, ed. Nannerl O. Keohane, Michele Z. Rosaldo, and Barbara C. Gelpi. Chicago: University of Chicago Press.

Kelly, George. 1955. *The Psychology of Personal Constructs*. 2 vols. New York: Norton.

Kelly, L., and J. Radford. 1987. "The Problem of Men: Feminist Perspectives on Sexual Violence." In *Law, Order and the Authoritarian State: Readings in Critical Criminology*, ed. Phil Scraton. Philadelphia: Open University Press.

Kennedy, Mark C. 1976. "Beyond Incrimination: Some Neglected Facets of the Theory of Punishment." In *Whose Law? What Order?: A Conflict Approach to Criminology*, ed. William J. Chambliss and Milton Mankoff. New York: Wiley.

Kessley, Semour, and Rudolph H. Moos. 1970. "The XYY Karotype and Criminality: A Review." *Journal of Psychiatric Research* 7(3): 153–70.

Kidder, Robert. 1983. *Connecting Law and Society: An Introduction to Research and Theory*. Englewood Cliffs, NJ: Prentice-Hall.

Kim, Daeshik, and Kyung Sun Shin. 1983. *Judo*. Dubuque, IA: Wm. C. Brown.

Kinberg, Olof. 1935. *Basic Problems of Criminology*. Copenhagen: Levin and Munksgaard.

King, Michael. 1978. "A Status Passage of the Defendant's Progress through the Magistrates Court." *Law and Human Behavior* 2(3): 183–221.

King, Michael. 1981. *The Framework of Criminal Justice*. London: Croom Helm.

Kinsey, Richard. 1979. "Despotism and Legality." In *Capitalism and the Rule of Law*, ed. Bob Fine et al., 76–89. London: Hutchinson.

Kinsey, Richard, et al. 1986. *Losing the Fight Against Crime*. Oxford: Basil Blackwell.

Kitsuse, John I. 1964. "Societal Reaction to Deviant Behavior; Problems of Theory and Method." In *The Other Side*, ed. Howard Becker, 87–102. New York: Free Press.

Kitsuse, John J., and David C. Dietrick. 1970. "Delinquent Boys: A Critique." In *Society, Delinquency, and Delinquent Behavior*, ed. Harwin L. Voss. Boston: Little, Brown.

Klein, Dorie. 1980 [1973]. "The Etiology of Female Crime: A Review of the Literature." In *Women, Crime and Justice*, ed. Susan K. Datesman and Frank R. Scarpitti, 70–105. New York: Oxford University Press.

Kline, Marlee. 1989. "Race, Racism and Feminist Legal Theory." *Harvard Women's Law Journal* 12: 115–150.

Kline, Paul. 1981. *Fact and Fantasy in Freudian Theory*. New York: Methuen.

Klockars, Carl B. 1974. *The Professional Fence*. New York: Free Press.

Klockars, Carl B. 1979. "The Contemporary Crisis of Marxist Criminology." *Criminology* 16: 477–515.

Knopp, Fay Honey. 1991. "Community Solutions to Sexual Violence: Feminist/Abolitionist Perspectives." In *Criminology as Peacemaking*, ed. Harold Pepinsky and Richard Quinney, 181–93. Bloomington: Indiana University Press.

Knorr-Cetina, Karin. 1981. "Introduction: The Micro-Sociological Challenge of Macro-Sociology: Towards a Reconstruction of Social Theory and Methodology." In *Advances in Social Theory and Methodology: Toward an Integration of Macro- and Micro-Sociologies*, ed. Karin Knorr-Cetina and Aaron Cicourel. London: Routledge and Kegan Paul.

Knorr-Cetina, Karin, and Aaron Cicourel. 1981. *Advances in Social Theory and Methodology: Toward an Integration of Macro- and Micro-Sociologies*. London: Routledge and Kegan Paul.

Kobrin, Solomon. 1959. "The Chicago Area Project—A 25-year Assessment." *The Annals of the American Academy of Social Science* 322: 20–29.

Kobrin, Solomon. 1971. "The Formal Legal Properties of the Shaw-McKay Delinquency Theory." In *Ecology, Crime and Delinquency*, ed. Harwin L. Voss and David M. Peterson. New York: Appleton Century Crofts.

Kornhauser, Ruth R. 1978. *Social Sources of Delinquency*. Chicago: University of Chicago Press.

Kors, Alan C., and Edward Peters, eds. 1972. *Witchcraft in Europe 1100–1700*. Philadelphia: University of Pennsylvania Press.

Kraepelin, Emil. 1883. *Psychiatrie*. Leipzig: Barth.

Kramer, Ronald. 1984. "Corporate Criminality: The Development of an Idea." In *Corporations as Criminals*, ed. Ellen Hochstedler. Beverly Hills, CA: Sage.

Kramer, Heinrich, and Jakob Sprenger. 1971 [1485]. *The Malleus Maleficarum*. Trans. Montague Summers. New York: Dover.

Kretch, D., and R. S. Crutchfield. 1948. *Theory and Problems of Social Psychology*. New York: McGraw-Hill.

Kretschmer, Ernest. 1925. *Physique and Character*. New York: Harcourt Brace.

Krisberg, Barry. 1975. *Crime and Privilege: Towards a New Criminology*. Englewood Cliffs, NJ: Prentice-Hall.

Krohn, Marvin. 1991. "Control and Deterrence Theories." In *Criminology: A Contemporary Handbook,* ed. Joseph F. Sheley, 295–313. Belmont, CA.: Wadsworth.

Krohn, Marvin D., and J. Massey. 1980. "Social Control and Delinquent Behavior: An Examination of the Elements of the Social Bond." *Sociological Quarterly* 21: 529–43.

Kuhn, Thomas. 1970. [1962]. *The Structure of Scientific Revolutions*. Chicago: University of Chicago Press.

Lacan, Jacque. 1977. *Ecrits*. Trans. Alan Sheridan. New York: Norton.

LaGrange, Randy, and Helen R. White. 1985. "Age Differences in Delinquency: A Test of Theory." *Criminology* 23: 19–45.

Laing, R. D. 1965 [1959]. *The Divided Self*. Harmondsworth, England: Penguin.

Laing, R. D. 1967. *The Politics of Experience and the Bird of Paradise*. Harmondsworth, England: Penguin.

Lander, Bernard. 1954. *Toward an Understanding of Juvenile Delinquency*. New York: Colombia University Press.

Layland, J. 1990. "On the Conflicts of Doing Feminist Research into Masculinity." In *Feminist Praxis*, ed. L. Stanley, 125–33. London: Routledge.

Lea, H. C. 1906. *History of the Inquisition of the Middle Ages*. London:

Lea, John, and Jock Young. 1984. *What Is to Be Done About Law and Order?* Harmondsworth, England: Penguin.

LeGrande, Camile. 1973. "Rape and Rape Laws: Sexism in Society and Law." *California Law Review* 61: 919–41.

Lemert, Edwin M. 1951. *Social Pathology*. New York: McGraw-Hill.

Lemert, Edwin. 1964. "Social Structure, Social Control and Deviation." In *Anomie and Deviant Behavior*, ed. Marshall B. Clinard. New York: Free Press.

Lemert, Edwin M. 1967. *Human Deviance, Social Problems and Social Control*. Englewood Cliffs, NJ: Prentice-Hall.

Lemert, Edwin M. 1981. "Diversion in Juvenile Justice: What Has Been Wrought." *Journal of Research in Crime and Delinquency* 18: 34–46.

Leonard, Eileen B. 1982. *Women, Crime and Society: A Critique of Criminological Theory*. New York: Longman.

Lewontin, R. C., Steven Rose, and Leon J. Kamin. 1984. *Not in Our Genes*. New York: Pantheon.

Liazos, Alexander. 1972. "The Poverty and the Sociology of Deviance: Nuts, Sluts and Perverts." *Social Problems* 20: 103–120.

Liddle, M. 1989. "Feminist Contributions to an Understanding of Violence Against Women—Two Steps Forward, Three Steps Back." *Canadian Review of Sociology and Anthropology* 26(5): 759–75.

Lilly, J. Robert, Francis Cullen, and Richard A. Ball. 1989. *Criminological Theory: Context and Consequences*. Newbury Park, CA: Sage.

Liska, A., and M. D. Reed. 1985. "Ties to Conventional Institutions and Delinquency: Estimating Reciprocal Effects." *American Sociological Review* 50: 547–60.

Little, Alan. 1963. "Professor Eysenck's Theory of Crime: An Empirical Test on Adolescent Offenders." *British Journal of Criminology* 4: 152–62.

Livingston, Jay. 1992. *Crime and Criminology*. Englewood Cliffs, NJ: Prentice-Hall.

Locke, John. 1689. "Essay Concerning Human Understanding." In *The Works of John Locke,* Vol. 1. London: Arthur Bettesworth.

Locke, John. 1964 [1690]. *Two Treatises of Government*. Cambridge: Cambridge University Press.

Lofland, John H. 1969. *Deviance and Identity*. New Jersey: Prentice-Hall.

Lombroso, Cesare. 1876. *L'Uomo Delinquente*. Milan: Hoepli.

Lombroso, Caesar, and William Ferrero. 1900. *The Female Offender*. New York: Appleton.

Longmoor, Elsa S., and Erle F. Young 1936. "Ecological Interpretations of Juvenile Delinquency, Dependency and Population Mobility: A Cartographic Analysis of Data from Long Beach, California." *American Journal of Sociology* 41: 598–610.

Los, Maria. 1990. "Feminism and Rape Law Reform." In *Feminist Perspectives in Criminology*, ed. Loraine Gelsthorpe and Allison Morris, 160–72. Milton Keynes, England: Open University Press.

Lottier, Stuart. 1938-39. "Distribution of Criminal Offenses in Metropolitan Regions." *Journal of Criminal Law and Criminology* 29: 39–43.

Love, Barbara, and Elizabeth Shanklin. 1978. "The Answer Is Matriarchy." In *Our Right to Love*, ed. Ginny Vida. Englewood Cliffs, NJ: Prentice-Hall.

Lovibond, Sabina. 1989. "Feminism and Postmodernism." *New Left Review* 178: 5–28.

Lowman, John. 1986. "Conceptual Issues in the Geography of Crime: Toward a Geography of Social Control." *Annals of the Association of American Geographers* 76: 81–94.

Lowman, John, and Brian D. MacLean. 1992. *Realist Criminology*. Toronto: University of Toronto Press.

Lynch, Michael J., and W. Byron Groves. 1986. *A Primer in Radical Criminology*. New York: Harrow and Heston.

MacDonald, Arthur. 1893. *Criminology*. New York: Funk and Wagnalls.

Macfarlane, Alan. 1970. *Witchcraft in Tudor and Stuart England: A Regional and Comparative Study*. London: Routledge and Kegan Paul.

MacGill, Helen. 1938. "The Oriental Delinquent in the Vancouver Juvenile Court." *Sociology and Social Research* 22(5): 428–38.

MacKinnon, Catherine. 1982. "Feminism, Marxism, Method, and the State: An Agenda for Theory." *Signs* 7(2): 515–44.

MacKinnon, Catherine. 1983. "Feminism, Marxism, Method, and the State: Toward Feminist Jurisprudence." *Signs* 8(4): 635–58.

MacKinnon, Catherine. 1987. *Feminism Unmodified: Discourses on Life and Law*. Cambridge, MA: Harvard University Press.

MacKinnon, Catherine. 1989. *Toward a Feminist Theory of the State*. Cambridge, MA: Harvard University Press.

MacLean, Brian D. 1991a. "The Origins of Left Realism." In *New Directions in Critical Criminology*, ed. Brian D. MacLean and Dragan Milovanovic, 9–14. Vancouver: Collective Press.

MacLean, Brian D. 1991b. "In Partial Defense of Socialist Realism: Some Theoretical and Methodological Concerns of the Local Crime Survey." *Crime, Law and Social Control: An International Journal* 15(3): 213–54.

MacLeod, Jay. 1987. *Ain't No Makin' It*. Boulder, CO: Westview Press.

Maestro, Marcello T. 1973. *Cesare Beccaria and the Origins of Penal Reform*. Philadelphia: Temple University Press.

Mahan, Sue. 1984. "Imposition of Despair—An Ethnography of Women in Prison." *Justice Quarterly* 1: 357–83.

Mair, Lucy. 1969. *Witchcraft*. New York: McGraw-Hill, World University Library.

Malinowski, Bronislaw. 1944. *A Scientific Theory of Culture and Other Essays*. Chapel Hill, NC: The University of North Carolina Press.

Mama, Amina. 1989. "Violence Against Black Women: Gender, Race and State Responses." *Feminist Review* 32: 30–48.

Mankoff, Milton. 1971. "Societal Reaction and Career Deviance: A Critical Analysis." *Sociological Quarterly* 12: 204–218.

Mankoff, Milton. 1978. "On the Responsibility of Marxist Criminology: A Reply to Quinney." *Contemporary Crisis* 2: 293–301.

Manning, Peter K. 1988. *Symbolic Communication: Signifying Calls and the Police Response.* Cambridge: MIT Press.

Manning, Peter K. 1989. "Critical Semiotics." *The Critical Criminologist* 1(4): 7–8, 16–18.

Markle, Gerald E., and R. J. Troyer. 1979. "Smoke Gets in Your Eyes: Cigarette Smoking as Deviant Behavior." *Social Problems* 26: 611–25.

Martin, Randy, Robert J. Mutchnick, and W. Timothy Austin. 1990. *Criminological Thought: Pioneers Past and Present.* New York: Macmillan.

Martindale, Don. 1960. *The Nature and Types of Sociological Theory.* Cambridge, MA: Houghton Mifflin.

Marx, Gary. 1988. *Undercover: Police Surveillance in America.* Berkeley, CA: University of California Press.

Marx, Karl. 1964 [1844]. *The Economic and Philosophical Manuscripts of 1844.* New York: International.

Marx, Karl. 1984 [1852]. "The Eighteenth Brumaire of Louis Bonaparte." In *The Portable Marx*, ed. Eugene Kamenka. Harmondsworth, England: Penguin.

Marx, Karl. 1859. "'Preface' to a Contribution to the Critique of Political Economy." In *Selected Works*, Vol. 1, ed. Karl Marx and Friedrich Engels, 502–506. Moscow: Progress.

Marx, Karl. 1868. *Capital.* 3 vols. New York: International.

Marx, Karl. 1868. "Thesis on Feurbach, No. 6." In *Collected Works*, ed. Karl Marx and Frederick Engels. New York: International.

Massey, J. L., and Marvin D. Krohn. 1986. "A Longitudinal Examination of an Integrated Social Process Model of Deviant Behavior." *Social Forces* 65: 106–34.

Masson, Jeffrey. 1984. *Assault on the Truth: Freud's Suppression of the Seduction Theory.* New York: Farrar, Straus and Giroux.

Masters, Ruth, and Cliff Roberson. 1990. *Inside Criminology.* Englewood Cliffs, NJ: Prentice-Hall.

Matsueda, Ross L., and Karen Heimer. 1987. "Race, Family Structure, and Delinquency: A Test of Differential Association and Social Control Theories." *American Sociological Review* 52: 826–40.

Matthews, Roger. 1987. "Taking Realist Criminology Seriously." *Contemporary Crisis* 11: 371–401.

Matthews, Roger, and Jock Young, eds. 1986. *Confronting Crime.* Beverly Hills, CA: Sage.

Matthews, Roger, and Jock Young, eds. 1992. *Issues in Realist Criminology.* Beverly Hills, CA: Sage.

Matza, David. 1964. *Delinquency and Drift.* New York: Wiley.

Matza, David. 1969. *Becoming Deviant.* Englewood Cliffs, NJ: Prentice-Hall.

Matza, David, and Gresham Sykes. 1961. "Juvenile Delinquency and Subterranean Values." *American Sociological Review* 26: 712–19.

Maudsley, Henry. 1874. *Responsibility in Mental Disease.* London: Macmillan.

Mayhew, Henry. 1861. *London Labour and the London Poor.* London: Griffin.

Mayhew, Henry. 1981. "A Visit to the Rookery of St. Giles and Its Neighbourhood." In *Crime and Society: Readings in History and Society*, ed. Mike Fitzgerald, Gregor McLennan, and Jennie Pawson, 148–159. London: Routledge and Kegan Paul.

McCahery, Joseph. 1993. "Modernist and Postmodernist Perspectives on Public Law in British Critical Legal Studies." *Social and Legal Studies* 2(4): 397–421.

McCarthy, John D., and Meyer N. Zald. 1987. *Resource Mobilization and Social Movements in an Organizational Society.* New Brunswick, NJ: Transaction Books.

McDonald, Scott. 1986. "Does Gentrification Affect Crime Rates?" In *Crime and Justice—An Annual Review of Research*, Vol. 8, ed. Albert J. Reiss, Jr., and Michael Tonry, 163–201. Chicago: University of Chicago Press.

McGee, Linda, and Michael D. Newcomb. 1992. "General Deviance Syndrome: Expanded Hierarchical Evaluations at Four Ages from Early Adolescence to Adulthood." *Journal of Consulting and Clinical Psychology* 60(5): 766–76.

Mead, George Herbert. 1934. *Mind, Self and Society*, ed. C. W. Morris. Chicago: University of Chicago Press.

Mednick, Sarnoff A. 1979. "Biosocial Factors and Primary Prevention of Anti-Social Behavior."
    In *New Paths in Criminology: Interdisciplinary and Intercultural Explanations*, ed. S. A. Mednick
    and S. G. Shoham. Lexington, MA: D. C. Heath.

Mednick, Sarnoff A. 1985. "Crime in the Family Tree." *Psychology Today* (March): 58–61.

Mednick, Sarnoff A., and Karl O. Christiansen. 1977. *Biosocial Bases of Criminal Behavior*. New
    York: Gardiner Press.

Mednick, Sarnoff A., and Karen M. Finello. 1983. "Biology Factors and Crime: Implications for
    Forensic Psychiatry." *International Journal of Law and Psychiatry*, 6(1): 1–15.

Mednick, Sarnoff, W. Gabrielle, and Barry Hutchings. 1984. "Genetic Influences in Criminal
    Convictions: Evidence from an Adoption Cohort." *Science* 224(4651): 891–94.

Mednick, Sarnoff, W. Gabrielle, and Barry Hutchings. 1987. "Genetic Factors in the Etiology of
    Criminal Behavior." In *The Causes of Crime: New Biological Approaches*, ed. Sarnoff S.
    Mednick, T. Moffitt, and Susan Stack, 74–91. Cambridge: Cambridge University Press.

Mednick, Sarnoff A., and J. Volavka. 1980. "Biology and Crime." In *Crime and Justice: An Annual
    Review of Research,* Vol. 2, ed. Norvil Morris and Michael Tonry. Chicago: Chicago
    University Press.

Mednick, Sarnoff A., et al. 1982. "Biology and Violence." In *Criminal Violence*, ed. Marvin
    Wolfgang and Neil Alan Weiner, 46–52. Beverly Hills, CA: Sage.

Mednick, Sarnoff A., Patricia Brennan, and Elizabeth Kandel. 1988. "Predisposition to
    Violence." Special Issue on *Current Theoretical Perspectives on Aggressive and Antisocial Behavior.
    Aggressive Behavior* 14(1) 25–33.

Meier, Robert F. 1989. *Crime and Society*. Boston: Allyn and Bacon.

Megill, Allan. 1985. *Prophets of Extremity: Nietzsche, Heidegger, Foucault, Derrida*. Berkeley:
    University of California Press.

Melichar, Kenneth E. 1988. "Deconstruction: Critical Theory or an Ideology of Despair?"
    Humanity and Society 12: 366–85.

Melossi, Dario, and M. Pavarini. 1981. *The Prison and the Factory: Origins of the Penitentiary System.*
    Totowa, NJ: Barnes and Noble.

Melville, K. 1972. *Communes in the Counterculture*. New York: William Mason.

Menzies, Robert, and Dorothy Chunn. 1991. "Kicking Against the Pricks: The Dilemmas of
    Feminist Teaching in Criminology." *Critical Criminologist* 3(1): 7–8, 14–15.

Merry, Sally. 1988. "Legal Pluralism." *Law and Society Review* 22: 869–96.

Merton, Robert K. 1938. "Social Structure and Anomie." *American Sociological Review*, 3: 672–82.

Merton, Robert K. 1957. *Social Theory and Social Structure*. New York: Free Press.

Merton, Robert K. 1968. *Social Theory and Social Structure*. Enlarged ed. New York: Free Press.

Merton, Robert K. 1959. "Social Conformity, Deviation, and Opportunity-Structures: A
    Comment on the Contributions of Dubin and Cloward." *American Sociological Review* 24:
    177–88.

Merton, Robert K. 1961. "Social Problems and Sociological Theory." In *Contemporary Social
    Problems*, ed. Robert K. Merton and Robert A. Nisbet. New York: Harcourt Brace
    Jovanovich.

Merton, Robert K. 1964. "Anomie, Anomia, and Social Interaction: Contexts of Deviant
    Behavior." In *Anomie and Deviant Behavior: A Discussion and Critique*, ed. Marshall B.
    Clinard. New York: Free Press.

Merton, Robert K., and M. F. Ashley-Montague. 1940. "Crime and the Anthropologist."
    American Anthropologist 42: 384–408.

Messerschmidt, James W. 1986. *Capitalism, Patriarchy, and Crime: Toward a Socialist Feminist
    Criminology*. Totowa, NJ: Rowan and Littlefield.

Messerschmidt, James W. 1993. *Masculinities and Crime: Critique and Reconceptualization of Theory*.
    Boston: Rowman and Littlefield.

Messner, Steven F., Marvin D. Krohn, and Allen E. Liska, eds. 1989. *Theoretical Integration in the
    Study of Deviance and Crime: Problems and Prospects*. Albany, NY: State University of New
    York Press.

Mestrovic, Stjepan G., and Helene M. Brown. 1985. "Durkheim's Concept of Anomie as

Dereglement." *Social Problems,* 33: 81–99.

Michael, Jerome, and Mortimer J. Adler. 1933. *Crime, Law and Social Science.* New York: Harcourt Brace Jovanovich.

Michalowski, Ray J. 1976. "Repression and Criminal Justice in Capitalist America." *Sociological Inquiry* 46: 99–110.

Michalowski, Ray J. 1977. "Perspective and Paradigm: Structuring Criminological Thought." In *Theory in Criminology,* ed. Robert Meier, 17–39. Beverly Hills, CA: Sage.

Michalowski, Ray J. 1985. *Order, Law and Crime: An Introduction to Criminology.* New York: Random House.

Michalowski, Ray J., and Edward W. Bohlander. 1976. "Repression and Criminal Justice in Capitalist America." *Sociological Inquiry* 46: 95–106.

Miles, Maria. 1983. "Toward a Methodology for Feminist Research." In *Theories of Women's Studies,* ed. Gloria Bowles and Renate Duelli Klein. Boston: Routledge and Kegan Paul.

Miller, Alden D., and Lloyd E. Ohlin. 1985. *Delinquency and Community: Creating Opportunities and Controls.* Beverly Hills, CA: Sage.

Miller, Eldon S. 1981. "Crime's Threat to Land Value and Neighborhood Vitality." In *Environmental Criminology,* ed. Paul J. Brantingham and Patricia L. Brantingham, 111–18. Beverly Hills, CA: Sage.

Mills, C. Wright. 1940. "Situated Actions and Vocabularies of Motive." *American Sociological Review,* 5: 904–913.

Mills, C. Wright. 1956. *The Power Elite.* New York: Oxford University Press.

Mills, C. Wright. 1969. *Power, Politics and People.* New York: Oxford University Press.

Milovanovic, Dragan. 1989. "Critical Criminology and the Challenge of Postmodernism." *Critical Criminologists* 1(4): 9–10, 17.

Milovanovic, Dragan. 1992. *Post Modern Law and Disorder: Psychoanalytic Semiotics, Chaos and Juridic Exegeses.* Merseyside, England: Deborah Charles.

Milovanovic, Dragan. 1994. "Law Ideology, and Subjectivity: A Semiotic Perspective on Crime and Justice." In *Varieties of Criminology: Readings from a Dynamic Discipline,* ed. Gregg Barak, 231–51. Westport, CT: Praeger.

Milovanovic, Dragan, and Stuart Henry. 1991. "Constitutive Penology." *Social Justice* 18(3): 205–24.

Minor, M. William. 1980. "The Neutralization of Criminal Offense." *Criminology* 18: 103–120.

Minow, Martha. 1990. *Making All the Difference: Inclusion, Exclusion and American Law.* Ithaca, NY: Cornell University Press.

Molitch, M. 1937. "Endocrine Disturbance in Behavior Problems." *American Journal of Psychiatry* 93(5): 1176–80.

Monachesi, Elio D. 1955. "Cesear Beccaria." *Journal of Criminal Law Criminology and Police Science* 46: 439–49.

Monahan, John, and Henry J. Steadman. 1983. "Crime and Mental Disorder: An Epidemiological Approach." In *Crime and Justice and Annual Review,* ed. Michael Tonry and Norval K. Morris. Chicago: Chicago University Press.

Montague, M. F. Ashley. 1968. "Chromosomes and Crime." *Psychology Today* 2: 42–49.

Monte, C. F. 1980. *Beneath the Mask: An Introduction to Theories of Personality.* 2nd ed. New York: Holt, Rinehart and Winston.

Moor, L. 1972. "A Gene for Delinquency: Myth or Reality?" *Annales Medico-Psychologiques* 2(4): 520–27.

Moore, Joan W. 1978. *Homeboys.* Philadelphia: Temple University Press.

Morris, Allison. 1987. *Women, Crime and Criminal Justice.* Oxford: Blackwell.

Morris, Norval. 1974. *The Future of Imprisonment.* Chicago: University of Chicago Press.

Morris, Norval, and Gordon Hawkins. 1970. *The Honest Politician's Guide to Crime Control.* Chicago: University of Chicago Press.

Morris, Terrence P. 1957. *The Criminal Area: A Study in Social Ecology.* London: Routledge and Kegan Paul.

Moyer, K. E. 1976. *The Psychobiology of Aggression.* New York: Harper and Row.

Naffine, Ngaire. 1985. "The Masculinity-Femininity Hypotheses: A Consideration of Gender-based Personality Theories of Female Crime." *British Journal of Criminology* 25(4): 365–81.

Naffine, Ngaire. 1987. *Female Crime: The Construction of Women in Criminology.* London: Allen and Unwin.

Nelkin, Dorothy. 1993. "The Grandiose Claims of Geneticists." *Chronicle of Higher Education* (March 3): B1–B3.

Nelson, S. D. 1975. "Nature/Nurture Revisited II." *Journal of Conflict Resolution* 19: 734–61.

Nettler, Gwynn. 1984. *Explaining Crime.* 3rd. ed. New York: McGraw-Hill.

Newman, Graeme, and Pietro Marongiu. 1990. "Penological Reform and the Myth of Beccaria." *Criminology* 28(2): 325–46.

Newman, Oscar. 1972. *Defensible Space.* New York: Macmillan.

Newman, Oscar. 1973. *Architectural Design for Crime Prevention.* Washington, DC: National Institute of Law Enforcement and Justice, U.S. Department of Justice.

Nicholson, Linda J., ed. 1990. *Feminism/Postmodernism.* New York: Routledge.

Nielsen, Johannes. 1968. "The XYY Syndrome in a Mental Hospital." *British Journal of Criminology* 8(2): 186–203.

Nielsen, Johannes. 1971. "Prevalence and a 2½ Years Incidence of Chromosome Abnormalities Among All Males in a Forensic Psychiatric Clinic." *British Journal of Psychiatry* 119(552): 503–12.

Nye, Ivan F. 1958. *Family Relationships and Delinquent Behavior.* New York: Wiley.

O'Conner, James R. 1973. *The Fiscal Crisis of the State.* New York: St. Martin's Press.

O'Malley, Pat, and Stephen Mugford. 1994. "Crime, Excitement, and Modernity." In *Varieties of Criminology: Readings from a Dynamic Discipline,* ed. Gregg Barak, 189–211. Westport, CT: Praeger.

Olson, M. 1965. *The Logic of Collective Action.* Cambridge, MA: Harvard University Press.

Olsen, Marvin E. 1965. "Durkheim's Two Concepts of Anomie." *Sociological Quarterly* 6: 37–44.

Omand, Donald. 1977. "Exorcism: An Adjunct to Christian Counseling." *Counseling and Values* 21(2): 84–88.

Packer, Herbert L. 1968. *The Limits of the Criminal Sanction.* Stanford, CA: Stanford University Press.

Page, Sydney H. 1989a. "The Role of Exorcism in Clinical Practice and Pastoral Care." *Journal of Psychology and Theology* 17(2): 121–31.

Page, Sydney H. 1989b. "Exorcism Revisited: A Response to Beck and Lewis and to Wilson." *Journal of Psychology and Theology* 17(2): 140–43.

Pahl, R. E. 1984. *Divisions of Labor.* Oxford: Blackwell.

Park, Robert E., and Ernest Burgess. 1924. *Introduction to the Science of Sociology.* 2nd. ed. Chicago: University of Chicago Press.

Park, Robert E., and Ernest Burgess. 1925. *The City.* Chicago: University of Chicago Press.

Parmelee, Maurice. 1918. *Criminology.* New York: Macmillan.

Parsons, Talcott. 1937. *The Structure of Social Action.* New York: McGraw-Hill.

Passingham, R. E. 1972. "Crime and Personality: A Review of Eysenck's Theory." In *Biological Bases of Individual Behavior,* ed. V. D. Nebylitsyn and J. A. Gray. London: Academic Press.

Paternoster, Raymond, and Ruth Triplett. 1988. "Disaggregating Self-reported Delinquency and Its Implications for Theory." *Criminology* 26: 591–625.

Pearce, Frank. 1976. *Crimes of the Powerful.* London: Pluto Press.

Pearson, Frank S., and Neil A. Weiner. 1985. "Toward an Integration of Criminological Theories." *Journal of Criminal Law and Criminology* 76(1): 116–50.

Peoples, James, and Garrick Bailey. 1988. *Humanity: An Introduction to Cultural Anthropology.* St. Paul MN: West.

Pepinsky, Harold. 1976. *Crime and Conflict: A Study of Law and Society.* Oxford: Martin Robertson.

Pepinsky, Harold. 1978. "Communist Anarchism as an Alternative to the Rule of Criminal Law." *Contemporary Crisis* 2: 315–27.

Pepinsky, Harold. 1991. *The Geometry of Violence and Democracy*. Bloomington: Indiana University Press.

Pepinsky, Harold, and Paul Jesilow. 1985. *The Myths That Cause Crime*. Cabin John, MD: Seven Locks Press.

Pepinsky, Harold, and Richard Quinney, eds. 1991. *Criminology as Peacemaking*. Bloomington: Indiana University Press.

Pfohl, Stephen J. 1977. "The Discovery of Child Abuse." *Social Problems* 24: 310–23.

Pfohl, Stephen J. 1985. *Images of Deviance and Social Control: A Sociological History*. New York: McGraw-Hill.

Pfohl, Stephen. 1992. *Death at the Parasite Cafe: Social Science (Fictions) and the Postmodern*. New York: St. Martin's Press.

Pfohl, Stephen. 1993a. "Twilight of the Parasites: Ultramodern Capital and the New World Order." *Social Problems* 40(2): 125–51.

Pfohl, Stephen. 1993b. "Revenge of the Parasites: Feeding Off the Ruins of Sociological (De)Construction." In *Reconsidering Social Constructionism: Debates in Social Problems Theory*, ed. James A. Holstein and Gale Miller, 403–440. New York: Aldine de Gruyter.

Pfuhl, Erdwin H. 1992. "Crime Stoppers: The Legitimation of Snitching." *Justice Quarterly* 9(3): 505–28.

Pfuhl, Erdwin H., and Stuart Henry. 1993. *The Deviance Process*. 3rd ed. New York: Aldine.

Pike, Luke Owen. 1876. *The History of Crime in England*, Vol. 2. London: Smith, Elder.

Phillipson, Michael. 1971. *Sociological Aspects of Crime and Delinquency*. London: Routledge and Kegan Paul.

Piliavin, I., and S. Briar. 1964. "Police Encounters with Juveniles." *American Journal of Science* 69: 206–14.

Pitch, Tamar. 1985. "Critical Criminology and the Construction of Social Problems and the Question of Rape." *International Journal of the Sociology of Law* 13: 35–46.

Platt, Anthony. 1969. *The Child Savers*. Chicago: University of Chicago Press.

Platt, Tony. 1974. "Prospects for a Radical Criminology in the United States." *Crime and Social Justice* 1: 2–10.

Plummer, Ken. 1979. "Misunderstanding Labelling Perspectives." In *Deviant Interpretations,* ed. David Downes and Paul Rock. Oxford: Oxford University Press.

Pollak, Otto. 1950. *The Criminality of Women*. Philadelphia: University of Pennsylvania Press.

Portes, Alejandro, and Alex Stepick. 1993. *City on the Edge: The Transformation of Miami*. Berkeley: University of California Press.

Proudhon, Pierre-Joseph. 1876. *What Is Property? An Inquiry into the Principle of Right and Government*. New York: H. Fertig.

Quandagno, J. S., and R. J. Antonio. 1975. "Labeling Theory as an Oversocialized Conception of Man." *Sociology and Social Research* 60: 33–45.

Quetelet, L. Adolphe. 1831. *Research on the Propensity for Crime at Different Ages*. Trans. S. Sylvester. Cincinnati: Anderson, 1984.

Quetelet, L. Adolphe. 1835. *Physique Sociale: Ou, Essai sur le Developpement des Facultes de L'Homme*. 2 vols. Brussels: Muquardt.

Quinney, Richard. 1969. "Toward a Sociology of Law." In *Crime and Justice in Society*, ed. Richard Quinney, 1–30. Boston: Little, Brown.

Quinney, Richard. 1970. *The Social Reality of Crime*. Boston: Little, Brown.

Quinney, Richard. 1974. *Critique of the Legal Order*. Boston: Little, Brown.

Quinney, Richard. 1975a. *Criminology*. Boston: Little, Brown.

Quinney, Richard. 1975b. "Crime Control in a Capitalist Society." In *Critical Criminology*, ed. Ian Taylor, Paul Walton, and Jock Young. London: Routledge and Kegan Paul.

Quinney, Richard. 1977. *Class, State, and Crime*. New York: David McKay.

Quinney, Richard. 1978. "The Production of Marxist Criminology." *Contemporary Crisis* 2: 277–92.

Quinney, Richard. 1980. *Class, State, and Crime*. 2nd ed. New York: Longman.

Quinney, Richard. 1984. "Journey to a Far Place: The Way of Autobiographical Reflection." *Humanity and Society* 8: 182–98.

Quinney, Richard, and John Wildeman. 1991. *The Problem of Crime: A Peace and Social Justice Perspective.* 3rd ed. Mountain View, CA: Mayfield.

Quinton, Anthony. 1977. "Causality." In *The Fontana Dictionary of Modern Thought,* ed. Alan Bullock and Oliver Stallybrass, 91–92. London: Fontana Books.

Rafter, Nicole Hahn. 1983. "Prisons for Women 1790–1980." In *Crime and Justice,* Vol. 5, ed. Michael Tonry and Norval Morris, 129–81. Chicago: University of Chicago Press.

Rafter, Nicole Hahn. 1985. *Partial Justice.* Boston: Northeastern University Press.

Rafter, Nichole Hahn. 1992. "Criminal Anthropology in the United States." *Criminology* 30: 525–45.

Rankin, Joseph H., and L. Edward Wells. 1990. "The Effect of Parental Attachments and Direct Controls of Delinquency." *Journal of Research in Crime and Delinquency* 27: 140–65.

Reckless, Walter C. 1940. *Criminal Behavior.* New York McGraw-Hill.

Reckless, Walter C. 1973 [1950]. *The Crime Problem.* Englewood Cliffs, NJ: Prentice Hall.

Reckless, Walter C. 1961. "A New Theory of Delinquency and Crime." *Federal Probation* 25: 42–46.

Reckless, Walter C., Simon Dinitz, and Ellen Murray. 1956. "Self-Concept as an Insulator Against Delinquency." *American Sociological Review* 21: 744–56.

Redl, Fritz, and David Wineman. 1951. *Children Who Hate.* New York: Free Press.

Redl, Fritz, and David Wineman. 1952. *Controls from Within.* New York: Free Press.

Reiff, Philip. 1961. *Freud: The Mind of the Moralist.* Garden City, NJ: Doubleday.

Reiman, Jeffrey. 1979. *The Rich Get Richer and the Poor Get Prison.* New York: Wiley.

Reiss, Albert J. 1951. "Delinquency as the Failure of Personal and Social Controls." *American Sociological Review* 16: 196–207.

Reiss, Albert J., and A. Lewis Rhodes. 1961. "The Distribution of Delinquency in the Social Class Structure." *American Sociological Review* 26: 720–32.

Reiss, Albert J. 1983. "Crime Control and the Quality of Life." *American Behavioral Scientist* 27(1): 43–58.

Renner, Karl. 1949 [1904]. *The Institutions of Private Law and Their Social Functions.* London: Routledge and Kegan Paul.

Rennie, Ysabel. 1978. *The Search for Criminal Man.* Lexington, MA: D. C. Heath.

Renzetti, Claire M. 1993. "On the Margins of the Malestream (or, They Still Don't Get It, Do They?): Feminist Analyses in Criminal Justice Education." *Journal of Criminal Justice Education* 4(2): 219–34.

Rex, John, and Robert Moore. 1967. *Race, Community and Conflict: A Study in Sparkbrook.* Oxford: Oxford University Press.

Reynolds, Morgan O. 1973. *The Economics of Criminal Activity.* Introductory Economics Series, Module 12, 1–27. Andover, MA: Warner Modular.

Rice, Marcia. 1990. "Challenging Orthodoxies in Feminist Theory: A Black Feminist Critique." In *Feminist Perspectives in Criminology,* ed. Loraine Gelsthorpe and Allison Morris, 57–69. Milton Keynes, England: Open University Press.

Ritzer, George. 1980. *Sociology: A Multiple Paradigm Science.* Boston: Allyn and Bacon.

Robinson David, and Henry Stuart. 1977. *Self-help and Health: Mutual Aid for Modern Problems.* Oxford: Martin Robertson.

Robison, Sophia M. 1936. *Can Delinquency Be Measured?* New York: Columbia University Press.

Robson, Brian T. 1969. *Urban Analysis: A Study of City Structure with Special Reference to Sunderland.* London: Cambridge University Press.

Rosen, George. 1968. *Madness in Society.* New York: Harper Torchbooks.

Rosenau, Pauline M. 1992. *Postmodernism and the Social Sciences—Insights, Inroads, and Intrusions.* Princeton, NJ: Princeton University Press.

Rosenthal, David. 1975. "Heredity in Criminality." *Criminal Justice and Behavior* 2(1): 3–21.

Roshier, Bob. 1989. *Controlling Crime: The Classical Perspective in Criminology.* Philadelphia: Open University Press.

Rousseau, Jean Jaques. 1962 [1762]. *The Social Contract*. New York: Oxford University Press.

Rowe, David C., and D. Wayne Osgood. 1984. "Heredity and Sociological Theories of Delinquency: A Reconsideration." *American Sociological Review* 49: 526–40.

Rubington, Earl, and Martin S. Weinberg. 1968. *Deviance: The Interactionist Tradition*. New York: Macmillan.

Rubington, Earl, and Martin S. Weinberg. 1987. *Deviance: The Interactionist Tradition*. 5th ed. New York: Macmillan.

Rusche, Georg, and Otto Kirchheimer. 1939. *Punishment and Social Structure*. New York: Columbia University Press.

Rushton, J. Philipe. 1987. "Population Differences in Rule-Following Behavior: Race Evolution and Crime." Paper presented at the 39th Annual Meeting of the American Society of Criminology, Montreal.

Rushton, J. Philipe. 1990. "Race and Crime: A Reply to Roberts." *Canadian Journal of Criminology* 32(2): 315–34.

Ryan, Kevin and Jeff Ferrell. 1986. "Knowledge, Power, and the Process of Justice." *Crime and Social Justice* 25: 178–95.

Sagarin, Edward. 1969. *Odd Man In: Societies of Deviants in America*. Chicago: Quadrangle Books.

Sagarin, Edward, and Jose Sanchez. 1988. "Ideology and Deviance: The Case of the Debate over the Biological Factor." *Deviant Behavior* 9(1): 87–99.

Samenow, Stanton E. 1978. "Dr. Samenow Responds." *American Journal of Correction* 40(6): 28–29.

Samenow, Stanton E. 1979. "Author/Researcher Takes Issue with O. J. Keller." *Corrections Today* 41(3): 12–19.

Samenow, Stanton E. 1984. *Inside the Criminal Mind*. New York: Times Books.

Sampson, Robert J. 1987. "Communities and Crime." In *Positive Criminology*, ed. Michael R. Gottfredson and Travis Hirschi, 91–114. Newbury Park, CA: Sage.

Sampson, Robert J., and W. Byron Groves. 1989. "Community Structures and Crime: Testing Social Disorganization Theory." *American Journal of Sociology* 94: 774–802.

Sampson, Robert J., and William Julius Wilson. 1993. "Toward a Theory of Race, Crime and Urban Inequality." In *Crime and Inequality*, ed. John Hagan and Ruth Peterson. Stanford, CA: Stanford University Press.

Sanders, William B. 1983. *Criminology*. Reading, MA.: Addison-Wesley.

Santos, Boaventura de Sousa. 1985. "On Modes of Production of Law and Social Power." *International Journal of the Sociology of Law* 13: 299–336.

Santos, Boaventura de Sousa. 1987. "Law: A Map of Misreading. Toward a Postmodern Conception of Law." *Journal of Law and Society* 14: 279–302.

Sarbin, Theodore R., Jeffrey E. Miller. 1970. "Demonism Revisited: The XYY Chromosomal Abnormality." *Issues in Criminology* 5(2): 195–207.

Schafer, Stephen. 1976. *Introduction to Criminology*. Reston, VA: Reston.

Scharf, Peter. 1977. "The Just Community." *New Society* (April 21): 104–105.

Scheff, Thomas J. 1966. *Being Mentally Ill: A Sociological Theory*. Chicago: Aldine.

Schervish, Paul G. 1973. "The Labeling Perspective." *American Sociologist* 8: 47–56.

Schlapp, Max G., and Edward H. Smith. 1928. *The New Criminology*. New York: Boni and Liveright.

Schlossman, Steven, and Michael Sedlak. 1983. *The Chicago Area Project Revisited*. Santa Monica, CA: Rand Corporation.

Schmid, Calvin. 1960. "Urban Crime Areas: Part 1." *American Sociological Review* 25: 527–42.

Schmidt, Peter, and Ann D. Witte. 1984. *An Economic Analysis of Crime and Justice: Theory, Methods, and Applications*. Orlando, FL : Academic Press.

Schuerman, Leo, and Solomon Kobrin. 1986. "Community Careers in Crime." In *Communities and Crime* series, *Crime and Justice: An Annual Review of Research,* Vol. 8, ed. Albert J. Reis, Jr., and Michael Tonry, 76–100. Chicago: University of Chicago Press.

Schur, Edwin M. 1965. *Crimes without Victims: Deviant Behavior and Public Policy*. Englewood Cliffs, NJ: Prentice-Hall.

Schur, Edwin M. 1969. *Our Criminal Society*. Englewood Cliffs, NJ: Prentice-Hall.

Schur, Edwin M. 1971. *Labeling Deviant Behavior: Its Sociological Implications*. New York: Harper and Row.

Schur, Edwin M. 1973. *Radical Non-Intervention: Rethinking the Delinquency Problem*. Englewood Cliffs, NJ: Prentice-Hall.

Schur, Edwin M. 1980. *The Politics of Deviance: Stigma Contests and the Uses of Power*. Englewood Cliffs, NJ: Prentice-Hall.

Schur, Edwin M., and Hugo Adam Bedau. 1974. *Victimless Crimes*. Englewood Cliffs, NJ: Prentice-Hall.

Schutz, Alfred. 1967 [1932]. *The Phenomenology of the Social World*. Evanston, IL: Northwestern University Press.

Schutz, Alfred. 1971 [1970] [1964]. *Collected Papers*, 3 vols., ed. Maurice Natanson. The Hague, Netherlands: Martinus Nijhoff.

Schwartz, Martin D. 1989. "The Undercutting Edge of Criminology." *Critical Criminologist* 1(2): 1, 2, 5.

Schwartz, Martin D. 1991. "The Future of Criminology." In *New Directions in Critical Criminology*, ed. Brian MacLean and Dragan Milovanovic, 119–24. Vancouver: Collective Press.

Schwartz, Marty, and Todd Clear. 1980. "Toward a New Law on Rape." *Crime and Delinquency* 28(2): 171–91.

Schwendinger, Herman, and Julia Schwendinger. 1970. "Defenders of Order or Guardian of Human Rights?" *Issues in Criminology* 5: 123–57.

Schwendinger, Herman, and Julia Schwendinger. 1991. "Feminism, Criminology and Complex Variations." In *New Directions in Critical Criminology*, Brian D. MacLean and Dragan Milovanovic, 39–44. Vancouver: Collective Press.

Schwendinger, Julia, and Herman Schwendinger. 1982. "Rape, the Law and Private Property." *Crime and Delinquency* 28(2): 171–91.

Schwendinger, Julia, and Herman Schwendinger. 1983. *Rape and Inequality*. Beverly Hills, CA: Sage.

Scott, Marvin, and Stanford Lyman. 1970. "Accounts, Deviance and the Social Order." In *Deviance and Respectability*, ed. Jack Douglas, 89–119. New York: Basic Books.

Scott, Peter. 1973 [1956]. "Henry Maudsley, 1835–1918." In *Pioneers in Criminology*, 2nd ed., ed. Herman Mannheim. Montclair, NJ: Patterson Smith.

Scraton, Phil. 1981. *Class, Marginality and State Control*. London: Macmillan.

Scraton, Phil. 1990. "Scientific Knowledge or Masculine Discourses? Challenging Patriarchy in Criminology." In *Feminist Perspectives in Criminology*, ed. Loraine Gelsthorpe and Allison Morris, 10–25. Milton Keynes, England: Open University Press.

Scull, Andrew T. 1984. *Decarceration*. 2nd ed. Cambridge, England: Polity Press.

Seidman, Stever. 1989. "The Tedium of General Theory." *Contemporary Sociology* 18(3): 634–36.

Seidman, Stever. 1990. "Against Theory as Foundationalist Discourse." *Perspectives: The Theory Section Newsletter* 13(2): 1–3.

Sellin, Thorsten. 1937. "The Lombrosian Myth in Criminology." *American Journal of Sociology* 42(6): 898–99.

Sellin, Thorsten. 1938. *Culture Conflict and Crime*. New York: Social Science Research Council.

Sellin, Thorsten. 1973. [1960]. "Enrico Ferri 1856–1929." In *Pioneers in Criminology*, 2nd ed., ed. H. Mannheim. Montclair, NJ: Patterson Smith.

Shah, Saleem A., and Loren H. Roth. 1974. "Biological and Psychophysical Factors in Criminality." In *Handbook of Criminology*, ed. Daniel Glaser, 101–73. Chicago: Rand McNally.

Shaw, Clifford R. 1930. *The Jackroller*. Chicago: University of Chicago Press.

Shaw, Clifford. 1951. *The Natural History of a Delinquent Career*. Philadelphia: Albert Saifer.

Shaw, Clifford R., and Henry D. McKay. 1931. *Social Factors in Juvenile Delinquency. Report of the Causes of Crime*. National Commission on Law Observance and Enforcement, Report No. 13. Washington DC: U.S. Government Printing Office.

Shaw, Clifford R., and Henry D. McKay. 1942. *Juvenile Delinquency and Urban Areas: A Study of Delinquents in Relation to Differential Characteristics of Local Communities in American Cities.* Chicago: University of Chicago Press.

Shaw, Clifford R., and Henry D. McKay. 1969. *Juvenile Delinquency and Urban Areas: A Study of Delinquents in Relation to Differential Characteristics of Local Communities in American Cities.* Revised ed. with an introduction by James F. Short, Jr. Chicago: University of Chicago Press.

Sheldon, William H., S. S. Stevens, and W. B. Tucker. 1940. *The Varieties of Human Physique.* New York: Harper and Row.

Sheldon, William H., Emil M. Hartl, and Eugene McDermott. 1949. *Varieties of Delinquent Youth.* New York: Harper.

Sheley, Joseph F. 1985. *America's "Crime Problem."* Belmont, CA: Wadsworth.

Sheley, Joseph F. 1991. "Conflict and Criminal Law." In *Criminology,* ed. Joseph F. Sheley. Belmont, CA: Wadsworth.

Sherman, Lawrence W., Patrick R. Gartin, and Michael E. Buerger. 1989. "Hot Spots of Predatory Crime: Routine Activities and the Criminology of Place." *Criminology* 27(1): 27–55.

Short, James F. 1969. Introduction to *Juvenile Delinquency and Urban Areas: A Study of Delinquents in Relation to Differential Characteristics of Local Communities in American Cities.* Revised ed. by Clifford R. and Henry D. McKay. Chicago: University of Chicago Press.

Short, James. 1960. "Differential Association as a Hypothesis: Problems of Empirical Testing." *Social Problems* 8: 14–25.

Shover, Neal. 1979. *A Sociology of American Corrections.* Homewood, IL: The Dorsey Press.

Shover, Neal, and Werner J. Einstadter. 1988. *Analyzing American Corrections.* Belmont CA: Wadsworth.

Siegel, Larry J. 1989. *Criminology.* 3rd ed. St. Paul, MN: West.

Siegel, Larry J. 1992. *Criminology.* 4th ed. St. Paul, MN: West.

Simmel, Georg. 1904. "The Sociology of Conflict." *American Journal of Sociology* 9: 490–525, 672–89, 798–811.

Simmel, Georg. 1955 [1908]. *The Sociology of Conflict,* trans. Kurt H. Wolff, and *The Web of Group Affiliations,* trans. Reinhard Bendix. (Omnibus edition.) Glencoe, IL: Free Press.

Simon, Carl P., and Ann D. Witte. 1982. *Beating the System: The Underground Economy.* Boston: Auburn.

Simon, Rita. 1975. *Women and Crime.* Lexington, MA: D. C. Heath.

Simon, William, and John Gagnon. 1976. "The Anomie of Affluence: A Post Mertonian Conception." *American Journal of Sociology* 82: 356–78.

Simpson, Sally S. 1989. "Feminist Theory, Crime, and Justice." *Criminology* 27:(4): 605–631.

Singer, Simon I., and Murray Levine. 1988. "Power-Control Theory, Gender and Delinquency: A Partial Replication with Additional Evidence on the Effects of Peers." *Criminology* 26: 627–47.

Skinner, B. F. 1953. *Science and Human Behavior.* New York: Macmillan.

Skinner, B. F. 1971. *Beyond Freedom and Dignity.* New York: Knopf.

Smart, Carol. 1976. *Women, Crime and Criminology: A Feminist Critique.* London: Routledge and Kegan Paul.

Smart, Carol. 1979. "The New Female Criminal: Reality or Myth?" *British Journal of Criminology* 19: 50–59.

Smart, Carol. 1984. *The Ties That Bind: Law, Marriage and the Reproduction of Patriarchal Relations.* London: Routledge and Kegan Paul.

Smart, Carol. 1989. *Feminism and the Power of Law.* London: Routledge.

Smart, Carol. 1990. "Feminist Approaches to Criminology or Postmodern Woman Meets Atavastic Man." In *Feminist Perspectives in Criminology,* ed. Loraine Gelsthorpe and Allison Morris, 70–84. Milton Keynes, England: Open University Press.

Smart, Carol. 1992. "The Women of Legal Discourse." *Social and Legal Studies: An International Journal* 1: 29–44.

Smart, Carol, and Smart, Barry. 1978. "Accounting for Rape: Reality and Myth in Press Reporting." In *Sexuality and Social Control*, ed. Carol Smart and Barry Smart. London: Routledge and Kegan Paul.

Smith, Douglas A. 1986. "The Neighborhood Context of Police Behavior." In *Communities and Crime. Series in Crime and Justice An Annual Review of Research*, Vol. 8, ed. Albert J. Reiss and Michael Tonry, 313–341. Chicago: University of Chicago Press.

Smith, Douglas A., and Roger C. Jarjoura. 1988. "Social Structure and Criminal Victimization." *Journal of Research in Crime and Delinquency*, 25: 27–52.

Snider, Laureen. 1985. "Legal Reform and Social Control: The Dangers of Abolishing Rape." *International Journal of the Sociology of Law* 13(4): 337–56.

Snodgrass, Jon. 1976. "Clifford R. Shaw and Henry D. McKay: Chicago Sociologists." *British Journal of Criminology* 16(1): 1–19.

Soper, Kate. 1991. "Postmodernism and Its Discontents." *Feminist Review* 39: 97–108.

Southard, Samuel. 1986. "Demonizing and Mental Illness: II. The problem of Assessment, Los Angeles." *Pastoral Psychology* 34(4): 264–87.

Southard, Samuel, and Donna Southard. 1985. "Demonizing and Mental Illness: The Problem of Identification, Hong Kong." *Pastoral Psychology* 33(3): 173–88.

Sparks, Richard F. 1980. "A Critique of Marxist Criminology." In *Crime and Justice: An Annual Review of Research*, ed. Norval Morris and Michael Tonry. Chicago: University of Chicago Press.

Spelman, E. 1988. *Inessential Woman*. Boston: Beacon Press.

Spergel, Irving. 1964. *Racketville, Slumtown, Haulburg: An Exploratory Study of Delinquent Subcultures*. Chicago: University of Chicago Press.

Spitzer, Steven. 1975. "Towards a Marxian Theory of Deviance." *Social Problems* 22: 638–51.

Spitzer, Steven. 1980. "Left-Wing Criminology—An Infantile Disorder." In *Radical Criminology: The Coming Crisis*, ed. James Inciardi, 169–90. Beverly Hills, CA: Sage.

Srole, Leo. 1956. "Social Integration and Certain Corollaries: An Exploratory Study." *American Sociological Review* 21(6): 709–16.

Stanko, Elizabeth. 1985. *Intimate Intrusions: Women's Experience of Male Violence*. London: Virago.

Stanko, Elizabeth. 1990. *Danger Signals*. London: Pandora.

Stark, Rodney. 1987. "Deviant Places: A Theory of the Ecology of Crime." *Criminology* 25(4): 893–909.

Starkey, M. L. 1949. *The Devil in Massachusetts*. New York: Knopf.

Steffensmeier, Darrell J. 1978. "Crime and the Contemporary Woman: An Analysis of Changing Levels of Female Property Crime, 1960–75." *Social Forces* 57: 566–84.

Steffensmeier, Darrell J., and Michael J. Cobb. 1981. "Sex Differences in Urban Arrest Patterns." *Social Problems* 29: 37–50.

Steinberg, Laurence. 1993. *Adolescence*. 3rd ed. New York: McGraw-Hill.

Suchar, Charles S. 1978. *Social Deviance: Perspectives and Prospects*. New York: Holt, Rinehart and Winston.

Sudnow, David. 1965. "Normal Crimes: Sociological Features of the Penal Code in a Public Defender Office." *Social Problems* 12(3): 255–70.

Sullivan, Richard F. 1973. "The Economics of Crime: An Introduction to the Literature." *Crime and Delinquency* 19(2): 138–49.

Sumner, William Graham. 1906. *Folkways: A Study of the Sociological Importance of Usages, Manners, Customs, Mores and Morals*. Boston: Ginn.

Sutherland, Edwin H. 1929. "Crime and the Conflict Process." *Journal of Juvenile Research* 13: 38–48.

Sutherland, Edwin H. 1939. "Review of Hooton's Crime and the Man." *Journal of Criminal Law and Criminology* 30: 911–14.

Sutherland, Edwin H. 1939. *Principles of Criminology*. Philadelphia: Lippincott.

Sutherland, Edwin H. 1949. "The White Collar Criminal." In *Encyclopedia of Criminology*, ed. Vernon C. Branham and Samuel B. Kutash, 511–15. New York: Philosophical Library.

Sutherland, Edwin H. 1950. "The Diffusion of Sexual Psychopath Laws." *American Journal of Sociology* 56: 142–48.

Sutherland, Edwin H., and Donald R. Cressey. 1978 [1961] [1966]. *Principles of Criminology*. Philadelphia: Lippincott.

Suttles, Gerald. 1968. *The Social Order and the Slum*. Chicago: University of Chicago Press.

Suttles, Gerald. 1972. *The Social Construction of Communities*. Chicago: University of Chicago Press.

Sykes, Gresham M., and Francis T. Cullen. 1992. *Criminology*. 2nd ed. Fort Worth: Harcourt Brace Jovanovich.

Sykes, Gresham M., and David Matza. 1957. "Techniques of Neutralization: A Theory of Delinquency." *American Sociological Review* 22: 664–70.

Szasz, Thomas S. 1961. *The Myth of Mental Illness*. New York: Harper and Row.

Szasz, Thomas S. 1973. *The Manufacture of Madness*. New York: Dell.

Tappan, Paul W. 1947. "Who Is the Criminal?" *American Sociological Review* 12: 96–102.

Tannenbaum, David J. 1977. "Personality and Criminality: A Summary and Implications of the Literature." *Journal of Criminal Justice* 5: 225–35.

Tannenbaum, Frank. 1938. *Crime and the Community*. Boston: Ginn.

Tarde, Gabriel. 1886. *La Criminalité Comparée*. Paris: Alcan.

Tarde, Gabriel. 1903 [1890]. *G. Tarde's Laws of Imitation*. Trans. E. Parsons. New York: Henry Holt.

Taub, Nadine, and Wendy Williams. 1985. "Will Equality Require More than Assimilation, Accommodation or Separation from the Existing Social Structure?" *Rutgers Law Review* 37(4): 825–44.

Taylor, Ian, Paul Walton, and Jock Young. 1973. *The New Criminology: For a Social Theory of Deviance*. London: Routledge and Kegan Paul.

Taylor, Ian, Paul Walton, and Jock Young, eds. 1975. *Critical Criminology*. London: Routledge and Kegan Paul.

Taylor, Laurie. 1971. *Deviance and Society*. London: Michael Joseph.

Taylor, Laurie. 1972. "The Significance and Interpretation of Motivational Questions: The Case of Sex Offenders." *Sociology* 6: 23–29.

Taylor, Laurie, and Paul Walton. 1971. "Industrial Sabotage: Motives and Meanings." In *Images of Deviance*, ed. Stanley Cohen. Harmondsworth, England: Penguin.

Taylor, M. 1982. *Community, Anarchy and Liberty*. Cambridge: Cambridge University Press.

Telfer, Mary A., David Baker, and Gerald R. Clark. 1968. "Incidence of Gross Chromosomal Errors Among Tall Criminal American Males." *Science* 159: 1249–50.

Teubner, Geunther. 1988. *Autopoietic Law: A New Approach to Law and Society*. New York: Walter de Gruyter.

Teubner, Geunther. 1992. "The Two Faces of Janus: Rethinking Legal Pluralism." *Cardozo Law Review* 13: 1443–62.

Thomas, Jim. 1988. *Prisoner Litigation: The Paradox of the Jailhouse Lawyer*. Totowa, NJ: Rowman and Littlefield.

Thomas, William I. 1923. *The Unadjusted Girl*. Boston: Little, Brown.

Thornberry, Terrence P. 1987. "Toward an Interactional Theory of Delinquency." *Criminology* 25: 863–91.

Thrasher, Frederick M. 1927. *The Gang*. Chicago: University of Chicago Press.

Tierney, Kathleen J. 1982. "The Battered Women's Movement and the Creation of the Wife Beating Problem." *Social Problems* 29: 207–220.

Tifft, Larry L. 1979. "The Coming Redefinitions of Crime: An Anarchist Perspective." *Social Problems* 26: 392–402.

Tifft, Larry L., and Dennis Sullivan. 1980. *The Struggle to Be Human: Crime, Criminology and Anarchism*. Sanday, Orkney, England: Cienfuegos Press.

Tittle, Charles. 1980. *Sanctions and Social Deviance*. New York: Praeger.

Tittle, Charles R. 1983. "Social Class and Criminal Behavior: A Critique of the Theoretical Perspective." *Social Forces* 62: 334–58.

Tobias, J. J. 1972. *Nineteenth-Century Crime: Prevention and Punishment*. Harmondsworth, England: Penguin.

Toby, Jackson. 1957. "Social Disorganization and Stake in Conformity: Complementary Factors in the Predatory Behavior of Hoodlums." *Journal of Criminal Law, Criminology and Police Science* 48: 12–17.

Toby, Jackson. 1979. "The New Criminology Is the Old Sentimentality." *Criminology* 16: 516–26.

Tong, Rosmarie. 1989. *Feminist Thought: A Comprehensive Introduction*. Boulder: Westview Press.

Touraine, Alain. 1988. *Return of the Actor: A Social Theory in Post-Industrial Society*. Minneapolis: University of Minnesota Press.

Trasler, Gordon. 1962. *The Explanation of Criminality*. London: Routledge and Kegan Paul.

Turk, Austin T. 1966. "Conflict and Criminality." *American Sociological Review* 31: 338–52.

Turk, Austin T. 1969. *Criminality and the Legal Order*. Chicago: Rand McNally.

Turk, Austin T. 1976. "Law as a Weapon in Social Conflict." *Social Problems* 23: 276–91.

Turk, Austin T. 1980. "Analyzing Official Deviance: For Nonpartisan Conflict Analysis in Criminology." In *Radical Criminology: The Coming Crisis*, ed. James A. Inciardi. Beverly Hills, CA: Sage.

Turk, Austin T. 1982. *Political Criminality: The Defiance and Defense of Authority*. Beverly Hills, CA: Sage.

Turner, Jonathan H. 1986. *The Structure of Sociological Theory*. 4th ed. Chicago: Dorsey Press.

Turque, Bill, and Farai Chideya. 1991. "Society: Religion: The Exorcism of Gina." *Newsweek* (April 15): 62.

Unger, Robert M. 1976. *Law in Modern Society*. New York: Free Press.

Unger, Robert M. 1986. *The Critical Legal Studies Movement*. Cambridge: Harvard University Press.

Ursel, J. 1986. "The State and the Maintenance of Patriarchy: A Case Study of Family, Labour and Welfare Legislation in Canada." In *Family Economy and State: The Social Reproduction Process Under Capitalism,* ed. J. Dickinson and B. Russell. Toronto: Garamond Press.

Van den Haag, Ernest. 1975. *Punishing Criminals: Concerning Old and Very Painful Questions*. New York: Basic Books.

Virkler, Henry A., and Mary B. Virkler. 1977. "Demonic Involvement in Human Life and Illness." *Journal of Psychology and Theology* 5(2): 95–102.

Vold, George B. with Thomas Bernard. 1979 [1958]. *Theoretical Criminology*. 2nd ed. London: Oxford University Press.

Vold, George B., and Thomas J. Bernard. 1986. *Theoretical Criminology*. 3rd ed. New York: Oxford University Press.

Volkart, Edmund H. 1964. "Human Nature." In *A Dictionary of the Social Sciences,* ed. Julius Gould and William Kolb, 306–307. London: Tavistock.

Von Hirsch, Andrew. 1976. *Doing Justice: The Choice of Punishments*. New York: Hill and Wang.

Von Hirsch, Andrew, and Nils Jareborg. 1991. "Gauging Criminal Harm: A Living Standard Analysis." *Oxford Journal of Legal Studies* II(1): 1–38.

Waldo, Gordon P., and Simon Dinitz. 1967. "Personality Attributes of the Criminal: An Analysis of Research Studies, 1950–1965." *Journal of Research in Crime and Delinquency* 4: 185–201.

Walker, Jeffrey T. 1994. "Human Ecology and Social Disorganization Revisit Delinquency in Little Rock." In *Varieties of Criminology: Readings from a Dynamic Discipline*, ed. Gregg Barak, 47–78. Westport, CT: Praeger.

Walker, Nigel D. 1974. "Lost Causes in Criminology." In *Crime, Criminology and Public Policy*, ed. Roger Hood. London: Heineman.

Walters, Glenn D. 1992. "A Meta-Analysis of the Gene Crime Relationship." *Criminology* 30:(4): 595–613.

Walters, Glenn D., and Thomas W. White. 1989. "Heredity and Crime: Bad Genes or Bad Research?" *Criminology* 27: 455–85.

Ward, David, and Gene Kassebaum. 1965. *Women's Prison*. Chicago: Aldine.

Warming, E. 1909. *Oecology of Plants: An Introduction to the Study of Plant Communities*. Oxford: Oxford University Press.

Warren, Carol A. B. 1981. "New Forms of Social Control—The Myth of Deinstitutionalization." *American Behavioral Scientist* 24: 724–40.

Washburn, S. L. 1951. "Review of W. H. Sheldon, Varieties of Delinquent Youth." *American Anthropologist* 53(December): 561.

Weis, Joseph G., and J. David Hawkins. 1981. *Reports of the National Institute of the National Juvenile Justice Assessment Centers, Preventing Delinquency*. Washington, DC: U.S. Department of Justice.

Weis, Joseph G., and John Sederstrom. 1981. *Reports of the National Institute of the National Juvenile Justice Assessment Centers, The Prevention of Serious Delinquency: What to Do*. Washington, DC: U.S. Department of Justice.

Weiss, Robert. 1983. "Radical Criminology: A Recent Development." In *International Handbook of Contemporary Developments in Criminology: General Issues and the Americas*, ed. Elmer H. Johnson. Westport, CT: Greenwood Press.

Weiss, Robert P. 1987. "From 'Slugging Detectives' to 'Labor Relations.'" In *Private Policing*, ed. Clifford D. Shearing and Philip C. Stenning. Beverly Hills, CA: Sage.

Wells, Edward L., and Joseph H. Rankin. 1988. "Direct Parental Controls and Delinquency." *Criminology* 26: 263–85.

Wenger, Morton G., and Thomas A. Bonomo. 1981. "Crime, the Crisis of Capitalism and Social Revolution." In *Crime and Capitalism: Readings in Marxist Criminology*, ed. David F. Greenberg, 420–34. Palo Alto, CA: Mayfield.

Whitaker, Ian. 1965. "The Nature and Value of Functionalism in Sociology." In *Functionalism in the Social Sciences: The Strength and Limits of Functionalism in Anthropology, Economics, Political Science, and Sociology*, ed. Don Martindale, 127–43. Philadelphia: American Academy of Political and Social Science.

White, R. Clyde. 1932. "The Relation of Felonies to Environmental Factors in Indianapolis." *Social Forces* 10: 498–513.

Whyte, William Foote. 1943. *Street Corner Society: The Social Structure of an Italian Slum*. Chicago: University of Chicago Press.

Wieck, D. 1978. "Anarchist Justice." In *Anarchism*, ed. J. R. Pennock and J. W. Chapman. New York: New York University Press.

Wilbanks, William. 1987. *The Myth of a Racist Criminal Justice System*. Monterey, CA: Brooks/Cole.

Williams, Frank P., III, and Marilyn D. McShane. 1988. *Criminological Theory*. Englewood Cliffs, NJ: Prentice-Hall.

Wilson, James Q. 1975. *Thinking About Crime*. New York: Vintage.

Wilson, James Q., and Richard Herrnstein. 1985. *Crime and Human Nature*. New York: Simon and Schuster.

Wilson Vine, Margaret S. 1960. "Gabriel Tarde, 1843–1904." In *Pioneers in Criminology*, 2nd ed., ed. H. Mannheim, 292–304. Montclair, NJ: Patterson Smith.

Wilson, William Julius. 1987. *The Truly Disadvantaged: The Inner City, the Underclass and Public Policy*. Chicago: University of Chicago Press.

Wilson, William P. 1989. "Demon Possession and Exorcism: A Reaction to Page." *Journal of Psychology and Theology* 17(2): 135–39.

Wolfgang, Marvin E. 1972 [1960]. "Cesare Lombroso. 1835–1909." In *Pioneers in Criminology*, 2nd ed., ed. Herman Mannheim, 232–291. Montclair, NJ: Patterson Smith.

Wolfgang, Marvin E., and Franco Ferracuti. 1967. *The Subculture of Violence*. London: Tavistock.

Woodcock, George. 1963. *Anarchism: A History of Libertarian Ideas and Movements*. Harmondsworth, England: Penguin.

Woodcock, George. 1977. *The Anarchist Reader*. London: Fontana.

Wooton, Barbara. 1959. *Social Science and Social Pathology*. London: Allen and Unwin.

Wunderlich, Ray C. 1978. "Neuroallery as a Contributing Factor to Social Misfits: Diagnosis and Treatment." In *Ecologic-Biochemical Approaches to the Treatment of Delinquents and Criminals*, ed. L. Hippchen, 229–53. New York: Van Nostrand Reinhold.

Yablonsky, Lewis. 1990. *Criminology, Crime and Criminality.* 4th ed. New York: Harper and Row.

Yochelson, Samuel, and Stanton E. Samenow. 1976. *The Criminal Personality:* Vol. 1, *A Profile for Change.* New York: Jason Aronson.

Yochelson, Samuel, and Stanton E. Samenow. 1977. *The Criminal Personality:* Vol. 2. New York: Jason Aronson.

Young, Jock. 1971. "The Role of Police as Amplifiers of Deviancy, Negotiators of Reality and Translators of Fantasy." In *Images of Deviance*, ed. Stan Cohen. Harmondsworth, England: Penguin.

Young, Jock. 1979. "Left Idealism, Reformism and Beyond." In *Capitalism and the Rule of Law*, ed. Bob Fine et al., 13–28. London: Hutchinson.

Young, Jock. 1981. "Thinking Seriously About Crime: Some Models of Criminology. In *Crime and Society: Readings in History and Society*, ed. Mike Fitzgerald, Gregor McLennan, and Jennie Pawson, 248–309. London: Routledge and Kegan Paul.

Young, Jock. 1986. "The Failure of Criminology: The Need for a Radical Realism." In *Confronting Crime*, ed. Roger Matthews and Jock Young, 4–30. London: Sage.

Young, Jock. 1987. "The Tasks Facing a Realist Criminology." *Contemporary Crisis*, 11: 337–356.

Young, Jock. 1991. "Left Realism and the Priorities of Crime Control." In *The Politics of Crime Control*, ed. Keven Stenson and David Cowell. London: Sage.

Young, Jock, and Roger Matthews, eds. 1992. *Rethinking Criminology: The Realist Debate.* Newbury Park, CA: Sage.

Young, T. R. 1991. "Chaos and Crime." *The Critical Criminologist* 3(4): 3–4, 13–14.

Zedner, Lucia. 1991. "Women, Crime and Penal Responses: A Historical Account." In *Crime and Justice: A Review of Research,* Vol. 14, ed. Michael Tonry, 307–362. Chicago: University of Chicago Press.

Zilboorg, Gregory. 1949. "Psychoanalysis and Criminology." In *Encyclopedia of Criminology*, ed. Vernon C. Branham and Samuel B. Kutash, 398–405. New York: Philosophical Library.

Zorbaugh, Frederick. 1929. *The Goldcoast and the Slum.* Chicago: University of Chicago Press.

Zuckerman, M. 1979. *Sensation Seeking Beyond the Optimal of Arousal.* Hillsdale, NJ: Erlbaum.

NAME AND SUBJECT INDEX